BABYLON UNDER WESTERN EYES

A Study of Allusion and Myth

Babylon under Western Eyes

A Study of Allusion and Myth

ANDREW SCHEIL

UNIVERSITY OF TORONTO PRESS
Toronto Buffalo London

Toronto Buffalo London
www.utppublishing.com

ISBN 978-1-4426-3733-7

Library and Archives Canada Cataloguing in Publication

Scheil, Andrew P., 1968–, author
Babylon under western eyes : a study of allusion and myth / Andrew Scheil.

Includes bibliographical references and index.
ISBN 978-1-4426-3733-7 (cloth)

1. European literature – History and criticism. 2. Babylon (Extinct city) – In literature. 3. Allusions in literature. 4. Mythology in literature. 5. Popular culture in literature. I. Title.

PN701.S34 2016 809 C2015-908251-X

University of Toronto Press acknowledges the financial assistance to its publishing program of the Canada Council for the Arts and the Ontario Arts Council, an agency of the Government of Ontario.

Canada Council for the Arts | Conseil des Arts du Canada

Funded by the Government of Canada | Financé par le gouvernement du Canada | Canada

To my mother and the memory of my father;
to my sons, William and David.

Contents

Illustrations

Preface

Once upon a time, I taught at Harvard University as a lecturer and tutor in their superb honours undergraduate concentration in "History and Literature." It was an exhilarating and intense experience. Working with such fine young minds in such a collaborative program remains one of my most satisfying pedagogical experiences; however, I was also commuting from nearby Rhode Island (two hours, door-to-door), raising two infant boys, and finishing my first book. I often spent what little "down time" I had at Harvard in the Child Memorial Library; this would be Francis James Child (1825–96) of English ballad fame and Harvard's first Professor of English. The Child Memorial Library is where this book you hold was first conceived.

One day, preparing for a tutorial on Thomas Dekker's comic play *The Shoemaker's Holiday*, I paused at the point where the Falstaffian Simon Eyre gathers his rowdy apprentices Firk, Hodge, and Hans, shouting at them and calling them "Babylonian knaves" (III.4). My mind – certainly enjoying the play, but hazy from the chronic lack of sleep that comes with a newborn child – wondered: What in the world is a "*Babylonian* knave"? That is, what were the connotations of "Babylonian" in this phrase? The Child Library is a non-circulating English literature collection, a dusty place and a bit shabby – pleasantly so. Framed images of the diminutive Francis Child peered down at me as I got up to look into my Babylonian puzzle. The collection is a relatively small one, mainly consisting of standard scholarly editions and concordances, as well as selected monographs. Browsing to clear my head (and stay awake), I looked up "Babylon" in a number of major authors' concordances: Chaucer, Shakespeare, Spenser, Milton, Tennyson, Henry James, Melville, Whitman, Thomas Hardy, Dickens. They all had some entry for "Babylon."

Well, I thought, someone must have written a longitudinal study along the lines of "Babylon in English Literature"; something like W.B. Stanford's *The Ulysses Theme*, but for Babylon. After that day, as time permitted, I kept checking: apparently, no such book. Should I write on the subject? The wide-ranging intellectual atmosphere of History and Literature encouraged such work, as did other intellectual interests I began to see in such a project, and off I went. All things fall and cease (as did, eventually, my lectureship at Harvard), and now, finally, the present book is my long-deferred, overly complex (yet still partial) answer to my question: What could Eyre have meant by "Babylonian knaves"?[1]

Thanks, first, go to that inceptive environment. Then to the chairs of History and Literature in my time there, Stephen Greenblatt and Homi Bhabha; to the Director of Studies, Steve Biel; to the community of medievalists and the Medieval Doctoral Conference and other supportive friends in and around Harvard and Boston University at that time, some of whom listened to a very early version of this material: Daniel Donoghue, Joseph Harris, Nicholas Watson, James Engell, Patrick Ford, Nicholas Everett, Richard Moll, Chris Walsh, Andy Romig, Meegan Kennedy, Rebecca Schoff, the late, much-missed Nathan Alexander, and others.

The University of Minnesota has been my home for some time now, and I cannot imagine a better, more receptive interdisciplinary environment for my work. Thanks are thus due to my many helpful colleagues in the University of Minnesota's English department, in particular John Watkins, Andy Elfenbein, Nabil Matar, Michael Hancher, Edward Griffin, Donald Ross, and John Wright. Several chairs of English supported the project: Michael Hancher, Paula Rabinowitz (thanks to Paula as well for savvy advice on images), Geoffrey Sirc, and Ellen Messer-Davidow. Faculty and students at the Center for Medieval Studies, the Center for Early Modern History, the Consortium for the Study of the Premodern World, the Department of Classical and Near Eastern Studies, and the James Ford

1 After this book had entered production, two very good books came to hand: Michael Seymour's *Babylon: Legend, History, and the Ancient City* (London and NY: I.B. Tauris, 2014) and Kevin M. McGeough's *The Ancient Near East in the Nineteenth Century: Appreciations and Appropriations. III. Fantasy and Alternative Histories* (Sheffield: Sheffield Phoenix Press, 2015). Seymour examines the legend of Babylon from the classical world to the present, with a focus on art history and the history of archaeology. Since my focus is more literary, I believe our works are complementary. McGeough's study treats the general representation of the Near East in the nineteenth century, with a likewise different focus from what I set out here. I have inserted references to these works throughout my notes as appropriate.

Bell Library were supportive and helpful in many ways – in particular, Ruth Karras, J.B. Shank, Kay Reyerson, Maggie Ragnow, Margaret Borg, Oliver Nicholson, Susan Noakes, Mary Franklin-Brown, Anatoly Liberman, Ray Wakefield, Valentine Pakis, Renana Schneller, and James Parente.

I was fortunate to receive aid from several sources in the research and writing of this study: a National Endowment for the Humanities faculty fellowship, and several University of Minnesota programs – a Grant-in-Aid paid for the services of two fine graduate assistants (Erik Carlson and Christopher Flack); a Single-Semester Leave, and a College of Liberal Arts Research Fellowship Supplement; the support of my appointment as a McKnight Presidential Fellow, and my subsequent appointment as the Donald V. Hawkins Professor of English. Thanks as well to the libraries of the University of Minnesota, Boston University, and Harvard College for the use of their splendid resources.

I also spent a profitable academic year working on the book as a Solmsen Fellow in residence at the Institute for Research in the Humanities at the University of Wisconsin, Madison; many thanks to my colleagues there, especially Jack Niles, Susan Friedman (the very supportive director of the Institute), David Morgan, and my fellow Solmsen scholars that year, Bob Berkhoffer, Valerie Garver, and Catherine Gimelli Martin.

Portions of this book were given as invited lectures and conference papers in several places, including the annual meetings of the Medieval Academy, the International Congress on Medieval Studies at Western Michigan University, and the Association of Literary Scholars, Critics, and Writers. I'd like to thank the following people for their invitations, comments and questions on these and other varied occasions: Bill North, George Shuffleton, Hannibal Hamlin, Joe Pucci, Eleanor Cook, Eileen Joy, the late Nicholas Howe, Karl F. Morrison, David Wallace, Ryan Szpeich, and many others I have no doubt forgotten. The readers of the book for the University of Toronto Press offered quite valuable suggestions for refinement and improvement. My thanks to them, to Suzanne Rancourt, Barbara Porter, and Kel Pero at the Press, and, frankly, to anyone else I've ever talked to about Babylon in the course of this project. All errors and follies herein, of course, remain my own.

I dedicated my first book to my wife, Katherine West Scheil, superb Shakespeare scholar and my partner in all things. She remains the one without whom none of this is possible. But for this book's dedication I chose to single out my parents, George and Jeanne Scheil, as well as my two young sons, William and David. My love to you all: ἡ ἀγάπη οὐδέποτε πίπτει (I Corinthians 13:8).

Abbreviations

AHR	*American Historical Review*
ASE	*Anglo-Saxon England*
ASPR	*The Anglo-Saxon Poetic Records*, ed. G.P. Krapp and E.V.K. Dobbie, 6 vols. (New York: Columbia University Press, 1931–42)
AV	Authorized (King James) Version of the Bible
BCE	Before Common Era
Bosworth-Toller	*An Anglo-Saxon Dictionary*, ed. J. Bosworth and T.N. Toller (Oxford: Oxford University Press, 1898); *Supplement* by T.N. Toller (Oxford: Clarendon, 1921); *Enlarged Addenda and Corrigenda* to the *Supplement* by Alistair Campbell (Oxford: Clarendon, 1972)
CCSL	Corpus Christianorum, Series Latina
CE	Common Era
CSEL	Corpus Scriptorum Ecclesiasticorum Latinorum
DOE	*Dictionary of Old English*, ed. A. Cameron, et al.
EETS o.s.	Early English Text Society, old series
EETS s.s.	Early English Text Society, supplementary series
ES	*English Studies*
MH	*Medievalia et Humanistica*
JEGP	*Journal of English and Germanic Philology*
JMEMS	*Journal of Medieval and Early Modern Studies*
LCL	Loeb Classical Library
MGH	Monumenta Germaniae Historica
MGH, AA	Monumenta Germaniae Historica, Auctores Antiquissimi

MGH, Poet. Lat.	Monumenta Germaniae Historica, Poetae Latini Aevi Carolini
NM	*Neuphilologische Mitteilungen*
NLH	*New Literary History*
OED	*Oxford English Dictionary*
PLL	*Papers on Language and Literature*
PL	*Patrologia Latina*, ed. J.P. Migne
PMLA	*Publications of the Modern Language Association*
RS	Rolls Series
SEL	*Studies in English Literature, 1500–1900*
SLI	*Studies in the Literary Imagination*

In general, I have used the most readily available texts and translations for the reader's convenience: e.g., Loeb Classical Library volumes. When a translation is my own, I have noted so in the notes; I have also occasionally adjusted published translations, usually in the direction of a more literal rendering. I have also sometimes made minor textual modifications to primary sources, such as altered punctuation and spelling, to make the texts more reader-friendly.

Biblical quotations throughout are drawn from the Latin Vulgate Bible, via the Douay-Rheims translation; I also draw attention to interesting variants in the King James Bible (AV) when warranted. By using the Vulgate and the AV, I cover the two most influential versions of the Christian Bible in the West from antiquity to the present. I have also occasionally edited names in the Douay translation to their more familiar form (e.g., Ezechias to Hezekiah). When I refer to the Vulgate Psalm 136 (*Super flumina Babylonis*), the same text is Psalm 137 in the numbering of the AV.

In a broad study of this nature, the coverage of secondary sources must necessarily be selective. I have tried to cite only the most useful and relevant works, and I have thus generally confined the citation of secondary sources and attendant discussion to the notes.

BABYLON UNDER WESTERN EYES

Introduction

My heart failed, darkness amazed me: Babylon, my beloved, is become a wonder to me.

– Isaiah 21:4

[Paris] hung before him this morning, the vast bright Babylon, like some huge iridescent object, a jewel brilliant and hard, in which parts were not to be discriminated nor differences comfortably marked. It twinkled and trembled and melted together, and what seemed surface one moment seemed all depth the next.

– Henry James, *The Ambassadors* (1903)[1]

"If the City is a text, how shall we read it?"

– Joyce Carol Oates, "Imaginary Cities: America"[2]

Sometimes a single word conceals an entire conceptual universe. Take "Babylon," a word that bears a double life: "Babylon" denotes an ancient city of the historical Near East, but "Babylon" is also a complex fictive allusion with a wide variety of connotations in its long history, from the biblical Whore of Babylon to Hollywood Babylon. "Babylon" conceals a rich array of meanings beneath its surface: the word presides over a nexus of mythic narratives, and in this way endures in the West's cultural consciousness, bearing little resemblance to the real Babylon of history.

1 Henry James, *The Ambassadors*, 83.
2 Joyce Carol Oates, "Imaginary Cities: America," 11.

In what follows, I offer a map of this mythic place – Babylon as seen under Western eyes – from the ancient world to the present.[3]

The Matter of Babylon and its Hermeneutic

My subject is thus the "Matter of Babylon": a complex of related tropes, images, characters, and themes forming a roughly coherent, multifaceted myth of deep presence and adaptive power in Western culture. As a term, the "Matter of Babylon" calls to mind the more familiar medieval "Matter of Britain" or "Matter of Troy," and is similarly a complex, living myth of great capaciousness and flexibility. At its heart, *Babylon under Western Eyes* is a study of medieval Christian cultural traditions and their afterlives in an ongoing process of adaptation. In this regard, the Matter of Babylon tradition comprises places (the Tower of Babel, the plain of Shinar, the Tigris and Euphrates rivers, Babylon, and Nineveh); peoples, usually blurred together indiscriminately (Chaldeans, Babylonians, Assyrians); characters (Nimrod, Ninus, Semiramis, Nebuchadnezzar, Belshazzar, the Whore of Babylon); events (the foundation of empires and the conquest of cities; the subjugation, dispersion, and emancipation of nations). The Matter of Babylon has enjoyed an unbroken record of cultural reference, allusion, and adaptation in the West, and my aim here is to provide an analytical and synthetic study of this rich tradition from a literary and rhetorical perspective. Put simply, *Babylon under Western Eyes* offers answers to the following questions: How does Babylon function as an allusion or a reference in the West? What are the allusive meanings of Babylon, and how (and when) did these meanings enter

3 As an investigation of one or more semantically rich words or a phrase, this study of "Babylon" resembles Leo Spitzer's analysis of the word *Stimmung* ("harmony") in his *Classical and Christian Ideas of World Harmony*; William Empson's *Structure of Complex Words*; Raymond Williams's *Keywords*; and Karl F. Morrison's *"I Am You": The Hermeneutics of Empathy* (an unpacking of the phrase "I am you" in the history of Western thought). Roland Greene has also recently revived and updated this approach in a nuanced way, terming it "critical semantics" (see *Five Words*, 12–14, 175–6).

For introductions to the real history of Babylon see Georges Roux, *Ancient Iraq*; Boardman et al., ed., *Cambridge Ancient History*, vol. 3, part 2; Hallo and Simpson, *Ancient Near East*; Leick, *Mesopotamia*; Van De Mieroop, *History of the Ancient Near East*; Seymour, *Babylon*, 6–34. See also generally Finkel and Seymour, eds., *Babylon: Myth and Reality*, a beautiful and scholarly catalogue of a major travelling exhibit (2008–9) on the topic of the title organized by the British Museum, the Musée du Louvre and the Réunion des Musées Nationaux (Paris), and the Staatliche Museen zu Berlin.

various currents of Western thought? A phrase used here synonymously with the "Matter of Babylon" – "the Babylon myth" – foregrounds the basic conceptual unity of this material and the interconnectedness of varied elements under the sign of "Babylon." I also do not mean to imply that the Babylon myth displays an unchanging stasis throughout its long history; on the contrary, one of my broader arguments is the importance of dynamic adaptation in the creation, growth, and maintenance of premodern traditions.[4]

I use three key terms to describe the dynamic mechanisms of the Babylon myth in this study: *displacement, adaptation,* and *transformation.* I will often speak of "displaced" Babylons or "displaced elements" of the Babylon myth. *Displacement* refers to the way "mythical structures continue to give shape to the metaphors and rhetoric of later types of structure," to use Northrop Frye's formulation.[5] Along these lines, *Babylon under Western Eyes* demonstrates the continued vitality of the Babylon myth in displaced forms throughout Western culture. The process of *adaptation* allows elements of the displaced Babylon myth to replicate across centuries, cultures, and local environments. As a process dependent on displacement and re-creation, adaption sustains an inherent duality: that is, every secondary adaptation of a primary text exists alongside that "original," primary work in some fashion. All adaptations are paratexts, in this sense.[6] Allusions display a similar duality: discrete uses of the word "Babylon" as an allusion not only function within their local context, but also bear with them a second level of meaning referring back to prior originals and their traditions. Allusions thus have a paratextual quality similar

---

4 For an overview of myth, see Coupe, *Myth.* My use of the term "myth" has been guided by the work of scholars such as Harold Fisch and Northrop Frye: see, e.g., Fisch, *A Remembered Future* and his concept of "historical archetypes" (1–19); and Frye (below, note 5). Cf. Richard Slotkin's description of myth in *Regeneration through Violence,* 7: myth is "an intellectual or artistic construct that bridges the gap between the world of the mind and the world of affairs, between dream and reality, between impulse or desire and action. It draws on the content of individual and collective memory, structures it, and develops from it imperatives for belief and action."

5 Frye, *Great Code,* 35. For Frye's concept of displacement, see also his *Anatomy of Criticism,* 136–7, 155–6; and *Words with Power,* 141–2, 148–9. Frye's notion of mythic structure is especially useful for my purposes, given his argument (citing Blake here) that the Bible is the "Great Code of Art": that is, the mythic structures of the Christian Bible reside, in displaced form, as a powerful immanent presence in Western literature. On the enduring influence of the Bible in this sense see also Norton, *History of the Bible as Literature;* Fisch, *Biblical Presence;* Schneidau, *Sacred Discontent.*

6 My thinking on adaptation is guided by Hutcheon, *Theory of Adaptation.*

to adaptations. And finally, *transformation* is a useful term for the "result" of the process begun by displacement and adaptation, because the word "transformation" suggests a result that encompasses both continuity and change. When a cultural tradition is transformed, it implies not a replacement or an utterly new genesis, but rather the incorporation of the old into a new configuration, the retention of prior structures in new forms. Transformed elements look both back to a prior state and ahead to a renewed beginning. As a Western myth of long-standing power, the matter of Babylon operates through a linked process of displacement, adaptation, and transformation.

Reception History, Medievalism, Adaptation

As it lays out the often-surprising ubiquity of Babylon in the following chapters, *Babylon under Western Eyes* testifies to the powerful afterlife of biblical, classical, and medieval paradigms in Western culture. Although I argue that the Middle Ages constitute the most important phase in the genesis of mythic Babylon, my broader aim is to demonstrate the long, vibrant afterlife of Babylon beyond the Middle Ages. In this regard, this is a study in reception history.[7] I show, through the example of just one word and its meanings, that the overemphasized epistemic ruptures of modernity – whether that shifting horizon of modernity is placed in the Renaissance, in the Enlightenment, in the nineteenth-century age of Empire, or in the watershed moments of the twentieth century – and the scholarly emphasis on these supposed moments of modernity's aggressive inception have obscured the deeper, more complex *continuity* of the modern world with its premodern past. The curious and deformative process by which "the modern" is constructed at the expense of "the medieval" is no news to scholars of the medieval world.[8] By focusing on a specific powerful Western symbol – one rich word, in fact – we can see instead the deep, abiding, and complex temporal relationship between the modern and the premodern.

This long tradition of mythic Babylon in the West, derived particularly from Christian modes of thought, manifests even in completely secular contexts. The Christian conceptual basis of Babylon's myth is never truly

7 For just a few sample studies in this mode, see Waswo, *Founding Legend*; Donoghue, *Lady Godiva*; Maguire, *Helen of Troy*; Ziolkowski, *Gilgamesh Among Us*.

8 See, e.g., Robinson, "Medieval, the Middle Ages"; Patterson, "On the Margin"; Holsinger, *Neomedievalism*.

left behind, no matter how secular the later displacements – an argument about the influence of biblical culture that has been made before in various contexts.[9] Again, what I shall delineate in these pages is not a static process, with the Bible or Christianity replicating itself mechanically at every turn, generating archetypal ghosts in the machine. Instead, the mythology of Babylon endures through a dynamic process: its adaptive tradition is an achieved state, constantly mediated and renegotiated through displacement, adaptation, and transformation.

Allusion and Traditional Referentiality

In the main, *Babylon under Western Eyes* shows *what* were the uses of the Babylon myth, and *why* the myth was put to such uses; in my conclusion I also suggest some idea of *how* the tradition grew and was transmitted across the centuries, enduring even now. Thus a secondary agenda in this study is to explore the dynamics involved in building and disseminating an allusive mythic tradition, with Babylon simply as a case study. As we shall see in the following chapters, my evidence generally turns on textual references, citations, quotations, and allusions to the Matter of Babylon. The first three terms – "reference," "citation," "quotation" – while often perhaps technically correct in the examples to follow, do not quite do justice to the complexity of Babylon's myth. As we shall see, the word "Babylon" has accrued connotations independent of any one source, leaving these terms wanting; something more complex and rich is at play here, involved in the creation and dissemination of tradition. I adapt and redefine two terms in order to track this process: "allusion" and "traditional referentiality." *Babylon under Western Eyes* examines the dynamics of textual allusion as a figure, and finds (among other things) that the word "Babylon" always has some of the metaphorical richness and reach of allusion, even if the explanatory

9 For example, in *Natural Supernaturalism* M.H. Abrams demonstrates the deep ties that Romanticism and its modern reflexes have with Christian theological traditions, as new secular contexts adapted and transformed displaced religious ideas. Northrop Frye, Robert Alter, and Harold Fisch have argued similarly with regard to literature, as has Michael Walzer in relation to historical and political writing (*Exodus and Revolution*). For Frye and Fisch, see above, notes 4–5. Alter argues that "the very presuppositions by which we read, our expectations of what literature can do, are predetermined by the decisive early model of the Bible" (*World of Biblical Literature*, 85; see also 87). On the afterlife of Christian tropes in modern horror fiction, see Aguirre, *Closed Space*.

power of the term falls short in some ways.[10] Allusions point beyond their specific textual instantiation to augment the meaning of the texts in which they are deployed by reference to extra-textual materials.[11] In this manner, a Babylon textual reference/citation/quotation *alludes* to the greater Matter of Babylon.[12] Allusions are also temporal displacements, momentarily unmooring the reader in time to connect with a prior textual moment or tradition, often in complex and contradictory ways. Allusions to Babylon thus playfully depend upon and produce a "busy afterlife" for our myth.[13]

However, proceeding in tandem with this process of textual allusion is a second constitutive – but in this case non-textual – operation that generates and disseminates the Babylon mythic tradition. To describe this second process, I borrow and adapt the term "traditional referentiality" from the oral tradition scholar John Miles Foley.[14] "Traditional referentialty" refers to the metonymic process by which oral traditions produce meaning through story; in oral traditions, any one instantiation of an oral "text" (e.g., a singular performance, or at a microscopic level, a singular epithet or word) generates meaning by metonymically accessing

10 My thinking on allusion has been guided mainly by Brower, *Pope: Poetry of Allusion*; Hollander, *Figure of Echo*; Alter, *Pleasures of Reading*, 111–40; Pucci, *Full-Knowing Reader*; Cook, *Against Coercion*, 99–155; Ricks, *Allusion to the Poets*; and Machacek, "Allusion."

11 See Orr, *Intertextuality*, on the difference between quotation and allusion: "Quotation ... is both extraneous ornament and reference of the most overt and saturated kind. It can be a homage, an authority or a complex shorthand which also counters authenticating functions by means of parody, counter-example or ironic questioning ... Quotation, then, is foreign and integrally familiar matter, like sand in the oyster that forms the pearl" (130). "Like any signifier, allusion is not self-referential as it points beyond itself. However, allusion does not disperse or defer meanings either. Like quotation, it intensifies meaningfulness, but extensively rather than intensively. Allusion gathers up the many inferences of the referent as if by the way, to navigate meanings to another port" (139).

12 Hollander and Cook both urge better understanding of the specific subcategories of allusion. As useful as this is, I follow Cook in retaining "allusion" as a general term encompassing several related terms: references, citations, quotations, echoes, and so forth (see *Against Coercion*, 101).

13 The quoted phrase is from Felski, "Context Stinks!," 580; she argues for the "busy afterlife of the literary artifact" and its "possibilities of transtemporal connection and comparison" as aspects of literary experience that militate against the determining power of historicized understanding. I believe that allusion as a figure of speech also enhances this "transtemporal" dimension of literature.

14 On traditional referentiality, see Foley, *Immanent Art*, 38–60.

a much broader oral field of traditional semantic associations available to the audience. From this perspective, the Matter of Babylon is an oral tradition as well as a textual tradition; in the West, down through the centuries, people have just always "known" some meanings of Babylon, in many cases without being able to recite the chapter and verse of some textual source. We will return to allusion and traditional referentiality more directly in my conclusion, but suffice to say here that in addition to *what* Babylon means, and *why* it means what it does, this study also suggests *how* Babylon is transmitted as a myth: through the intertwined and mutually enabling processes of textual figure (allusion) and oral dissemination (traditional referentiality).

Babylon and the Urban Symbolic

Babylon under Western Eyes also naturally contributes something to the study of the city's image in literature.[15] Cities are one of humanity's most ancient and rich symbols, a primal representation of human community, for both good and ill. Babylon stands as an urban symbol in at least two senses. It is part of a fundamental urban dyad: in the Western tradition, particularly in the Middle Ages, it is difficult to talk about Babylon without considering its bright opposite, Jerusalem.[16] The two cities are paired together most powerfully in the patristic writings of the Western Church Fathers, especially Augustine: the City of Man – Babylon, and the City of God – Jerusalem.[17] Following Augustinian tradition, opposed binary images tend to dominate Western representations of the City: the city as a paradisiacal utopia (Jerusalem) and the city as a nightmare dystopia (Babylon). Between the poles of this opposition, the city can stand for

15 This is an enormous field of study. For a selection of interesting representative works covering a variety of periods, all of which I have found useful in thinking about Babylon, see Weimer, *City as Metaphor*; Wheatley, *City as Symbol*; R. Williams, *Country and the City*; Byrd, *London Transformed*; Dougherty, *Fivesquare City*; Jaye and Watts, eds. *Literature and the Urban Experience*; Pike, *Image of the City in Modern Literature*; Paster, *Idea of the City in the Age of Shakespeare*; Tinkler-Villani, ed., *Babylon or New Jerusalem?*; Alter, *Imagined Cities*; McNutt, *Urban Revelations*; P. Yeager, ed., "Cities," a special topic issue of *PMLA*; Fitzpatrick, ed., *Idea of the City: Early-Modern, Modern and Post-Modern*; Peer, ed., *Romanticism and the City*.

16 On the connection between the medieval city and medieval world views, see Lilley, *City and Cosmos*. For a study of Jerusalem in medieval literature, focusing mostly on late medieval England, see S. Yeager, *Jerusalem in Medieval Narrative*.

17 See chapter 2, 48–54.

the experience of humanity in the world, a "strident assertion of mankind against time itself."[18]

But in the premodern world, Babylon is also linked to a second fundamental urban symbol: the Tower of Babel. The fusion of Babylon with the Tower of Babel was a Western commonplace deriving from a reading of Genesis 10–11. After the great Flood, Noah's son Ham begets Cush, who in turn begets the fearsome Nimrod, mighty hunter before the Lord. Genesis 10 tells us that "the beginning of [Nimrod's] kingdom was Babylon ... in the land of Sennaar [Shinar]" (Genesis 10:10).[19] The very next chapter in Genesis gives us the Tower of Babel story and the sundering of tongues: the descendants of Noah journeyed from the east and "found a plain in the land of Sennaar, and dwelt in it" (Genesis 11:2). Upon this plain they declare their ambition: "Come, let us make a city and a tower, the top whereof may reach to heaven: and let us make our name famous, before we be scattered abroad into all lands" (Genesis 11:4). God confounds their ambition, toppling the tower into the city and splitting their one common language into many:

> And so the Lord scattered them from that place into all lands, and they ceased to build the city. And therefore the name thereof was called "Babel" because there the language of the whole earth was "confounded" [*confusum*]: and from thence the Lord scattered them abroad upon the face of all countries. (Genesis 11:8–9)

As Robert Alter explains, the biblical narrator here makes a polemical pun upon the Akkadian word *Bâbilu* (i.e., "Babylon"), by associating it with the Hebrew verb *bālāl* ("to mix or confuse," i.e., "confounded").[20]

---

18 Max Weber, *The City*, 10: "There are moments in every city dawn when the circles, rectangles, polygons, and triangles – the geometry of the city – seem to float in the mist, like the essence of the human spirit emancipated from the earth. There are times, on starlit nights, when its towers and spires ram upward as if to tear the darkness loose from its riveting stars and the city seems to be a strident assertion of mankind against time itself."

19 Here the AV reads "And the beginning of his kingdom was Babel, and Erech, and Accad, and Calneh, in the land of Shinar" (Genesis 10:10).

20 The Akkadian word probably means "gate of God" (Alter, *Genesis*, 47). The entry for Babylon in the *New Catholic Encyclopedia* summarizes the linguistic situation well: "[Babylon's] original name was perhaps the Akkadian term *bābu ellu* (holy gate) – which term had been transferred from its processional gate to the section of the city near the gate and then to the whole city – or it was a pre-Semitic, non-Sumerian word; but at

Taking their cue from the biblical text, subsequent commentators naturally connected Nimrod's founding of Babylon on the plain of Shinar in Genesis 10 with the rising tower of Babel on the same plain of Shinar in Genesis 11. Therefore, the fundamental medieval equation was Babylon = Babel and Babylon/Babel = "confusion" [*confusio*]. This commonplace fusion of Babel and Babylon stretches from the fifth century to at least the seventeenth: that is, from Augustine's *City of God* – "This city, which was called 'Confusion,' is Babylon itself, whose marvellous construction is praised also by pagan historians. In fact, 'Babylon' means 'confusion'"[21] – to Jacques-Bénigne Bossuet's *Discourse on Universal History* (*Discours sur l'histoire universelle*, 1681):

> Shortly after the first division of mankind the fierce Nimrod became the first conqueror because of his violent nature; and such is the origin of conquests. He established his kingdom at Babylon, the very place where the tower had been started and was already quite high, though not quite high enough to satisfy human pride.[22]

As we shall see, the myth of Babylon – in and of itself, and through myriad displacements – underwrites a host of urban representations in the West.

Myths and their Genealogies

Babylon under Western Eyes is a selective study, not a comprehensive chronological history of mythic Babylon in all its iterations and incarnations.[23] References and allusions to Babylon in Western culture are

---

an early period this name was changed by folk etymology to *bāb-ilim* [gate of the god (Marduk)] ... In Genesis 11.9 the Hebrew name *bābel* is explained by folk etymology as if the city were thus called because Yahweh there 'confused' (*bālāl*) the language of the builders of the Tower of Babel. From the neo-Babylonian name of the city *bāb-ilāni* (gate of the gods) is derived its Greek name Βαβυλών" (s.v. "Babylon, City of").

21 *De civitate Dei*, 16.4: Ista ciuitas, quae apellata est confusio, ipsa est Babylon, cuius mirabilem constructionem etiam gentium commendat historia. Babylon quippe interpretatur confusio. Augustine, *De civitate Dei*, ed. Dombart and Kalb; trans. Dyson, *Augustine: The City of God*. Cf. Isidore, *Etymologiae*, XV.1.4: "It [Babylon] takes its name from 'confusion,' because there the languages of those building the tower were confused and confounded" (Vocabulum autem sumpit a confusione, eo quod ibi confusae sint atque permixtae linguae aedificantium turrem).

22 Bossuet, *Discourse on Universal History*, 11.

23 Nothing like the four volumes and two thousand, three hundred, and twenty pages of Arno Borst's *Der Turmbau von Babel: Geschichte der Meinungen über Ursprung und Vielfalt*

simply too pervasive to write a comprehensive sequential history of the topic. I have even tried to avoid the term "history" in describing the form and structure of this book. The traditional form of diachronic history almost invariably imparts a narrative *telos* to the material under consideration, deploying a narrative shape that is also an interpretation, a generalization, and (quite often) a simplification. While a useful structuring device in other contexts, such a narrative *telos* would not be faithful to the complex Babylon myth and its allusive character. I have found there is no simple dominant chronological story to tell, Babylon meaning one thing in the medieval world, another thing in the nineteenth century, and yet another in the modern world, for example. The twin processes of adaptation and allusion foregrounded in this study in fact tend to short-circuit such teleologies of narrative history and their accompanying generalizations. Instead, the Babylon myth is one of rough continuity, expanding incrementally and unpredictably under pressure from the recursive force of adaptation and allusion on the one hand, as well as the pressure of successive, localized historical contexts on the other.

A better term or image for my purposes therefore is the "genealogy," and the following chapters thus present several overlapping genealogies intrinsic to mythic Babylon. A genealogy is always a partial representation: "family trees" could be, in theory, expanded indefinitely; the picture of Babylon I present here is similarly partial and not exhaustive. A genealogy also maps out the connections among elements, but without a pre-existing scheme in mind; in its random lines of connection, a genealogy schematizes relationships, but without recourse to a teleological explanation of the phenomenon under study. A genealogy also demonstrates both continuity and change over time: different "family members," but an overall "family resemblance"; the introduction of new elements, yet continuity in the face of ongoing expansion. This study does have a diachronic historical component in the way my individual genealogies show change over time; but I offer several parallel and overlapping genealogies in order to illuminate and represent better the total complex formation of the Babylon mythic tradition.[24]

---

der Sprachen und Völker is attempted here. On the Tower of Babel story in Anglo-Saxon literature and culture, see Tristan Major, *Literary Developments of the Table of Nations and the Tower of Babel in Anglo-Saxon England*. PhD dissertation, University of Toronto, 2010.

24 My use of "genealogy" is partially inspired by Foucault's well-known (and pervasively influential) post-structuralist notion of genealogy as an alternative to traditional historical enquiry: see Foucault, "Nietzsche, Genealogy, History." Foucault's aversion

Such a structure also allows me to investigate more adequately the dynamics of adaptation and allusion; in many ways, *Babylon under Western Eyes* is a "case study" of these two rhetorical figures. Adaptation and allusion have a transtemporal aspect: they are derived, secondary manifestations of a prior (or primary) text. Both modes defy time, in a sense: they bear the weight of an entire tradition of meaning, and their use signals a moment of interface, a contiguity among multiple times and places. The structure of the book accommodates and mimics this transtemporal dimension of adaptation and allusion.[25] And so I divide this study into three main sections, each focused on a complex classical/Christian/medieval topical tradition related to the "Matter of Babylon"; the chapters in each of these sections move chronologically and selectively from the premodern world to the present as they develop complex genealogies of Babylon's displaced myths. By moving back and forth across time and across topical traditions in the overall arc of this study, the book's structure better engages the analogous temporal dynamics of allusion and adaptation.[26] My hope is that the deployment of this study's argument in this way points to an alternate mode of writing literary history – one that eschews exclusively diachronic or synchronic teleology and operates instead through a more complex understanding of temporality.

The three main sections of the book thus constitute three thematic genealogies, each one examining distinct aspects of the Babylon myth in its discreet trajectory. Each section also corresponds to a different

---

to teleology and the search for origins in historical method generally fits well with this study's analysis of the Babylon myth: the history of Babylon under Western eyes is messy, recursive, marked by accident, misunderstanding (see, e.g., chapter 7, on Babylon and Cairo), and "the errors, the false appraisals, and the faulty calculations that give birth to those things that continue to exist and have value for us" (Foucault, "Nietzsche," 81). I believe, however, that at a certain point Foucault's focus on discontinuities, on the disruption of "pretended continuity" (88) and the "dissipation of identity" (95), simply substitutes an alternative teleological imperative and ideological narrative in place of a putative traditional search for origins.

25 The book's complication of direct linear time and history derives some inspiration from the field of postcolonial literary studies. See in particular Wallace, *Premodern Places* and Campbell, *Literature and Culture in the Black Atlantic*. Campbell refers to his mixing of past and present, medieval writers and Anglophone Caribbean writers as "temporally synchronous hybridity" (1).

26 The book's argumentative structure thus enters current scholarly debates over method in literary studies, particularly the growing discontent with historical contextualization as the *sine qua non* of literary interpretation: see, for example, the essays in *NLH* 42.4 (2011), a special issue on "Context?" and Felski, *Uses of Literature*.

governing mechanism of reproduction: Babylon as *metaphor* (Part I), Babylon as *archetype* (Part II), and Babylon as *topos* (Part III). Beneath these three rubrics I construct my genealogies, stretching from the ancient world to the present. When choosing my texts and examples, I have generally gravitated towards influential, typical, or representative authors and textual traditions. My selective principle of importance and influence has not been absolute – there are some surprises in these pages, examples too interesting to pass up, as well as materials that were once popular and influential, but now have fallen silent in the cultural record. Nevertheless, it has seemed prudent to illuminate with the most important sources, seeking out other angles of sight from time to time with more obscure texts. There is an emphasis in these pages on the medieval tradition and on the English tradition; however, I cast my net beyond these areas to incorporate classical and late antique texts (mainly in Latin) as well as selected later examples from other European traditions as needed. Again, this book does not claim to be a comprehensive study, but rather a vivid sketch that does, however, claim representative status in defining the Matter of Babylon's main currents in the West.

Moreover, in order to focus on representative and influential texts, *Babylon under Western Eyes* also deliberately mixes what are sometimes distinguished as "high culture" and "low culture" (or popular culture) texts. In these pages the reader will find Herodotus and H.P. Lovecraft, Voltaire and the modern horror film, and many other vertiginous pairings. In this way, the book derives inspiration from the legacy of cultural studies, which looks for cultural patterns regardless of where they may reside, and also draws upon the field of adaptation studies and reception history, which adopts a similarly tolerant and eclectic attitude towards cultural evidence.

Part I, "Babylon as Political Metaphor," examines the use of Babylon in political contexts and as political discourse, broadly construed. The three chapters in this section, moving collectively from Herodotus to the contemporary American evangelical "Left Behind" apocalyptic fiction, demonstrate Babylon's association with a range of political subjects such as empire, conquest, and tyranny; political power and its abuses; slavery and dissent; exile, emancipation, and restoration; polemic and prophecy. I trace the way Babylon has acquired a metaphoric cast and evolved into a metaphoric expression regularly connected to and co-opted by political themes and ideologies charged with apocalyptic intensity and immediacy. Chapter 1 looks at pre-Christian classical sources and the Bible, establishing many of the basic features of the West's understanding of political Babylon. Chapter 2 moves to late antique and early medieval case studies of political Babylon. This chapter begins with the most important figure in this period of Babylon's imaginative history – Saint Augustine of Hippo (354–430) and his supremely influential metaphoric use of Babylon in his theological concept of the "Two Cities." Augustine consolidates the mimetic and metaphoric traditions inherited from classical antiquity and the Bible and extends the tradition in important ways, animating the Babylon myth as a way to understand both sacred history and the inner workings of the self. The remaining authors in this chapter display variations on the inherited Augustinian formula, case studies in the adaptation of Babylon's political myth: Paulus Orosius (fl. early 5th c.) and his *Seven Books of History against the Pagans*; the anonymous Old English poem *Daniel* (c. 700–1000); and the exegetical writings of the venerable Bede (c. 673–735). Chapter 3 carries the genealogy of political Babylon forward in time to the present. This chapter argues for the importance of the fourteenth-century Great Schism of the papacy and the Reformation in the later promulgation of Babylon as a commonplace metaphor within political/religious rhetoric. Taken as a whole, these first three chapters comprising Part I show how Babylon has been an enduring and important metaphoric component of Western political language deriving from a late antique/early medieval synthesis of the Babylon myth.

Part II, "Babylon as Degenerate Archetype," moves to a different genealogy: the commonplace connection between Babylon and luxuriant, deviant, and contagious "racial" degeneracy. I use "archetype" in this section with no reference to Joseph Campbell or C.G. Jung or Frye, or any type of immemorial, essential unchanging forms; rather I take "archetype" here in something closer to its etymological meaning as "original form" or "primary model."[27] The two chapters in this section demonstrate that a potent and influential tradition of "racial degeneracy" originates in the medieval Matter of Babylon. In this tradition, Babylon is the archetypal

27 The *OED* tells us that the definition of "archetype" as an "original pattern or model from which copies are made; a prototype" dates from the early modern period, prior, of course to Jung's early twentieth-century appropriation of the term. Etymologically, "archetype" derives from Latin *archetypum*, which itself comes from Greek *ἀρχέτυπον*, < *ἀρχε-* = *ἀρχι-* first + *τύπος* impress, stamp, type (*OED*, s.v. "archetype").

source of an ancient tainted human lineage: in the Christian imagination a line of racial degeneracy begins even before the founding of Babylon with Cain (history's first murderer, exile, and founder of cities) and his progeny, and then descends directly to Ham (the cursed son of Noah), and thence to Nimrod (archetypal tyrant, founder of Babylon and architect of the Tower of Babel). In early Christian tradition these biblical representatives of primordial evil were connected as the archetypal founders of a cursed, inhuman strain of humanity – the "kin of Cain," as the *Beowulf* poet describes the lineage of Grendel and his mother. The shadow of Babylon presided over the delineation of a cursed, degenerate strain of humanity in which the original vigour and purity of God's people has fallen into corruption and decline. The chapters in this section thus argue that scholarship on the concept of "race" in the Western tradition up to the present day needs to take better account of the powerful afterlife of the medieval archetype of the cursed, degenerate race – the children of Babylon. Although "race" as a concept is often seen exclusively as an eighteenth- or nineteenth-century invention, these chapters establish an important medieval paradigm and precedent for somatic, racial logic in the West. In displaced form, this pattern would become the foundation for a way of thinking about the "family of man" and its outcasts in later centuries, even when the "Babylonian" connection was long lost.

Part III, "Babylon as Sublime Topos," establishes two distinct but parallel genealogies. "Topos" is often a loose synonym for "theme" or "subject" in literary criticism, but my intent in these two chapters is to play upon the original etymological sense of topos as a *location* or *place*; these chapters analyze aspects of the imaginative topography of Babylon. In other words, Babylon in these chapters is a sublime place, rather than a political metaphor or an archetype of degeneracy. By examining two distinct – even opposed – senses of place (*topoi*) derived from the Babylon myth – the Ruined City and the City of Eastern Romance – these two chapters argue for a sublime "aesthetics of Babylon." Thus, beyond its political uses (Part I), and beyond its associations with degeneracy (Part II), Babylon is finally a figure of beauty and exotic magnificence, even as it is also an awe-inspiring image of decay and ruin (Part III). Chapter 6 tracks the idea of Babylon as the origin of the ruined/haunted/lost city *topos*; chapter 7 investigates Babylon as a metonymic representation of the sublime East and a figure for unbounded distance in the romance tradition.

PART I

Babylon as Political Metaphor

De seculo veni; Babilone versatus sum.

[I have come from the world; I have experienced Babylon.]
– Petrarch, *On Religious Leisure* (*De otio religioso*)[1]

"Ah! Konstantin Dmitrich! You've come back to our depraved Babylon," she said, giving him her tiny yellow hand and recalling the words he had spoken once at the beginning of winter, that Moscow was Babylon. "Has Babylon become better, or have you become worse?" she added, glancing at Kitty with a mocking smile.
– Countess Nordston to Levin in Tolstoy, *Anna Karenina* (1873–7), trans. Pevear and Volokhonsky, 49

1 Franceso Petrarca, *Opere Latine*, I.696, ed. Bufano et al.; Petrarch, *On Religious Leisure*, trans. Schearer, 82.

Chapter One

The Political Image of Babylon in Antiquity

Alas! alas! that great city, Babylon, that mighty city: for in one hour is thy judgment come.

– Revelation 18:10

Alexander [the Great] preferred Babylon, since he saw that it far surpassed [other cities], not only in its size, but also in all other respects.

– Strabo, *Geography*, XV.3.10

Babylon, which is the capital of the Chaldaean races, long held an outstanding celebrity among the cities in the whole of the world.

– Pliny, *Natural History*, VI.121

Prior to the Middle Ages, the image of Babylon in the West was a composite drawn primarily from two traditions: the literature of classical Greece and Rome, and the books of the Bible. Both sources were influential, setting out patterns that would endure as the varied myths of Babylon developed in the Middle Ages. We shall see that classical Babylon and biblical Babylon contain strongly congruent, analogous, and mutually reinforcing images. This chapter accordingly has two main areas of focus. The first might be called the "metaphoric potential" of Babylon. In the classical and biblical traditions, the word "Babylon" designates a historical city; but there is also, right from the beginning of the tradition, a sense in which "Babylon" is a metaphor accruing connotations beyond its denotative referent. The second element that becomes clear in this chapter, a consequence of this metaphoric potential, is the city's early association with a number of political themes, such as imperial power and the decadence of tyranny; conquest and the terror of subjugation; enslavement and emancipation; and renovation and transition. Overall, these political themes might also well be described as apocalyptic in their general orientation; therefore, a final argument across these three chapters will be that these metaphoric and political dimensions of Babylon tend to be charged with the intensity of feeling and emotional immediacy typical of apocalyptic thought.

Babylonian Power in Western Classical Sources

The vast might of Babylon – as both a city and as a larger political entity – impressed classical authors. Babylon had a reputation as a "superpower" of the past – a city and empire reputed to be of great power and antiquity. A description of the city's massive size is a standard topic in numerous histories and geographies.[2] Babylon moves Herodotus (c. 490–25 BCE) to superlatives; the city appears mainly in two places in his *Histories*: near the end of Book I when he details the conquest of the city by Cyrus of Persia in 539 BCE, and near the end of Book III when he narrates the second taking of the city by Darius in 521 BCE during a rebellion of its inhabitants. In Book I he tells us that Babylon is the "most renowned and strongest" of Assyria's "vast number of great cities."[3] He explains that "such is its size, [that] in magnificence there is no other city that approaches to it";[4] he notes that "the fruitfulness of Babylonia must seem incredible to those who have never visited the country."[5] After Herodotus, the size, beauty, and power of the city become a commonplace. Aristotle (384–22 BCE), for example, also notes the city's immensity, and the Greek geographer Strabo (64 BCE–24 CE) passes on an influential

2 E.g., Herodotus, *Histories* I.178–87; Strabo, *Geogrwaphy* XVI.1.5; Diodorus Siculus, *Library of History*, II.7.2–II.10.6; Pliny, *Natural History*, VI.121–2. For a later example see Aethicus Ister, *Cosmography*, 108.2–6. Ctesias of Cnidus also wrote of Babylon in his lost *Persica*; his information about the city was incorporated by Diodorus Siculus in his *Library of History*. On Babylon in classical sources see also Seymour, *Babylon*, 51–78. For a general survey of the classical idea of the city in Horace, Juvenal, and Plautus, see Paster, *Idea of the City*, 33–57.

3 *Histories*, I.178.

4 *Histories*, I.178.

5 *Histories*, I.193. The rich fecundity of Babylonian land is noted by many sources: e.g., by Strabo, who notes that the city is situated in "a very prosperous land" (*Geography*, XV.3.5); see also XVI.1.14 (on Babylon's production of barley); Pliny, *Natural History*, VI.121–2; Orosius, *History*, II.6.8.

anecdote from Herodotus, marveling that the width of Babylon's walls is so great that four-horse chariots can easily pass each other when driven along the top, a description many later authors repeat; Strabo acclaims the massive walls and the Hanging Gardens as one of the Seven Wonders of the World.[6] Herodotus and Aristotle both explain that Babylon was so enormous that when the outer walls were breeched by the Persians, the inhabitants of the central part of the city were not aware for some time that the city had been lost.[7] The historian Quintus Curtius (late first century/early second century CE) praises Babylon as the richest of cities (*urbem opulentissimam*), a place of beauty and antiquity (*pulchritudo ac vetustas*); he describes the massive walls as a "prodigious work" (*ingens opus*) and notes that the bridge of Babylon built over the Euphrates is among the "marvels of the Orient" (*mirabilia Orientis*).[8] Pliny, in the epigraph to this chapter, sums up the city's reputation and influence in his encyclopedic *Natural History*: "Babylon, which is the capital of the Chaldaean races, long held an outstanding celebrity among the cities in the whole of the world, and in consequence of this the remaining part of Mesopotamia and Assyria has received the name of Babylonia."[9]

Moreover, Babylon's awe-inspiring reputation was soon used metaphorically, as a figure or symbol for great and prodigious works. In the sixth book of Lucan's (39–65 CE) *Civil War*, Caesar surrounds Pompey's forces at Dyrrachium with a vast earthwork; Lucan uses Babylon as an epic comparison for the vast size of the military undertaking:

> [L]et ancient legend praise the walls of Troy and ascribe the building to the gods; let Parthians, who fight retreating, marvel at the brick walls round Babylon. Behold! a space as great as is surrounded by the Tigris or swift

6 Aristotle, *Politics*, II.1265a and III.1276a; Strabo, *Geography*, XVI.1.5; Herodotus, *Histories*, I.179. See also Quintus Curtius, *History of Alexander*, V.i.25; Pliny, *Natural History*, VI.121 2; Vitruvius, *On Architecture*, I.5.8; Orosius, *History*, II.6.10. Cf. Juvenal, *Satires*, X.168–72.

7 Herodotus, *Histories*, I.191; Aristotle, *Politics*, III.1276a.

8 *History of Alexander*, V.i.7, V.i.24, V.i.16, V.i.29.

9 *Natural History*, VI.121: Babylon Chaldaicarum gentium caput diu summam claritatem inter urbes obtinuit in toto orbe, propter quam reliqua pars Mesopotamiae Assyriaeque Babylonia appellata est. For further references to the size and power of Babylon see Strabo, *Geography*, XV.3.10; Pliny, *Natural History*, VI.121–2; Solinus, *Collectanea Rerum Memorabilium*, 227; Martianus Capella, *De Nuptiis Philologiae et Mercurii*, VI.70 (Pliny, Solinus, and Martianus Capella all use Pomponius Mela, *De chorographia*, I.63.52 as a source); Ammianus Marcellinus XXIII.VI.23; Orosius, *History* II.6.6–11; Aethicus Ister, *Cosmography*, 108.2–6. Cf. Lucan, *Bellum Civile*, I.10–12.

Orontes – a space large enough to form a kingdom for the Assyrian nations of the East – is here enclosed by works hastily thrown up in the stress of war.[10]

In this passage, Lucan gives Babylon status equal to Troy as a place of wondrous urban accomplishment. Troy and Babylon are both, in fact, proverbial images of civilization's might and power. Babylon's mighty reputation in these early classical sources sets the groundwork for later mythmaking.

These basic classical tropes of Babylon – the size of the city walls, the power and rich prosperity of the empire, the marvellous, almost decadent, opulence of the city – formed a composite image that was replicated again and again in the geographical and historical traditions of late antiquity and the early Middle Ages, through a host of intermediary texts and authors – texts such as Solinus's *Collection of Memorable Things* (*Collectanea Rerum Memorabilium*), a third century geographical compendium based on Pliny that saw enormous circulation throughout the Middle Ages into the seventeenth century; or Justin's Latin *Epitome* (second or third century CE) of the lost Latin *Phillipic History* composed by Pompeius Trogus sometime near the end of the first century CE; or Saint Jerome's Latin translation of Eusebius of Caesarea's *Chronicon* (early fourth century), the latter a Greek text deriving its Babylon lore from Herodotus. For us, this sounds like a roll call of obscure names and titles; but such texts were mainstream, canonical sources widespread throughout late antiquity and the early Middle Ages.[11] Works such as these

10 Lucan, *Bellum Civile*, VI.48–54:

Nunc vetus Iliacos attollat fabula muros
Ascribatque deis; fragili circumdata testa
Moenia mirentur refugi Babylonia Parthi.
En quantum Tigris, quantum celer ambit Orontes,
Assyriis quantum populis telluris Eoae
Sufficit in regnum, subitum bellique tumultu
Raptum clausit opus.

For similar statements in the *Bellum Civile* see also VIII.222–5 and VIII.298–300.

11 Pompeius Trogus wrote his Latin history of the Macedonian empire sometime during the reign of Augustus, the *Historiae Philippicae* (*Phillipic History*), in forty-four books; this work was lost, but selections survive in Pliny and especially in the Latin *Epitome* by Justin (c. 200 CE). Justin's *Epitome* of Pompeius Trogus was an exceptionally popular work in the Middle Ages, used by Augustine, Orosius, Cassiodorus, and Isidore. More than 200 medieval manuscripts survive (Justin, *Epitome*, trans. Yardley and Heckel, 1).

ultimately stand behind the pervasive medieval genres of universal history and encyclopedic compendia such as Isidore's *Etymologies.* Through these genres the classical traditions of Babylon are transmitted, with very little variation, to the later Middle Ages and ultimately to the modern world.

Imperial Origins: The Tyranny of Ninus and Semiramis

In tandem with Babylon's sheer size and magnificence, tyranny and imperial political aspirations are also an early part of the classical tradition. Diodorus Siculus (first century BCE) devotes the second book of his *Library of History* (based in part on Ctesias of Cnidus's late fifth-century BCE history of Persia) to Assyria; he notes that the very earliest kings of Asia are unknown, but the first infamous name passed down to posterity belongs to Ninus of Assyria, one of the earliest conquering kings in history and a precursor to the Babylonian imperial rulers:

> In the earliest age, then, the kings of Asia were native-born, and in connection with them no memory is preserved of either a notable deed or a personal name. The first to be handed down by tradition to history and memory for us as one who achieved great deeds is Ninus, king of the Assyrians ... For being by nature a warlike man and emulous of valour, he supplied the strongest of the young men with arms, and by training them for a considerable time he accustomed them to every hardship and all the dangers of war.[12]

But the warlike Ninus, Diodorus explains, is then "seized with a powerful desire to subdue all of Asia."[13] His imperial ambitions are a new thing in the history of the world: Pompeius Trogus tells us that prior to Ninus, men did not seek to expand their territory at others' expense.[14] Thus an imperial innovator, Ninus expands his empire and founds Nineveh as a monument to his political power, as Diodorus explains:

> For having accomplished deeds more notable than those of any king before him, he was eager to found a city of such magnitude [τηλικαύτην κτίσαι τὸ μέγεθος

On Orosius's use of Justin's *Epitome* see Hagendahl, "Orosius und Iustinus." For general introductions to Justin and Pompeius Trogus see Alonso-Núñez, *La Historia Universal de Pompeyo Trogo*; Justin, *Epitome*, trans. Yardley, 1–34; Yardley, *Justin and Pompeius Trogus.*

12 Diodorus Siculus, *Library of History*, II.1.4.

13 Diodorus Siculus, *Library of History*, II.2.1; see also Pompeius Trogus I.1.4–8.

14 Pompeius Trogus I.1.3. On the figure of Ninus in Pompeius Trogus see Alonso-Núñez, *La Hista Universal*, 64–5: Ninus is "el rey asirio fundador de la primera

> πόλιν], that not only would it be the largest of any which then existed in the whole inhabited world, but also that no other ruler of a later time should, if he undertook such a task, find it easy to surpass him.[15]

Ninus's name would be associated with tyranny throughout the Middle Ages, paired (in a competing Christian tradition) with Nimrod, as we shall see in the next chapter.[16] The imperial ambitions of Ninus set the stage for Babylon's glory: the classical tradition invariably links Ninus with his wife Semiramis, who will surpass her husband's imperial ambitions and found Babylon. Nineveh's unprecedented size and power under Ninus are important precursors to the myth of Babylon: as Diodorus explains, "a city its [i.e., Nineveh's] equal, in respect to either the length of its circuit or the magnificence of its walls, was never founded by any man after his time."[17] In later traditions the separate strands of Assyrian, Babylonian, Parthian, and Persian history, as well as their cities and rulers (Babylon, Nineveh, Ninus, Semiramis, Nebuchadnezzar, Belshazzar), will tend to blur together into one archetypal City of the ancient Orient in the mythic imagination, presided over by ancient despotism and imperial ambition.

Although Diodorus Siculus claims that no man will found a larger city than Nineveh, a woman did indeed surpass Ninus's imperial ambitions: his wife, Semiramis. The imperial couple dominates the earliest history of Assyria and Babylonia; as Strabo notes, in the early history of the world, "[t]hese two gained the mastery of Asia."[18] In the classical view of ancient Asian history, Ninus and Semiramis form a linked pair: Ninus

---

monarquía universal ... De este modo Pompeyo trogo establece una secuencia de acontecimientos y vincula los orígenes de la historia propiamente dicha a la figura ne Nino" (64–5; see also 96–7, 116–17). He describes Ninus's expansion of his kingdom as "imperialista" (96).

15 Diodorus Siculus, *Library of History*, II.3.1.This tyranny of Ninus becomes a standard feature of later world histories: see, e.g., Pompeius Trogus I.1.3–8; Book I of Eusebius/Jerome, *Chronicon*: "King Ninus son of Belus first reigned over all Asia except for the Indies, for fifty-two years. In the forty-third year of the rule of this Ninus, Abraham was born" (Primus omnis Asiae rex exceptis Indis regnavit Ninus, Beli filius, annis LII. Huius XLIII imperii anno sui natus est Abraham); Latin text from *Eusebius Werke*, vol. VII: *Die Chronik des Hieronymus*, ed. Helm, 16.

16 The twelfth-century Latin poet Walter Map, for example, gives us a Ninus "whose tyranny and hostility to his neighbors can be read about in history" (de cuius tirannide quam inuide satis exercuit et cupide contra finitimos, liquet in auctoribus): Walter Map, *De nugis curialium*, ed. and trans. James, Dist. iii, c. 3.

17 Diodorus Siculus, *Library of History*, II.3.3.

18 Strabo, *Geography*, XVI.1.2.

begins the first imperial project, founding Nineveh; Semiramis continues and completes the task, founding the greater city of Babylon.[19] She too then becomes regularly associated with Babylon's construction in classical sources: in the *Metamorphoses* of Ovid (43 BCE–17 CE), Pyramus and Thisbe live in "houses side by side, in the city [of Babylon], which Semiramis is said to have surrounded with walls of brick."[20] Like Ninus, Semiramis is an ambitious imperial leader; she also burns to have her name live on in great monumental works. According to Diodorus Siculus:

> Semiramis, whose nature made her eager for great exploits and ambitious to surpass the fame of her predecessor on the throne, set her mind upon founding a city in Babylonia, and after securing the architects of all the world and skilled artisans and making all the other necessary preparations, she gathered together from her entire kingdom two million men to complete the work.[21]

The sense of transcendent space here is important: the resources of the entire world were leveraged into Babylon's construction.[22] Pomponius Mela (early first century) notes that there are many signs (*multa insignia*) of Semiramis's works in the world; particularly well known are two things: that she diverted the course of the Tigris and Euphrates rivers through the desert, and that she founded the city great and wondrous city of Babylon (*constituta urbs mirae magnitudinis Babylon*).[23] The Latin

---

19 See Herodotus, *Histories*, I.184; Strabo, *Geography*, II.1.31 and XVI.1.2; Didodorus Siculus, *Library of History*, II.4.1, II.7.3, and ff.; Pompeius Trogus I.2.1–11; Ammianus Marcellinus XXIII.6.3; Vitruvius, *On architecture*, VIII.3.8. On Ninus and Semiramis in Diodorus, see Seymour, *Babylon*, 60–4.

20 Ovid *Metamorphoses*, IV.57–8: "contiguas ... domos, ubi dicitur altam / coctilibus muris cinxisse Semiramis urbem." They will make a romantic rendezvous by Ninus's tomb (IV.88); or "Ninny's tomb," as Shakespeare's mechanicals mangle it in *A Midsummer Night's Dream* (II.1.84).

21 *Library of History*, II.7.2; see also Pompeius Trogus I.2.8–9; Eusebius/Jerome, *Chronicon*, 17: "Semiramis, wife of Ninus, ruled over the Assyrians, of whom innumerable things are recounted. She also held Asia, and constructed mud banks, because of a flood, restoring very many of the cities of Babylonia" (Assyriis imperauit uxor Nini Semiramis, de qua innumerabilia narrantur, quae et Asiam tenuit et propter inundationem aggeres construxit plurima Babyloniae urbis instaurans).

22 Diodorus Siculus emphasizes in great detail the munificence of Semiramis's city (II.8.3). On Semiramis as a builder of towers see also Claudian, *Panegyric on Probinus and Olybrius* in *Claudian*, ed. and trans. Platnauer, I.2–23, lines 161–3.

23 Pomponius Mela, *De Chorographia*, ed. Parroni, I.63; trans. Romer, *Pomponius Mela's Description of the World*, 52.

poet Claudian (fl. 395–404) points out that both Carthage and "proud Babylon with her hundred gates, are both said to have been built by a woman's effort (*femineus labor*)."[24] Semiramis and her femininity become part of Babylon's mythic image along with the city's sense of excess and vaunting ambition. We shall see that the association of Babylon with tyranny and over-proud ambition will be adapted to Christian mythology through the figure of Nimrod, founder of Babylon in the Christian tradition. But this original association of Babylon with femininity makes the developing image of Babylon consonant with later elements of the Babylon myth, such as the apocalyptic Whore of Babylon and general notions of sexual degeneracy, effeminacy, and decadence.

The Babylonian Transitus

The Babylon of Ninus and Semiramis thus achieves a certain imperial monumentality in the classical sources; it is the image of a vast polity rooted deeply in the earliest depths of recorded human time and the original source of despotic, decadent empire. There was surely an attendant sense of wonder attached to this greatest polity of earliest history, an immovable city and empire immensely old and immensely powerful.

Yet as dominant as this image of great power, stasis, and monumentality might be, it also proceeds, in the classical sources, in step with a certain sense of Babylon's *transitus*, the city's passing or receding from history: the Western classical authors who note the power of Babylon usually do so in the shadow of that power's eventual loss. Like Troy in the Western imagination, Babylon exists as a paradoxical image of simultaneous power and desuetude, strength and transience. From the Western perspective, Babylon's great glory is already in the past: it is the image of a marvel lost to time. Control of Semiramis's city and the first empire of history passes to the Medes, then to the Persians, and finally to the Macedonians and the Parthians. This transition would inform the idea of imperial power's destined movement down through world history – the great Western *translatio imperii*, in which the heritage and right of empire and civilization migrate from Babylon to Persia and Greece, and on to Rome, Great Britain, France, and the United

24 Claudian, *Against Eutropius* (*In Eutropium*) in *Claudian*, ed. and trans. Platnauer, I.138–229; Book I, lines 335–6: creditor et centum portis Babylona superbam / femineus struxisse labor.

States.[25] The *translatio imperii* theme pervaded the understanding of Babylon in late antiquity and the early Middle Ages, as we shall see in the next chapter; but it begins here, with the classical world's dual image of Babylon's might and the shadow of its passing.

In summary, classical sources initiate several enduring elements of the Babylon myth. First, the antiquity of Babylon's polity: Babylon is the original empire. From the political perspective of Greece, Macedonia, or Rome, Babylon is the great precursor and model, the historical precedent for abounding imperial power and conquest. Second, power: the impressive details of Babylonian might stand as a testament to human political achievement. The monumental size of the walls, the vast bridges over the Tigris and Euphrates, the city's technological sophistication, the fecundity of Shinar's plain: all exemplify unbounded human ambition and the swelling power of civilization. Third, the vicissitudes of empire: for all its power, Babylon fell to ruin, its imperial power passing to younger nations. We might therefore characterize the classical image of Babylon as moving between two opposed poles: the static image of a great monumental empire, and the mutable image of that empire's passing. In all these ways, Babylon displays a tendency towards metaphoric expression as it accrues a set of political meanings.

The classical traditions sketched here would later merge with biblical representations, and this amalgam of political associations would be further modified during the Middle Ages. But these standard images of Babylon first constructed by writers of the ancient world had a long, powerful afterlife. Edward Gibbon (1737–94) captures this same composite image of Babylon in his *History of the Decline and Fall of the Roman Empire* (1776–88) when he introduces the history of Persia and the great, ancient realms of the East:

> In the more early ages of the world, whilst the forest that covered Europe afforded a retreat to a few wandering savages, the inhabitants of Asia were already collected into populous cities, and reduced under extensive empires, the seat of the arts, of luxury, and of despotism. The Assyrians

25 For brief overviews see *The Classical Tradition*, ed. Grafton et al., s.v. "Translatio Imperii" and Trompf, *Idea of Historical Recurrence*, 222–9. A more detailed history of the concept can be found in Goetz, *Translatio imperii*.

> reigned over the East, till the sceptre of Ninus and Semiramis dropt from the hands of their enervated successors. The Medes and the Babylonians divided their power, and were themselves swallowed up in the monarchy of the Persians, whose arms could not be confined within the narrow limits of Asia.[26]

Babylonian Power in the Bible

How is Babylon depicted in the Bible?[27] Such a question assumes a conceptual unity to "the Bible" that is of course, from certain angles, illusory. Historically speaking, the Bible is not one book but many books (Greek *τὰ βιβλία*, "the books") written over many centuries in different languages by a mix of authors. As well, from the Christian perspective, the Bible also has a unique two-part structure; the "Old Testament" of the Hebrew Scriptures, complemented and completed by the gospel of the "New Testament," a characterization of the Hebrew Bible rejected, of course, by Judaism.[28] Because I focus specifically on the afterlife and influence of Christian mythology in the West from the Middle Ages to the present, I refer to the Bible in this chapter and elsewhere as a coherent imaginative whole, since that assumption of unity has generally governed the understanding and influence of the Bible in the West.[29] While I draw my primary evidence from the biblical text, what "the Bible" stands for here in effect is the deep influence of biblical textuality in its various forms. The dissemination of "biblical textuality" or "the biblical tradition" is not therefore confined to the reading of one sacred book; "the Bible," in this adaptive sense, is a far more fragmented and elusive mode of influence. Knowledge of biblical language and images has entered Western consciousness at a deep level through a variety of channels: liturgical forms, art, sacred history, full Bibles, partial Bibles, translations, paraphrases, and adaptations in textual forms as varied as

---

26 Gibbon, *Decline and Fall of the Roman Empire*, ed. Bury, I.216–17.

27 For partial studies see Sals, *Die Biographie der "Hure Babylon"*; Bellis, "Changing Face of Babylon"; and Seymour, *Babylon*, 36–51 for an overview. On urban imagery in the Bible see Frye, *Great Code*, 156–60; on the biblical fear and suspicion of cities see Schneidau, *Sacred Discontent*, 5–6.

28 Given my primary focus on the Christian Western tradition, I thus set aside the obvious historical distinction between the Hebrew Scriptures and the Christian gospels and use the traditional terminology of Old and New Testaments here.

29 On the unity of the Bible in this regard see Frye, *Great Code*, xiii and Josipovici, *Book of God*, 36–49, 306–7. Cf. the skeptical discussion in Norton, *History of the Bible as Literature*, II.349–99.

poetry, sermons, and drama. In this study, "the Bible" thus serves as a shorthand designator for the wide range of materials used to transmit the full power of biblical textuality.[30]

Babylon's image in the Bible parallels, complements, and extends the composite picture of Babylon in classical sources. The following pages make several interrelated arguments about biblical Babylon. First, biblical Babylon alternates between a mimetic and a metaphoric mode of representation. By "mimetic," I mean that the Bible often represents Babylon in a simple, unadorned fashion. In an effort to chronicle history and represent reality realistically, certain biblical texts represent Babylon as simply a "real" city, Babylonia a "real" kingdom, and the Babylonians as a "real" nation: Babylon is just one of many places and peoples in the historical world represented by the Bible. This historiographic representational mode strives for mimetic simplicity: it is matter-of-fact, unremarkable, commonplace. However, the second, complementary representational mode is metaphoric or prophetic in character. This metaphoric mode represents Babylon in a rhetorically baroque fashion, with a florid discourse supplementing and interpenetrating the spare mimetic representations of Babylon. In this more stylistically ornate mode, Babylon's name accrues obvious symbolic capital and comes to stand for more than itself: Babylon becomes a metaphor, a process we saw beginning in the classical sources as they mused upon the greatness that is (or was) Babylon. This metaphoric/apocalyptic Babylon of the biblical prophets and Revelation is a figure of rhetorical flourish and of wonder, a poetic Babylon conjuring up images of divine wrath and retribution, exile, tyranny, servitude, corruption, and regeneration. As it occurs in the Bible, then, Babylon is thus presented in two senses: as part of the world of history, and as part of the poetic world of metaphor – as both mimetic object and as imaginative figure.

My second argument is that the Bible places Babylon within a set of political ideas and subjects. Across the interplay between the mimetic and metaphoric modes of representation, biblical Babylon stands at the centre of images, themes and narratives that are either essentially political in nature or are particularly amenable to political adaptation in

30 See Norton, *History of the Bible as Literature*, I.2: "the crucial point is that 'the Bible' designates a huge range of books and is not even to be confined to books. In a very real sense there is no such thing as *the* Bible. Instead, there are Bibles. Even so, it still makes good sense to talk of 'the Bible': what is referred to is the meaning contained within the variety of verbal forms" (emphasis in original).

later traditions. The biblical Babylon inescapably calls to mind tyranny and empire, political power and its abuses, servitude and dissent, exile and restoration, polemic and prophecy; these subjects are also, broadly speaking, apocalyptic in character. My third argument, a consequence of the first two propositions, looks forward to the adaptation of biblical Babylon in later traditions (detailed in the next two chapters) and asks, Why would later centuries find Babylon such an easily adaptable figure, especially in political contexts? Is there something inherent in the structure of the reference itself that makes Babylon such an adaptable allusion? I conclude that the internal dynamics of the political Babylon complex – its situation in the interplay between mimesis and metaphor – gives Babylon a strong proleptic character. Prolepsis sees the future in the instant, as Lady Macbeth puts it; the always-already fallen Babylon is a proleptic figure, temporally "present" in the here-and-now of the mimetic mode while it is simultaneously projected into the future as prophecy and metaphor. If, in later traditions, Babylon can stand as a metaphor for Rome or London, or Paris or New York, it is in part the proleptic character of the city's representation in the Bible that lays the groundwork for those later metaphoric appropriations of the city. Such prolepsis is also a typical feature of apocalyptic thought – specifically, of apocalyptic time: that an *imminent* End casts an *immanent* shadow over the present, rendering the imperatives of political Babylon with an apocalyptic intensity.[31]

Captivity: The Mimetic Babylon

The word "Babylon" occurs far more frequently in the Old Testament than in the New Testament. In the Hebrew Scriptures we find Babylon at the centre of a great epic of conquest, exile, and return: the Babylonian Captivity of the Jews. According to the Bible, after the apogee

31 On the proleptic character of apocalyptic time see Kermode, *Sense of an Ending*, e.g. 6 and 83–9, from which I draw my *Macbeth* example. Apocalypticism – ancient, medieval, and modern – is a subject simply too vast to do more with it than provide some basic starting places here. Excellent broad overviews can be found in O'Leary, *Arguing the Apocalypse* and E. Weber, *Apocalypses*. For the Middle Ages, Bernard McGinn provides a good orientation in his two annotated anthologies, *Apocalyptic Traditions in the Middle Ages* and *Apocalyptic Spirituality*. For sample studies focused on the premodern world see Emmerson, *Antichrist in the Middle Ages*; Emmerson and Herzman, *Apocalyptic Imagination*; Firth, *Apocalyptic Tradition in Reformation Britain*; Christianson, *Reformers and Babylon*.

of Israel's power under Solomon, the nation divides into the northern and southern kingdoms of Israel and Judah. Both kingdoms fall into idolatry, and eventually the southern kingdom of Judah brings the wrath of God down upon itself in the person of Nebuchadnezzar, the lord of Babylon, who captures Jerusalem in 586 BCE, destroys and despoils the Temple, and carries the Jews off to the seventy years of the Babylonian Exile. Babylon in turn would fall to the Persians under Cyrus, who then ends the Exile as God redeems the Jews from their Captivity: this cycle of punishment and redemption is a pattern repeated throughout the Old Testament. This mythic fall of Jerusalem and the Babylonian Captivity fired the imagination of late antiquity and the medieval Christian West far more pervasively and imaginatively than the New Testament Whore of Babylon, or Babylon in Revelation generally.[32] The discrete elements of this "Captivity epic" – the cycle of sin and punishment expressed in the destruction of one great city by another; tyranny, exile, and oppression; the cycle of redemption and emancipation – the rhythms of this narrative, in both detailed and abstract form, were essential elements of the medieval storehouse of myth, and found their way through that connection into the mainstream of Western culture.

The Bible does not narrate the Babylonian Captivity in one specific book or place; rather, it is presented in a fragmented fashion, spread out over a number of historical and prophetic books.[33] As the Bible represents Babylon's conquest of the Jews in all these scattered places, generally these moments are relatively unremarkable and stylistically spare, particularly in the historical books. Babylon is simply mentioned as a narrative element, without much rhetorical adornment. In these instances Babylon is represented by a style that strives for mimetic fidelity deriving from the world of chronicle and historiography. For example, in the

32 For example, in medieval Christian thought the event marked a major phase in the traditional chronology of sacred history. The Babylonian Captivity designated the end of the so-called Fourth Age of the world and the beginning of the Fifth Age, according to the influential Six Ages of the World temporal design of Augustine. On the Six Ages of the World in Augustine and others see Dean, *World Grown Old in Later Medieval Literature*, 39–46 and Allen, "Universal History 300–1000," 31–5.

33 The fortunes of Israel are related by the historical books: Joshua, Judges, Ruth, 1 and 2 Samuel, 1 and 2 Kings (these latter four books comprising a more closely titled sequence in the Vulgate: that is, the four Books of Kings), 1 and 2 Chronicles (1 and 2 Paralipomenon in the Vulgate), Ezra, Nehemiah, and Esther (adding Tobit and Judith in the Vulgate). For a general survey of what historical information about Babylon can be gleaned from the Hebrew Prophets, see Vanderhooft, *Neo-Babylonian Empire*, 115–202.

canonical sequence of biblical books, the first reference to the Babylonian Captivity comes in the last Book of Kings. At the end of Hezekiah's reign, messengers from Babylon arrive bearing gifts for the king. In an ominous foreshadowing, Hezekiah orders them to be given a tour of Jerusalem's riches. The prophet Isaiah then asks the unsuspecting king: "'What said these men? Or from whence came they to thee?' And Hezekiah said to him: 'From a far country they came to me out of Babylon'" (4 Kings 20:14). The informed reader knows that this unassuming moment will eventually lead to Desolation and Captivity; but, stylistically, this first citation of Babylon is not framed by an elaborate rhetoric of prophecy.[34] This is the mimetic Babylon deployed by the historiographic voice, characterized by understatement and simple reportage. Even the ultimate destruction of Jerusalem as narrated in the Book of Kings does not approach the rhetorical flare of the prophets:

> At that time the servants of Nabuchodonosor king of Babylon came up against Jerusalem, and the city was surrounded with their forts. And Nabuchodonosor king of Babylon came to the city with his servants to assault it ... And he carried away all Jerusalem, and all the princes, and all the valiant men of the army, to the number of ten thousand into captivity, and every artificer and smith: and none were left, but the poor sort of the people of the land. (4 Kings 24:10–11, 14)

Such is the spare, understated style of biblical historical narrative; the Babylonian Captivity in this representational mode is part of the sober world of historical record.[35] Thus, in one respect, any reader of the Bible would encounter "Babylon" as a simple place, not singled out more than any other city, just as for classical authors Babylon was (or could be) simply a city of the real world (albeit a very powerful one). Yet these simple mimetic representations of the Captivity only appear to be "simple" in relation to the baroque representation of Babylon found in the prophetic rhetoric of the Old Testament and Revelation. Just as Babylon in the classical world was both a city and The City, so too the Bible

34 A similar understatement can be seen in passages such as the following summary of the Captivity from *Ezra and Nehemiah*: "But after that our fathers had provoked the God of heaven to wrath, he delivered them into the hands of Nabuchodonosor the king of Babylon the Chaldean: and he destroyed this house, and carried away the people to Babylon" (1 Ezra 5:12).

35 On the reticent nature of biblical narrative see Alter, *Art of Biblical Narrative*, 114–30.

represents Babylon both mimetically and as a complex figure charged by metaphoric, apocalyptic language.

Captivity: The Metaphoric Babylon

Interwoven with the historical representations of the Captivity throughout the Bible is a parallel version of the same tale of exile and return, but related in the prophetic idiom.[36] The florid language of biblical prophecy tells the story of the Captivity in an allusive, metaphoric and poetic mode, a representational strategy quite different in effect from the sober reportage of mimetic historiography. For example, contrast the prosaic account of Jerusalem's destruction from the Book of Kings quoted above with Jeremiah's rendering of the very same event, but this time suffused by the rhetoric of prophecy:

> Behold, I will send, and take all the kindreds of the north, saith the Lord, and Nabuchodonosor the king of Babylon my servant: and I will bring them against this land and against the inhabitants thereof, and against all the nations that are round about it: and I will destroy them, and make them an astonishment and a hissing and perpetual desolations. And I will take away from them the voice of mirth, and the voice of gladness, the voice of the bridegroom and the voice of the bride, the sound of the mill and the light of the lamp. And all this land shall be a desolation and an astonishment: and all these nations shall serve the king of Babylon seventy years. And when the seventy years shall be expired, I will punish the king of Babylon and that nation, saith the Lord, for their iniquity, and the land of the Chaldeans: and I will make it perpetual desolations. (Jeremiah 25:9–12)

Quite a difference. Jeremiah embeds the Matter of Babylon in all the baroque stylistic trappings of biblical prophecy.[37] In this passage, God's voice speaks through the prophet with the unrelenting immediacy of the first-person, embellished by cascading paratactic syntax, and the kalei-

---

36 On the rhetoric of prophecy I am guided by Alter, *Art of Biblical Poetry*, 171–204; Dougherty, *Fivesquare City*, 1–22, passim; the essays on the prophetic books in Alter and Kermode, eds., *Literary Guide to the Bible*; Peckham, *History and Prophecy*, 133–517; A. Cook, *Burden of Prophecy*; Lundbom, *Hebrew Prophets*, 165–207.

37 On Babylon as an important, complex metaphoric construct in Jeremiah see Hill, *Friend or Foe?*; Sals, *Biographie der "Hure Babylon,"* 331–466.

doscope of vivid images. Such vivid rhetoric forms a counterpoint and contrast to the spare style of Old Testament historical representations of Babylon.

This elevated language and style gives us a "poetic" Babylon, in the sense that Babylon accrues extra-textual meaning and stands for more than itself; whether the poetic dimension of the word is labelled "metaphoric" or "symbolic" is not as important as the process of moving beyond the mundane literal denotation. In the same way that Babylon becomes a commonplace metaphoric figure of imperial power in the classical tradition, the prophetic mode of Babylon in the Bible endows the word with a similar excess of meaning, beginning the enduring process of adorning Babylon with layered connotations in Western culture. Take, for example, this series of rapid-fire metaphors:

> How is the hammer of the whole earth broken, and destroyed! How is Babylon turned into a desert among the nations! ... Babylon hath been a golden cup in the hand of the Lord, that made all the earth drunk: the nations have drunk of her wine, and therefore they have staggered. (Jeremiah 50:23; 51:7)

Babylon the hammer, Babylon the desert, Babylon the golden cup: the baroque expressions of the prophetic mode provoke the imagination and push us towards a rich, mythic conception of Babylon. This metaphoric Babylon is a fantastic alternate to the mimetic and mundane city of history and chronicle. Jeremiah's powerful imagery recurs in this typical passage:

> For thus saith the Lord of hosts, the God of Israel: The daughter of Babylon is like a threshing-floor. This is the time of her threshing: yet a little while, and the time of her harvest shall come. Nabuchodonosor king of Babylon hath eaten me up; he hath devoured me; he hath made me as an empty vessel; he hath swallowed me up like a dragon; he hath filled his belly with my delicate meats, and he hath cast me out. The wrong done to me, and my flesh be upon Babylon, saith the habitation of Sion; and my blood upon the inhabitants of Chaldea, saith Jerusalem. Therefore thus saith the Lord: Behold I will judge thy cause, and will take vengeance for thee, and I will make her sea desolate, and will dry up her spring. And Babylon shall be reduced to heaps, a dwelling-place for dragons, an astonishment and a hissing, because there is no inhabitant. They shall roar together like lions, they shall shake their manes like young lions.

> In their heat I will set them drink: and I will make them drunk, that they may slumber, and sleep an everlasting sleep, and awake no more, saith the Lord. I will bring them down like lambs to the slaughter, and like rams with kids. How is Sesach taken, and the renowned one of all the earth surprised? How is Babylon become an astonishment among the nations? (Jeremiah 51:33–41)

This passage exemplifies the Bible's poetic apprehension of Babylon, and the language obviously appeals to the visionary apocalyptic tradition replicated in Revelation (e.g., Revelation 18:1–10) and adapted by later authors. For a cultural touchstone such as Babylon to have an enduring life and adaptability, it must have rich metaphoric poetic potential.[38]

If the metaphoric potential of biblical Babylon sets up a range of connotations for the city, what are those connotations? Some of these, as we have noted, are identical with classical traditions: Babylon as a figure for beauty and power (an idea we will pursue further in chapter 7). The biblical Babylon is also a figure for ruin and desolation (a theme we will track more extensively in chapter 6). Some of these connotations are political in nature, as we shall see in the latter part of this chapter; and the successive reanimation of these political concerns across the centuries will be the subject of the next two chapters. But supplementing all of the above are apocalyptic or eschatological images of Babylon – metaphors of utter destruction and finality.

Babylon is a figure of elemental devastation and destruction. As both a tool of God's power and, in turn, an offending object of that same power, the biblical Babylon stands for complete and utter devastation. This destruction is sometimes conveyed in water imagery, an echo of Noah's flood: "The sea is come up over Babylon: she is

---

38 See Alter's comments on the "archetypifying force of vocative poetry in the Prophets" (183): "the language of poetry in this and most other biblical prophecies ... tends to lift the utterances to a second power of signification, aligning statements that are addressed to a concrete historical situation with an archetypal horizon ... In this fashion, a set of messages framed for a particular audience of the eighth century B.C.E. is not just the transcription of a historical document but continues to speak age after age, inviting members of otherwise very different societies to read themselves into the text" (*Biblical Poetry*, 182–3). He notes that prophetic poetry in the Bible "exhibits a certain predilection to mythologize its historical subjects, setting the here and now in cosmic perspective" (183).

covered with the multitude of the waves thereof" (Jeremiah 51:42); "Because the Lord hath laid Babylon waste, and destroyed out of her the great voice: and their wave shall roar like many waters: their voice hath made a noise" (Jeremiah 51:55). Along with water come images of devastating fire:

> For I have set my face against this city for evil, and not for good, saith the Lord: it shall be given into the hand of the king of Babylon, and he shall burn it with fire. (Jeremiah 21:10)

> Thus saith the Lord of hosts: That broad wall of Babylon shall be utterly broken down, and her high gates shall be burnt with fire, and the labours of the people shall come to nothing, and of the nations shall go to the fire, and shall perish. (Jeremiah 51:58)

In the first quotation above, Babylon will destroy Jerusalem with fire; in the second example, Babylon herself will be incinerated. This association with fire as both subject and object will anticipate and drive the late antique and medieval Christian exegetical understanding of Babylon as a figure for the fires of hell – here on earth or in the next world.

The apocalyptic desolation of Babylon is an image of complete annihilation, resulting in a world barren of human inhabitants: "And Babylon shall be reduced to heaps, a dwelling-place for dragons, an astonishment and a hissing, because there is no inhabitant" (Jeremiah 51:37). Babylon is a space of the void, an apocalyptic image of destruction in which humanity disappears entirely: "And the land shall be in a commotion, and shall be troubled: for the design of the Lord against Babylon shall awake, to make the land of Babylon desert and uninhabitable" (Jeremiah 51:29). Babylon-as-annihilation will be adapted in many ways in the later Babylon traditions. Revelation, for example, picks up and complements this imagery of destruction, intensifying it in an apocalyptic key, as the angel from heaven cries out before John: "Babylon the great is fallen, is fallen; and is become the habitation of devils and the hold of every unclean spirit and the hold of every unclean and hateful bird" (Revelation 18:2). In terms of its political resonance, the image of a world devoid of human action is one of a place where the fleeting human "experiment" of community and polity has failed and the resulting wasteland embodies the darkest fears of the human generational spirit's failure.

Rounding out our inventory of Babylon's apocalyptic imagery in the Bible, the city is also personified as a woman.[39] Giving Babylon a feminine gender was commonplace, due to the fact that *civitas* is a feminine noun, as is Latin *Babylon*, Greek *βαβυλών*, and Hebrew לבב. The prophetic books play upon this femininity through images of the city as a fallen woman – once fair, but now cast down and shamed, as in this succession of mournful images:[40]

> Come down, sit in the dust, O virgin daughter of Babylon, sit on the ground: there is no throne for the daughter of the Chaldeans, for thou shalt no more be called delicate and tender. (Isaiah 47:1)

> Declare to many against Babylon, to all that bend the bow: stand together against her round about, and let none escape; pay her according to her work: according to all that she hath done, do ye to her: for she hath lifted up herself against the Lord, against the Holy One of Israel. (Jeremiah 50:29)

> Babylon is suddenly fallen and destroyed: howl for her, take balm for her pain, if so she may be healed. (Jeremiah 51:8)[41]

Revelation takes up this imagery of the fallen woman to deliver us the famed Whore of Babylon (Revelation 17:1–18), with whom the "kings of the earth ... have committed fornication" and upon whose head is written "A mystery: Babylon the great, the mother of the fornications and the abominations of the earth" (Revelation 17:2, 5; see also 18:3, 9).[42] It is also worth noting how this biblical image of Babylon as a woman resonates with elements of the classical tradition, whereby Babylon was founded by Semiramis, a woman herself associated with incestuous sexual depravity and sinful corruption.[43] *In toto*, this composite feminine Babylon, derived from classical sources and the Bible – corrupt and sinful

---

39 On the feminine representation of Babylon see Hill, *Friend*, 166–8; also Reimer, *Oracles Against Babylon*, 204–8; Vanderhooft, *Neo-Babylonian Empire*, 181–2; Sals, *Biographie der "Hure Babylon."*

40 On the lament genre and its rhetoric see Dobbs-Allsopp, *Weep, O Daughter of Zion*; for the "weeping goddess" figure see 75–90.

41 See also Jeremiah 50:42 and Isaiah 21:9: "Behold, this man cometh, the rider upon the chariot with two horsemen, and he answered, and said: Babylon is fallen, she is fallen, and all the graven gods thereof are broken unto the ground."

42 See the comprehensive study by Sals, *Biographie der "Hure Babylon."*

43 See also chapter 4, 127–9.

avatar of the feminine body – would make it easy for pervasive medieval Christian traditions to connect this aspect of the Babylon myth to the entire contiguous tradition of sins associated with sexuality and the body.

Biblical Babylon: Political Themes

The images detailed above have a long afterlife in Western culture, and have their own genealogies of influence. What is important is not only the multifaceted metaphorical dimensions of Babylon illustrated above, but also their intensifying of Babylon's connection to political subjects: tyranny and empire, political power and its abuses, servitude and dissent, exile and restoration, polemic and prophecy. The Bible adapts, extends, and augments the embryonic political resonance of Babylon in classical texts, and then endows these political subjects with the intense metaphoric immediacy of apocalyptic thought.

We saw that, according to classical authors, Ninus and Semiramis were behind the first imperial powers in history: Assyria and Babylon. Likewise in the Bible, Babylon is the great Power, the great tyrannical force. In the epic of the Captivity, Babylon is the focus of heathen power and the unstoppable enemy of Israel, an almost impersonal force and presence as the agent of Israel's destruction. Babylon is associated both with the sack of Jerusalem and with its own destruction. The sack of Jerusalem, the destruction of the temple and the deportation of the Jews to Babylon were all signs of God's judgment against sinning Israel, a logic of retribution that would provide a durable answer to a central political question: Why do great national disasters happen? Answer: we have angered the Divine. This logic of retribution – its apocalyptic intensity never far in the background – has been an enduring way for Western cultures to understand the unfolding of dire events in the social and political arenas.[44]

With the sack of Jerusalem and the deportation of the Jews, the Babylonian Captivity epic modulates from tyrannical empire to a story of exile and slavery, highlighted by the enduring themes of political resistance and appeasement in the face of oppression and the pressure of assimilation.[45] The Babylonian Captivity has always captured the imagination of

---

44 On this pattern see Frye, *Great Code*, 169–72. See also Trompf, *Early Christian Historiography*; the phrase "logic of retribution" is Trompf's.

45 On Babylon as a metaphor for exile and death in Jeremiah see Hill, *Friend or Foe?*, 55–72.

readers as a metaphorical expression of slavery and exile (as we shall see in the next two chapters). Perhaps the most famous biblical expression of servitude and exile during the Captivity is Psalm 136 (I give the AV version, Ps. 137, below), with its plangent mix of nostalgia, sadness, and rage:

> By the rivers of. Babylon, there we sat down, yea, we wept, when we remembered Zion.
> We hanged our harps upon the willows in the midst thereof.
> For there they that carried us away captive required of us a song; and they that wasted us required of us mirth, saying, Sing us one of the songs of Zion.
> How shall we sing the LORD's song in a strange land?
> If I forget thee, O Jerusalem, let my right hand forget her cunning.
> If I do not remember thee, let my tongue cleave to the roof of my mouth; if I prefer not Jerusalem above my chief joy.
> Remember, O LORD, the children of Edom in the day of Jerusalem; who said, Rase it, rase it, even to the foundation thereof.
> O daughter of Babylon, who art to be destroyed; happy shall he be, that rewardeth thee as thou hast served us.
> Happy shall he be, that taketh and dasheth thy little ones against the stones.

This famous psalm has been adapted and cited as allusion throughout the centuries of Western culture, from medieval poetry to Elizabeth Smart.[46] Ever relevant, Psalm 136 has spoken powerfully and movingly to many people about the imperatives of political life: servitude and the cultural loss derived from assimilation; the nature of tyranny over a minority and concomitant dissent; the fragility of cultural memory and coherence in bondage; the longing voice of freedom and redemption.

Although the exilic songs of Babylon may be plaintive and painful, nevertheless an important part of the Captivity narrative is the eventual emancipation and deliverance of the Jews out of bondage in Babylon through the mercy of the Lord: "Fear not because of the king of Babylon, of whom you are greatly afraid. Fear him not, saith the Lord: for I am with you, to save you, and to deliver you from his hand" (Jeremiah 42:11). If Babylon is an image of misery and slavery, it is also bound up with a

46 See generally Norton, *History of the Bible as Literature*, I.274–90; on Psalm 136 see Scheil, *Footsteps of Israel*, 134–41 and Hamlin, *Psalm Culture and Early Modern English Literature*, 218–52. Elizabeth Smart, *By Grand Central Station I Sat Down and Wept* (1945).

sense of hope and renewal in which the world shall yet revolve, and in that revolution the oppressor shall be cast down and the oppressed set free.[47] Isaiah proclaims that when turnabout comes, "Thou shalt take up this parable against the king of Babylon, and shalt say: 'How is the oppressor come to nothing, the tribute hath ceased?'" (14:4).[48] Babylon is thus not exclusively a symbol of destruction; it can also be, paradoxically, a figure for the joy that comes at the end of exile:

> Come forth out of Babylon, flee ye from the Chaldeans, declare it with the voice of joy: make this to be heard, and speak it out even to the ends of the earth. Say: The Lord hath redeemed his servant Jacob. (Isaiah 48:20)

In the Hebrew Scriptures, the rhythm of bondage and emancipation is the foundation of the lachrymose model of Jewish history: the Babylonian Captivity is but one stage in Israel's unfolding relationship with God in a cycle of pride, chastisement, and reconciliation. Psalm 136 asks many existential political questions, which are also asked by the Captivity as a whole in the Bible. When will freedom come? How have we merited the loss of home? How can I be sustained in the face of exile's loss and longing? Which is better: to live and survive no matter the cost, or to live only in keeping with protocols of faith? To what degree is assimilation proper before one loses one's identity (personal, social, political) and ceases to be? When will a new home, a new polity, emerge? These questions, embedded in miniature within the verses of Psalm 136, and in the Captivity writ large, will resonate down through the centuries in succeeding contexts of political oppression. In much the same way that the Exodus story of Hebrew deliverance from Egypt has served as a political model and touchstone in the West, so too the Babylonian Captivity becomes part of the Western language of political action, at both the social level and at the level of the individual – both social groups and individuals endure their moments of slavery (their own "Babylonian exile") and their corresponding joys of emancipation.[49]

---

47 Hill, *Friend or Foe?*, 87: "Babylon is ... represented in its topography simultaneously as a place of exile and a place of hope. From Babylon will come a new people to again enter and take possession of the land."

48 The AV (Isaiah 14:4): reads: "Thou shalt take up this proverb against the king of Babylon, and say, 'How hath the oppressor ceased! the golden city ceased!'"

49 On the Exodus story as an adaptive political myth see Walzer, *Exodus*.

But there is yet a further resonant characteristic of political Babylon in the Bible. Classical texts described Babylon's great political power and its passing; the Bible expands the ultimate ephemerality of Babylonian tyranny by adding an important dimension: an ambiguity about the source of political power. Does political power – or any human endeavour in the world – derive from humanity's self-determination or from God's will? The answer to this question for the Bible, of course, is God; and this injection of the Divine into the matrix of human politics is an important feature of the Babylon political myth in the Christian tradition.

In the Bible, Babylon is a great worldly power, but it is also, in the end, only an instrument of a yet greater power: God's will. The mightiest of earthly empires, Babylon nevertheless is subject to divine control and direction. The Babylonian conquest of the Jews and the destruction of the Temple are part of God's plan, part of the logic of retribution. Like Egypt, Babylon serves ultimately as God's weapon, an instrument of divine wrath for the punishment of his chosen people, as Jeremiah prophesizes:

> For thus saith the Lord: Behold I will deliver thee up to fear, thee and all thy friends. And they shall fall by the sword of their enemies, and thy eyes shall see it, and I will give all Juda into the hand of the king of Babylon: and he shall strike them with the sword. And I will give all the substance of this city, and all its labour, and every precious thing thereof, and all the treasures of the kings of Juda will I give into the hands of their enemies: and they shall pillage them, and take them away, and carry them to Babylon ... And after this, saith the Lord, I will give Sedecias the king of Juda, and his servants, and his people, and such as are left in this city from the pestilence, and the sword, and the famine, into the hand of Nabuchodonosor the king of Babylon, and into the hand of their enemies, and into the hand of them that seek their life. And he shall strike them with the edge of the sword, and he shall not be moved to pity, nor spare them, nor shew mercy to them. (Jeremiah 20:4–5, 21:7)

There will be no pity or mercy for Israel when Babylon serves as the weapon of God's punishment; but in the emancipation of the Jews from the Captivity, Babylon herself will in turn be conquered and cast down. The implication is clear: no earthly power has utter autonomy; God's hand is behind all political events. The example of Babylon thus demonstrates the limits of human political power, even for the greatest of empires. A clear political precept echoes through the biblical Matter of Babylon: that earthly power (especially imperial power) is granted by God, not Man, and God periodically asserts his awful prerogative. In the book of Daniel, for example, Nebuchadnezzar exults in the apogee of his power, mistakenly locating the source of political power within human hands:

> And the king answered, and said: Is not this the great Babylon, which I have built to be the seat of the kingdom, by the strength of my power, and in the glory of my excellence? (Daniel 4:27)

Yet the prophetic voice, speaking for God, knows that Nebuchadnezzar's boast is mere illusion and tells the truth about the source of mundane political power, as in Jeremiah' s prophecy to Jehoiakim:

> I made the earth, and the men, and the beasts that are upon the face of the earth, by my great power and by my stretched-out arm: and I have given it to whom it seemed good in my eyes. And now I have given all these lands into the hand of Nabuchodonosor king of Babylon, my servant: moreover also the beasts of the field I have given him to serve him. And all nations shall serve him, and his son and his son's son, till the time come for his land and himself: and many nations and great kings shall serve him. But the nation and kingdom that will not serve Nabuchodonosor king of Babylon, and whosoever will not bend his neck under the yoke of the king of Babylon: I will visit upon that nation with the sword, and with famine, and with pestilence, saith the Lord: till I consume them by his hand. Therefore hearken not to your prophets, and diviners, and dreamers, and soothsayers, and sorcerers, that say to you: You shall not serve the king of Babylon. For they prophesy lies to you: to remove you far from your country, and cast you out, and to make you perish. (Jeremiah 27:5–10)

At the end of the cycle of the Captivity, with the destruction of Babylon, it is clear that the lesson is about the sources of political power in the world. The biblical moral of Babylon echoes the Tower of Babel's moral – humanity builds its works upon this earth, and glories in might and splendor; but the world and its powers are subject to a greater force, a greater determination. The biblical Babylon thus stands as an emblem for the recurring narrative of humanity's limitations.

Unlike the comparatively simple depictions of Babylon's power and passing in the classical tradition, the rise and fall of biblical Babylon is part of a shaping divine plan stretching from Nimrod's Babylon in Genesis to the Whore of Babylon in Revelation. This underwriting of Babylon as an instrument of divine will implies that human political actions are always overdetermined, influenced by factors unseen. In later Christian traditions, this aspect of the biblical Babylon renders the city an essential part of the language of Christian theology and history, at once historical in character as well as paradigmatic in seemingly endless application.

In this chapter I have offered two main propositions about Babylon in the antiquity of classical culture and in the Bible: 1) that Babylon oscillates between a mimetic and a metaphoric mode of representation; 2) that Babylon is at the centre of a cluster of political themes and images riven by apocalyptic imagery and intensity. I now wish to combine these observations to explore one final question: why Babylon as a political metaphor had such an appeal for adaptation and transformation in subsequent centuries, as the next chapters will show. The pervasive influence of biblical Babylon could simply be ascribed to the cultural omnipresence and influence of the Bible itself, and in some cases also to local historical and rhetorical situations. However, I believe the mobility of Babylon as a paradigm or as a metaphor, with its seemingly endless adaptability, is also due precisely to its combination of mimetic and metaphoric modes of representation and its apocalyptic charge.

"Babylon" is a way to talk about political life. We might say that the historical mimetic mode gives us the representation of human events as they are in the present, while the prophetic mode gives us the interpenetration of God's power in human history, breaching the veil of the present to offer a glimpse of human events as they might be in the future. Consequently, this interplay of mimesis and metaphor has important consequences for the destiny of Babylon as political rhetoric. The representation of political life intrudes simultaneously upon these two domains: the harsh reality of life in the world of history; and parallel poetic dreams of how life should be, could be, or must not be – unsettled reveries of paradise and corruption. Babylon is thus a way of talking about politics not only due to the political subject matter it traditionally encompasses, but also (and more importantly) due to the contours of the allusion's representational and hermeneutic structure.

The proleptic nature of apocalyptic thought has an important role here as well. Prophecy itself is inherently proleptic, as is the visionary experience of apocalypse: both jump forward from the present moment to look into the future. Taken as a whole, throughout the books of the Bible, the political struggle between Babylon and Jerusalem is presented proleptically. We constantly flash-forward to the spoiling of Jerusalem and the Captivity; we also look even farther ahead to the destruction of Babylon in turn. Any discrete reference to Babylon thus inhabits the present and the future simultaneously. This proleptic interplay between present and future is a prime reason the city began its long afterlife as political metaphor: Babylon is both a concrete historical example in the "present" (the mimetic mode) and a mobile prophecy for the future (the metaphoric mode). This temporal duality is an essential part of Babylon's endurance and potential as political language in the West.

In fact, we see this proleptic potential of Babylon as early as the New Testament's apocalyptic adaptation of prophecy. In other words, reading Babylon allusively and politically, as a template for future political situations, begins in the Bible itself.[50] In the New Testament's symbolic economy, Babylon stands for Rome; Revelation supplements and complements the Babylon tradition of the Old Testament. Babylon's Old Testament political associations become the paradigm for political discourse about a second Babylon – Rome during the era of early Christian persecution when Revelation was composed – adapting the Old Testament prophetic voice to a new political situation in a passage quoted earlier:

> And he cried out with a strong voice, saying: Babylon the great is fallen, is fallen; and is become the habitation of devils, and the hold of every unclean spirit, and the hold of every unclean and hateful bird. (Revelation 18:2)

This is a prophecy of the future when Babylon/Rome will fall; yet the prophecy is certainly powered, as prophecy, by the simultaneous hopeful awareness that the Babylon of old has indeed, already fallen and passed away – as it always has in the Western tradition.

Finally, as I have shown, the political image of Babylon embeds an interrogation of earthly power into its proleptic structure and apocalyptic expectations. In the Bible, the power and plans of God continually circumscribe the great events of human history; thus, any reference to Babylon also questions the self-determination and efficacy of human actions.

50 Alter, *World of Biblical Literature*, 117: "In the Bible, however, the matrix for allusion is often a sense of absolute historical continuity and recurrence, or an assumption that earlier events and figures are timeless ideological models by which all that follows can be measured."

This treatment of political power complements the proleptic structure of the Babylon image. For if Babylon refers not only to the here-and-now, but also to the what-is-to-come, that temporal scheme maps powerfully onto the idea of both tradition and reform, the dynamic of stasis and change defining political institutions and actions throughout history. As a result, Babylon will become a powerful, endlessly generative paradigm for political thinking, and part of the West's political language for centuries to come.

Chapter Two

Political Babylon in Late Antiquity and the Early Middle Ages

How is Babylon become an astonishment among the nations?

–Jeremiah 51:41

We shall not linger over details; but the city of Rome was founded as a kind of second Babylon; the daughter, as it were, of the former Babylon, through whom it pleased God to conquer the whole earth.

– Augustine, *City of God*, XVIII.22

Late Antiquity and the Early Middle Ages (c. 300–c. 1000 CE) constitute an important period of synthesis for the political understanding of Babylon. By the end of this period, an elaborate Christian understanding of Babylon had developed, solidified into a tradition, and spread widely as it became part of the theological and political language of Western Christian communities. In the works of patristic and early medieval authors, the classical Babylon and the biblical Babylon merge and evolve in important ways, establishing an influential paradigm for understanding Babylon as a political metaphor.

This chapter begins with the most important representative of patristic culture – Saint Augustine of Hippo (354–430 CE) and his supremely influential metaphoric use of Babylon in his theological concept of the "Two Cities": Jerusalem, the City of God, and Babylon, the City of Man. Augustine represents the dominant understanding of Babylon in the patristic tradition, as he consolidates the mimetic and metaphoric traditions inherited from classical antiquity and the Bible and extends them in fascinating ways. Representing Augustine's voluminous writings on the subject will be *The City of God* (*De civitate Dei*), composed between 416 and 422 CE.

The remaining texts in this chapter represent adaptations and transformations of the inherited Augustinian archetype – case studies of political Babylon's displacement. Of first importance is Paulus Orosius (early fifth century CE) and his monumental *Seven Books of History against the Pagans* (*Historiarum libri VII contra paganos*), a canonical late-antique history of the world complementing the theology presented in Augustine's *City of God.* Under the inspiration of Augustine, the *translatio imperii* ideology, and other influences, Orosius adapts the Babylon myth to a scheme of Christian sacred history, imparting symmetry, shape, and order (*ordo*) to the political myth of Babylon. Augustine provides a theoretical account of Babylon's significance in human history, and Orosius works out – according to narrative protocols – a historiographic understanding of political Babylon that would shape historical accounts of the Babylonian empire throughout the Middle Ages and into the modern world.

As representative case studies of the patristic and historiographic traditions of late antiquity, Augustine and Orosius provide evidence for the widespread promulgation of the political Babylon myth in powerful new cultural forms. From these two late antique figures, the chapter then moves to a corresponding pair of early medieval examples from Anglo-Saxon England: the anonymous Old English poem *Daniel* (date unknown, but c. 700–1000 CE) and the Latin exegetical writings of the venerable Bede (c. 673–735 CE). These case studies present a more focused picture of political Babylon's adaptation in specific generic and historical contexts.

The Old English *Daniel* is a stylized displacement and adaptation of the historiographic dimensions of the political Babylon myth, taking up the political themes of Babylon derived from Orosius and Augustine and adapting them in a poetic idiom. In contrast to the poetic *Daniel,* Bede's exegetical commentaries on the Bible privilege not the historiographic Babylon, but rather the symbolic or metaphorical understanding of the city deriving from Augustine and the patristic exegetical tradition; Bede's Babylon fulfills the metaphoric potential of Babylon we have found in classical texts and the Bible. In other words, *Daniel* adapts one dimension of the Two Cities theory, one that is primarily historiographic in nature; Bede's work, representing a typical Christian, allegorical or symbolic understanding of Babylon, allows us to see the other side of the Two Cities paradigm, the one that is primarily metaphorical in nature. In these examples, we see a developing connection between Babylon and politics through the influence of narrative teleologies, the imaginative demands of poetry, and the pressure of local historical, rhetorical, and generic circumstances.

Augustine

Chapter 1 demonstrated the duality of Babylon's representation: the interwoven mimetic and metaphoric modes of understanding, and the interplay of denotation and connotation. This incipient duality of Babylon was likely one of the elements that drew Augustine to the city as he formulated his enormously influential political/theological doctrine of the Two Cities in the fifth century.[1] Augustine's Two Cities doctrine was absorbed into medieval culture in a variety of fundamental ways, as either a primary source or at one or more removes through intermediary traditions.[2]

Although Augustine explicates his Two Cities doctrine in many texts, his most sustained and influential work on the subject was in *The City of God*, an inherently polemical work composed as a response to mid-fifth century Roman political calamities. Augustine's opponents saw Rome's political troubles and the afflictions of the empire as a result of the universal adoption of Christianity in the fourth century; plainly, so the argument went, Rome had chosen the wrong path, and the empire was being punished by the gods for its apostasy. The monumental *City of God* was Augustine's formidable answer to this charge: in composing the work, he provided a comprehensive view of history and humanity that placed the current Roman political crisis against a vast backdrop of Christian thought, doctrine, and sacred history.

The City of Man and Tyranny

In the *City of God,* Augustine promises to unfold "the origin, progress and proper ends of the two cities, one of which, the City of God, dwells in the other, the city of this world, as far as the race of men is concerned, but

1 On Augustine's Two Cities concept and its background see Markus, *Saeculum,* 45–71; Dougherty, *Fivesquare City,* 23–53; Brown, *Augustine of Hippo,* 312–29. The exhaustive study of the sources of Augustine's doctrine is van Oort, *Jerusalem and Babylon.* On the vast subject of Augustine's political philosophy, begin with Weithman, "Augustine's Political Philosophy."

2 For Augustine's influence see Marrou, *St. Augustine and His Influence,* 147–80; Hillgarth, "L'Influence de la Cité de Dieu"; Matthews, ed., *Augustinian Tradition;* Stone, "Augustine and Medieval Philosophy" and Matthews, "Post-medieval Augustinianism." For a classic analysis of Augustine's influence on literature, see Robertson, *Preface to Chaucer,* see also Dahlberg, *Literature of Unlikeness.*

as a pilgrim" (XVIII.1).[3] For Augustine, "Babylon" and "Jerusalem" refer metaphorically to two types of human communities, each defined by a particular tendency in the human heart. He explains that the word *civitas* ("city") denotes not just an urban, physical city, but also a "political community"; likewise he defines a "people" (*populus*) as a group of human beings united in the object of their love (XIX.24). Thus the City of Man, Babylon, is a *populus* defined by the "love of self extending even to contempt of God"; the City of Man "glories in itself ... [and] seeks glory from men" (XIV.28).[4] Babylon, wherever it may be found in human affairs and in the psyche, is defined by "perverted" love, in the etymological sense of that word: love that is "turned away" from its proper object (God), and misdirected to the love of the self. The City of God (Jerusalem), on the other hand, is a *populus* united in the love of God and things eternal. Augustine's treatise aims to explicate the nature of this duality and, more importantly, show its presence and manifestation in human history.

Augustine explains that earthly imperial tyranny and conquest are naturally the ultimate expressions of the City of Man, since it is through tyranny and conquest that the highest terrestrial glory is sought; tyranny in the political realm is a real-world reflex of the operation of the City of Man in the heart. The self-love of the City of Man and its habitual alienation from God can be expressed anywhere, from an individual's ethical choices to the vast self-interest of Empire – it is all the operation of the City of Man, the workings of Babylon. Tyranny is thus the ultimate expression of self-love or terrestrial love: "In the Earthly City, princes are as much mastered by the lust for mastery as the nations which they subdue are by them" (XIV.28).[5] Imperial ambition in turn is the supreme earthly expression of the self-love endemic to Babylon, as

3 De ciuitatum duarum, quarum Dei una, saeculi huius est altera, in qua est, quantum hominum genus pertinet, etiam ista peregrina, exortu et procursu et debitis finibus me scripturum esse promisi.

4 amor sui usque ad contemptum Dei ... in se ipsa ... gloriatur ... quaerit ab hominibus gloriam.

5 Illi in principibus eius uel in eis quas subiugat nationibus dominandi libido dominatur. As Weithman summarizes, "This restless love for power explains the sway of history's great empires and Rome's hegemony over Augustine's own world. Indeed love and conflict are central to Augustine's discussion of politics. Augustine's identification of a love which defines one of the cities with one of the driving forces in political history suggests that history unfolds as a result of a contest between the Earthly City and the City of God. In fact nothing could be further from Augustine's view than this facile dualism. Though people may differ in their most fundamental orientations, every human being has a divided will" (Weithman, "Augustine's Political Philosophy," 237).

Augustine asks: "But, once established in the minds of the proudest, how can such lust for mastery rest until, by the usual succession of offices, it has reached the highest power [i.e., tyrannical rule over an empire]?" (I.31).[6] In other words, the deepest antithesis of the love for God that should unite a *populus* is a love of the self so great that it leads to the subjugation of others in a demonic parody of the proper relationship between God and humanity. For Augustine, politics and history are thus epiphenomena of the more powerful forces that guide human ethics.[7]

Augustine's City of Man and its misdirected tendencies are simply part of the human condition, consequences of Adam's fall. This tendency towards self-love is a slippery slope – it leads to the excessive elevation of the self and eventually, step by step, to one society trying to dominate another. In the following passage, worth quoting at length, Augustine tracks the endemic self-love of the metaphorical City of Man all the way to its inevitable expression in the tyrannical empires of history – specifically Rome and Babylon. He begins with the sociopolitical organization of earliest recorded history, post-Adam, and proceeds to Babylon:

> The society of mortals, then, was diffused throughout all lands; and, despite of all diversity of place, was linked by a kind of fellowship of common nature, even though each section of mankind pursued devices and desires of its own. In this condition, not everyone, and perhaps no one, completely attains what he desires, because not all men seek the same end; and so mankind everywhere is generally divided against itself, and when one part is the stronger, it oppresses another ... Thus – and this does not happen without the providence of God, in Whose power it lies to determine who in war shall be subjugated and who shall subjugate them – certain peoples have been entrusted with kingdoms, while some have been placed under the rule of others. But the society whose goal is earthly advantage or desire – the city to which we assign the general name of "the city of this world" [i.e., the City of Man, "Babylon"] – has been divided into a great number of kingdoms. And we note that, of these, two kingdoms have won a renown greatly surpassing that of all others: that of the Assyrians first, and then that of the Romans. These are ordered and distinguished in relation to one another in terms of both time and place. For the former arose earlier, and the latter later;

6 Nam quando illa quiesceret in superbissimis mentibus, donec continuatis honoribus ad potestatem regiam perueniret?

7 See Weithman, "Augustine's Political Philosophy," 249: "what seems to interest Augustine about politics is what it shows about the divine and psychological forces which govern human life but which human reason cannot fully penetrate or control."

the one in the East, and the other in the West. Again, the beginning of the one came immediately after the other's end; and I should say that all other kingdoms and kings are like appendages to those empires. (XVIII.2)[8]

Augustine explains that all early human societies shared a "fellowship of common nature" (*unius naturae communione*): this is the destructive, fallen self-love of the City of Man, in which humans pursue their personal, selfish desires. This produces conflict because "not all men seek the same end"; humanity is therefore divided against itself (as in the Tower of Babel story). Thus, under the will of God, the stronger assert their self-desires over the weaker – some people rule, some are ruled. As Augustine ends the passage, he notes that two societies in history have surpassed all others in this aggressive political manifestation of the City of Man – Babylon ("the Assyrians") and Rome.[9] And he notes that these two empires are

8 Societas igitur usquequaque mortalium diffusa per terras et in locorum quantislibet diuersitatibus unius tamen euiusdemque naturae quadam communione deuincta utilitates et cupiditates suas quibusque sectantibus, dum id quod appetitur aut nemini aut non omnibus sufficit, quia non est id ipsum, aduersus se ipsam plerumque diuiditur, et pars partem, quae praeualet, opprimit ... Hinc factum est, ut non sine Dei prouidentia, in cuius potestate est, ut quisque bello aut subiugetur aut subiuget, quidam essent regnis praediti, quidam regnantibus subditi. Sed inter plurima regna terrarum, in quae terrenae utilitatis uel cupiditatis est diuisa societas (quam ciuitatem mundi huius uniuersali uocabulo nuncupamus), duo regna cernimus longe ceteris prouenisse clariora, Assyriorum primum, deinde Romanorum, ut temporibus, ita locis inter se ordinata atque distincta. Nam quo modo illud prius, hoc posterius: eo modo illud in Oriente, hoc in Occidente surrexit; denique in illius fine huius initium confestim fuit. Regna cetera ceterosque reges uelut adpendices istorum dixerim.

9 Cf. *City of God*, XVIII.2: "Thus, we must give the name of Assyrian kings where necessary, in order to show how Babylon, the first Rome, as it were, pursues its course alongside the City of God on pilgrimage in this world; but the things which we must insert into this work for the sake of comparing the two cities, that is, the earthly and the heavenly, must be derived rather from Greek and Latin history, in which Rome herself is like a second Babylon" (ob hoc debemus, ubi opus est, Assyrios nominare reges, ut appareat quem ad modum Babylonia, quasi prima Roma, cum peregrina in hoc mundo Dei ciuitate procurrat; res autem, quas propter comparationem ciuitatis utriusque, terrenae scilicet et caelestis, huic operi oportet inserere, magis ex Graecis et Latinis, ubi et ipsa Roma quasi secunda Babylonia est, debemus adsumere).

Sometimes the City of Man refers to a historical social institution such as the Roman Empire, but it also can refer to misdirected individuals within that social entity; i.e., there can be righteous people following the path of the City of God, who nevertheless live in (for example) the Roman Empire. See Markus, *Saeculum*, 59–62, on the overlapping spheres of the City of Man in Augustine's conception: e.g., "'Babylon' is both the city of the impious, and the secular sphere in which good pious Christians may discharge important functions" (59).

connected, images of each other, and that all other kingdoms are mere "appendages" to these two great polities.[10]

Nimrod and Babylon's Tyranny

As he explicates human history in this fashion, Augustine shows that the real-world Babylon is a manifestation of the metaphorical Babylon. The City of Man leaves an imprint in the historical record; or, from another perspective, the historical record itself is the story of the City of Man. In the pre-Christian classical tradition, as we have seen, Ninus and Semiramis were the first acquisitive tyrants and the founders of Babylon. Augustine follows this general idea, but integrates Christian biblical history into his timeline. He explains that "three great kingdoms of the Gentiles [the Sicyonians, the Egyptians, and the Assyrians] ... rose to great power under the lordship of the fallen angels" (a reference to Genesis 6:1–4); this was "the city of the earth-born – that is, the society of men who live according to man," and the empire of the Assyrians was "by far the most mighty and exalted" of the three, "for king Ninus, son of Belus, had subjugated the peoples of the whole of Asia with the exception of India" (XVI.17).[11] Assyria's capital was Babylon:

> In Assyria, then, the lordship of the ungodly city prevailed. Its capital was that Babylon whose name, "Confusion," is most apt for the city of the earth-born. Ninus was reigning there at this time, after the death of his father Belus, who had reigned for sixty-five years as the first king there. His son Ninus, who succeeded to the kingdom on the death of his father, reigned for fifty-two years; and he had possessed the kingdom for forty-three years when Abraham was born. This was about 1,200 years before Rome was founded as a second Babylon, as it were, in the West. (XVI.17)[12]

10 Isidore similarly explains that all other reigns and kings are just appendages (*adpendices*) to the empires of Babylon and Rome (*Etymologiae,* IX.3.2).

11 Per idem tempus eminentia regna errant gentium, in quibus terrigenarum ciuitas, hoc est societas hominum secundum hominem uiuentium, sub dominatu angelorum desertorum insignius excellebat, regna uidelicet tria, Sicyoniorum, Aegyptiorum, Assyriorum. Sed Assyriorum multo erat potentius atque sublimius. Nam rex ille Ninus Beli filius excepta India uniuersae Asiae populous subiugauerat.

12 In Assyria igitur praeualuerat dominatus impiae ciuitatis; huius caput erat illa Babylon, cuius terrigenae ciuitatis nomen aptissimum est, id est confusio. Ibi iam Ninus regnabat post mortem patris sui Beli, qui primus illic regnauerat sexaginta quinque annos. Filius vero eius Ninus, qui defuncto patri successit in regnum,

But in an important innovation, Augustine, following Josephus and other sources, adapts this genealogy of Assyrian tyranny to Christian history by asserting that Nimrod, the biblical "great hunter before the Lord," was the founder of Babylon prior to Ninus, and thus was the first true tyrant after the great Flood.[13] Augustine explicates "Babel" (*confusio*) in the following passage to make this point:

> This city which was called "Confusion" is Babylon itself, whose wondrous construction is mentioned by historians of all nations. The name "Babylon" indeed means "confusion." Hence it may be inferred that the giant Nimrod was its founder, as was briefly suggested above. For when the Scripture mentions him, it says that "the beginning of his kingdom was Babylon": that is, Babylon was the city which took precedence over all others, where the king had his dwelling, as in a capital city ... (XVI.4)[14]

The "historians of all nations" that Augustine mentions here include classical authors we have already examined, such as Herodotus and Pompeius Trogus, and their descriptions of Babylon's "wondrous construction" (*mirabilem constructionem*). In the Christian patristic tradition, Nimrod becomes the legendary founder of Babylon, in apparent direct conflict with the classical tradition of the city's founding by Ninus and Semiramis. Nimrod seems a likely candidate for history's first tyrant because he is a "mighty hunter before the Lord" (*robustus venator coram Domino*): Augustine, explicating this epithet, accordingly asks, "[W]hat is a 'hunter,' if not a deceiver, an oppressor, a slayer of earth-born creatures?" (XVI.4).[15] It is a natural move in the exegetical imagination from Nimrod as a hunter (oppressor of animals) to Nimrod as a proud tyrant (oppressor of human beings).

---

quinquaginta duo regnauit annos, et habebat in regno quadraginta tres, quando natus est Abraham, qui erat annus circiter millensimus ducentensimus ante conditam Romam, ueluti alteram in occidente Babyloniam.

13 For a further discussion of Nimrod and his reception in the West, see chapter 4, 149–51 and chapter 5, 159, 162–3, 170.

14 Ista ciuitas, quae appellata est confusio, ipsa est Babylon, cuius mirabilem constructionem etiam gentium commendat historia. Babylon quippe interpretatur confusio. Vnde colligitur, gigantem illum Nebroth fuisse illius conditorem, quod superius breuiter fuerat intimatum, ubi, cum de illo scriptura loqueretur, ait initium regni eius fuisse Babylonem, id est quae ciuitatum ceterarum gereret principatum, ubi esset tamquam in metropoli habitaculum regni.

15 Quid autem hic significatur hoc nomine, quos est *venator,* nisi animalium terrigenarum deceptor oppressor extinctor?

Patristic and later-derived early medieval traditions thus re-inscribe the classical origin of imperial tyranny into a biblical source. Moreover, in this syncretic adaptation Babylon is simultaneously mimetic and metaphoric: in Augustinian terms, the historical Babylon exemplifies the meaning of the metaphorical Babylon, and the metaphorical Babylon explains the character of the historical Babylon. In Nimrod, the historical Babylon and the metaphorical Babylon become one: the self-love endemic to the City of Man manifests in the first city built after the flood, and generates the first tyrant.

Augustine's formulation of the Two Cities metaphor and its syncretic explication in the historical record were crucial moments in the history of Babylon as political discourse. In his synthesis of the classical and biblical traditions, Augustine adapts and transforms the incipient metaphoric and mimetic capacities of Babylon by making the city a trans-historical metaphor. After Augustine, the metaphorical aspect of Babylon was firmly established as a commonplace with particular political associations; Babylon would most often be seen as part of an inevitable dyad with Jerusalem, giving Babylon a further tendency towards binary political applications – Us vs. Them. And, after Augustine, Babylon could be used to interrogate personal morals, especially when those personal ethics were related to a larger social polity. At its inception, the Babylon/Jerusalem dichotomy was Augustine's polemical answer to a political dilemma; the Augustinian precedent would in turn be an important first step in the use of Babylon as a mobile Christian political metaphor.

Paulus Orosius

The work of Augustine's contemporary Paulus Orosius (fl. early fifth century CE) shows the clear, if erratic, influence of Augustine's thought. Orosius's universal history *The Seven Books of History Against the Pagans* (*Historiarum libri VII contra paganos*) attempts to complement Augustine's *City of God*, even if Orosius often cannot fully match his mentor's subtlety and nuance.[16] If Augustine provided the theoretical framework to

16 See Mommsen, "Orosius and Augustine." While acknowledging the close relationship between Orosius and Augustine, Mommsen also stresses the way the two men diverge in their views of history and other matters. For further discussion see Fainck, *Paul Orose et sa conception de l'histoire*, 119–35; Markus, *Saeculum*, 2, 54, 161–3; Lacroix, *Orose et ses idées*, 193–207; Trompf, *Early Christian Historiography*, 292–309, esp. 292–4; Brown, *Augustine of Hippo*, 294. Recently, James O'Donnell has called Orosius "the

understand human history through the operation of the Two Cities, then Orosius's book – an influential work of history throughout the Middle Ages, extant in hundreds of manuscripts and a pervasive source – would attempt to track the specific demonstration of Augustine's ideas in the historical record.[17] Like Augustine, Orosius uses Babylon to comment on the near-apocalyptic crisis of fifth-century Roman political conditions.[18] And with Augustine as an inspiration, Orosius shapes history according to certain mutually reinforcing narrative teleologies: sacred history, divine intention, symmetry and patterns, and the *translatio imperii* motif.

Orosius had an important precursor and source for his narrative shaping of biblical history in the work of the first-century Jewish historian Flavius Josephus (c. 37–c. 100 CE), who wrote two influential histories in Greek. The first is *The Jewish War* (*Περί του Ιουδαϊκού πολέμου*; *Bellum Judaicum*), an eyewitness account in seven books of the Jewish War against the Romans, including the sack of Jerusalem in 70 CE.[19] The second work is the *Antiquities of the Jews* (*Ιουδαϊκή Αρχαιολογία*; *Antiquitates Iudaei*), a long work in twenty books that traces the history of the Jews from their scriptural origins down to the beginning of the Jewish War. For this history, Josephus used the Greek Septuagint as his biblical source, and supplemented the scriptural material with a variety of additional materials ranging from Herodotus's *Histories* to haggadah (oral Jewish lore). A Latin translation of the *Antiquities* was initiated by Cassiodorus in the sixth century, and this Latin translation of Josephus was widely read and disseminated in the Middle Ages.[20]

---

boneheaded disciple [Augustine] never managed to disown" (*Classical Tradition*, ed. Grafton et al., s.v. "Augustine"). Latin edition of Orosius edited by Zangemeister; citations by book, chapter and sentence number. Translation is by Fear, *Seven Books of History against the Pagans.*

17 Fear notes that Orosius's *History* is extant in more than two hundred medieval manuscripts and was translated into many vernaculars, including Old English and Arabic; see Fear, trans., Orosius, *Seven Books of History*, 24–5. On Orosius's influence see also Lacroix, *Orose et ses idées*, 207–10; Hillgarth, "*Historiae* of Orosius in the Early Middle Ages."

18 Fear describes the *History* as "patriotic [i.e., Roman] Christian polemic" (Orosius, *Seven Books of History*, 24; see also 11, 16).

19 Josephus took part in the Jewish war of 66 CE, but switched sides after he was taken prisoner by the Romans. He subsequently became attached to the retinues of the emperors Vespasian and Titus. The *Jewish War* was translated into Latin twice in the fourth century: first by "Pseudo-Hegesippus," in a free rendition and condensation sometimes wrongly attributed to Ambrose in antiquity; and second by Rufinus in a more literal version sometimes wrongly attributed to Jerome.

20 See Cassiodorus, *Institutes*, XVII.1. The Latin text was widely read in the Middle Ages. In his partial edition of the Latin text, Franz Blatt describes 171 manuscripts, not including

Josephus's main contribution to the Babylon myth lies in his narrative skill. To bring order to the mass of disordered, scattered materials comprising the biblical Captivity narrative, Josephus provides a sequential historical narrative of the Captivity that would be of deep influence. Book X of the *Jewish Antiquities* covers the Babylonian captivity, beginning with the reign of Hezekiah, moving through the siege of Jerusalem and the destruction of the Temple by the Babylonians under Nebuchadnezzar, continuing to the deportation of the Jews to Babylon and the story of Daniel, and finally ending just prior to the emancipation of the Jews under Cyrus (at the beginning of Book XI). Book X of the *Jewish Antiquities* thus forms a coherent narrative unit centred on the Captivity; Josephus's "Matter of Babylon" in Book X synthesizes disparate materials from several biblical books into a coherent narrative sequence. As a historian trained in the protocols of ancient narrative history, Josephus narrates the struggle of the Jews against Babylon by firming up the untidy diverse materials of the Bible and other sources into a coherent – and influential – whole. Josephus amplifies some biblical details and omits others, usually with an eye to fleshing out the characters, motivations, and the inertia of the narrative. Josephus tends to fill in the "gaps" to create a compelling narrative; he also explains and comments on the action with a combination of dispassion and engagement. Using the narrative protocols of historiography seems a simple innovation, but Book X of Josephus's *Antiquities* was perhaps the first Western text to establish a compact, coherent "epic" narrative of the Babylonian captivity, with all the rhetorical power that aesthetic entails.

For example, the Bible never directly narrates the actual siege of Jerusalem by Nebuchadnezzar in any substantial way. Josephus, however, amplifies the sparse biblical source and renders the siege of Jerusalem with vivid, epic details:

> Now the Babylonian king applied himself very strenuously and zealously to the siege of Jerusalem; he built towers on great earthworks from which he kept back those stationed on the walls, and also erected round the whole

---

excerpts and fragments: Blatt, ed., *Latin Josephus*, 25–94. The *Jewish Antiquities* was also translated into Hebrew, Syriac, Slavic, Armenian, Georgian, and Arabic. Josephus's work had a wide influence even beyond the Middle Ages: "The writings of Josephus played an important role in the culture of the Radical Reformation. If Puritan arrivals to New England possessed a book in addition to their Bibles, it was usually Josephus" (Wacholder, "Josephus, Flavius"). See also Schreckenberg and Schubert, *Jewish Historiography*, 2–138.

> circuit (of the city) many earthworks equal in height to the walls. But those within bore the siege with courage and spirit, for they did not weaken under either famine or disease, but, although plagued internally by these afflictions, opposed stout hearts to the war; neither were they dismayed at the devices and engines of their foes, but on their side devised engines to check all those used by the enemy, so that the contest between the Babylonians and the people of Jerusalem was wholly one of cleverness and skill, one side thinking that the capture of the city could be more easily effected in this way, while the other placed its hope of deliverance solely in not wearying or giving up the search for counter-devices by which the engines of their foes might be rendered useless. And thus they held out for eighteen months until they were exhausted by the famine and by the missiles which the enemy hurled at them from the towers. (*Jewish Antiquities*, X.131–4)[21]

This expansion of the biblical source material was no doubt inspired in part by Josephus's own experience as an eye-witness to the siege of Jerusalem by the Romans and the sack of the Second Temple in 70 CE. Josephus's mandate is to amplify and adapt the biblical matter of Babylon to create vivid and compelling narrative history.

Among the many narrative protocols Josephus contributed to Orosius's understanding of the Captivity narrative, an important element was a manifest sense of God's design at work behind human political events. For example, after narrating the final fall of Jerusalem and the captivity of Zedekiah, Josephus pauses to comment on the significance of the moment:

> These things, then, which we have related should make sufficiently clear to those who do not know, how varied and manifold is the nature of God and how those things which He foretells must come to pass, duly take place at the appointed hour, and should also make clear the ignorance and disbelief of these men, by which they were prevented from foreseeing any of these future events and, when they were delivered over to disaster, were taken off their guard, so that any attempt to escape from it was impossible for them. Thus, then, did the kings of David's line end their lives. (*Jewish Antiquities*, X.142–3)

21 I use the Loeb Classical Library edition and translation by Thackeray et al.: Josephus, *Jewish Antiquities*, by book and section numbers.

In a similar moment, at the end of Book X, once Daniel's prophecies have come true in the fall of Belshazzar, Josephus ends the Captivity narrative with a similar excursus, noting the truth of Daniel's divinely inspired prophecies, including the rise of "the empire of the Romans and that Jerusalem would be taken by them and the temple laid waste" (X.276). He explains that such events prove the workings of God's providential foresight (*πρόνοιαν*) in human affairs and that historical events therefore do not proceed in a random or rudderless fashion (X.277–81).

I have digressed on the nature of Josephus's narrative because he was an important source and precedent for Orosius; from the Jewish historian Orosius not only gleaned important historical information, but at the level of form he also learned from Josephus (and other historians) the need to assert the protocols of narrative in history writing and to use sources synthetically, to harmonize disparate, untidy narrative source elements and subjugate them to a shaping design. He also derived from Josephus a precedent for seeing God's hand behind human history.

Design and ordo in the History of Orosius

We can see the proclivity for design and pattern in the understanding of historical events in Orosius's prologue. The prologue sets out his polemical purpose: to write against the pagans – "strangers from the city of God" (*alieni a ciuitate Dei*) who lament the evil times of the present and long for the past, when their gods were venerated rather than Christ (I.preface.9). He argues that the farther one goes back in time from the advent of Christianity, and thus "from the salvation of True Religion" (*a remedio uerae religionis*; I.prologue.14.), the more clearly history shows how terrible was the plight of humanity in those benighted days. However, with the coming of Christ, the old ways began to pass away: "For when Religion spreads forth its light, death is confounded; death is imprisoned, when Religion is strong; indeed, in the profoundest sense death will not exist when Religion alone reigns."[22] The balanced oppositions and chiastic structure of this sentence (clear in the Latin: *ista / illam ... illam / ista*) reflect in miniature the broader sense of symmetric design governing Orosius's grand narrative. This sense of progression is an important part of Orosius's rhetorical program; in a viewpoint deriving from

22 I.prologue.14: ista [i.e., religio] inlucescente, illam [i.e., mors] constupuisse; illam concludi, cum ista iam praeualet; illam penitus nullam futuram, cum haec sola regnabit.

his Augustinian sensibility, he argues that if one steps back far enough and sees the whole picture of history, one can then see the intentional guiding force of God's hand in the patterns of human endeavour.[23] As part of his polemical purpose, he explains that the pagans do not have this "big picture": they are men who "do not look to the future and have either forgotten or are ignorant of the past [and] besmirch the present as a time particularly full of evils."[24] In order to understand the role of Babylon in Orosius's history of empires, we must outline the design Orosius constructs in his understanding of world political history.

Book II begins with an elaborate introduction designed to show that though history may *appear* chaotic and devoid of any divine guidance, there nevertheless *is* divine order in the world. Orosius first asserts that no one doubts that God made man; thus if God made us, he loves us. He then asks: "Who can better order and control it [i.e., His creation – humanity] than He who has made and loves it?).[25] With strength and wisdom God is able to order and control (*ordinare et regere*) our world; therefore all power and all order (*omnem ordinationem*) come from God.[26] *Ordo/ordinatio* and its variants will continue to be key words for Orosius, an index to his narrative teleology and his understanding of historical events.

Having established that both power (*potestas*) and order (*ordinatio*) come from God, Orosius then proceeds to make an argument based on analogy. He posits that "if power comes from God, this is especially the case with kingdoms from which all other power proceeds."[27] This is an argument based on scale: if A is true (i.e., that God is the source of power), then how much truer is B (i.e., that the authority of human kingdoms is based on power), given that A is the greater, divine original

23 Here it is accurate to say that Orosius was inspired by Augustine, but certainly differs in application, whether through Orosius's misunderstanding or the influence of other sources and models. Augustine, for example, places more emphasis on the inscrutability of God's plan and does not have the same simplistic sense of Christian progressive history as Orosius.

24 I.prologue.9: qui cum futura non quaerant, praeterita autem aut obliuiscantur aut nesciant, praesenti a tamen tempora ueluti malis.

25 II.1.2: quis autem *ordinatius* regit, quam is qui et fecit et diligit?

26 II.1.2–3: quis uero sapientius et fortius ordinare et regere facta potest, quam qui et facienda prouidit et prouisa perfecit? quapropter omnem potestatem a Deo esse omnemque ordinationem.

27 II.1.3: si potestates a Deo sunt, quanto magis regna, a quibus reliquae potestates progrediuntur.

source of power and B thus only an earthly copy of that power, since B derives from A. He then extends this argument of "natural" hierarchy to the disposition and rank of earthly polities, explaining that "if there are a number of kingdoms, it is right that there is one supreme kingdom under which all the sovereignty of the rest is placed. In the beginning, this was the kingdom of Babylon, then the kingdom of Macedon, after that the African kingdom, and finally that of Rome, which remains in place to this day."[28] Just as God is at the top in terms of *ordo*, so too it makes sense that lesser polities do homage to the greater polity of empire. This, for Orosius, is the way of the world. What Orosius has done is set forth his proposition, made an argument by analogy, and then extended this argument to historical example – in this case, the Babylonian empire and its successors.

Babylon and the translatio imperii

Having established a political theory and paradigm, Orosius now turns to history proper and the sequence of empires beginning with Babylon, with pattern and symmetry foremost in his mind. Babylon has an important place in Orosius's expression of the *translatio imperii* motif – Babylon was the empire preeminent in power (*potestas*) and first in order (*ordinatio*):

> Through this same ineffable ordering of things, the four principal kingdoms which have been pre-eminent to differing degrees, have occurred at the four cardinal points of the world: the kingdom of Babylon to the east; that of Carthage to the south; that of Macedon to the north; and that of Rome to the west. Between the first and the last of them, that is to say Babylon and Rome, just as in the interval of time between an old father and his young son, come the short-lived and intermediate periods of the African and Macedonian kingdoms.[29]

28 II.1.4: si autem regna diuersa, quanto aequius regnum aliquod maximum, cui reliquorum regnorum potestas uniuersa subicitur, quale a principio Babylonium et deinde Macedonicum fuit, post etiam Africanum atque in fine Romanum quod usque ad nunc manet.

29 II.1.5: eademque ineffabili ordinatione per quattuor mundi cardines quattuor regnorum principatus distinctis gradibus eminentes, ut Babylonium regnum ab oriente, a meridie Carthaginiense, a septentrione Macedonicum, ab occidente Romanum: quorum inter primum ac nouissimum, id est inter Babylonium et Romanum, quasi inter patrem senem ac filium paruum, Africanum ac Macedonicum breuia et media.

In Orosius's conception, the African empire of Carthage and the Macedonian realm of Alexander the Great are minor intervals between the first empire of Babylon and the present empire of Rome.[30] As he begins to work out this history, analogies or resemblances between Babylon and Rome function as hermeneutic keys. If he sees symmetry in history, he judges this to be the ordering and shaping intention of God.[31]

Orosius draws out a series of symmetrical correspondences and analogies between the first and last empires – between the father and son, Babylon and Rome. He notes that all the ancient histories begin with Ninus, first king of Assyria/Babylon, and all the Roman histories begin with Procas (II.2.4). This is further symbolically significant because in the same year that Procas began to rule the Romans, Arbatus the Mede killed Sardnapalus and the original ancient kingdom of Babylon, the kingdom of Ninus, fell to the Medes (II.2.2–3). Moreover, there were sixty-four years between the reign of Ninus and the restoration of Babylon under Semiramis; likewise, the span running from the first year of Procas's reign to the founding of Rome by Romulus also tallied sixty-four years (II.2.5). Thus Orosius concludes that "[i]n Procas's reign, therefore, the seed of future Rome was sown, although it had not yet begun to germinate," while the original kingdom of Babylon came to an end.[32] The power of Babylon lasted for a total of one thousand, one hundred and sixty-four years, from Ninus to Arabatus and the sack of the city by the Medes; similarly, the same number of years elapsed from the beginning of Rome until the sack of the city by Alaric and the Goths.[33] The parallels continue in the later history of the two empires. Orosius notes that Babylon was conquered by Cyrus the Persian in the same year in which

30 Orosius's innovative fourfold scheme of empire is not found in Augustine (Mommsen, "Orosius and Augustine," 339); see also Merrills, *History and Geography in Late Antiquity*, 50–64 for an analysis of this passage.

31 Thus in Book II.2 he notes that the Babylonian kingdoms of Ninus and Semiramis was turned over to the Medes in the same year in which Procas began to rule among the Latins.

32 II.2.5: ita regnante Proca futurae Romae sementis iacta est, etsi nondum germen apparet. eodem anno regni ipsius Procae Babylonis regnum defecit, etsi adhuc Babylon ipsa consistit.

33 II.3.2–3; none of these symmetries are in Orosius's source for this information, Pompeius Trogus. Cf. also the end of Orosius, *History*, Book I: "power passed in one way or another to the Scythians and the Chaldaeans, and then returned by the same route to the Medes" (per uarios prouentus ad Scythas Chaldaeosque et rursus ad Medos parili uia rediit; I.19.2).

"Rome was first liberated from the rule of the Tarquin kings."[34] In this way, Orosius brings Babylon into a narrative pattern deriving from the *translatio imperii* ideology and Augustinian thought. He cannot look at the history of Babylon and Rome and see anything other than uncanny, obvious symmetries:

> So it was this exact conjunction of time that the one fell and the other rose. The former suffered the heel of foreign domination for the first time, while the latter threw off the haughty rule of her masters for the first time. The former, like a dying man, abandoned its inheritance, the latter, though but a youth, recognised itself as its heir. It was at this time that the Empire of the East perished and that of the West arose.[35]

Yet once Orosius establishes this stunning series of parallels, he notes the one, all-important distinction: Babylon was pagan, but Rome became Christian. And this makes all the difference:

> Behold, how Babylon and Rome had a similar beginning, similar powers, a similar size, a similar age, similar goods, and similar evils, but their ends and decline are not similar. Babylon lost her kingdom; Rome retains hers. Babylon was left an orphan on the death of her king, Rome is secure and her emperor safe. And why has this happened? Because there punishments for its disgraceful lusts were visited upon the person of the king, but here the restrained moderation of the Christian Religion was preserved in the person of the king. There, where there was no reverence for religion, licentious frenzy eagerly took its fill of desires; here there were Christians who gave pardon, Christians who were pardoned, and Christians through whose memory and in whose memory pardon was given.[36]

---

34 II.2.9: primum Roma a Tarquiniorum regum dominatione liberata est.

35 II.2.10: siquidem sub una eademque conuenientia temporum illa cecidit, ista surrexit; illa tunc primum alienorum perpessa dominatum, haec tunc primum etiam suorum aspernata fastidium, illa tunc quasi moriens dimisit hereditatem, haec uero pubescens tunc se agnouit heredem; tunc Orientis occidit et ortum est Occidentis imperium.

36 II.3.6–7: ecce similis Babyloniae ortus et Romae, similis potentia, similis magnitudo, similia tempora, similia bona, similia mala; tamen non similis exitus similisue defectus. illa enim regnum amisit, haec retinet; illa interfectione regis orbata, haec incolumi imperatore secura est. et hoc quare? quoniam ibi in rege libidinum turpitudo punita, hic Christianae religionis continentissima aequitas in rege seruata est; ibi absque religionis reuerentia auiditatem uoluptatis licentia furoris impleuit, hic et Christiani fuere, qui parcerent, et Christiani, quibus parcerent, et Christiani, propter quorum memoriam et in quorum memoria parceretur.

He concludes by urging his pagan opponents to "cease to execrate Religion and exasperate the patience of God" (*desinant religionem lacerare et lacessere patientiam Dei*), and instead to reflect on the horrific times of the past, recognizing that God allowed such things to happen by his hidden justice (*occulta iustitia*) and will mercifully assure that such things will not come to pass again (II.3.8–10). Orosius is, as he explains, unfolding his history in an orderly (*per ordinem*) fashion, because nothing in history happens without a divine reason.[37]

According to Orosius these parallels exemplify the powerful hand of God at work: the "order of all these parallels between these two cities ... was brought about by mystic decree"; all these events "came to pass through the ineffable mysteries and the deepest judgements of God," rather than by accident or the power of humanity.[38] He explains that through these parallels he hopes to in part reveal the "ineffable judgments of God" (*ineffabilium iudiciorum Dei*) at work in history from ancient Babylonian times to the fifth-century present (II.3.5). For Augustine, it is difficult to speak of Babylon without Jerusalem; for Orosius, it is difficult to speak of Babylon without Rome.

In the end, Orosius leverages this shaping design to make an argument about real-world political themes – the rise and fall of empires – by extrapolating from Augustine's Two Cities teleology. Orosius concludes that there is a divine symmetry to the passing of empires; Babylon's fall is here used to understand the current political turmoil of Rome:

> It is not my task here to expatiate on the unstable nature of changeable things: whatever is built by the work of man's hands, collapses and is consumed by old age as the capture of Babylon shows. Hers was the first and mightiest empire, and so it was the first to come to an end in order that, as if in obedience to some law of the succession of ages, her due inheritance could be handed on to the next generation who would, in their turn, follow this same law of succession. In this way great Babylon and mighty Lydia fell on Cyrus's first attack – the most powerful limbs of the East falling along with its head and collapsing through the outcome of one single battle. And the people of our time are looking round in unreflecting distress and asking

37 I.3.10: quae modo a me plenius ab ipso Vrbis exordio, reuolutis per ordinem historiis, proferentur.

38 II.3.4: quamuis in tantum arcanis statutis inter utramque urbem conuenientiae totius ordo seruatus sit. II.2.4: ut autem omnia haec ineffabilibus mysteriis et profundissimis Dei iudiciis disposita, non aut humanis uiribus aut incertis casibus accidisse perdoceam.

> whether the once-mighty foundations of the Roman state are now tottering not from the blows of foreign foes, but rather from the weakness of its own old age.[39]

To find a design behind the history of Babylon, to extrapolate or abstract a teleology from the messy, chaotic events of human history enhances Babylon's conceptual, metaphorical mobility, particularly when used as political discourse. Thus, in the early Middle Ages, as the political dimensions of the Matter of Babylon become Christianized and expanded, authors such as Orosius build upon the metaphorical inheritance of Babylon by adding the vital element of teleology: Babylon, in its political dimensions, is part of a plan, a design in the understanding of Christian history. To speak of Babylon in political terms was, at some level, a mandate to speak of the awesome guidance of God's hands in human affairs.

Tyranny and Mutability

Augustine's influence on Orosius can also be seen in the *History*'s representation of Babylonian political tyranny and its passing. Like Augustine, Orosius also casts Babylon as part of the history of tyranny, the City of Man manifest in the world. In his desire to depict past history as alternating periods of bloodshed and stability, Orosius depicts the forerunners of Babylon as examples of worldly power run amok. Orosius likewise synthesizes the classical and Christian origins of tyranny, explaining that Babylon "was founded by the giant Nebrot and refounded by Ninus or Semiramis."[40] Ninus introduces conquest into the world: he ruled with a lust for power (*dominationis libidine*) and waged war throughout Asia in

39 II.6.13–14: Exaggerare hoc loco mutabilium rerum instabiles status non opus est: quidquid enim est opere et manu factum, labi et consumi uetustate, Babylon capta confirmat; cuius ut primum imperium ac potentissimum exstitit ita et primum cessit, ut ueluti quodam iure succedentis aetatis debita posteris traderetur hereditas, ipsis quoque eandem tradendi formulam seruaturis. ita ad proxima aduentantis Cyri temptamenta succubuit magna Babylon et ingens Lydia, amplissima Orientis cum capite suo bracchia unius proelii expeditione ceciderunt: et nostri incircumspecta anxietate causantur, si potentissimae illae quondam Romanae reipublicae moles nunc magis inbecillitate propriae senectutis quam alienis concussae uiribus contremescunt.

40 II.6.7: namque Babylonam a Nebrot gigante fundatam, a Nino uel Samiramide reparatam multi prodidere.

his "bloodstained life" (*cruentamque uitam*; I.4.1). His propensity for war and conquest spread like a savage influence: for example, the Scythians, although barbaric, had been a peaceful race, but Ninus taught them to stir up their dormant savagery (*torpentem saeuitiam*) and drink the blood of men rather than the milk of animals: " as he conquered them, he taught them how to conquer."[41] Semiramis continues her husband's work. Her people now accustomed to the desire for blood (*usu sanguinis*), she led them further "in the slaughter of other tribes" (*caedibus gentium*).[42] Orosius portrays Ninus and Semiramis as conquerors, lords of the primal empire: Ninus at that time was the only warlike king (*solo bellatore*) and his wife was a woman not content with her borders (*non contenta terminis mulier*).[43] Orosius replicates these tropes from the classical myth of Babylon and uses them to comment on the politics of his own time:

> At that time hunting down and slaughtering peoples who lived in peace was a more cruel and serious matter than it is now, because among them there were neither great conflagrations of war abroad nor such a great cultivation of greed at home.[44]

Yet even as Orosius narrates the origins of Babylonian tyranny, he incorporates the tradition of Babylon's passing, again following his personal adaptation of Augustinian thought. For Augustine, the City of Man, as something terrestrial, is also an entity perishable and transitory; it is only the City of God that is eternal and unchanging. In some ways, then,

---

41 I.4.2: a meridie atque a Rubro mari surgens, sub ultimo septentrione Euxinum pontum uastando perdomuit, Scythicamque barbariem, adhuc tunc inbellem et innocentem, torpentem excitare saeuitiam, uires suas nosse, et non lacte iam pecudum sed sanguinem hominum bibere, ad postremum uincere dum uincitur edocuit. Cf. the similar account of Ninus's career in Justin, *Epitome*, I.1.1–10.

42 I.4.4: huic mortuo Samiramis uxor successit, uirum animo, habitu filium gerens, auidosque iam usu sanguinis populos, per duos et quadraginta annos caedibus gentium exercuit.

43 I.4.5: non contenta terminis mulier, quos a uiro suo tunc solo bellatore in quinquaginta annis adquisitos susceperat, Aethiopiam bello pressam, sanguine interlitam, imperio adiecit.

44 I.4.6: quod eo tempore ideo crudelius grauiusque erat quam nunc est, persequi et trucidare populos in pace uiuentes, quia tunc apud illos nec foris erant ulla incendia bellorum, nec domi tanta exercitia cupiditatum. Fear notes in his translation that "Orosius's point of comparison here is probably the Gothic sack of Rome which he is at pains to play down throughout the *Histories*" (*Seven Books of History*, 51n 144).

any history written by the hand of man about humanity is a history of the City of Man, and thus will be necessarily a record of failure, falling-off, and fading away. Orosius reflects this Augustinian perspective by opening his history not with the rise of the great Assyrian/Babylonian empires, but rather with the primal failure: Adam's fall.[45] In his first chapter he explains that he will not begin his history with Ninus, king of Assyria, as most historians do (e.g., Pompeius Trogus), but rather will "trace the beginning of men's misery from man's original sin."[46] This is clearly an Augustinian perspective: the City of Man, according to Augustine, begins with Adam's sin. By beginning with Adam, Orosius shows that from the beginning of postlapsarian history (*ab initio hominis*) humanity has lived under the shadow of Babylon; as a result of Adam's fall, the City of Man – human history itself – has been defined by "alternating good and bad times" (*per bona malaque alternantia*).[47] Flux, rather than stability, defines Babylon, in both the metaphoric and literal senses, as Orosius records the passing of Babylonian power to successive empires in history.

Augustine notes that the love of domination in the City of Man will ultimately be futile; any polity constructed out of such an impetus or desire is inherently doomed (*City of God*, XV.4). Everything built by the hand of man will eventually shake itself apart. For Orosius, Babylon is the prime example of this axiom. Following classical tradition, he describes Babylon in familiar exalted terms, noting that "When they are described, the solidity and size of [Babylon's] walls hardly sound credible" and "[t]he houses within were of twice-four stories and marvelous for their menacing height."[48] Cyrus, he tells us, "captured a city which scarcely seemed possible to have been built by human hands or to be brought low by human endeavour."[49] He explains that this size and power, this *potestas*, did not endure: "The great Babylon, however, the first city to be founded

45 Mommsen notes that Orosius's innovation in this regard was an "important change in the development of Christian historiography" ("Orosius and Augustine," 331).

46 I.1.1–4: et quoniam omnes propemodum tam apud Graecos quam apud Latinos studiosi ad scribendum uiri, qui res gestas regum populorumque ob diuturnam memoriam uerbis propagauerunt, initium scribendi a Nino Beli filio, rege Assyriorum ... ego initium miseriae hominum ab initio peccati hominis ducere institui.

47 I.I.10: iure ab initio hominis per bona malaque alternantia, exerceri hunc mundum sentit quisquis per se atque in se humanum genus uidet.

48 II.6.8, 10: murorum eius uix credibilis relatu firmitas et magnitudo ... domus intrinsecus quatergeminae habitationis minaci proceritate mirabiles.

49 II.6.6: cepitque urbem, quam uel humano opere exstrui potuisse uel humana uirtute destrui posse utrumque paene incredibile apud mortales erat.

after the restoration of the human race, was at that time captured and overthrown with hardly any delay."[50] Orosius's Babylon speaks to the medieval sense of time and the transitory world of the flesh; it is one way the Augustinian Two Cities could be adapted in the register of historiography, transformed according to the narrative teleologies of Christian history.

The Old English *Daniel*

Augustine and Orosius stand as examples of two important traditions of thinking about Babylon in late antiquity: Augustine represents the tradition of patristic exegetical commentary with its important contributions to the metaphoric conception of Babylon; Orosius represents the dominant tradition of historiography with its narrative inflection of the Babylon myth in the mainstream tradition of Christian history. In the following two examples, we move to more focused case studies in order to complement the sweeping paradigms of the Augustinian and Orosian traditions. The following examples from Anglo-Saxon England demonstrate the creative adaptation and transformation of the metaphoric and mimetic traditions of the political Babylon myth. As we shall see, the Old English poem *Daniel* belongs to the tradition of historiography; the biblical commentaries of Bede extend the metaphoric patristic tradition in the realm of figural interpretation or allegory. These case studies will allow us to view the continuing powerful synthesis of political Babylon in the early Middle Ages as the contours and dynamics of the tradition are established as commonplaces for later centuries.

The anonymous Old English poem *Daniel* survives in one copy in the "Junius manuscript" of Old English poetry (Oxford, Bodleian Library, manuscript Junius 11), an illustrated miscellany of Old English religious verse.[51] *Daniel* follows the composite Genesis poem (*Genesis A* and *B*) and the poem *Exodus*, but precedes the final poem in the codex, *Christ and Satan*. The Old English *Daniel*'s main source is the biblical Book of Daniel (in what exact state that source was encountered is still an open scholarly question), but the poem is a free paraphrase, treating only the first five chapters of the biblical source.[52] *Daniel* begins with the epic destruction

50 II.6.11: et tamen magna illa Babylon, illa prima post reparationem humani generis condita, nunc paene etiam minima mora uicta capta subuersa est.

51 I use the edition by Krapp, *The Junius Manuscript*, ASPR I, 111–32, with occasional readings from the edition by Farrell. All translations from Old English are my own.

52 On the sources of *Daniel* see Remley, *Old English Biblical Verse*, 231–434.

of Jerusalem and deportation of the Jews to Babylon, but much of the poem focuses on the agonistic interaction between Nebuchadnezzar and Daniel, the ordeal of three dissenting Hebrew youths cast into Nebuchadnezzar's fiery furnace, and the debasement of Nebuchadnezzar and his empire's ultimate doom. The poem is incomplete in its extant copy, breaking off just after Belshazzar's feast and the prophecy of Babylon's destruction. Like Josephus and Orosius, the anonymous author of *Daniel* imposes narrative order upon recalcitrant source material (in this case, the Book of Daniel itself), and supplements that narrative with a variety of poetic additions, omissions, expansions, and contractions. *Daniel* is above all a poem in the historiographic mode, a poem of sacred history.

One of the most satisfying moments in *Daniel* comes in a lingering pause just prior to Nebuchadnezzar's punishment by God.[53] Nebuchadnezzar has been confronted by the evidence of God's abounding might: three Hebrew youths who defied the king's command to worship false idols have been preserved from harm in the Babylonian fiery furnace. But even when confronted by the limits of his own terrestrial power, the lord of Babylon still glories in his own apparently limitless rule and ignores Daniel's warning that God will soon drive him from power and send him friendless into exile (*wineleasne on wræc*, 568). Just before God debases Nebuchadnezzar, reducing him to something like a witless beast, the king delivers a prideful boast. Our poet delights in this fateful moment of pause, expanding the laconic Latin biblical source to give us a picture of imperial possessiveness and complacency in the City of Man:

> Then, when the Chaldean king ruled the fortress,
> and looked upon the city of Babylon in its glory,
> towering high and extending far over the plain of Shinar,
> he began to declaim with great boasting
> that he, the war-king, had built it for his host
> through a great marvel. Then he became headstrong
> and arrogant beyond all men because of the special gift
> God had given him: a kingdom of men and a world
> as a possession, in the days of mankind:
> "You are my great and famed city which I wrought

53 For a history of the real-life Nebuchadnezzar see Wiseman, *Nebuchadrezzar and Babylon*. For a reception history of Nebuchadnezzar see Sack, *Images of Nebuchadnezzar*. See also Seymour, *Babylon*, 44–9.

for my glory with my vast power. I wish to possess
a resting-place, a dwelling and home, in you."[54]

In the very next lines, God takes away Nebuchadnezzar's "special gift" as well as his human reason: he drives the debased king into wasteland exile for seven years, destroying his mind and reducing him to a "fellow-councilor of the animals" (*wilddeora gewita*, 623a). Only when he finally looks up through the coursing clouds and acknowledges the authority of God is he released and restored to his throne. We might say that Nebuchadnezzar's two extremes, the heights of *imperium* and the depths of *exilium*, represent opposite ends of the spectrum for the individual in medieval political terms: an imperial centre of earthly power set above the domain of lesser kings, and its shadowed, wasteland margins of exile.

We have established the general political valences of Babylon in the preceding pages; this tradition was certainly part of the Anglo-Saxon cultural library. What happens, therefore, if we examine *Daniel* as a "Babylon poem," as an adaptation of the "Matter of Babylon"? Critics have generally interpreted *Daniel* as a general moral exemplum of one sort or another – perhaps a warning against pride or idolatry or drunkenness, turning on the dynamic of Nebuchadnezzar's transformation; thus, interpretive readings of the poem tend to be binary in nature: the idolatry or pride of Nebuchadnezzar vs. the faith or humility of the

---

54 Lines 598–611:

Ongan ða gyddigan þurh gylp micel
Caldea cyning þa he ceastre weold,
Babilone burh, on his blæde geseah,
Sennera feld sidne bewindan,
heah hlifigan, þæt se heretyma
werede geweorhte þurh wundor micel;
wearð ða anhydig ofer ealle men,
swiðmod in sefan, for ðære sundorgife
þe him god sealde, gumena rice,
world to gewealde in wera life:
"Ðu eart seo micle and min seo mære burh
þe ic geworhte to wurðmyndum,
rume rice. Ic reste on þe,
eard and eðel, agan wille."

I restore the manuscript reading *ceastre weold*, following Farrell. Cf. Bately, ed., *Old English Orosius*, II.iiii, 43–4.

Hebrews, for example.[55] But as a reflex of the "Matter of Babylon," *Daniel* becomes a rather more political text, a deeper poetic engagement with political subjects and ideologies. As a "Babylon poem," *Daniel* meditates upon ideas of empire, tyranny, despotism and the limits of rule; the role of law and counsel in governance; the genesis and administration of divine and secular power. We can see this focus in a few areas in which the poet has apparently departed from or augmented the biblical source materials; such moments reveal the poem's adaptation of the Babylon political mythology. These areas include the poet's exploration of Nebuchadnezzar's political character as a tyrant or absolutist ruler; and the evidence for alternative ideologies of sovereignty in the poem.

It is clear that Nebuchadnezzar is a less-than-benevolent king; however, the Babylonian context allows us to see a more politically specific dimension to his character: that is, the tyrant. As we have already noted, Babylon is the *locus classicus* of tyranny, whether the first tyrant is Ninus or Nimrod. Isidore, following Christian tradition, asserts that Nebuchadnezzar's city and kingdom were founded by Nimrod, the first tyrant.[56] He tells us that Nimrod's name is in fact synonymous with tyranny: "'Nimrod' means 'tyrant,' for first he seized unprecedented tyranny among the people, and then himself advanced against God to build the tower of impiety."[57] In his *Jewish Antiquities*, Josephus explains that Nimrod "little by little transformed the state of affairs into a tyranny (*εἰς τυραννίδα*), holding that the only way to detach men from the fear of God was by making them continuously dependent upon his own power" (I.114). Bede also relates the novelty of Nimrod's tyranny, explaining that Nimrod was a man

> who corrupted [*perverteret*] the condition of the human way of life by a new kind of living. So long as he was puffed up by his remarkable power, he at first lived by hunting; then, having gathered an army, he strove to exert an unaccustomed tyranny upon the peoples. Finally, in the verses that follow [in Genesis] we read that he possessed a kingdom and built great cities.[58]

55 See Remley, *Old English Biblical Verse*, 243–4.

56 Isidore, *Etymologiae*, XV.1.4: Primus post diluvium Nembroth gigans Babylonem urbem Mesopotamiae fundavit [First after the flood Nimrod the giant built the city Babylon of Mesopotamia].

57 Isidore, *Etymologiae*, VII.6.22: Nembroth interpretatur tyrannus. Iste enim prior arripuit insuetam in populo tyrannidem, et ipse adgressus est adversus Deum impietatis aedificare turrem.

58 Latin text: Bede, *In Genesim*, ed. Jones, II.10.8–9 (by book number, chapter and verse): qui statum humanae conuersationis nouo uiuendi genere peruerteret.

A poem in the same manuscript as *Daniel*, the Old English *Genesis A*, represents Nimrod as a great imperial leader in the native, formulaic language of Anglo-Saxon poetry, demonstrating this commonplace connection between Nimrod and tyranny in the early Middle Ages:

> Afterwards, a man of wide renown,
> the first-born child of Cush,
> ruled his inherited throne, as books tell us,
> so that he had the greatest might and power of mankind
> in those long-ago days. He was the founder of the kingdom,
> the foremost of princes; he advanced the power
> of his homeland, expanded and exalted it.[59]

The entire complex of ideas concerning Babylonian tyranny stands behind any depiction of Babylon's political hegemony in the Middle Ages and thus also behind the Old English *Daniel* and the character of its ruler: in *Daniel*, Nebuchadnezzar is a "modern Nimrod." In his Genesis commentary, Bede in fact places Nebuchadnezzar along with Ninus and Semiramis in Nimrod's line; all are latter-day lords of Babylon "born from his [i.e. Nimrod's] own lineage" (*progenito ex sua stirpe*; III.11.8–9). The question remains: How does a vernacular poet adapt and transform this particular Babylon political tradition?

The character of Nebuchadnezzar himself seems to have caught our poet's imagination, particularly with regard to his tyranny; many critics have noted that the poem seems to centre on the Babylonian king, rather than on Daniel, regardless of the poem's modern editorial title.[60] In the poem,

---

Dum singulari potentia elatus, primum uenatu uiueret; dein, collecto exercitu, insolitam in populos tyrannidem studuit exercere. Denique in sequentibus regnum habuisse et ciuitates maximas aedificasse legitur; trans. Kendall, 218.

59 *Genesis A*, in ASPR I, 1 87, lines 1628b–35a:

> Frumbearn siððan
> eafora Chuses yrfestole weold,
> widmære wer, swa us gewritu secgeað,
> þæt he moncynnes mæste hæfde
> on þam mældagum mægen and strengo.
> Se wæs Babylones bregorices fruma,
> ærest æðelinga; eðelðrym onhof,
> rymde and rærde.

60 Both Gillian Overing ("Nebuchadnezzar's Conversion") and Antonina Harbus ("Nebuchadnezzar's Dreams") have usefully explored the poet's focus on the psychology of the ruler.

Nebuchadnezzar is a strong king who takes his power beyond appropriate limits and becomes a tyrant. The poet emphasizes that Nebuchadnezzar is not simply a king, but rather an emperor placed above tributary kings. He accordingly gathers his host from across a wide domain, "from south and north" (*suðan and norðan*, 52b), and leads an "army of heathen kings" (*herige hæðencyninga*, 54a) against the Hebrews: that is, not just his own army, but an army comprised of other, lesser kings. The sense of muster here implies not just a ruler gathering his personal followers for a war, but rather something greater: an imperial ruler.

In a number of poetic expansions from the source material, the poet depicts Nebuchadnezzar as proud, rash, headstrong and terrifying, in keeping with the early medieval understanding of tyrants: he is arrogant, resolute, bold (*swiðmod, anmod* and *bræsna*);[61] he is "fierce and gallows-minded" (*grim and gealhmod*, 229a); he is "mighty and powerful upon the earth, terrifying to the children of men."[62] He does not heed the law, but instead lives in foolish pride (*in oferhygde*, 107a);[63] he is "cruel and lacking in guidance" (*reðe and rædleas*, 177a) when he acts in opposition to God's favour (*ofer metodes est*, 174b).[64] In one of the poet's more striking compounds, Nebuchadnezzar is a "king with a wolf's heart" (*wulfheort cyning*).[65] This compound occurs only here in *Daniel* (three times) and is probably the poet's invention.[66] Like Plato's despotic man as detailed in *The Republic*, the Babylonian king suffers from the unbalanced tyranny of certain internal passions and appetites that drive his external political tyranny.[67]

---

61 *swiðmod*: 100a, 268a, 449a; *anmod*: 224a; *bræsna*: 448a.

62 105–6a: *mære and modig ofer middangeard, / egesful ylda bearnum.*

63 See also 489b for *oferhygd* again; he is "not wise" (*gleaw*) at 176a.

64 Ælfric's *Grammar* also glosses a *tyrannus* as one who is "reðe oððe wælhreow" (cruel and bloodthirsty); *Ælfrics Grammatik und Glossar*, ed. Zupitza, 294.1–3).

65 See 135a, 246a; the adjective is also used substantively at 116a. Cf. also *Maxims II*, ed. Dobbie, ASPR VI, 55–7; 18b–19a: "wulf sceal on bearowe, / earm anhaga" (a wolf must be in the woods, a wretched exile); the wolf-hearted Nebuchadnezzar is also described as an exile (*wræcca*, 633a) in *Daniel*. On the epithet *wulfheort* see Caie, "Old English *Daniel*," 6n7.

66 In one of the poem's typical ironies, the bestial behavior in the king's heart will be externalized later as he is reduced to nothing more than an animal as punishment: see Overing, "Nebuchadnezzar's Conversion," 10.

67 Overing, "Nebuchadnezzar's Conversion" and Harbus, "Nebuchadnezzar's Dreams," have examined the king's character and psychology in detail; Manish Sharma has recently gone further and connected the psychological boundary-crossing of Nebuchadnezzar with structural principles of the poem ("Nebuchadnezzar and the Defiance of Measure").

Nebuchadnezzar's imperial power and status are stressed through the rich variety of Old English terms used to designate his rank. The Latin source does not offer much here: overwhelmingly, Nebuchadnezzar is simply called a "king" (*rex*) in the Vulgate; the poet accordingly responds by designating him a *cyning* ("king") seventeen times,[68] but also devises a variety of alternative renderings of *rex*.[69] Nebuchadnezzar is a *weard* ("guardian") sixteen times in various collocations;[70] a *þeoden* ("prince") eight times;[71] a *drihten* ("lord") six times;[72] *Nebuchadnezzar* six times; an *aldor* ("ruler") five times;[73] *ætheling* ("prince") four times;[74] a *brego* ("ruler"), a *wisa* ("leader") and a *frea* ("lord") three times each;[75] a *folctoga* ("commander") twice (108a, 655a); here and there, he is simply the *hæþen* ("heathen": e.g., 433b, 539a). Four terms get one use each: *wyrrestan eorðcyninga* ("the worst of earthly kings," 304b–5a); *se rica* ("the mighty one," 595a), *ræswa* ("councilor," but in the sense of "king" or "leader," 486b), and *heretyma* ("war-leader," 602b). Given the moderate length of the poem (764 lines), this seems to render a high proportion of lexical exploration on the part of the poet when representing Nebuchadnezzar's political office.

As the *Daniel* poet works out the character of Nebuchadnezzar, he is impressed enough by the traditional status of Babylon's fabled ruler to use a number of different political designations for him. It is as if he is searching for the right constellation of vocabulary to describe adequately a legendary

68 *cyning* (95a, 129b, 148b, 165b, 416b, 430a); *Caldea cyning* (599a, 667a); *wulfheort cyning* (135a, 246a); *swiðmod cyning* (100a, 161b, 268a, 528a), *anmod cyning* (224a); *leoda cyninges* (435a), *winburge cyning* (621b). Belshazzar is also called a *cyning* at 701a.

69 For a discussion of Nebuchadnezzar's epithets see Ishiguro, "*Daniel*," 472–5.

70 *Babilone weard*: 99b, 104b, 117a, 167a, 209b, 228b, 448b, 460a, 487a, 641a; *burge weard* (173b), *gumrices weard* (176b), *weredes weard* (551a), *ana eallum eorðbuendum / weard and wisa* (564–5a), *middangeardes weard* (596a), *gumena weard* (635a). God is called a *weard* six times (with a possible seventh, ambiguous example at 234a).

71 93b, 109b, 188b, 190a, 205a, 241a, 419a, 467a.

72 *drihten*: 130b, 547b, 593b, 612b; also *mandrihten* twice (157a, 636b). The poetic word *mandrihten* is not a common word; it is used only four times in the Old English corpus (only in poetry): twice in *Daniel* and once each in *Beowulf* and in *Genesis A*.

73 *aldor* (183b, 753a); *gumena aldor* (548a); *leoda aldor* (645b); *aldor ðeoda* (757b); ealdor þeode (409b, an emendation) may count as a sixth. The word is also used of Belshazzzar (*burga aldor*, 676b, 712b), the ruler of the Medes (*Meda aldor*, 687a) and of God at 466b.

74 489a, 524a, 550b, 637b.

75 *Babilones brego* (47a), *Babilone brego* (255a), *brego Caldea* (427b); *hæðen heriges wisa* (203a); *heriges wisa* (539b); *weard and wisa* (565a); *frea*: (159b, 185b, 585a).

despot of the mightiest empire in history. In a sense, whether the poet is consciously searching for a variety of epithets for Nebuchadnezzar or simply following the opportunities of metre, alliteration, and variation in coming up with these terms is beside the point: this lexical wealth demonstrates that the result of thinking or conceptualizing *in poetic form* is fundamentally different from doing so in other discursive modes, e.g., historiography or exegetical commentary. The generation of poetry is not simply the technical rendering of a source in Old English poetic formulae, but rather the creation of an object of a different ontological category altogether. Every poem presents its own unique thought-world, and the thinking that goes on there is *sui generis* and inseparable from the alchemy that is the poem itself.[76]

Bluntly put, poetic expression can do strange things to its expressed subject; poetic language has a way of slipping its moorings in peculiar ways. Poetry tends to open questions, rather than resolve them. How could it not? If it did not have a certain range of reference and intertextual richness of connotation, it would not be poetry. In the case of *Daniel*, this should urge us to take a careful look at the poem's expression of its political subjects, measuring the poem's language against the informing context of external traditions; when we do, I would argue that we find some of this curious indeterminacy or slippage. For example, while everything about the Babylon tradition tells us that Nebuchadnezzar is a terror and a tyrant, as presented in *Daniel* he also has some attributes that might be admired in an Anglo-Saxon political context: to paraphrase the beginning of *Beowulf* and its praise of the legendary Danish king Scyld, Nebuchadnezzar expands his territory, terrifies neighbouring peoples, and becomes great under the skies until tribes all around are despoiled of their treasure. Might in some ways the Anglo-Saxons thus be inclined to judge him, like Scyld, as a "good king"? Is there, in other words, room to interpret Nebuchadnezzar in a sympathetic fashion, against the grain of tradition, given the inherent ambiguities of poetry? Admittedly, he is the very model of an evil pagan ruler, but he is nevertheless granted a vision of God and reforms his ways. Klaeber noted in his third edition of *Beowulf* that the Babylonian king in *Daniel* could be a model for Heremod, a good king tragically turned bad.[77] In the Old English translation of Gregory the Great's Latin treatise *Pastoral Care*, Nebuchadnezzar is

76 Robert Alter argues this point strongly throughout *Biblical Poetry*, as does Helen Vendler in *Poets Thinking*. See also Scheil, "Sacred History and Old English Religious Poetry."

77 Klaeber, ed., *Beowulf*, 3rd ed. with first and second supplements, cx–cxi.

an example of a distracted king, one with (perhaps) good intentions, but who cannot take the pressures of rule. The text explains that Nebuchadnezzar was "very puffed up in his spirit" (*swiðe upahæfen on his mode*); Gregory blames this on the "weakness of (such kings') hearts" (*untrymnesse hira heortan*).[78] In *Daniel*, Nebuchadnezzar's poetic character is rather more complex than a stock villain or simple exemplum.

Thus Nebuchadnezzar's abasement is not just a figure for the punishment of "the proud" as an abstract moral category; not just an example of what happens justly to bad kings; but an exploration of the political rise and fall of a tyrant and the process of illegitimate power: the poem suggests a tragic arc from strong and successful leader to strong and tyrannical king. The sense of process encoded in the political category of "tyrant" is perhaps captured even in Isidore's seminal definition of a *tyrannus*:

> Tyrants in Greek are the same as "kings" in Latin, because among the ancients there was no distinction between a king and a tyrant ... And so strong kings were called tyrants, because a *tiro* is a strong young man ... Now in later days the practice has come to pass of using the word "tyrants" for the worst wicked kings, who enact upon their people their lust for luxurious domination and the cruelest lordship.[79]

Isidore acknowledges the historical transformation of the political term *tyrannus* over time: it once simply meant a strong king, but "now" denotes a wicked king; the term is a mobile category, one dependent upon changing political contexts and historical circumstances. If Nebuchadnezzar is a tyrant, a tyrant is a name given to a certain localized, contextual definition of a ruler: the ruler in process, in change, transformed from a context of approved political limits to a context of transgressive political authority. Thus central to the Old English *Daniel* is the question

78 *King Alfred's West-Saxon Version of Gregory's Pastoral Care*, ed. Sweet, 38, 40.

79 *Etymologiae*, IX.3.19–20: Tyranni Graece dicuntur. Idem Latine et reges. Nam apud veteres inter regem et tyrannum nulla discretio erat ... Fortes enim reges tyranni vocabantur. Nam tiro fortis ... Iam postea in usum accidit tyrannos vocari pessimos atque inprobos reges, luxuriosae dominationis cupiditatem et crudelissimam dominationem in populis exercentes.

Note how close Isidore's phrase *pessimos inprobos reges* is to *Daniel*'s *wyrrestan eorðcyninga* (304b–5a). For further background references (primary and secondary) to tyranny in classical/late antique culture, see Trompf, *Early Christian Historiography*, 318 n. 93.

of Nebuchadnezzar's power: his power to conquer and despoil Jerusalem; his power to dictate worship; his power to enforce his will upon the Hebrews; the insolence of his ambitions for power in the face of God; and finally the loss and restoration of his power, his sins then replicated in another power-hungry generation.

How does this adaptation of the Babylonian tyranny myth operate within more specific early medieval and Anglo-Saxon debates over the nature of secular power and sovereignty? In other words, what might be the historical context for such an exploration of power provoked by an adaptation of the Babylon political myth? In the Middle Ages, the formula *rex Dei gratia* ("king by the grace of God") is part of the powerful ideological tradition of theocratic kingship, whereby the king is only granted his power through God and has no intrinsic right to his own secular authority; as a corollary, the people have no right to demand anything of the king, since his power resides not in himself, but in God.[80] In some ways, our poem seems to follow this vision of kingship: *Daniel* summarizes the hard truth for Nebuchadnezzar just before his exile: "that there is one lord for all men, / a ruler and power, who is in heaven."[81] It is the illusion of men that power is theirs; the poem continually emphasizes that the beginning and end of power, the *ord and ende* (162a), as our poet puts it, lies with God.

So when we ask, "What is the informing political ideology of *Daniel*?" one main axiom seems clear: power, whether sub-lunary or super-lunary, comes from God, and that power is absolute, able to shape actively the to-and-fro strivings of humanity. But to push this further we might ask, "What ideological preconditions does the poem deploy in order to assert that monolithic voice? What, if any, competing ideologies does this hegemonic voice supplant or incorporate? Does the polyvalent mode of the poetic object allow us to glimpse these alternative paths?"

In late antiquity and the early Middle Ages we might say that two general theories of political power prevailed: an ideology of absolute/theocratic secular rule (part of the inheritance of Rome), and countervailing ideologies pulling in different directions: the Christians of the early Church, for example, asserted that the meek and the humble were sources of political power; likewise, the traditions of law located an alternate source of power outside the ruler; the division between *imperium*

---

80 See Ullmann, *Medieval Political Thought*, 53–8.

81 578–9: þæt sie an metod eallum mannum / reccend and rice, se on roderum is.

and *sacerdotium* spoke to the issue as well.[82] In other words, the ideology of theocratic power was not uncontested, if for no other reason than the fact that inept or tyrannical rulers and their disastrous actions put the whole notion of God's benevolence in doubt. We often think of kingship as an uncomplicated political category, but the nature of kingship was an open question in the post-Roman Europe of the early Middle Ages.[83]

For example, one early medieval variant of the theocratic model of power saw the ruler, whether a good or bad king, as divinely sanctioned and anointed; good kings were a gift from God, bad kings were a punishment from God – but either way, the king was a divine instrument, a representative of His will, and would retain, no matter the circumstances, some of that sacred character. This discourse posits divine power as an intrinsic attribute of the earthly ruler, rather than seeing the ruler as simply a disposable vessel for God's power on earth. Augustine uses the example of rulers such as Nero and cites Proverbs 8:15: "It is through me that kings rule and through me that tyrants (*tyranni*) possess the land" (*City of God*, V.19). The biblical precedent is Saul, cited in this fashion by the Old English translator of Gregory the Great's *Pastoral Care*; although Saul was a bad king, David did not allow him to be harmed because he retained that intrinsic, essential sacral dimension. Gregory concludes therefore that "when we sin against our lords, we sin against the God who created the authority."[84] According to this theory, Nebuchadnezzar, a king-turned-tyrant sent by God, should be judged accordingly as shaped and sanctified by God's power. And thus, in *Daniel*, Nebuchadnezzar is touched by God's hand: he is the instrument of God's retribution against the Hebrews at the beginning of the poem; he *does* receive divine visions from God; he *does* in the end acknowledge God's superior might. There is a sense in which Nebuchadnezzar is a manifestation of God in his more vengeful aspect. Yet the poem then complicates this possibility by so dramatically abasing Nebuchadnezzar as helpless before God's power, juxtaposing the king's far-reaching imperial vision with his unknowing bestial gaze cast upward to the heavens. God gives and takes,

82 On these "descending" and "ascending" theories of political power in the Middle Ages, see Ullmann, *Principles of Government and Politics in the Middle Ages*, esp. 19–26 and Ullmann, *Medieval Political Thought*. Ullmann's model is moderately complicated and contested in *The Cambridge History of Medieval Political Thought*, ed. Burns, 6–7, and passim. On *imperium* and *sacerdotium* in particular see Marcus, "Latin Fathers," 92–102.

83 See Wormald, "Kings and Kingship," 575. See also Nelson, "Kingship and Empire."

84 *Old English Pastoral Care*, ed. Sweet, 200: ðonne we agyltað wið ða hlafordas, ðonne agylte we wið ðone God þe hlafordshipe gescop.

preserves or destroys Nebuchadnezzar's kingdom with ease, even as he transforms Nebuchadnezzar from man to beast. So the text seems to raise the notion of the tyrant as a sanctified instrument of the divine, charged with numinous power, but ultimately forestalls that ideology and asserts the greater power of God and the more purely theocratic vision of rule.

A second alternative to theocratic power is the ideology of rule by law, the tradition that sovereign power is not absolute, endowed for good or ill solely to the ruler through the ruler's ineffable connection to God, but rather that there is a competing locus of power – the "populist" tradition of law, and its derivative, good counsel.[85] This brings us back to some fascinating innovations by the *Daniel* poet. The poem continually emphasizes that Nebuchadnezzar is a poor ruler because he does not keep, or ignores, or does not have access to, the appropriate traditions of law, wisdom, and counsel. Nebuchadnezzar orders his men to find young Hebrew men "wisest in the books of the law" (*gleawost ... boca bebodes*); he wants the youths to learn "skill" (*cræft*, a key term of political valence in the Old English *Boethius*) so that they can give him wisdom (*snytro*).[86] These youths are repeatedly associated with wisdom: they are *freagleawe* (divinely wise? 88b, a hapax legomenon) and *æfæste*, 271a, "firm in observing the law"; they resolve to keep the law of God (*æ godes*, 219a) when pressured by idolatry. The Babylonians, in contrast, worship the idol of Dura because they do not know a "more noble counsel" (*wræstran ræd*, 182b) and therefore they turn to "ill counsel" (*unræd*, 186a) and commit "injustice" (*unrihtdom*, 183a; another hapax legomenon). A number of epithets describe Nebuchadnezzar's unwise nature (e.g., *rædleas*, 177a; *ne gleaw*, 176a).[87]

---

85 Cf. an analogous argument in Trilling, "Sovereignty and Social Order."

86 81b–2a, 83b, 84a. The prologue of the poem designates the fall of the Hebrews as the result of their not keeping their *wær* ("covenant" or "promise," 10b) with God; they forsake the *æcræftas* ("the skills of the law," 19a) and the *drihtnes domas* ("decrees/judgments of the Lord," 32a).

87 Likewise the Babylonian wise men are unable to find the true knowledge, the *wyrda gerynu* (149a) through prophecy (*þurh witigdom*, 146a). Much of the narrative tension revolves around the inability of the Babylonian counselors to divine the substance and meaning of Nebuchadnezzar's dreams, dreams that are political prophecies; the interpreters of the king's dreams are in effect political counselors. In contrast, the wise Daniel (*snotor*, 151a) prudently (*wislice*, 160a) tells the king the meaning of his dream; in order to do this, God has given Daniel "the skills of wisdom" (*snyttro cræftas*, 485b).

But the possibility of a countervailing ideology of rule by law is best exemplified by the poet's wholesale invention of a new character, an unnamed Babylonian councilor, a *ræswa*, who stands as the poem's textual embodiment of law and counsel. After the ordeal of the Three Youths, Nebuchadnezzar stands puzzled by the invulnerability of the Hebrews within the fire, but the king seems almost as puzzled by the fact that he sees a fourth man (really God's angel) in the furnace. As Nebuchadnezzar commands his counselors to explain the mystery, our poet's invented *ræswa* intrudes:

Then a councilor of the king spoke,
a man intelligent and wise of speech:
"That is a thing of marvels that we see there
with our own eyes. Consider, my prince, your proper duty.
Understand well who gave that gift to the young companions!
They praise the one eternal God and constantly
they speak to him joyfully by each of his names;
with bold words they give thanks for (His) power,
they say that he alone is God almighty,
the wise glory-king of earth and heaven."[88]

The poetic invention of the *raeswa* and his wise counsel combines with the text's overall emphasis on law and good counsel, allowing us to glimpse the medieval political theory of law as a counterpoint to imperial power. But yet again, the poem closes off this possibility by emphasizing that such law, in the end, derives ultimately from God, as does the related ability to understand Nebuchadnezzar's dreams and

---

88 Lines 416–26:

Ða cwæð se ðe wæs cyninges ræswa,
wis and wordgleaw: "þæt is wundra sum
þæt we ðær eagum on lociað.
Geðenc, ðeoden min, þine gerysna!
Ongyt georne hwa þa gyfe sealde
gingum gædelingum! Hie god herigað,
anne ecne, and ealles him
be naman gehwam on neod sprecað,
þanciað þrymmes þristum wordum,
cweðað he sie ana ælmihtig god,
witig wuldorcyning, worlde and heofona."

give good counsel: in Nebuchadnezzar's own words, Daniel was able to interpret his dreams and advise him well, "because God almighty sent an augmented spirit, wise skills, into his mind."[89] Any sense of reciprocal power or contractual power deriving from an interface between ruler and traditions of law is briefly raised by the *raeswa*'s wise advice, but then is sublimated by the poem's theocratic ideology. An analogous ideological dynamic might be seen in Coifi, the pagan priest and councilor to Edwin in Bede's *Ecclesiastical History*; in his celebrated speech, Coifi advises Edwin regarding their shared ineffectual pagan beliefs and then urges the king to adopt Christianity: like Daniel's *raeswa*, Bede's pagan priest is an ideological invention designed to body forth and then undermine his own constitutive ideology from within.

Daniel is a poetic text produced at the fault-line measure of competing ideologies of political power. Like all fault lines of this sort, the monolithic solution provides a comforting resolution to these issues; for *Daniel*, this solution is the emphasis on God's power behind all human events. However, in the very raising of alternate political ideologies (even if, ultimately, they are superseded), the inherent ambiguities of the poetic text give them a marginal life, leaving textual traces of their sublimation. Poetry *qua* poetry always displays at some level the awareness of its own artifice; when applied to a political subject, the ideologies represented poetically consequently carry at least a hint of their own status as fabrications.[90]

Concluding this localized case study, it might be interesting to speculate about a more specific historical context for this adaptation of the Babylon myth, even in the absence of a known date or place of origin for the poem. If *Daniel* is in part a response to political theory, is there a historical Anglo-Saxon context for such a work? Can we find a specific stimulus for the ideological response that is the poem? Not easily. It is fair to say that every period of Anglo-Saxon history was interested in or anxious about the dynamics of rule and sovereignty. But I will suggest two things.

First, the ninth century is an appealing candidate: from the Carolingian renovation of empire in the early part of the century to the Alfredian polity at its end, from the decline of Mercia to the rise of Wessex, this would be a time when new, grander political conceptions were in the air,

89 Lines 484–5: forþam ælmihtig eacenne gast / in sefan sende, snyttro cræftas.

90 Cf. Steiner, *Grammars of Creation*, 29: "The work of art, of poetics, carries within it, as it were, the scandal of its hazard, the perception of its ontological caprice."

or under attack, or under discussion – power was a concept in flux, in crisis as well as growth.[91] The translational program of Alfred also provides a context for a vernacular rendering of such matters. The Alfredian or immediately post-Alfredian environment could produce a text like the hypothetical archetype of *Daniel*, a text that is a response to the ideologies of legitimate rule and its pressing questions.

The second, perhaps safer conclusion is to note that the political responsiveness of the *Daniel* tradition lends itself to adaptation and transformation in many different historical contexts. It is likely that a multiphased, reworked poetic *Daniel* tradition stretching back at least into the earlier tenth century eventually led to the text found in Junius 11.[92] It is possible that a poem that spoke to the concerns of political ideology could lead to this sort of protean tradition as successive historical contexts – in the eighth, ninth or tenth centuries – found their ideological anxieties or needs addressed by this poetic reimagining of the origins and ends of power in long-lost Babylon.

Our detour into close reading and the specifics of word choice, character invention, and historical contexts in this discussion of *Daniel* is an example of the creative way that aspects of the Babylon political myth could be adapted and transformed in the early medieval West. The Old English *Daniel* responds to a coherent set of political themes central to the Babylon myth in the historiographic tradition: *translatio imperii* ideology, tyranny, captivity, exile, slavery and dissent, political prophecy, political redemption and restoration. As an adaptation of the Babylon myth according to the Orosian historiographic tradition, *Daniel* responds creatively to its historical moment and to the rhetorical exigencies of vernacular poetic form.

Bede

We turn now to the close reading of another localized Anglo-Saxon case – Babylon in the exegetical writings of the Venerable Bede. Bede's modern reputation rests on his *Ecclesiastical History of the English People*, a history of England's church from the conversion of the pagan Anglo-Saxons to the early eighth century. Yet in the early Middle Ages, Bede was perhaps more influential through the volume of his exegetical works: eighteen

91 See Godden, "King and Counsellor in the Alfredian Boethius."
92 See Remley, "*Daniel*, the Three Youths Fragment."

extant commentaries on scripture that digest the best of patristic thought and transmit that material (with Bede's own sometimes-original stamp) to later Western traditions. In these exegetical commentaries Bede explicates the typological, allegorical, and tropological levels of scripture, yet he also attends to the literal level of historical detail. Following Augustine, Isidore, and general patristic tradition, he conflates the Tower of Babel in Genesis with Babylon, making the tower a spire of the city.[93] As Bede encounters Babylon in the Bible, and responds to the city in his various works, he usually gives some basic historical facts about the city/empire/region and, in particular, the historical details of the Babylonian Captivity of the Jews. If the Old English *Daniel* is an example of the adaptation of mimetic historiographic motifs in the Babylon political tradition, then Bede's work will serve as an example of the extension, use, and adaptation of the metaphoric Babylon promulgated by Augustine and patristic tradition.

Even as he attends to literal, factual information about Babylon in his explication, Bede is far more interested in the figural interpretation of Babel, Babylon, and the Captivity. Almost every time Babylon appears under Bede's eye, he follows patristic tradition by explaining the etymology of the city's name as *confusio.* For example, in his commentary on Genesis he summarizes the basic significance of Babylon: "And the fact is that Babylon with the cities of which it is the head signifies the proud glory of this world, which is liable to confusion; for 'Babel' means confusion."[94] He often extends or qualifies this meaning, e.g., as "the confusion of this world" or a similar modifying phrase ("confusion of sin," "confusion of vices," "the confusion of error," "the confusion of the present life").[95] In a familiar Augustinian fashion, Jerusalem usually also appears as the other half of the dyad, as the opposite of Babylon – Jerusalem as

93 E.g., Bede, *In Genesim,* III.11.8–9.

94 Bede, *In Genesim,* III.10.10; trans. 219: Quia uero Babylon cum ciuitatibus quarum caput est, superbam huius mundi gloriam, quae confusioni obnoxia est, designat; Babel enim confusio dicitur.

95 E.g., in his commentary on Revelation 9:14, Bede notes that the Euphrates is a river in Babylon and that it "stands for the power of the worldly kingdom, and the waves of persecutors" (*mundani regni potentiam et persecutorum indicat undas*). See also his commentary on Revelation 18:10, and 18:21: Babylon is "the city of this world" (*Ciuitas saeculi*) cast down by "the weight of sinners and their error" (*pro peccatorum pondere et errore*); cf. commentary on Revelation 18:2 and 18:9. Latin text: Bede, *Expositio Apocalypseos,* ed. Gryson; Bede, *Commentary on Revelation,* trans. Wallis, 172, 241.

the *visio pacis* ("vision of peace") in direct contrast to Babylon, the "confusion of the world":

> And this city, in which languages are divided and people scattered, is deservedly called Babylon, that is, "confusion"; that city is called Jerusalem, that is, "vision of peace," in which the languages of all the peoples are united in the praise of God and harmony is established.[96]

The inheritance of the Augustinian Two Cities is obvious here. Much of Bede's understanding of Babylon's metaphoric meaning derives from this interpretation of Babylon as "confusio," a multivalent Latin word only partially captured by the modern English "confusion."

Babylon is prominent in Bede's commentary on Genesis, particularly around the Tower of Babel story and the appearance of the great tyrant Nimrod. Acting according to his historian's instincts, Bede spends some time explaining the literal or historical details of these episodes, relying on the traditional historiographic explanations: that Nimrod was the first tyrant and Babylon the first empire (III.11.8–9; see also III.10.10). But he then moves to an extended figural interpretation of Nimrod: for Bede, the great hunter symbolizes the devil, and thus in the spiritual sense Babylon is the "devil's city, that is, the whole condemned human race."[97] Bede applies an Augustinian perspective, explaining that Babylon is the "city of the devil ... that is, the whole multitude of the wicked [that] wanders about like a vagabond through the dissolute corruption of the present life."[98] He contrasts the wicked metaphorical city of Babylon with the architectural purity of the metaphorical city of the Church, "built of living stones" (*de uiuis aedificatur lapidibus*, III.11.8–9; trans. 234). Bede then proceeds incrementally through the relevant Genesis verses, allowing this basic opposition to guide his understanding. His summary adapts the Augustinian notion of misdirected love powering

96 Bede, *In Genesim*, III.11.1; trans. 228: Meritoque haec ciuitas, in qua linguae diuisae ac gentes sunt dispersae, Babylon, id est "confusio"; illa dicitur Hierusalem, id est "uisio pacis," in qua, adunatis in Dei laudem loquelis uniuersarum gentium, est facta concordia. See also III.11.8–9; trans. 231.

97 *In Genesim*, III.11.8–9; trans. 233: Babylon est diaboli ciuitas, hoc est reproba hominum multitudo uniuersa. See also *Expositio Apocalypseos*, 18.2, and 14:8: Babylon is "the ruined city of the devil" (Ciuitatem diaboli ruinosam; trans. 211).

98 *In Genesim*, III.11.8–9; trans. 234: ciuitas diaboli ... hoc est uniuersa reproborum multitudo, per fluxam corruptionem uitae praesentis uagabunda oberrat.

and defining the City of Man: "All the wicked make a city for themselves whenever, ignoring the protection of God's commandments, they follow the feelings and desires of their own heart in doing or saying whatever they please. They build the city of Babylon whenever they do shameful deeds [literally: 'deeds deserving of *confusio*']."[99] As traditional as this metaphorical Augustinian approach might be, nevertheless there is also a hint of real-world political application when Bede connects the sundering of tongues at Babel to this figural interpretation of Babylon. The builders of Babylon, he explains, are the figural equivalents of heretics, the "instigators of heresies" (*magistri errorum*, III.11.8–9; trans. 233) who lead people into wickedness. With the reference to these "heretics," here and elsewhere in this explication, there is an obvious potential to connect figural (metaphorical) understanding to the exigencies of lived experience in Bede's world, where heresy and deviation from orthodoxy – real or imagined – was part of the social matrix.

Aside from Babylon's appearance in Genesis, the other main figural interpretation of Babylon comes in Bede's interpretation of the Babylonian Captivity. Again, Bede is not blind to the literal or historical nature of the event, and in his various commentaries and treatises he explains the basic facts of the Captivity. However, his main interest again is in a figural interpretation of the narrative, and he is quite consistent in this understanding across various commentaries. A statement in the prologue to his commentary on Ezra and Nehemiah gives us the basic interpretation:

> It is appropriate, then, that those who were held as captives in Babylonia as a result of wicked works are freed after seventy years, and that they rebuild God's house and the holy city. For often those who were separated because of their sins from the communion and society of the Holy Church and joined to the fate and number of infidels, in turn through the gift of the Holy Spirit exercise themselves zealously in the pursuit of good works and in this way regain the fellowship of the faithful, i.e. the Lord's house and city from which they were cast out. For it should be noted that the rebuilding of the Lord's house after it was burnt down, the restoration of Jerusalem after its destruction, the return of the people to their homeland after their

99 *In Genesim*, III.11.8–9; trans. 237: Faciunt sibi ciuitatem omnes reprobi cum, neglecto praesidio praeceptorum Dei, sensus ac desideria sui cordis in agendis siue loquendis quae ipsos libet sequuntur. Aedificant ciuitatem Babyloniam cum opera confusione digna faciunt.

captivity, and the recovery of the stolen holy vessels to their house all typologically denote this one and the same return of penitents to the Church.[100]

The narrative of exile and return, of ruin and redemption, moves Bede's exegetical imagination here. In this interpretation Nebuchadnezzar, like Nimrod before him, represents the devil (II.1022–33; trans. 119),[101] luring the good away from the path of righteousness to the captivity and confusion of this world and its sins. Ezra, the Jewish priest/ scribe who leads the people back to Jerusalem after the Captivity, represents God or Jesus (II.1957–97; trans. 151), because it is "only those whom God is with who can journey from the confusion of sins to works of virtue as though from the slavery of Babylon to freedom in Jerusalem."[102] However, Bede also augments this basic interpretation with slight transformations and dilations: for example, he argues that in some sense, the Captivity can be considered a sort of fortunate fall, a warning given by God that will ultimately strengthen the believer, both then and now:

> Also, we should note and very frequently remind ourselves how much good the evil of captivity brought to the people, for when they were freed from it, they are all shown to have attended to heavenly devotions with greater determination than they had ever before. But today too, it has been beneficial for many who had lived negligently in the peace of the Church to have suddenly gone astray and fallen into some sins, provided that after their fall they were raised up by repenting and began to serve the Lord more vigilantly.[103]

---

100 Bede, *In Ezram et Neemiam*, ed. Hurst, I.65–78 (book and line numbers): Vnde apta significatione qui per opera peruersa in Babiloniam fuerant captiuati post septuaginta annos liberantur ac domum Dei et ciuitatem sanctam reaedificant quia non numquam hi qui per sua peccata a communione ac societate sanctae ecclesiae separati infidelium sorti ac numero copulabantur rursum per donum sancti spiritus studio se bonae operationis exercent ac per hoc consortium fidelium domus uidelicet et ciuitatis domini de qua fuerant eiecti recipiunt. Notandum enim quod unam eandemque paenitentium ad ecclesiam reuersionem et domus domini reaedificata post incendium et ciuitas restaurata Hierusalem post destructionem nec non et populus post captiuitatem patriam remissus et uasa sancta quae ablata erant domum reducta typice denuntient. Translation by DeGregorio, *Bede: On Ezra and Nehemiah*, 8–9.

101 See also *In Genesim*, III.11.8–9; trans. 231–2, connecting Nimrod to Nebuchadnezzar.

102 Bede, *In Ezram et Neemiam*, I.233–5; trans. 15: solos illos cum quibus Deus est de confusione peccatorum ad uirtutum opera quasi de seruitio de Babylone in Hiersolimam ad libertatem posse transire.

103 Bede, *In Ezram et Neemiam*, I.1491–7; trans. 64: Notandumque et crebrius rememorandum quantum boni populo malum captiuitatis contulerit de qua eruti

As he adapts and transforms the metaphoric Babylon tradition, Bede and his exegesis share some of the dilating originality the *Daniel* poet uses in adapting the historiography of the Babylon myth.

Moreover, as in *Daniel*, there is a sense that this interpretation of the Captivity had a potential application for Bede's immediate social situation, for believers "today" (*hodie*), as the passage above puts it. Two further examples demonstrate this real-world political application of the metaphoric Babylon. First, after noting that Nebuchadnezzar represents the devil in the Captivity narrative, Bede explains that learned clergy must save souls led astray by the devil into the confusion of the world and guide them back to restoration and redemption through the sacrament of penance: "Equally, those who by sinning have been drawn away from the Church's fellowship into the devil's servitude, and who by remaining in their sins have fallen into the captivity of the king of Babylon, must be reconciled to the Holy Church by doing penance *through the office of a priest*" (emphasis added).[104] This bit of Babylon exegesis supports the essential mediating and pastoral role of clergy in Bede's own social milieu. He then expands this idea further to include a comment on those people recently converted to the Church: "We too, then, when we are teaching peoples new to the Church to renounce the devil and to believe in and confess the true God, it is as though we are going out from Babylon."[105]

A second example of this localized political application comes from Bede's treatise *Thirty Questions on the Book of Kings*. The verse Bede interprets here is the Vulgate 4 Kings 24:14 [modern 2 Kings 24:14]: "And he [Nebuchadnezzar] carried away all Jerusalem; and all the princes; and all the valiant men of the army, to the number of ten thousand into captivity; and every artificer and smith. And none were left, but the poor sort of the people of the land." Bede explains the historical or literal meaning of this

tanta omnes intentione quanta numquam antea caelestibus obsequiis operam dare probantur. Sed et hodie multis qui in pace eccelsiae neglegenter uixerant subito errasse et in flagitia aliqua cecidisse profuit dum post casum paenitendo erecti uigilantius domino seruire coeperunt.

104 Bede, *In Ezram et Neemiam*, II.1345–50; trans. 130: quicumque ad consortium sanctae eccelsiae pertingere desiderant, per sacerdotum aeque officium debent reconciliari sanctae ecclesiae paenitendo qui ab eius societate peccando recesserant et in seruitium diaboli qui in captiuitatem Babylonii regis in peccantis perseuerando deciderant.

105 Bede, *In Ezram et Neemiam*, II.1400–3; trans. 131: Et nos ergo cum nouos ecclesiae populos diabolo renuntiare et Deum uerum credere ac confiteri docemus quasi ... de Babylone ... egredimur.

verse: that the Babylonians took back to Babylon all the skilled artisans and smiths of Israel so that such skills would serve Babylon (or no one at all). He then pauses and delivers his figural interpretation, highlighting the contemporary relevance of the figure:

> Because the allegory of so lamentable a history fits so well *with the negligence of our own time*, it must not – I believe – be passed over in silence. For it is clear that Jerusalem and the land of Israel here stand for the city of Christ – which is the Holy Church – and that Babylon and the Chaldeans (and also the Philistines) stand for the city of the devil – which is the whole multitude of evil humans and angels.[106] (emphasis added)

The interpretation of the Babylonian captivity "fits the negligence of [Bede's] own time." Bede further explains that a believer "travels to Babylon" and is held captive there whenever he or she is led astray by (and into) the confusion of the world and its vices. The Captivity can even apply, most calamitously, to learned clergy:

> But Nebuchadnezzar leads Jerusalem, all its princes, and its army's ten thousand valiant men into captivity when the world's temptations, or its calamities, suddenly overwhelm *even the people's teachers* and those who have been seen to serve the Lord with invincible spirit and to keep the Ten Commandments faithfully in love of God and neighbour. And so, they either defile themselves with wicked deeds or, by turning away toward heresy, incur the mark of open apostasy."[107] (emphasis added).

These moments, in which the local and political push into the hermetic world of exegesis, do not simply replicate the Two Cities of Augustinian

106 Bede, *In Regum XXX Quaestiones*, ed. Hurst, 30.15–21 (question and line numbers): Cuius tam deflendae historiae quia multum neglegentiae nostri temporis congruit non opinor allegoriam esse reticendam. Constat namque quia Hierusalem et terra Israhel ciuitatem Christi, id est ecclesiam sanctam, Babylon autem et Chaldaei siue Philisthei ciuitatem diaboli, id est omnem malignorum siue homium siue angelorum. Translation from *Bede: A Biblical Miscellany*, trans. Foley and Holder, 136–7.

107 Bede, *In Regum XXX Quaestiones*, 30.25–32; trans. 137: Abducit autem Nabuchodonosor Hierusalem et uniuersos principes fortesque exercitus decem milia in captiuitatem cum *etiam magistros populorum* et eos qui inuincibili animo domino seruire ac decalogum legis fideliter uidebantur in Dei ac proximi amore conseruare subito siue illecebris mundi seu aduersitatibus subacti aut maioribus se facinoribus pollunt aut certe in heresim declinando apertae apostasiae notam incidunt.

thought, but rather demonstrate an imaginative adaptation of the Babylon political myth, applying it, in this case, to local political issues of education and doctrinal orthodoxy. As the next chapter will show, the mobility and applicability of Babylon exemplified by Bede's exegesis are essentially the same application of political Babylon used by the Western tradition to the present, but with some important watershed moments along the way. We see that it is a natural tendency of metaphorical or figural interpretation to move inexorably towards a localized application or adaptation; the natural movement of the Augustinian paradigm of Babylon, as it was expanded in the medieval West, was to use the metaphor to comment on individual lives in ethical or existential fashion.

As this chapter demonstrates, by the early Middle Ages "Babylon" had become a word rich in allusive meaning and a central commonplace image in the Christian language of metaphor. This last aspect is especially important as we turn to the latter-day reception of Babylon as political invective. The sign of Babylon integrated both mimetic and metaphoric modes of representation, until it evolved to a master signifier under Augustine's Two Cities motif. Early medieval Christian narrative teleologies provided conceptual frameworks for universalizing claims in terms of the city's metaphorical reach. The late antique/early medieval synthesis and development of the Babylon political myth provides a shared understanding of the word for later centuries; this period established the necessary enabling discursive context from which Babylon could then be displaced and adapted to endlessly different rhetorical and political situations in subsequent centuries. Thus, even when we are in an ostensibly secular context, and we speak of "Hollywood Babylon" or off-handedly call New York, Moscow, Paris, or Las Vegas a "modern Babylon," we are still accessing that age-old Christian paradigm in a latter-day, displaced form.

Chapter Three

Political Babylon from the Great Schism to the Present

Prepare yourselves against Babylon round about, all you that bend the bow. Fight against her, spare not arrows: because she hath sinned against the Lord.

–Jeremiah 50:14

In forming our idea of the great capital of the British Empire and of the nineteenth century, we naturally look for models in the great cities of the past, and the centres of other empires. We compare London with Imperial Rome; and when we would express in one word the idea of her greatness, we call her "the Modern Babylon." It is natural, then, that in trying to form an idea of London we should think of that great Assyrian capital, with her lofty walls, her hundred brazen gates, her magnificent palaces, and wonderful hanging gardens.

– Anonymous, "London, As It Strikes a Stranger" (1862)[1]

Having established, in the previous chapters, a set of inceptive paradigms and dynamics governing the political myth of Babylon, this chapter carries the history of this complex from the later Middle Ages to the present. In the post-medieval West, Babylon is a pervasive political metaphor in countless historical and rhetorical circumstances. However, the sample evidence gathered in this chapter does not suggest a simple story of mechanical replication; rather, in the midst of continuity we see some changes in the configuration of the Babylon political myth when we examine the post-medieval tradition from a diachronic perspective.

The case studies in this chapter display several tendencies. We see an intensifying use of Babylon as a figure for political/theological polemic

1 *Temple Bar* 5 (June 1862): 381, quoted in Nead, *Victorian Babylon*, 3.

rising in tandem with the late medieval/early modern internal struggles of Christianity. A key watershed moment in the polemic use of Babylon is during the late medieval Great Schism of the Avignon papacy (1309–77). Early modern Protestant writers, building upon this legacy, not only adapted the Babylon tradition to their own political contexts, but in so doing, they also transformed Babylon in key ways. In the case studies gathered here there are two observable trends. One is a continuing emphasis on Babylon as a flexible metaphor used to explore aspects of the moral self, echoing a Protestant emphasis on individual salvation. The second tradition moves in the opposite direction: there is a tendency in radical Protestant traditions to emphasize the literal characteristics of political Babylon in prophecy and apocalyptic thought, over and against a metaphorical tradition. In the context of political/theological polemic, the Protestant tradition adapted the general structure of the Augustinian Two Cities tradition, but in a way that would initiate a more simplistic, dualistic ideology, reducing the medieval Augustinian complexities to a simple binary vision of good versus evil, the saved versus the damned. These twin processes fueled a displacement of Babylon from an elaborate Christian conceptual apparatus to a more secular metaphoric context.

Dante, Petrarch, and the Avignon Papacy

By the early Middle Ages Babylon had become a commonplace allusion in Western political discourse. It is not possible to track all the uses of political Babylon throughout the Middle Ages and beyond, but we can pause at one historical moment to read a case study that stands as both an exemplum of typical later medieval uses of political Babylon, and also functions as an important precedent for the widespread Protestant adaptation of Babylon in early modern Europe. I speak here of the Great Schism and the Avignon papacy, the crisis of the late fourteenth-century Church in which the papacy was split between rival claimants to the Holy See in Rome and in Avignon.[2]

Dante Alighieri (1265–1321) saw the early phases of the Great Schism, as Pope Boniface VIII aggressively asserted the power of his office in

2 On the history of the Schism see Favier, *Les papes d'Avignon*; for a concise summary of the conflict, see Norwich, *Absolute Monarchs*, 202–26. On the literary context see Blumenfeld-Kosinski, *Poets, Saints, and Visionaries.*

both temporal and spiritual matters. In response to these shifting political winds, Dante fled Florence in 1303. While in exile, Dante uses Babylon as part of a political language of dissent in his letters. *Epistola VI* (31 March 1311) addresses Dante's home city of Florence, which was resisting the sovereignty of the Holy Roman Empire. Dante laments that rather than submitting to the legitimate authority of the Emperor Henry VII – the supreme ruler and God's representative on earth – the Florentines have "chosen to rise up (*insurgere*) in the madness of rebellion (*in rebellionis vesaniam*)."[3] Dante then constructs an analogy between the Holy Roman Empire and natural hierarchy as established by God: the rebellion of the Florentines against their rightful earthly sovereign replicates a rebellion against God and the natural order of things (an analogical argument similar to Orosius's *History*, as we have seen). Dante asks "Wherefore, then, being disabused of such an idle conceit, do you abandon the Holy Empire, and, like the Babylonians once more, seek to found new kingdoms, so that there shall be one polity of Florence, and another of Rome?"[4] The rest of the letter threatens a Babylon-style apocalyptic devastation upon Florence for its transgression; the Florentine rebellion will fail and the emperor, like God, will come in his anger and the "neo-Babylonian" Florentines will fall "into the dungeon of slavery" (*servitutis in ergastula*).[5] This is a very specific use of metaphoric Babylon in a political dispute: similar to Bede's social commentary in the previous chapter, but in a much more direct fashion.

Dante addresses another letter, *Epistola VII*, to the Holy Roman Emperor rather than to the Florentines. In this letter Dante hopes for an end to political discord and division, the *confusio* endemic to the City of Man, but he explains that the devil holds sway over the lands of Italy due to the emperor's neglect of the area. He represents the Italian city states as Jewish exiles in Babylon: "Wherefore we have long wept by the waters of Confusion, and unceasingly prayed for the protection of the

3 *Dantis Alagherii Epistolae: The Letters of Dante*, ed. and trans. Toynbee; Latin by line numbers, English translation by page numbers: *Epistola VI*, lines 31–6; trans. 77.

4 *Epistola VI*, 49–52; trans. 78: "Quid fatua tali opinione submota, tamquam alteri Babylonii, pium deserentes imperium nova regna tentatis, ut alia sit Florentina civilitas, alia sit Romana?" I have adjusted Toynbee's translation here, which reads "men of Babel" for "Babylonii." Toynbee's note (68, n.8) explains that "By *Babylonii* here Dante evidently means the builders of the Tower of Babel." I have restored the reading "Babylonians" since it makes clear the fusion of Babel and Babylon in the period.

5 *Epistola VI*, lines 87–95, at 95; trans. 79; cf. *Epistola VIII*, lines 1–16; trans. 143.

just king, who should destroy the satellite of the cruel tyrant, and should stablish us again under our own justice."[6] The phrase "waters of Confusion" (*flumina confusionis*) combines an allusion to Psalm 136 (*Super flumina Babylonis*) with the patristic tradition that *Babylon est confusio.* Dante longs for a redemption from the "captivity" of Babylon – i.e., the political *confusio* of the late fourteenth century engulfing the squabbling Italian city-states. He returns to the same psalm at the end of the letter, when he makes a final plea to the Emperor for political aid:

> Up then! make an end of delay ... and Israel shall be delivered. Then our heritage which was taken away, and for which we lament without ceasing, shall be restored to us whole again. But even as now, remembering the most holy Jerusalem, we mourn as exiles in Babylon, so then as citizens, and breathing in peace, we shall think with joy on the miseries of Confusion.[7]

In 1309 Pope Clement V would move the papacy to Avignon in the ongoing struggle over papal power and politics in Europe. What is important here for our purposes is that Dante's use of Babylon in the context of political dissent would be adapted and elaborated by Petrarch in the next stage of the Schism. And in turn, this use of the Babylon metaphor in an internecine Catholic conflict would provide a later precedent for using Babylon in analogous Protestant rhetoric against the Catholic Church. The Avignon papacy was of course not simply a precedent for the Reformation; my interest here centers only on the use of Babylon as a metaphor in similar (and linked) polemic contexts. Once used in the context of the Schism, by authors such as Dante and Petrarch – writers of enormous later influence across early modern Europe – it became that much easier to use Babylon in an analogous religious conflict in subsequent centuries.

With Dante's Babylon as a precedent, then, Petrarch (1304–74) uses the figure polemically against Avignon in his poetry and his letters

6 *Epistola VII*, lines 10–15; trans. 101: Hinc diu super flumina confusionis deflevimus, et patrocinia iusti regis incessanter implorabamus, qui satellitium saevi tyranni disperderet, et nos in nostra iustitia reformaret.

7 *Epistola VII*, lines 177–90; trans. 105: Eia itaque, rumpe moras ... et liberabitur Israel. Tunc hereditas nostra, quam sine intermissione deflemus ablatam, nobis erit in integrum restituta. At quemadmodum sacrosanctae Ierusalem memores, exules in Babylone, gemiscimus; ita tunc cives, et respirantes in pace, confusionis miseries in gaudio recolemus.

(the *Liber Sine Nomine*).[8] In a torrent of invective, sonnet 138 of the *Rime sparse* directly addresses Babylon/Avignon:

> Fountain of sorrow, dwelling of wrath, school of errors, and temple of heresy, once Rome, now false wicked Babylon, for whom there is so much weeping and sighing:
>
> O foundry of deceits, cruel prison where good dies and evil is created and nourished, a hell for the living: it will be a great miracle if Christ does not finally show his anger against you.
>
> Founded in chaste and humble poverty, against your founders you lift your horns, you shameless whore! And where have you placed your hopes?
>
> In your adulterers, in your ill-gotten riches that are so great? Constantine will not come back now. But since Hell shelters him, may it carry you off, too![9]

As in the Old English *Daniel*, this is a poetic adaptation of the political Babylon myth: note the familiar elements – the Whore of Babylon, the Horned Beast, the equation of Rome with Babylon, the sense of apocalyptic

8 Latin text of the *Liber sine Nomine* from *Petrarcas 'Buch Ohne Namen' und die Päpstliche Kurie*, ed. Piur, by page and line numbers. Translations are from *Petrarch's Book Without a Name*, trans. Zacour, by page numbers. On Babylon in Petrarch's poetry and its connection to the Augustinian Two Cities, see Hallock, "The Pre-Eminent Role of *Babilonia*" and Alexander Lee, "Sin City?." See also O'Rourke Boyle, *Petrarch's Genius*, 74–112 for Petrarch's writings on the Avignon Papacy (with discussion of Babylon as well).

9 Fontana di dolore, albergo d'ira,

> scola d'errori et templo d'eresia,
> già Roma or Babilonia falsa et ria,
> per cui tanto si piange et si sospira,
> o fucina d'inganni, o pregion dira
> ove 'l ben more e 'l mal si nutre et cria,
> di vivi inferno: un gran miracol fia
> se Cristo teco alfine non s'adira.
> Fondata in casta et umil povertate,
> contra' tuoi fondatori alzi le corna,
> putta sfacciata! Et dove ài posto spene?
> Negli adulteri tuoi, ne le mal nate
> ricchezze tante? or Constantin non torna.
> Ma tolga il mondo tristo che 'l sostene!

Text and translations from *Petrarch's Lyric Poems*, ed. and trans. Durling, by poem number. Poems 136, 137, 138 are the "Babylonian" sonnets.

imminence, the subtext of Psalm 136 beneath the weeping, sighing, and waters (*fontana*) of the first stanza. For Petrarch, Avignon is Babylon, a traitor to the true faith, a spiritual and doctrinal, and therefore political enemy, a tyrant to be overthrown. His poetic imagination plays with this rhetorical situation with all the imaginative resources of the Babylon tradition.

The almost playful elaboration of the Babylon political elements is Petrarch's distinctive contribution to this tradition. For example, in residence in Avignon, Petrarch (a Roman loyalist) laments his situation: "now the Gallic world holds me, and the western Babylon (than which the sun shines on nothing more deformed) ... I, an angry exile from Jerusalem, living by the rivers of Babylon, have written these things to you in great haste."[10] Avignon is a "western Babylon" (*occiduus Babilon*); Babylon itself the "inferno" (*infernum*).[11] In *Letter* 8 Petrarch elaborates the Babylon political metaphor into a full-scale overwrought motif, speaking of his personal torment of living in Babylon/Avignon:

> Whatever you may have read of the Babylons of Assyria or Egypt, of the four labyrinths, of the portals of Avernus and the forests and sulphrous marshes of the lower world, is all child's play compared with this hell. Here you may see Nimrod, a turret-rearing terror; Semiramis armed with her quiver, merciless Minos, Rhadamanthus, and all-consuming Cerberus; 'here is Pasiphaë coupled with the bull,' to quote Vergil, 'and the mongrel offspring and two-formed progeny, the Minotaur, memorial of her foul love.' Finally you may see here every disorder [*confusum*], gloom, or horror to be found or imagined anywhere.[12]

---

10 *Letter 5*: 185.5–6; Zacour 58: Nunc me Gallicus orbis habet et occidentalis Babilon, qua nichil informius sol uidet ... *Letter 9*: 196.24–5; Zacour 71: Hec tibi raptim Hierosolymitanus exul inter et super flumina Babilonis indignans scripsi.

11 *Letter 8*: 193.1; Zacour 67 and *Letter 14*: 215.2; Zacour 90. For further references to Avignon as Babylon in *Letter 14* see 210.19–211.1 (Zacour 85); 211.5–7 (Zacour 86); 215.1–2 (Zacour 90).

12 *Letter 8*: 193.13–17; Zacour 67–8: Quicquid de Assiria uel Egiptia Babilone, quicquid de quatuor laberinthis, quicquid denique de Auerni limine deque Tartareis siluis sulphureisque paludibus legisti, huic Tartaro admotum fabula est. Hic turrificus simul atque terrificus Nembroth, hic pharetrata Semiramis, hic inexorabilis Mios, hic Rhadamantus, hic Cerberus uiniuersa consumens, hic *tauro supposita Pasiphae mixtumque genus*, quod maro ait, *prolesque biformis Minotaurus inest, Veneris monimenta nefande*, hic postremo quicquid confusum, quicquid atrum, quicquid horribile usquam est aut fingitur aspicias.

Following tradition, Petrarch includes familiar elements of the Babylon political myth such as the great Semiramis, Nimrod the "turret-rearing terror" of Babel (highlighted by a nice wordplay in the Latin: *turrificus terrificus*), and the disorder (*confusum*) one would expect in the City of Confusion.[13] In a typical humanist fashion, Petrarch blends Babylonian elements with classical references to create a vivid image of "disorder, gloom, and horror."

Letter 10 displays a similar rhetorical exuberance. Petrarch explains that his "home address" is "Babylon":

> You are surprised by the addresses on my letters. As well you might be. Since you have read of only two Babylons, the Assyrian one of long ago enshrining the famous name of Semiramis, and the Egyptian one founded by Cambyses which still flourishes in our own day, you wonder about this unheard-of Babylon with which you are now confronted. You know that some of our authors declared Rome to be another Babylon, so to speak, on account of a similarity of government and climate; but since, as you say, I usually refer to Rome as our holy mother, queen of cities, you are now puzzled by this newest of Babylons.[14]

---

13 Nimrod's appearance should not surprise us. Another writer of the Schism, Philippe de Mézières (1327–1405), also uses Nimrod as the ruler of a land of confusion in his *Letter to King Richard II* (*Epistre au Roi Richart*; 1395). In this allegorical treatise, Mézières pleads for peace between France and England, for an end to the papal schism, and for a new crusading order to unite the West against the East. He explains that the discord of war and religious schism has led to social disorder of a Babylonian level; in his *Letter* he describes an allegorical "Garden of Perils," standing for England and France, riven by the plague of Babel: "This garden of perils, because of its great marvels, should be called Two-faced Fortune and *Perilleuse Garde*. The true name of the King of this garden was Nimrod, the same who built the tower of Babel and was the first tyrant in the world, who subjugated all the people of his time to his tyrannous rule. Would to God that, in his office, this Nimrod had been barren and had not had so many descendants, who, today, follow to the letter and too well his example." [Cestui jardin perilleux, par l'efect de ses oeuvres merveilleuses, doit estre appele fortune a ii. visages, et la perilleuse garde. Mais le roy du jardin doit estre appele par son droit nom Nemproch, qui edifia la tour Babel, et fu le premier roy tirant en ce monde, qui sousmit a soy et a sa tirannie les pueples de son temps. Et Dieu vausist que en son office le dit Nemproch eust este brehaignes, et qu'il n'eust pas eu tant de successeurs en son cruel office, qui au jour duy, helas, a la lettre gardent trop bien ses loys.] Philippe de Mézières, *Letter to King Richard II*, ed. and trans. Coopland, 59 (English translation); 133 (French text).

14 *Letter 10*: 197.1–198.4; Zacour 71: Subscriptiones epistolarum mearum miraris. Nec immerito. Non nisi geminam enim Babilonam cum legeris, alteram quidem apud

In this passage Petrarch deliberately highlights the mobility of Babylon as a metaphor: there are "many Babylons": the Assyrian, the Egyptian, the Roman, and now a "new Babylon."[15] In Petrarch's adaptation of the political motif, there is a familiar sense of teleology and design, like the succession of empires depicted in Orosius: Babylon re-appears again and again in human history, this time on the Rhone rather than the Tiber or the Euphrates.[16]

The letter further dilates the Babylonian conceit, as Petrarch explains how Avignon is a new Babylon:

> This part of the world has its own Babylon. For where, I ask, may the "city of confusion" be more appropriately located than in the west? We do not know who founded it, but it is well known who inhabits it – those, surely, from whom for the best of reasons it derives this name. Believe me, this place has its Nimrod too, 'powerful in the land and robust hunter against the Lord,' reaching heavenward with his proud turrets; here is Semiramis armed with her quiver.[17]

The more extended and baroque Petrarch's adaptation of the Babylon myth, the more obvious is its metaphorical character. Petrarch highlights the self-conscious nature of Babylon as a metaphor, citing Augustine's explanation of the city's meaning:

> I shall not refer you to the poets – no need of the Muses here – nor to the historians. Look to catholic authors, especially to Augustine's commentary

---

Assirios olim, ubi clarum Semiramis nomen habet, alteram apud Egiptios nostra etate florentem, que Cambissem habet auctorem, cuius nunc Babilonis inauditum tibi nomen ingeritur tecum uoluis. Non quod nescias quosdam ex nostris Romam quasi alteram Babilonem propter proportionem imperiorum et climatum stauisse; quam quia me almam, sanctam et reginam urbem uocitare solitum tenes, huius nouissime Babilonis tibi nunc etiam stupor manet.

15 On the Egyptian Babylon (i.e., Cairo), see chapter 7.

16 Cf. also *Letter 10*:199.10–200.1; Zacour 72: "After you read it [i.e., his letter] you will agree that the name [Babylon] fits the Rhone as well as it does the Euphrates or the Nile" (Quod cum legeris, dices non minus Rodano quam Euphrati debitum, quam Nilo.).

17 *Letter 10*: 198.5–199.2; Zacour 71–2: Et sua Babilon huic terrarum tractui est. Vbi enim, queso, dignius quam in occidentali plaga *ciuitas confusionis* existeret? A quibus quidem condita incertum, sed a quibus habitata notissimum. Certe ab his, a quibus iure optimo nomen hoc possidet. Et suus hic, michi crede, *Nembroth, potens in terra et robustus uenator contra dominum* ac superbis turribus celum petens, hic pharetrata Semiramis.

> on that psalm which begins in the same way I end some of my letters to you [i.e., Psalm 136]. There you will find out what the name Babylon meant to him. After you read it you will agree that the name fits the Rhone as well as it does the Euphrates or the Nile.[18]

It is no surprise to see Petrarch using Babylon in this way, given the influence of Augustine upon his thought.[19]

In his attention to the metaphoric capacity of Babylon, Petrarch moves from direct political commentary on the external world to a self-consciousness about the metaphoric nature of Babylon as he adapts and transforms the conceit, and finally ends up connecting the political to the personal through the figure itself. *Letter 15* shows the application of Babylon goes beyond simply designating a metaphorical city of exile, and shades effortlessly into speaking of the "Babylon within." In *Letter 15* Petrarch's addressee goes to Babylon (Avignon), but does not care for the city. Petrarch enthusiastically concurs: "Nowhere else is rational thought less fruitful. That's the one place on earth where there is no room for thoughtful counsel, where everything goes round aimlessly and without purpose."[20] This abstract language pushes us beyond a specific political situation to a deeper existential and personal dilemma. He goes further down this path in the following lines:

> There is no light anywhere, no one to lead you, no sign to guide you along the twisted paths, but only gloom on all sides and confusion everywhere. It is only too true, this is Babylon, that powerful chaos of things – "a vast night of crime," to quote Lucan. A night of eternal darkness, I may add, devoid of stars.[21]

---

18 *Letter 10*: 199.5–200.3; Zacour 72: Non ego te ad poetas, neque enim Pierium opus est, non te ad historicos mittam. Consule catholicos tractatores, sed precipue Augustinum super eo Psalmo, qui sic incipit ut epistolarum ad te mearum alique desinunt. Inuenies quid sibi Babilonicum nomen uelit. Quod cum legeris, dices non minus Rodano quam Euphrati debitum, quam Nilo.

19 On Petrarch's relationship to Augustine see Quillen, *Rereading the Renaissance*.

20 *Letter 15*: 215.19–21; Zacour 91: nusquam minus cogitata respondent. Vnus enim in terris est locus, ubi nullus consilio locus est, ubi omnia temere fortuitoque uoluuntur.

21 *Letter 15*: 216.4–7; Zacour 91–2: Nulla ibi preterea lux, nullus dux, nullus index amfractuum, sed caligo undique et ubique confusio, ne parum uera sit Babilon ac perplexitas rerum mira utque Lucani uerbo utar: *Nox ingens scelerum*. Tenebrosa, inquam, et eterna nox, experssiderum. (Lucan, *Bellum Civile*, VII.571.)

Petrarch's metaphoric dilations clearly encourage the idea that he is speaking not only of the physical city of Avignon as Babylon, but also the city as the errant way of life on a personal scale, like Dante's dark wood in the beginning of the *Inferno*. This application of Babylon to the moral/ethical self will be a pervasive latter-day adaptation of Augustinian thought. Petrarch notes that Avignon, as a city (*civitas*), is not a place, per se: it is instead an Augustinian community (*populus*), the City of Man: "Confess that it is not so much the city they inhabit that is evil, as they themselves who are vile and deceitful. As a matter of fact, the features of both people and place look the same: repulsive, offensive, deformed."[22] There is a difference, however: as expressed here, Petrarch's language seems to be a simplification of Augustine's doctrines, creating a rather more simplistic, binary understanding forged in a heated political/theological context: Babylon's denizens are (and can only be) repulsive, deformed, wrong – the ungodly set against the virtuous, wrong and right. The drawing of theological battle-lines in this late medieval papal controversy led to a simplistic binary adaptation of the medieval Two Cities metaphor, along with an intensified use of Babylon to describe the moral "place" of the individual.

The use of Babylon as political invective by such esteemed laureates as Dante and Petrarch in this medieval Christian conflict did not go unnoticed in the later early modern West. Given Petrarch's reputation and influence in particular, his use of Babylon in this way would provide later Reformation authors with a powerful precedent for the use of Babylon in internecine Christian polemic.[23]

Early Modern Politics, Babylon, and the Language of the Self

Dante and Petrarch provided a warrant for the use of Babylon as political discourse during the polemics of the western European Reformation: it was a small leap from the use of Babylon in the "inter-Catholic" Great Schism,

22 *Letter 15*: 216.12–14; Zacour 92: neque magis ciuitatis infande uicos quam ciues ipsos fedos ac lubricos fateare. Vna prorsus est hominum ac locorum facies obscena, tristis, informis . . .

23 The scholarly literature on Petrarch's influence is vast, but usually concentrates on poetic influence ("Petrarchism") rather than on political ideas. For sample literary studies, see Dubrow, *Echoes of Desire*; Braden, *Petrarchan Love*, 61–161; Kennedy, *Site of Petrarchism*; *Les Poètes Français de la Renaissance et Pétrarque*, ed. Balsamo; *Petrarch in Britain: Interpreters, Imitators, and Translators over 700 Years*, ed. McLaughlin and Panizza.

to the use of Babylon in the struggle between Catholic and Protestant. For Protestants, it was thus a simple commonplace to speak of the Catholic Church as Babylon or the Whore of Babylon. In lieu of detailing these countless political applications of Babylon during the Reformation, I instead have selected a few key examples of the early modern discourse of political Babylon in the work of Martin Luther (1483–1546), John Milton (1608–74), and John Donne (1572–1631).[24] Luther and Milton exemplify the extension of the Babylon political tradition into the arena of Catholic-Protestant disputation and invective; Donne shows us the continuing evolution of the "Babylon within": Babylon as a figure for the moral self, in a Protestant context.

In his polemical treatise *The Babylonian Captivity of the Church* (1520), Luther rails against the "tyranny of Rome" (11).[25] He "know[s] for certain that the papacy is the kingdom of Babylon and the power of Nimrod, the mighty hunter."[26] The Catholic Church as a whole is "wicked and despotic" (27), but it is the ecclesiastical hierarchy that is most to blame, not the misled common people: "It was not the church which ordained these things, but the tyrants of the churches, without the consent of the church, which is the people of God" (23). These wayward clergy/tyrants are the "princes of Babylon" (88) and their church a tyranny (117). It is the "popish flatterers" who have been guilty of impiety and slander; it is the "Romans [i.e., Catholics] who are the heretics and godless schismatics" (24). In the

24 My evidence here is highly selective: sixteenth and seventeenth century Europe was such a place of Christian ferment that any one of the many Christian sects could accuse any other group of being "Babylon" at any time. A search for "Babylon" in *Early English Books Online* (EEBO), covering books published between 1473 and 1700, yields 30142 hits. A typical literary example would be Thomas Dekker's play *The Whore of Babylon* (1607). Composed after the Gunpowder Plot, the play is an allegory of the antagonism between Titania, the Faerie Queen (England), and the Whore of Babylon (Rome). On the political allegory in Dekker's play see Gasper, *Dragon and the Dove*, 80–108; Krantz, "Thomas Dekker's Political Commentary."

25 Luther, *Babylonian Captivity of the Church*, trans. Steinhäuser; revised by Ahrens and Wentz in *Luther's Works*, vol. 36, ed. Wentz, 3–126. The translation is based on *Luthers Werke. Kritische Gesamtausgabe*, ed. Martin; parenthetical references in the text are by page numbers of the English translation. The treatise is an explication of the Eucharist and the entire system of sacraments.

26 Luther, *Babylonian Captivity*, 12. For a related political reading of Genesis 6, see also Luther, *Lectures on Genesis: Chapters 6–14*, trans. Schick in *Luther's Works*, vol. 2, ed. Pelikan, 32–3, where Luther asserts that the "giants on the earth" of Genesis represent arrogant men who usurp spiritual and temporal power, like the pope. He also compares the pope to Ham, the evil son of Noah (177) and to the tyrant Nimrod (197).

face of such Babylonian tyranny, Luther's treatise will aid the reader's inner spirituality in order to dissent from this oppression and begin the process of emancipation; his work will "instruct men's consciences so that they may endure the Roman tyranny" (28).

In addition to Nimrod's tyranny, Luther's treatise adapts the narrative of the Babylonian Captivity and its associations. The Babylonian tyranny of the Catholic Church has been God's punishment for a chosen people: he explains that the chosen faithful can "see how great is God's wrath with us, in that he has permitted godless teachers to conceal the words of this testament from us, and thereby to extinguish this same faith, as far as they could" (46–7). The Catholic "godless superstition of works" is the result of this loss of faith and thus: "By them we have been carried away out of our own land, as into a Babylonian captivity, and despoiled of all our precious possessions" (47). The analogy is clear here: (proto-) Protestants are like the ancient Hebrews, chastised by God for their sins by deporting them to a metaphorical city of Babylon, into a "Babylonian captivity" of false doctrine.[27] Like Petrarch, Luther continues to augment and imaginatively dilate the Babylon motif, in prophetic language:

> Behold, then, our miserable captivity. "How lonely sits the city that was full of people! How like a widow has she become, she that was great among the nations! She that was a princess among the cities has become a vassal. She has none to comfort her; all her friends have dealt treacherously with her." (73; Lamentations 1:1–2)[28]

Jerusalem is the lonely City, captive in Babylon. Luther warns that unless the Roman church hierarchy changes its tyrannical ways, "they are guilty of all the souls that perish under this miserable captivity, and the papacy is truly the kingdom of Babylon and of the very Antichrist ... All this the papal tyranny has fulfilled, and more than fulfilled, these many centuries" (72). Luther's statement is profoundly sweeping: by "this miserable captivity" enduring for "many centuries" he means nothing less than the entire history of the Catholic Church, in all lands: all men have been unwittingly living in Babylon, and it is only now, under the guidance of Luther and other Protestant reformers, that they may awaken to a new day.

---

27 For more references to Psalm 136, see 78, 83.

28 On the "prophetic mode" in early modern literature, see Collinson, "Biblical Rhetoric" and Richey, *Politics of Revelation.*

Milton follows medieval tradition by equating Babylon with *confusio,* and like Luther, he uses Babylon to rail against the Church of Rome.[29] In his prose treatise *Of True Religion, Haeresie, Schism, and Toleration* (1673), Milton argues against the power of the pope, charging the papacy with infringing upon individual nations' sovereignty; he explains that in England's past, the pope drained the country's wealth "to maintain the Pride and Luxury of his Court and Prelates: and now since, through the infinite mercy and favour of God, we have shaken off his Babylonish Yoke."[30] Likewise in his politically charged sonnet "On the Late Massacre in Piedmont," Milton begs God to avenge the Protestant "slaughtered saints" in Italy, persecuted and killed by the Catholic "bloody Piedmontese"; he prays, with apocalyptic intensity, that their "martyred blood and ashes" will sow the fields where the "triple tyrant" (the Pope), rules and that from these bloody seeds a "hundredfold" new believers will spring up, forsake the Catholic Church, and flee this "Babylonian woe."[31] It is not just the Catholic Church that is Babylon, however: in the *The Reason of Church-Government urg'd against prelaty* (1642), Milton rails against the "true merchants of Babylon" who would support the English royalist cause, and thereby sell the English into sin.[32] Luther and Milton intensify the use of Babylon in the context of Protestant political and theological polemic. As clear lines were drawn between Catholic and Protestant, who truly lived "in Babylon" and who did not – and how one might escape from a "Babylonian captivity" – became pressing questions of personal faith and politics, expressed and understood here through the use of Babylon as a multivalent, apocalyptic symbol.

It is this exploration of the inner self – the Protestant emphasis on personal ethics and individual salvation – that authors such as Donne explore through the figure of Babylon. Donne uses a variety of references

29 For Babylon as *confusio* see *Paradise Lost,* XII.342–3; cf. also Michael's narration of the Tower of Babel story (XII.43–62), in which the cast-down tower is "Confusion named" (XII.62). References to Milton's poetry are to *Complete Poetry and Essential Prose,* ed. Kerrigan et al.

30 *Of True Religion, Haeresie, Schism, and Toleration* in *The Complete Prose Works of John Milton,* ed. Wolfe et al., VIII.429–30 (volume and page number). Cf. also *Eikonoklastes* in *Complete Prose Works,* III.498.

31 "Sonnet 18" in *Complete Poetry and Essential Prose,* 155–6. For more on Babylon, cf. also the early Latin poem *In quintum Novembris,* lines 155–6 in *Complete Poetry and Essential Prose,* 210; *Paradise Regained,* IV.44–7. Cf. Marvell, *The First Anniversary,* lines 113–14 (equating "the Whore" of Babylon with Rome).

32 *The Reason of Church Government* in *Complete Prose Works,* I.851.

to Babylon throughout his sermons; it is clear that for him the word has great semantic flexibility in a variety of contexts. He can implore his audience not to "drinke the cup of Babylon," i.e., live a sinful life.[33] In a sermon from 1616, he writes about visiting a house of Anabaptists on the continent and compares the experience to Daniel's exile in Babylon (II.3.112–13). In another sermon, using a traditional exegetical scheme, he identifies Jesus as the cornerstone of the church, a stone that brings Jerusalem and Babylon together.[34] But beyond these scattered references, Donne's primary use of Babylon is to map the interior topography of the soul.

Donne's sermons use Babylon to examine the moral, ethical, and religious life of the self in the context of a Protestant tradition. For example, the following sermon from 1617 explicates Mary and Joseph's temporary loss of the young Jesus in Jerusalem after Passover (Luke 2:40–7). Donne interprets this narrative figuratively to mean that even the most righteous may "lose Christ in Jerusalem," when we only pretend to give Him service, or if we even think about past or future sins; that is, even when supposedly safe and living a righteous life under the proper form of Christian religion – a life "in Jerusalem" – the dangers of sin still lurk. But if this is the case for the individual "in Jerusalem," then what if we live "in Babylon"? How much *greater* the peril is for those who live a life in that "place," i.e., as a Catholic (or worse):

> [If] we may lose him at *Jerusalem*, how much more, if our dwelling be a *Rome* of Superstition and Idolatry, or if it be a *Babylon* in confusion, and mingling God and the world together, or if it be a *Sodome*, a wanton and intemperate misuse of Gods benefits to us.[35]

Donne bases his exegesis on the Augustinian Two Cities, but augments the motif. Rome, Babylon, and Sodom all represent states of sin or potential sin. These are "places" of the soul, places of the heart: do

33 *The Sermons of John Donne*, ed. Simpson and Potter, by volume, sermon, and page numbers: III.10.239 and VII.16.409. Other miscellaneous uses of Babylon: see also V.2.70; V.9.184; V.14.273; VIII.4.122; IX.16.369.

34 "Hee is such a Corner stone, as hath united heaven, and earth, Jerusalem and Babylon together" (II.8.185); preached on 21 February of 1618 or 1619.

35 "A sermon preached to Queen Anne at Denmarke-house, December 14, 1617": *Sermons*, I.5.245–6.

you live in Babylon or Jerusalem, in the vision of peace or in the turmoil of *confusio*?[36] Or in Protestant terms: are you saved or damned?

For Donne, as for most Protestant writers, the "residence" of the religious self had the most dire implications. In another sermon, Donne explains that the words Ezekiel aimed at the "*Chaldean Babylon*" are also "applicable to the condition of our *Fathers* in the *Italian Babylon, Rome*" (X.7.159; Ezekiel 34:19). Just as God led the Jews out of Babylon, so too he led the true church out from the shadow of Rome (X.7.160). He explains that "the whole prophecy of the deliverance of *Israel*, from *Babylon*, belongs to the Christian Church, both to the *Primitive* Church, at first, and to the *Reformed* since" (X.7.171). There is thus a "conformity of the *Jewish Priests* in the *Chaldean Babylon*, and these prelates in the Roman *Babylon*" (X.7.172). The entire sermon turns on this metaphorical resemblance or "conformity." He summarizes: "They therefore that aske now, *Where was your Church before Luther?* would then have asked of the *Jews* in *Babylon*, Where was your Church before *Esdras?* that was in *Babylon*, ours was in *Rome*" (X.7.170). Donne employs the Captivity narrative to establish the lineage of Protestant Christianity – it is not a "new" thing (and therefore possibly illegitimate); rather, the true Church has been in captivity under the tyranny of the Roman Catholic Church for ages.[37]

The conclusion to the sermon turns the metaphoric complex further inward:

> Our life is a warfare; other wars, in a great part, end in mariages: Ours in a divorce, in a divorce of body and soule in death. Till then, though God have brought us, from the *first Babylon*, the darknesse of the Gentiles, and from the *second Babylon*, the superstitions of Rome, and from the *third Babylon*, the confusion of tongues, in bitter speaking against one another, after all this, every man shall finde a *fourth Babylon*, enough to exercise all his forces, The civill warre, the rebellious disorder, the intestine confusion of his own Concupiscencies. (X.7.176)

36 Another Donne sermon speaks of "Babylon ... that Church of confusion, that makes the word of God and the word of Man equall" (IX.17.375). On Babylon as "confusion" see also X.7.171, 173, 174.

37 Sermon X.6 covers much the same ground, including phrases such as the "conformity between the *two Babylons*, the *Chaldean* and the *Italian*" and "the *Italian Babylon*" again and again (X.6.143, 145, 146, 148, 149, 153, 154, 155, 156, 158; see also IX.14.331; IX.15.343).

In this passage, successive metaphoric Babylons link personal history to salvation history: the Babylon of paganism, the Babylon of the Catholic Church, the Babylon of strife (*confusio*) against fellow men, and finally the Babylon of the Self, the "intestine confusion of Concupiscencies." This final Babylon is an adaptation of the Augustinian City of Man, where love's gaze aims at the self, rather than up to God: "This is a transmigration, a transportation layd upon us all, by *Adams* rebellion, from Jerusalem to Babylon, from our innocent state in our Creation, to this confusion of our corrupt nature" (X.7.176). For Donne, then, as it was for Bede, the Captivity is a type of *felix culpa*, a fortunate fall: he explains that "God would have his children first brought to Babylon, before he would be glorifyed in their deliverance": one must perceive "a holy sense of the miseries" attached to the fallen world of sin and corruption before being set free (X.7.176). He explains that all men are "not naturalized but borne Babylonians," "not *Incolae* but *Indigenae*," due to original sin (X.7.177). At some point the voice of God will call one forth and say (as he did to Abraham): "Get thee out of thy Country, and from thy kindred, unto the land I will shew thee; Come out of Babylon to Jerusalem"; or like Christ's command to Lazarus, the voice of God will say "come forth of your Tombs in Babylon, to this Jerusalem, come forth from your troubled waters, your waters of contention, of anxiety, of envy, of solicitude, and vexation for worldly encumbrances, and come ... to the waters of rest, the application of the merits of Christ, in a true Church" (X.7.177). Not unlike Dante and Petrarch, Donne plays rapid variations on the meditative Matter of Babylon, wringing change after change, metaphor upon metaphor as the chain of associations leads onward and inward. It is not surprising that the poet in Donne saw this great potential in a word such as "Babylon." In his equation of Babylon with the self, Donne achieves an eloquent, sublime evolution of the Augustinian Two Cities, an intensity of expression particularly enabled by Protestant tradition: "I am a reciprocall plague; passively and actively contagious; I breath corruption, and breath it upon my selfe; and I am the Babylon that I must goe out of, or I perish" (IX.13.311).The Babylon metaphor here imparts a lofty grandeur to the small confine of the self.

These representative early modern cases demonstrate both continuity and change in the political myth of Babylon. Poets and preachers worked from long-established texts and traditions dating back to late antiquity, yet they adapted and transformed those traditions, giving political Babylon a powerful afterlife to a wide audience. In the great Christian controversies of the fourteenth through seventeenth centuries Babylon came to be a dynamic political figure of rhetoric, charged by apocalyptic intensity. This political intensity also migrated from the political world into the realm of personal expression, as the Christian tradition developed ever more imaginative ways to adapt Babylon's metaphoric imperatives to the language of the self.

Political Babylon in the Modern World

London as Babylon: Innocence and Experience

Rome, Paris, Moscow, New York: as we have seen, any large urban centre can be a "Babylon" in the systems of Western thought. As we move beyond the heated religious politics of the sixteenth and seventeenth centuries, how does this political Babylon change and adapt to new contexts? We might look to London in the nineteenth century as a representative case study of the urban Babylon metaphor in the modern (i.e., post-1700) world.

For William Blake (1757–1827), Babylon was a rich symbol.[38] Babylon and Jerusalem bear a complex idiosyncratic significance in Blake's poetry: inspired by standard Christian traditions, but interpreted through his own personal imaginative universe. Blake found "Babylon in the opening Streets of London" and "Jerusalem in ruins wandering about from house to house,"[39] but just exactly what Babylon stands for across Blake's corpus is somewhat elusive. Blake's Babylon, as Jerusalem's shadow, certainly hearkens back to Augustine's Two Cities; but in Blake's quasi-allegorical poetry, Babylon represents a greater variety of meanings: Babylon stands for the forces of empire, war and lust; Babylon is the world at large, including Natural Religion; Babylon is Vala,

---

38 I base my summary of Blake's thought here on Damon, *Blake Dictionary*, s.v. "Babylon"; cf. s.v. "Babel"; on Blake and Babylon see also Seymour, *Babylon*, 167–70. For a discussion of the city in Blake's poetry, see also Byrd, *London Transformed*, 157–77; Johnson, "Blake's Cities."

39 *Jerusalem*, 74.16–17. Blake, *Complete Poems*, ed. Ostriker; references to *Jerusalem* are by plate and line numbers. I retain, as does Ostriker, Blake's spelling and punctuation. As the poem's speaker sees "London blind & age-bent begging thro the Streets / of Babylon" (84.11–12), the corruption of the city blurs the line between biblical past and modern present. The speaker laments that in precincts of London, "We builded Jerusalem as a City & a Temple" (84.3), but now "Jerusalem lies in ruins & the Furnaces of Los are builded there / You are now shrunk up to a narrow Rock in the midst of the Sea / But here we build Babylon on Euphrates" (84.6–8).

the goddess of Nature. At other times, Blake follows standard Christian tradition by using Babylon to comment on current political subjects: in *Vala, or the Four Zoas*, for example, he places "Jerusalems Children in the dungeons of Babylon" where they "play before the Armies before the hounds of Nimrod" (2.31–2), a poetic quasi-allegorical comment on the exploitation of the British textile industry.[40] Other uses of Babylon are more self-referential. In *Jerusalem*, Albion (England) turns his back on the "Divine Body" and leaves for the "Wastes of Moral Law" (*Jerusalem* 24.23–4), where "Babylon is builded in the Waste, founded in Human desolation" (*Jerusalem* 24.25):

> The Walls of Babylon are Souls of Men: her gates the Groans
> Of Nations: her Towers are the Miseries of once happy Families.
> Her Streets are paved with Destruction, her Houses built with Death
> Her Palaces with Hell & the Grave; her Synagogues with Torments
> Of ever-hardening despair squard & polishd with cruel skill (*Jerusalem* 24.31–5)

On one level, Babylon here speaks to the moral decay Blake the radical sees around him in London; but Babylon is also, in his personal mythology, Albion's fall and division, and his subsequent search for unity, an attempt to rescue his emanation Jerusalem from the Babylon of her dark hiding place. Even in this careful tip-toeing through the thickets of Blake's thought, we can nevertheless see how Blake superimposes the Babylon tradition upon his own view of London's city streets, in a distinctive – albeit idiosyncratic – trajectory of the Christian tradition, as he adapts the Babylon myth, generally speaking, to speak of internal matters of the self.

In the nineteenth-century English novel, we see a similar – but simpler – progressive adaptation of the metaphorical "Babylon within," a transformation of the tradition in a literary direction.[41] London as Babylon

---

40 *Vala, or the Four Zoas*, in *Complete Poems*, by night and line numbers. As David Erdman explicates: "Instead of saying that the British textile industry strips wool from sheep, binds children to factory labor, and leads imperial armies as far as China in search of markets, he says the 'Daughters of Albion' with their 'Needlework' strip 'Jerusalems curtains from mild demons of the hills,' bind 'Jerusalems children in the dungeons of Babylon,' and 'play before the Armies, before the hounds of Nimrod,' in lightning voyages (i.e. like flying shuttles) 'Across Europe & Asia to China & Japan'" (Erdman, *Blake: Prophet Against Empire*, 332).

41 A search for the exact phrase "Modern Babylon" in the records of Google Books between 1800 and 1899 yields 7020 hits.

was a common figure for nineteenth-century British novelists looking to represent a protagonist's movement from innocence to experience, the typical arc of the *Bildungsroman.* Charles Kingley's *Alton Locke* (1850), the fictional autobiography of the eponymous protagonist – a lower-class Cockney tailor, poet, and religious dissident – opens with his childhood in London under the influence of his Baptist mother, a woman who "gloried in her dissent" and was "sprung from old Puritan blood."[42] Locke recounts how he would occasionally walk the London streets with his mother through the streets of the City of Man:

> She would have hoodwinked me, stopped my ears with cotton, and led me in [*sic*] a string, – kind, careful soul! – if it had been reasonably safe on a crowded pavement, so fearful was she lest I should be polluted by some chance sight or sound of the Babylon which she feared and hated. (10)[43]

Such a passage hearkens back to the early modern Protestant polemic against the Catholic Church, but serving literary interests here, as a metaphor deployed in character-building.[44]

Likewise, novelistic London-as-Babylon could also be mined for ironic, satiric, or comic effects. In Dickens's *David Copperfield* (1850), for example, Mr. Micawber worries that the young Copperfield (a newcomer to the city) will not be able to find his way back to Micawber's house:

> "Under the impression," said Mr. Micawber, 'that your peregrinations in this metropolis have not as yet been extensive, and that you might have some difficulty in penetrating the arcana of the Modern Babylon in the direction of the City Road – in short," said Mr. Micawber, in another burst

42 Kingsley, *Alton Locke, Tailor and Poet: An Autobiography*, ed. Cripps, 7.

43 Locke explains that the only books he knew growing up were the Bible and Bunyan's *Pilgrim's Progress*; accordingly, he says that "London was the City of Destruction, from which I was to flee" (10). Bunyan's *Pilgrim's Progress* had a powerful influence on the *Bildungsroman* form, and although *Pilgrim's Progress* does not have "Babylon" in its text (surprisingly), its allegorical temper, its City of Destruction, and Slough of Despond resonate easily with the myth of political Babylon, as in this passage. Cf. also George Eliot, *Daniel Deronda*, ed. Handley, 210.

44 In the nineteenth century, the standard equation between Roman Catholicism and Babylon is alive and well in Thackeray's *The Newcomes* (1853–5), in which the viscount Florac tells the protagonist Clive Newcome that Florac's wife "was of the reformed religion ... a dissident" and that she tormented Florac's Catholic mother with accusations of idolatry, called the Catholics "*des Romishes*, and Rome, Babylon; and the Holy Father ... a scarlet abomination" (William Makepeace Thackeray, *The Newcomes*, ed. Sanders, 354).

of confidence, "that you might lose yourself – I shall be happy to call this evening, and install you in the knowledge of the nearest way."[45]

Beyond the humour of Micawber's manner, there is also a note of experiential or moral seriousness (unintentional, of course, on Micawber's part) about Copperfield "losing himself" in the "arcana" of Babylon. Indeed, Copperfield is in the process of "finding himself" in the novel, like so many nineteenth-century protagonists.

We see this use of Babylon as a figure for "the world of experience" (and the wanderings of an innocent therein) in a variety of novels, particularly the coming-of-age story. Thackeray titles an entire chapter of *The History of Pendennis* (1848–50) "Babylon"; in it the young Arthur Pendennis leaves the country for London "to face the world and to make his fortune."[46] In Charlotte Brontë's *Villette* (1853), her enigmatic protagonist Lucy Snowe similarly travels to London early in the novel, having been thrust out into the world after the death of her patron Miss Marchmont. Chapter 5 of the novel ("Turning a New Leaf") is a moment of pause and transition, both in terms of the plot and in terms of Lucy's identity. Lucy is in a state of "inward darkness"; her mind tells her to "Leave this wilderness ... and go out hence," to strike out into the world.[47] She arrives in London and addresses the reader directly:

> My reader, I know, is one who would not thank me for an elaborate reproduction of poetic first impressions; and it is well, inasmuch as I had neither time nor mood to cherish such; arriving as I did late, on a dark, raw, and rainy evening, in a Babylon and a wilderness of which the vastness and the strangeness tried to the utmost any powers of clear thought and steady self-possession with which, in the absence of more brilliant faculties, Nature might have gifted me.[48]

Lucy is in a state of *confusio*, in all the mythic Babylon senses of the term: in the very next lines the London crowds in fact greet her with a confused babble/Babel of dialects: "When I left the coach, the strange

45 Dickens, *David Copperfield*, ed. Burgis, 134–5; see also 452.

46 William Makepeace Thackeray, *History of Pendennis*, ed. Sutherland, 349. See also 201 and 638, where London is "the dreadful modern Babylon."

47 Brontë, *Villette*, ed. Lilly, 103–4.

48 *Villette*, 105–6.

speech of the cabmen and others waiting round, seemed to me odd as a foreign tongue. I had never before heard the English language chopped up in that way."[49]

In the nineteenth-century novel, Babylon bears a clear, but transformed, genealogy back to Augustinian thought. The metaphoric capacity of Babylon used by Augustine to explore the connection between human motivations and God's plan descends through Christian medieval traditional as a figural language of the self in authors such as Bede. Then, enhanced by the polemical apocalyptic intensity of early modern Protestant traditions, the use of Babylon to describe the moral "place" of an individual becomes a standard feature of Christian thought in the modern world. And finally, by the nineteenth century, through a process of partial secularization, the Babylon complex appears in a denatured form as a generalized signifier for the corruption of "the world," taken in the broadest possible sense.[50] But even in these latter-day secular literary contexts, the word still bears the stamp of Christian religious tradition as it delineates a bifurcated world of purity and danger, with the tyranny of the corrupt majority set against dissent of the righteous few.

Babylon and Slavery in Nineteenth-Century America

Nineteenth-century American adaptations of political Babylon display a similar moral dynamic, but adapted in a very different historical context: the American Civil War and the national struggle over slavery. Herman Melville's poem "The Fall of Richmond" (1865), for example, deploys the familiar topos of the *transitus* of Babylon as Melville celebrates Robert E. Lee's Confederate retreat from Richmond. In the first stanza, a "Northern Metropolis" rejoices at the fall of the southern city:

What mean these peals from every tower,
And crowds like seas that sway?
The cannon reply; they speak the heart
Of the People impassioned, and say –

49 Brontë, *Villette*, 106.

50 For further interesting references to London as Babylon see also George W. M. Reynolds, *The Mysteries of London*, 4 vols. (1846–48), I.135, 151, 179; II.159; IV.68. Cf. Dickens, *Bleak House*, ed. Page, 902–3; Benjamin Disraeli, *Tancred* [1847], ed. Langdon-Davies, 448; Anthony Trollope, *Can You Forgive Her?*, ed. Swarbrick, 11.

A city in flags for a city in flames,
Richmond goes Babylon's way –
Sing and pray[51]

The stanza echoes and adapts the Two Cities metaphor: a northern "city in flags" opposed to a southern "city in flames," in a dichotomy fraught with the people's political "passion." To go "Babylon's way" is to go the fleeting way of all tyranny, as Nebuchadnezzar discovered in the Old English *Daniel*.

When we turn to nineteenth-century African-American authors, we see that the Babylonian Captivity provides a language to protest the plight of slaves. On 5 July 1852, Frederick Douglass (1818–95) addressed the Rochester, NY Ladies' Anti-Slavery Society in his celebrated "Fourth of July Oration."[52] Douglass begins in a patriotic fashion appropriate for the Fourth by praising the noble qualities of the Founding Fathers, particularly their political courage in the face of British imperial tyranny from abroad; but he also points out that they did not see their nascent American government as infallible or absolute and instead possessed the wisdom of dissent and self-reflection (361). In the second half of the speech, Douglass turns from positive patriotic sentiment to anger and speaks out like a biblical prophet against American political injustice and tyranny, asking his audience: "What to the Slave is the Fourth of July?" He argues that the blessings of liberty celebrated on the fourth are not celebrated by all Americans, and thus the invitation to speak on such an occasion constitutes a cruel insult:

> This Fourth of July is *yours*, not *mine*. *You* may rejoice, *I* must mourn. To drag a man in fetters into the grand illuminated temple of liberty, and call upon him to join you in joyous anthems, were inhuman mockery and sacrilegious irony. Do you mean, citizens, to mock me, by asking me to speak to-day? If so, there is a parallel to your conduct." (368; emphasis in original)

51 "The Fall of Richmond" in Melville, *Published Poems*, ed. Ryan et al., 99. Cf. also Melville's citation of Nebuchadnezzar's coronation at "Babylon the Tremendous" as an example of kingly splendor in *Mardi and A Voyage Thither*, ed. Hayford et al., 183; and also 604.

52 Douglass, *What to the Slave is the Fourth of July?* in *Frederick Douglass Papers*, ed. Blassingame et al., Series 1, II.359–88.

At this important rhetorical moment, Douglass pauses to set up this "parallel" to the conduct of the United States – a Babylonian political parallel:

> And let me warn you that it is dangerous to copy the example of a nation whose crimes, towering up to heaven, were thrown down by the breath of the Almighty, burying that nation in irrecoverable ruin! I can to-day take up the plaintive lament of a peeled and woe-smitten people! (368)

Douglass then quotes the entirety of Psalm 136 ("By the rivers of Babylon," [368]). In Douglass's "parallel" or "example," America is the new Babylon, and the "woe-smitten people" are the African-American slaves, singing their laments in a strange land like the Jews of old. American is like Babylon, "a nation whose crimes, towering up to heaven, were thrown down by the breath of the Almighty." We have here not only a blunt citation and incorporation of the Captivity narrative, but also an allusion to the Tower of Babel story, with American "towering" crimes "thrown down" to ruin by the Almighty. As he continues, Douglass adapts and transforms the language of Psalm 136 in his rhetoric, through direct citation and allusion:

> Fellow-citizens; above your national, tumultuous joy, I hear the mournful wail of millions! whose chains, heavy and grievous yesterday, are, to-day, rendered more intolerable by the jubilee shouts that reach them. If I do forget, if I do not faithfully remember those bleeding children of sorrow this day, "may my right hand forget her cunning, and may my tongue cleave to the roof of my mouth!" To forget them, to pass lightly over their wrongs, and to chime in with the popular theme, would be treason most scandalous and shocking, and would make me a reproach before God and the world. My subject, then fellow-citizens, is AMERICAN SLAVERY. (368)

Douglass's speech resonates with all the themes of political Babylon: tyranny, unjust rule, oppression, dissent, freedom and bondage.

In a similar fashion, the African-American poet James Monroe Whitfield, a contemporary of Douglass, expresses almost identical sentiments in his scathing poem "America" (1853).[53] The poet begins by addressing the country:

> America, it is to thee,
> Thou boasted land of liberty,
> It is to thee I raise my song,
> Thou land of blood, and crime, and wrong. (1–4)

53 Whitfield, "America," in his *America and Other Poems* (1853), 9–16, by line numbers.

He angrily rails against the country that has torn "the black man from his soil" (7) and forced him to work "Bound to a petty tyrant's nod, / Because he wears a paler face" (13–14). As in Douglass' speech, the subjects of Whitfield's poem are freedom and liberty, toil and tyranny, slavery, oppression, "unjust, oppressive laws," (44), the "fervent prayer of the oppressed" (72), prophecy and bondage. And Whitfield, like Douglass, compares the plight of the slaves to the captive Jews in Babylon:

Almighty God! 't is this they call
The land of liberty and law;
Part of its sons in baser thrall
Than Babylon or Egypt saw –
Worse scenes of rapine, lust and shame,
Than Babylonian ever knew,
Are perpetrated in the name
Of God, the holy, just, and true (127–34)

Whitfield's prophetic voice threatens a Babylon-like doom upon America for its unjust slavery and ends the poem by imploring his audience to pray for the moment when the voices of dissent will "burst the bonds of every slave" (158) and then "north and south, and east and west, / The wrongs we bear shall be redressed" (159–60).

There is a broader story to be written about the place of political Babylon in the history of race relations, beyond my brief sketches here; moving ahead from these nineteenth-century precursors, there remains a powerful legacy of related biblical rhetoric in African-American culture, in which Egypt and Babylon stand for the historical oppression and slavery. In an analogous fashion, political Babylon also has a resonant history in the resistance to Western colonial rule. In Jamaica, for example, the Rastafari movement designates the non-Rastafari world, in all its aspects, as "Babylon": a figure for the oppressive order or Establishment of the Western world. In Rastafari terms "beating down Babylon" and "steppin' out of Babylon" refer to the Rastafari resistance to Western colonialism and its legacies.[54] The reggae songs of Bob Marley (1945–81), such as "Babylon System" and "Chant Down Babylon," are lyrics of resistance, poems of freedom and liberty, and a call to rebel against "Babylon" the oppressor.

54 See Chevannes, *Rastafari: Roots and Ideology*, 208; Murrell, Spencer, and McFarlane, eds. *Chanting Down Babylon*, esp. Edmonds "Dread 'I' In-a-Babylon," 23–35; Edmonds, *Rastafari: From Outcasts to Culture Bearers*, 41–66. See also Seymour, *Babylon*, 232–5.

Protestant Evangelical Babylon

I would like close out this genealogy of political Babylon by examining two latter-day Protestant evangelical case studies of Babylonian political rhetoric, one nineteenth and one twentieth-century – influential apocalyptic texts that use the Babylon tradition in service of particular theological and political ends.

The first is Alexander Hislop's odd but influential little book, *The Two Babylons or Papal Worship Proved to be the Worship of Nimrod and His Wife* (1858). Hislop (1807–65), a Free Church of Scotland minister, published this anti-Catholic pamphlet in Edinburgh in 1853 and later expanded it into a larger treatise (1858); in the strange paths of books and their afterlives, this obscure text has proved very popular in radical evangelical Protestant circles even today, reprinted numerous times (since it has long passed into the public domain in the US and elsewhere), and now widely available on the internet.[55]

The Two Babylons purports to be a work of "historical" scholarship; Hislop argues that the Catholic Church is – and always has been – a secret pagan cult, the idolatry of ancient Babylon deviously disguised in a vast conspiracy and passed down through the ages as a seeming Christian religion when it is really no less than pagan blasphemy. I can best summarize the book's argument by quoting from the back cover blurb of a 1999 reprint, which itself contains an embedded quotation from Hislop's own original introduction:

> This amazing volume proves the Papal worship [i.e., Catholicism] to be actually the worship of Nimrod and his wife, complete in every detail ... 'The providence of God, conspiring with the Word of God, by light pouring in from all quarters, makes it more and more evident that Rome is in very deed the Babylon of the Apocalypse; that the essential character of her system, the grand objects of her worship, her festivals, her doctrine and discipline, her rites and ceremonies, her priesthood and their orders, have all been derived from ancient Babylon; and, finally, that the Pope himself is truly and properly the lineal representative of Belshazzar.' This volume offers proof for every statement, including more than 260 original sources of facts, citing page and place and date of publication of each.

55 Any internet search engine will find Hislop all over the web, at places such as biblebelievers.com. Even beyond the full-text availability, Hislop is quoted and used extensively in evangelical websites; see, for example, the many articles and pamphlets on tomorrowsworld.org.

3.1. "Mystic Egg of Astarte." Hislop's caption; "proof" that Easter eggs are pagan. From Hislop, *Two Babylons*, 109.

> Illustrated with 61 woodcuts from Nineveh, Babylon, Egypt, Pompeii, and other ancient lands.[56]

Hislop is not speaking metaphorically; he does not believe that the Catholic Church is "a kind of Babylon," as Petrarch or Luther understood it – he believes Catholicism is the *literal* unchanged, genetic descendant of pagan Babylon. With inspired ingenuity, he connects almost every element of Catholic doctrine and custom with a supposed Babylonian origin. For example, the Catholic veneration of the Virgin Mary (always rather suspect in Protestant eyes) is in reality the worship of the Babylonian mother goddess (an avatar of Semiramis, we're told). Hislop even reveals the Catholic tradition of Easter eggs as a sinister example of pagan worship (107–8), illustrated in the text by the "mystic egg of Astarte" (see Figure 3.1).

Hislop warns that the Catholic rosary is "almost universally found among Pagan nations" (187), and that the Catholic veneration of relics, "occup[ies] the very same place in the worship of the Papacy as the relics of Osiris in Egypt, or of Zoroaster in Babylon" (181) – and so on, descending into the

56 Alexander Hislop, *The Two Babylons or Papal Worship Proved to be the Worship of Nimrod and His Wife* (1858); repr. Brooklyn, NY: A & B Publishers, 1999. All citations are to this reprint, by page numbers.

3.2. "Egyptian Pontiff-King (under a Canopy) borne on Men's Shoulders." Hislop's caption; supposedly reminiscent of a papal procession. From Hislop, *Two Babylons*, 214.

dementia of conspiracy theory, with a veneer of nineteenth-century amateur archaeology and comparative mythology thrown in for good measure.

Hislop believes that, through Catholicism, innocent people are unsuspectingly worshiping pagan gods in pagan ways; he of course locates the sinister heart of the conspiracy in the Pope and the entire structure of Catholic ecclesiastical authority. Like Luther – but, to say the least, without Luther's nuance – Hislop sees the Pope as literally the direct ancestor of a high priest of Babylon, and he assembles "overwhelming" evidence for this accusation. For example, the Pope is traditionally carried atop a platform or litter during public processions; this is, according to Hislop, the same thing as the pagan procession of a Babylonian high priest (see Hislop's illustration in Figure 3.2).

The clincher, however, is the Pope's hat. Hislop argues that the distinctive papal headgear, the mitre, has a Babylonian origin:

> As the Pope bears the key of Janus, so he wears the mitre of Dagon. The excavations of Nineveh have put this beyond all possibility of doubt. The Papal mitre is entirely different from the mitre of Aaron and the Jewish high priests. That mitre was a turban. The two-horned mitre, which the Pope wears, when he sits on the high altar at Rome and receives the adoration of the Cardinals, is the very mitre worn by Dagon, the fish-god of the Philistines and Babylonians ... Thus was it in the East, at least five hundred years before the Christian era. (215; see Figure 3.3)

3.3. "Assyrian Dagon, with Fish-Head Mitre." Hislop's caption; apparently reminiscent of the papal mitre. From Hislop, *Two Babylons*, 215.

As unlikely as all this sounds, Hislop's work is charged not only with traditional apocalyptic invective familiar as a radical descendant of early modern Protestant rhetoric, but also with an attendant real-world political urgency – Babylon adapted, once again, as a language of contemporary politics. Hislop advises that, given his startling findings, true Protestants should not engage in any kind of ecumenical spirit; rather, they should utterly reject Catholicism as dangerous, non-Christian paganism: "If the position I have laid down can be maintained, she [i.e., Catholicism] must be stripped of the name of a Christian Church altogether" (3). He cites contemporary calamities such as the Crimean War (1853–6) and the general turmoil of the British empire in the later nineteenth century as evidence that good Protestants should vigorously take arms against the sea of pagan idolatry in the world, especially the dangerous Catholic Church: "Now, if the voice of God has been heard in the late Indian calamities, the Protestantism of Britain will rouse itself to sweep away at once and for ever all national support, alike from the idolatry of Hindostan and the still more malignant idolatry of Rome" (285). To say the least, Hislop is obviously thinking in rather literal ways about the connection between Babylon and Rome; one senses that Augustine would be mystified. Nevertheless, one can clearly trace an apocalyptic genealogy running from Avignon to Hislop and thence to all the twentieth and twenty-first century consumers on the internet and beyond.

This literalist understanding of political Babylon continues with my final example, the "Left Behind" series of apocalyptic evangelical

Christian novels by Tim LaHaye and Jerry Jenkins. This series is Tom Clancy or Robert Ludlum for the evangelical set: the popular suspense novel charged with the theology of premillenial dispensationalism.[57] The *Left Behind* novels dramatize the End Times: the Apocalypse is at hand; the literal events described in Revelation will come to pass; the Rapture will whisk away the faithful to heaven, leaving behind the doomed remnants of mankind behind to endure the terrible reign of the Antichrist, the Tribulation and the eventual triumph of Christ's Second Coming. Over sixty-three million copies of these novels have been sold; and the series has inspired various spin-offs: films, a video game, graphic novels, and a companion series for teens, *Left Behind: The Kids*: in summary, a very influential American religious phenomenon.

I confess that I do not find these books easy to read, not so much due to the often hair-raising theology they express as to their poor writing: the "Left Behind" novels read almost like an unintentional parody of the suspense/thriller genre beloved of airport bookstores. In the first novel (*Left Behind*, 1995), the faithful – true Christians who have, in the evangelical formulation, "accepted Jesus Christ as their personal Lord and Saviour" – disappear all over the world in an instant as they are suddenly transported to heaven in the Rapture, leaving behind only their empty clothes and the remnants of sinful humanity (i.e., non-evangelicals) to endure the seven-year period of the Tribulation. The series follows a group of heroes: repentant sinners who have been "left behind" and who now band together to fight the forces of evil as the "Tribulation Force." Among our main characters we have the intrepid reporter Cameron "Buck" Williams and the airline pilot Rayford Steele – names

57 All of the novels are by LaHaye and Jenkins; all are published by Tyndale House in Wheaton, IL. They are (in order): *Left Behind: A Novel of the Earth's Last Days* (1995); *Tribulation Force: The Continuing Drama of Those Left Behind* (1996); *Nicolae: The Rise of Antichrist* (1997); *Soul Harvest: The World Takes Sides* (1999); *Apollyon: The Destroyer Is Unleashed* (1999); *Assassins: Assignment: Jerusalem, Target: Antichrist* (1999); *The Indwelling: The Beast Takes Possession* (2000); *The Mark: The Beast Rules The World* (2000); *Desecration: Antichrist Takes the Throne* (2001); *The Remnant: On the Brink of Armageddon* (2002); *Armageddon: The Cosmic Battle of the Ages* (2003); *Glorious Appearing: The End of Days* (2004); *Kingdom Come: The Final Victory* (2007). The same authors have also published a series of prequels (*The Rising* (2005); *The Regime* (2005); *The Rapture* (2006). LaHaye and a series of co-authors have also produced an analogous, ongoing spin-off series, "Babylon Rising": *Babylon Rising* (2004); *The Secret on Ararat* (2006); *The Europa Conspiracy* (2007); *The Edge of Darkness* (2008). For an introduction to the phenomena of the *Left Behind* series see *Rapture, Revelation, and the End Times*, ed. Forbes and Kilde.

that read like action hero clichés. As the narrative unfolds, it embraces all the theological/political paranoia and ideology of late twentieth-century American evangelical Christianity: the Antichrist turns out to be the Romanian politician Nicolae Carpathia (*Dracula* allusion presumably intended), described as "a strikingly handsome blond who looked not unlike a young Robert Redford" (82) (i.e., a well-known "Hollywood liberal"). Carpathia suddenly rises to the secretary-generalship of the United Nations and establishes a New World Order (which he helpfully calls "the New World Order"), setting up a new universal currency and a one-world religion, the "Enigma Babylon One World Faith" – a fuzzy, false agnosticism. All of these elements are familiar target-paranoia triggers of American evangelical conservatism: one can almost hear the blades of the black helicopters hovering over the action. What is fascinating is how *Left Behind*'s evangelical authors use Babylon and its traditions to enable and validate a language for expressing twentieth-century American theological and political rhetoric. In the course of the series we get commentary on any number of political and social topics dear to the American evangelical community: marriage, abortion, Israel and the Jews, the media/press, infidelity, scepticism towards religious tolerance and multiculturalism.

As a modern adaptation of ancient Christian apocalyptic thought, *Left Behind* picks up on a long-standing element of apocalyptic Babylon: the identification of the city as the prophesied location of the Antichrist's birth.[58] Carpathia will rule the world as the Antichrist through the United Nations, but he will not keep the headquarters of his international organization in New York. Where would the Antichrist want

58 Babylon as the birthplace of Antichrist was a pervasive idea in the Middle Ages (see Emmerson, *Antichrist*, 80–1). Adso of Montier-en-Der's influential *Libellus de Antichristo* (*Book about the Antichrist*; late tenth century), for example, tells us that, "You have heard how he [the Antichrist] is to be born; now hear the place where he will be born. Just as Our Lord and Redeemer forsaw Bethlehem for himself as the place to assume humanity and to be born for us, so too the devil knew a place fit for that lost man who is called Antichrist, a place from which the root of all evil ought to come, namely, the city of Babylon. Antichrist will be born in that city, which once was a celebrated and glorious pagan center and the capital of the Persian empire": Adso, *Libellus de Antichristo*, trans. in McGinn, *Apocalyptic Spirituality*, 91; (*PL* 101: 1293). Adso's treatise was the main source for the Latin *Play of Antichrist* (*Ludus de Antichristo*), composed in Germany in the twelfth century, itself an interesting adaptation of the political Babylon myth (*Play of Antichrist*, trans. Wright).

to establish the capital of his New World Order? We find out in this dialogue:

> "He wants to move the U.N."
> "Move it?"
> Steve nodded.
> "Where?"
> "It sounds stupid."
> "Everything sounds stupid these days," Bailey said.
> "He wants to move it to Babylon."
> You're not serious."
> "*He* is."
> "I hear they've been renovating that city for years. Millions of dollars invested in making it, what, New Babylon?" (256)

This is the first appearance of Babylon in the *Left Behind* series, introduced in a clumsy fashion without any regard to internal narrative logic or consistency. But it is too easy to take cheap shots at "Left Behind." The irony here is that in the dominant traditions of the pre-modern world, a period often clichéd as backward and retrograde in its religiosity, there was a sophisticated metaphorical understanding of Babylon. For Augustine, Dante, Petrarch, Luther, Milton and Donne, Babylon was a historical city in the past *and* a living metaphor in the present; in *Left Behind* and Hislop's *Two Babylons*, any subtlety departs, leaving behind only a literal, one-dimensional political use of the Babylon political tradition.

The three syllables of Babylon have resounded across the terrain of the Western imagination, tuned to some of the enduring intricacies of political life. Babylon has passed from history to metaphor across the centuries of Western culture to reach an enduring place in the lexicon of politics. One simple word, but behind that word a rich history of intense human feeling illuminated by the radiance of metaphor.

PART II

Babylon as Degenerate Archetype

The old ones are gone like phantoms and the savages wander these canyons to the sound of an ancient laughter. In their crude huts they crouch in darkness and listen to the fear seeping out of the rock. All progressions from a higher to a lower order are marked by ruins and mystery and a residue of nameless rage.

–Judge Holden, in Cormac McCarthy, *Blood Meridian, or the Evening Redness in the West,* 146

Chapter Four

The Medieval Genealogy of Babylonian Degeneracy: The Cursed Race

And the Lord set a mark upon Cain, that whosoever found him should not kill him. And Cain went out from the face of the Lord, and dwelt as a fugitive on the earth, at the east side of Eden.

– Genesis 4:15–16

The first founder of the earthly city, then, was a fratricide; for, overcome by envy, he slew his brother, who was a citizen of the Eternal City and a pilgrim on this earth. It is not to be wondered at, then, that, long afterwards, at the foundation of that city [Babylon] which was to be the capital of the earthly city of which we are speaking, and which was to rule over so many nations, this first example – or as the Greeks call it, archetype – of crime was mirrored by a kind of image of itself.

– Augustine, *City of God*, XV.5

Babylon plays a surprising role in the concept of race in Western culture. This chapter and the next, comprising Part II, argue that the Matter of Babylon is an origin and organizing principle of an enduring Western archetype: the idea of the primeval cursed race. As in Part I, the medieval period was the important incipient phase of this genealogy's formation, and in the following pages I examine the late antique and medieval understanding of a linked series of biblical narratives and characters that together define a Babylonian lineage of racial degeneracy: Cain (kinslayer and the first murderer); the corrupt and degenerate antediluvian humanity destroyed by Noah's flood; the curse upon Noah's son Ham and his descendants; Nimrod the giant, founder of Babylon and the builder of the Tower of Babel; Nebuchadnezzar's inhuman debasement. These elements constitute the earliest Western archetype of a cursed line of humanity, and serve as a model for later displaced versions of the cursed race, as we shall see in the next chapter. This archetype of degenerate Babylon sounded a series of discordant notes as a counterpoint to the song of early human history in the Western Christian tradition.

In other words, what follows is a story of racial understanding in the West, represented through biblical and late antique texts and their medieval reception. "Race" can be a fraught term to use with reference to premodern texts and cultures. Scholars are divided as to whether there is a premodern concept of race; if there is, how that premodern concept differs from modern formulations of race; and finally, when and why the shift occurs from premodern to modern racial thought.[1] The genealogy I trace here – the odd intersection of Babylon's allusive connotations with theories of race – is by no means the only or even perhaps the most important theory of racial difference in the premodern West. Climate-based theories of human difference – the idea that varying zones of climate produced corresponding variations in human form and disposition – were of enormous importance. Furthermore, overlapping the climate-based theories of race was the racial tradition of Noachid dispersion: that the sons of Noah dispersed, after the Flood, each to one of the three continents of the world, where their progeny assumed racial differences over time – Japheth in Europe, Shem in Asia, and Ham in Africa.[2]

These medieval theories of race are well-known, but what I wish to do in this chapter (and the next) is to insert a third, less well-known theory of human difference into the medieval mix: the idea that a degenerate,

---

1 The scholarship on whether the Middle Ages possessed a concept of race and/or how that concept operated is enormous. For initial orientation on the subject see Heng, "Invention of Race I" and "Invention of Race II"; also the various essays in "Race and Ethnicity in the Middle Ages," a special issue of *Journal of Medieval and Early Modern Studies*, ed. Hahn. Ivan Hannaford contends that a biologically inflected idea of "race" is a purely modern concept, discernible only from the late seventeenth or early eighteenth century onwards, and thus there is no such thing as a premodern concept of race (*Race: History of an Idea*). Hannaford does seem, however, to argue that the period 1200–1600 saw the emergence of elements that would form (as he calls it) the "pre-idea" of race prior to the Enlightenment (8; 87–146).

In an argument parallel to the one presented in this and the next chapter, Colin Kidd asserts that Christianity had an important enduring role in the modern creation of race: even taking into account the many cultural influences on the concept of "race," nevertheless "scripture has been for much of the early modern and modern eras the primary cultural influence on the forging of races" (*Forging of Races*, 19).

2 On the importance of climate-based and Noachid theories of bodily difference in the later Middle Ages see, e.g., Akbari, *Idols in the East*, 24–50.

cursed strain of humanity, tainted by sin from earliest primeval times and thus set apart, moved in the margins of Christian history, wending its way even through Babylon. As I track in this book this distinctive element of Babylon's allusive image under Western eyes, the story makes an unexpected detour into the history of race as a concept. The foundational narrative I assemble here constructs a story of human origins, a premodern understanding of the "family of man" that would be subsumed by modern evolutionary thought; I say "subsumed" rather than overturned: this chapter and the next establish that although "race" in the modern sense of the term is generally thought of as an eighteenth or nineteenth century social construct, medieval ideas of race continued to influence racial thinking, often in displaced and sublimated form, beyond the Middle Ages.[3] Modern racial thought has incorporated medieval traditions about race, rather than replaced them. These chapters argue that in the Western Christian tradition, a vital part of the understanding of human origins and ethnic diversity was a representation of the ancestors and descendants of Babylon as an evil outcast people; a human strain placed outside the mainstream; an offshoot of the human family generating the very concept of a "mainstream."

This chapter defines and analyzes the medieval tradition of Babylonian degeneracy as one of many constituent elements of Western racial thought; the next chapter then follows that tradition's displaced transformations and interactions with modern forms of racial thought. The focus in these two chapters moves from direct representations of the city (as in the previous chapters) to the cast of characters traditionally associated with the overall Matter of Babylon; not the city itself, but rather Babylon's patriarchs, rulers, and monstrous children. As we have seen, Babylon designates more than a simple city; in the following chapters we shall see that the word also presides over a complex negotiation over what it means to be human. In our survey here, the concept of "the degenerate race" encodes several recurrent tropes, all presided over by the sign of Babylon: degeneracy (ethical, moral, sexual); somatic corruption (monstrosity, atavism, primitivism); sexual deviance, miscegenation, and contagion.

3 Thus in retaining the term "race" in reference to premodern texts and cultures (rather than substituting "ethnicity" or "cultural identity"), I follow the lead of scholars such as Heng, "Invention of Race I"; Isaacs, *Invention of Racism in Classical Antiquity*, 15–38; Buell, *Why This New Race*,13–21; McCoskey, *Race: Antiquity and Its Legacy*.

Babylon and Sexual Degeneracy

From earliest times, Western commentators depicted Babylon's inhabitants as decadent and corrupt, especially in their sexual mores. Generally speaking, Babylonian sexual excess spreads as a classical commonplace: Orosius, for example, explains that Babylon fell to the Persians in part due to the inhabitants' decadent unrestrained sexuality, indicative of their moral corruption and weakness.[4] Denigrating one's enemies as sexual deviants has a long history, and it is not surprising to see classical and biblical sources depict Babylon as a cesspool of vice. Herodotus, for example, explains that all the Babylonians "bring up their daughters to be courtesans"; he also relates the annual sexual rituals of the Babylonian women with prurient fascination: "The Babylonians have one most shameful custom. Every woman born in the country must once in her life go and sit down in the precinct of Aphrodite, and there consort with a stranger."[5] He describes the great temple of Bel, where a Babylonian woman continually waits, "chosen for himself by the deity out of all the women of the land"[6] for sexual pleasure. Barred from intercourse with mortal men, she lives only for the sexual pleasure of Bel in his sacred chamber. Strabo seems to adapt Herodotus's accounts:

> And in accordance with a certain oracle all the Babylonian women have a custom of having intercourse with a foreigner, the women going to a temple of Aphrodite with a great retinue and crowd; and each woman is wreathed with a cord round her head. The man who approaches a woman takes her far away from the sacred precinct, places a fair amount of money upon her lap, and then has intercourse with her; and the money is considered sacred to Aphrodite.[7]

This particular theme will endure in the long tradition of Babylonian degeneracy: miscegenation, the mixing of sexual "types." According to Herodotus and Strabo, the Babylonian women have sex with gods or foreigners, rather than "normal" sexual partners, as part of a sacred rite. We will see this displaced mingling of sexual "types" repeatedly in this tradition.

---

4 *History*, II.3.6: The disgraceful lust (*libidinum turpitudo*) of Sardanapulus, and the licentious frenzy of its inhabitants' desires (*uoluptatis licentia furoris*).

5 Herodotus, *Histories*, I.196, 199.

6 Herodotus, *Histories*, I.181–2.

7 Strabo, *Geography*, XVI.1.20.

Transgressive female sexuality also enters the myth of degenerate Babylon through Semiramis, a figure we have already met. In chapter one we examined legends of Semiramis and Ninus as founders of Babylon; but Semiramis was also known to later ages especially for her depraved sexuality, what Spenser would call "her fowle reproches."[8] Diodorus Siculus reports that some historians say Semiramis was a beautiful prostitute, and he recounts her habitual promiscuity: she "passed along time and enjoyed to the full every device that contributed to luxury; she was unwilling, however, to contract a lawful marriage, being afraid that she might be deprived of her supreme position, but choosing out the most handsome of the soldiers she consorted with them and then made away with all who had lain with her."[9] The Babylonian queen also practiced bestiality: Pliny claims that she had sex with a horse,[10] and an eleventh-century Latin poem from northern France notes that the queen coupled with a bull, and through her acts "[s]uch lewd disorder spread from Babylon." The poem asks, in disgust: "What prostitute in the whole world could have been more debased?"[11] Ammianus Marcellinus provides the further intriguing detail that Semiramis was the first person to castrate male youths, "doing as it were a violence to nature, and forcing it back from its appointed course."[12]

---

8 Edmund Spenser, *The Faerie Queene*, ed. Hamilton et al., I.v.50. On Semiramis, see further chapter 1, pp. 24–6 and the references there; on her degeneracy, see also Claudian, *In Eutropium* (*Against Eutropius*), I.338–45. For further references to Semiramis's sexuality see Samuel, "Semiramis in the Middle Ages" and Archibald, *Incest and the Medieval Imagination*, 91–3. Archibald explains that "A barbarian queen with such power as Semiramis would have been particularly horrifying to early Christian writers; the legend of her sexual appetites, combined with her residence in Babylon, would have made her seem a living incarnation of the Whore of Babylon so vividly described in Revelation and depicted in medieval Apocalypse manuscripts" (92).

9 *Library of History*, II.20; II.13.4. Diodorus seems to paint all the Assyrians/Babylonians as sexually suspect; he relates that Ninyas was just as degenerate as his mother: "he spent all his time in the palace, seen by no one but his concubines and the eunuchs who attended him, and devoted his life to luxury and idleness ... holding the end and aim of a happy reign to be the enjoyment of every kind of pleasure without restraint" (II.21.2).

10 *Natural History*, VIII.156: equum adamatum a Samiramide usque in coitum Iuba auctor est.

11 *Semiramis*, ed. and trans. Dronke in his *Poetic Individuality in the Middle Ages*, 66–75, at lines 11–12 (text), 71 (trans.): Prodiit a Babilon talis confusio stupri. / In terris quod plus potuit sordescere scortum?

12 Ammianus Marcellinus, *History*, XIV.vi.17: velut vim iniectans naturae, eandemque ab instituto cursu retorquens.

If prostitution, bestiality, and castration were not enough to induce a male nightmare of female transgressive sexuality, incest and cross-dressing were also standard components of the Queen of Babylon's legend throughout antiquity and the Middle Ages.[13] Pompeius Trogus tells us that after the death of her husband Ninus, Semiramis disguised herself as a man in order to pretend she was a son of Ninus (rather than his wife), and thus could retain rule of Babylon. Trogus admits that she ruled Babylon well, but explains that her end came about because she "conceived a criminal passion for her son" (*concubitum filii*), who subsequently killed her.[14] Augustine corroborates the queen's incest: "It is said that she was slain by her son, because she, his mother, had dared to defile him by incestuous intercourse."[15] Predictably, Dante places Semiramis in the second circle of Hell, her sin the vice of lust (*vizio di lussuria*).[16] Orosius summarizes the Babylonian queen's degenerate character in terms that would be familiar throughout the Middle Ages:

> This woman, ablaze with lust and thirsting for blood, lived amid unending fornication and murder. After she had killed all those with whom she had enjoyed pleasures of the flesh – men she had summoned as a queen, but detained as a prostitute – on illicitly conceiving a son, she vilely exposed him. Then, when she learnt that she had indulged in incest with him, she covered her personal disgrace by inflicting this crime on all her people. For

---

13 See Samuel, "Semiramis in the Middle Ages."

14 I.2.10. Cf. also the reputed effeminacy of Sardanapulus, the last king of Assyria.

15 *De civitate Dei*, XVIII.2: apud illos enim regnabat filius Nini post matrem Samiramidem, quae ab illo interfecta perhibetur, ausa filium mater incestare concubitu.

16 *Inferno*, trans. Mandelbaum, V.52–60. These elements of Semiramis endure at least through the sixteenth century: the great ekphrasis in canto 7 of Camões's *Lusiads* (1572) depicts

> … a great host of Assyrians,
> Subject to Semiramis, a queen
> As lovely as she was lewd;
> For there, at her burning flank,
> Was carved the great rutting stallion,
> Whose place her son had afterwards to dispute:
> So criminal her passion, so dissolute! (*The Lusiads*, trans. White, VI.53)

Cf. similar references in Chaucer's *Man of Law's Tale* and Boccaccio's *On Famous Women*.

> she decreed that there should be none of the natural reverence between parents and their children when it came to seeking a spouse and that everyone should be free to act as he pleased.[17]

The picture of Semiramis here, we noted previously, is congruent with the biblical Whore of Babylon: through these women Babylon was firmly associated with feminine sexuality and licentious, forbidden pleasure.[18] Taken as a whole, therefore, this evidence represents Babylon as a degenerate place of monstrous, transgressive sexual pleasure similar to corrupt and doomed biblical cities like Sodom and Gomorrah.[19] The Greek chronicle of George the Monk (ninth century), a Byzantine text of the Alexander the Great tradition, summarizes this general Western fantasy: "The Chaldeans and the Babylonians have different customs again, involving marrying their mothers, sibling infanticide, murder and all practices hateful to God: they regard these things as virtuous, even if they are far from their own country."[20]

One final tradition contributes to the myth of sexually degenerate Babylon: the legend of Alexander the Great. The Middle Ages knew Babylon as the place where Alexander the Great died; the Macedonian, notorious in some sources for his homosexuality, thus finds an appropriate place to die in sexually decadent Babylon. Within the Alexander tradition we can see an adaptation of the city's infectious effeminate sexuality in the influential twelfth-century Latin epic poem, the *Alexandreis* by Walter of Châtillon.[21] In Book VI Alexander and his army take up residence in Babylon, and though their spirit had been

---

17 I.4.7–8: haec, libidine ardens, sanguinem sitiens, inter incessabilia et stupra et homicidia, cum omnes quos regie arcessitos, meretricie habitos, concubitu oblectasset occideret, tandem filio flagitiose concepto, impie exposito inceste cognito priuatam ignominiam publico scelere obtexit. praecepit enim, ut inter parentes ac filios nulla delata reuerentia naturae de coniugiis adpetendis ut cuique libitum esset liberum fieret.

18 Fear (52 n. 145) notes that Orosius may have been influenced in this passage by the Whore of Babylon in Revelation 17:5.

19 See, e.g., the Old English *Vercelli Homily VII,* lines 46–51 (*Vercelli Homilies,* ed. Scragg, 133–8, at 135).

20 In Stoneman, *Legends of Alexander the Great,* 32.

21 Latin text: *Galteri de Castellione Alexandreis,* ed. Colker. Translation from Walter of Châtillon, *Alexandreis,* trans. Townsend.

pure and noble, the corrupting feminine influence of Babylon takes its toll on their Western virtue:

> Yet
> the wealth of Babylon, the slothful pleasures
> its populace enjoyed, made slack the workings
> of inborn virtue's rigor. Vile corruption
> stained all that city's customs; unmixed wine
> warmed every heart to Venus' venal evils.
> Men pimped their wives, and parents their own children,
> provided only sin was paid its price.
> By night the banquets saw those solemn revels
> that tyrants keep by long ancestral wont.
> Four days and thirty Alexander lingered
> amidst the idle wantonness of Babylon;
> his troops, who would subdue the world, were weaker
> for such a stay, had an unbridled foe
> burst in upon the slothful banqueters. (trans. Townsend, VI.21–35)[22]

---

22 Colker VI.18–32:

> Innatae uirtutis opus solitumque rigorem
> Fregerunt Babilonis opes luxusque uacantis
> Desidiae populi quia nil corruptius urbis
> Moribus illius. nichil est instructius illis
> Ad Veneris uenale malum cum pectora multo
> Incaluere mero: si tantum detur acerbi
> Flagicii precium, non uxores modo sponsi
> Sed prolem hospitibus cogunt prostare parentes.
> Sollempnes de nocte uident conuiuia ludos
> Quos patrio de more solent celebrare tyranni.
> Hos inter luxus Babilonis et ocia Magnum
> Ter deni tenuere dies et quatuor, unde
> Terrarum domitor exercitus ille futurus
> Debilior fuerat si post conuiuia mensae
> Desidis effrenum piger irrupisset in hostem.

See also the *capitula* for Book VI: "The sixth book shows an Alexander spoiled / By Babel's gilded luxury" (Townsend trans. Heading VI.1–2) (Sextus Alexandrum luxu Babilonis et auro / Corruptum ostendit) (Colker ed. capitula VI.1–2).

The "idle wantonness of Babylon" and its "slothful pleasures" corrupt the moral rectitude of Alexander and his men.[23] This is an early Western expression of the sexualized Orient that would become familiar to eighteenth- and nineteenth-century European culture; it is a vision of ancient sexual excess that would eventually incorporate Western fantasies of harems and other exotic Eastern pleasures.[24]

In all these instances, Babylon functions as a nexus for the sublimated anxiety over the sexual body: all sins of the flesh find a home Babylon. Early Western traditions depict Babylon and the Babylonians as sexual deviants: there is an easy congruence here, as well, between this tradition of sexual degeneracy and Babylon as the Augustinian City of Man, in which love is perverted, in the etymological sense of the word (*per-vertere*) – twisted or turned from its proper direction (God) and fixed upon an improper object (the self). Moreover, Babylonian degeneracy is dangerous because it is infectious: as Alexander and his men find, such deviance has a way of infesting even the upright heart and pure. But in the Christian tradition, Babylonian degeneracy runs deeper than infectious Eastern sexuality. Sexual deviance (putative or real) is also a common way to mark out racial alterity and promulgate that difference through monstrous fecundity. As we shall see in the following pages, Babylon was founded by a cursed line of humanity, a deviant branch of the human family tree especially known for its innate capacity for sexual transgression and monstrous procreation.

---

23 See also Quintus Curtius, *History of Alexander*, V.i.36–9. This tradition would have a long life: Gibbon's *Decline and Fall of the Roman Empire* similarly notes the corrupting sensuality of Babylon, this time defied by the upright character of the emperor Julian: "In the warm climate of Assyria, which solicited a luxurious people to the gratification of every sensual desire, a youthful conqueror preserved his chastity pure and inviolate: nor was Julian ever tempted, even by a motive of curiosity, to visit his female captives of exquisite beauty, who, instead of resisting his power, would have disputed with each other the honour of his embraces. With the same firmness that he resisted the allurements of love, he sustained the hardships of war" (*Decline and Fall*, II.483–4). And cf. Austen Layard's explanation for Babylon's "effeminate customs": "The vast trade, that rendered Babylon the gathering-place of men from all parts of the known world, and supplied her with luxuries from the remotest climes, had at the same time the effect of corrupting the manners of her people, and producing that general profligacy and those effeminate customs which mainly contributed to her fall" (*Discoveries in the Ruins of Nineveh and Babylon* [1853], 539).

24 See chapter 7.

The Cursed Race

The archetype of a cursed race in the Western tradition begins in the prehistory of Babylon, with the story of Cain and his descendants in the Book of Genesis.[25] This archetype consists of several linked biblical stories; or, to be more precise, stories that late antique and medieval traditions would connect: the story of Cain; the corrupting miscegenation of the "sons of God" and the "daughters of men" in the antediluvian world; the story of Noah, his three sons, and the Curse of Ham; Nimrod, the Tower of Babel, and the founding of Babylon; and Nebuchadnezzar's debasement in the Book of Daniel. I summarize the arc of these narratives here first and then explain their reception *seriatim* in the Christian late antique/medieval world. Again, the point here is to collect the constituent elements of a particular tradition – each of those elements connected in some way to Babylon – and then to show how this allusive tradition functions as one strand in the complex understanding of race in the West.

In Genesis 4 Cain kills his brother Abel; God places a mark upon Cain, the first murderer in the postlapsarian world, and he goes into exile, founding the first city. Cain's line descends through Enoch to Lamech, who in some traditions is similarly cursed when he in turn murders Cain, a second perverse kin-slaying.[26] Lamech then begets a variety of dubious offspring who set about inventing the trademarks of civilized life: Tubal, for example, invents music, Tubal-Cain metalworking. Meanwhile the line of Adam and Eve's next son, Seth (Abel's "replacement"), also flourishes. But these two strains of antediluvian humanity – the kin of Cain and the people of Seth – meet in Genesis 6 with disastrous consequences, the next key narrative of our archetype:

> And after that men began to be multiplied upon the earth, and daughters were born to them. The sons of God, seeing the daughters of men, that they were fair, took to themselves wives of all which they chose. And God said: "My spirit shall not remain in man for ever, because he is flesh, and his days shall be a hundred and twenty years." Now giants were upon the earth in those days. For after the sons of God went in to the daughters of

25 On the Cain legend in the Middle Ages and beyond see Emerson, "Legends of Cain"; Mellinkoff, *Mark of Cain*; Quinones, *Changes of Cain*.

26 See Isidore, *Etymologiae*, VII.vi.14.

> men, and they brought forth children; these are the mighty men of old, men of renown. And God, seeing that the wickedness of men was great on the earth, and that all the thought of their heart was bent upon evil at all times, it repented him that he had made man on the earth ... And the earth was corrupted before God, and was filled with iniquity. And when God had seen that the earth was corrupted (for all flesh had corrupted its way upon the earth,) He said to Noah: "The end of all flesh is come before me, the earth is filled with iniquity through them, and I will destroy them with the earth." (Genesis 6:1–6, 11–13)

The moral corruption of the pre-flood world and the sexual mingling of the sons of God and the daughters of men precipitate God's destruction of the human race. In the Flood's aftermath, Noah and his family are the only humans to survive; this would seem to imply that the cursed line of Cain and their corruption had all perished in the flood, and only the righteous line of Seth had survived through Noah. Yet although all of corrupt humanity was destroyed in the deluge, the cursed line of Cain (or at least the evil represented by him) did not die out: evil reappears after the Flood in the story of Noah's sons in Genesis 9.

Soon after the Flood, human corruption regenerates. In Genesis 9, Noah plants a vineyard, and ends up drunk from wine, insensate, and naked. His sons Shem and Japheth respectfully avert their eyes from their father's shame, but his third son Ham sees his father's nakedness (and in some medieval traditions, laughs, therefore compounding his transgression). In retaliation, Noah curses Ham's son Canaan: "Cursed be Canaan; a servant of servants shall he be unto his brethren" (Genesis 9:25). Although Noah's curse lights upon Ham's son and his descendants (the Canaanites), in later traditions the curse was soon transferred to Ham as well as his descendants and thought of as the "Curse of Ham." Thus through Ham, evil rises again in the world after the Flood, and through Ham the evil of Cain passes to Ham's direct descendant: Nimrod, the founder of Babylon and the Tower of Babel in Genesis 10–11. Thus, a primordial tainted strain of humanity marked by sin and transgression moves from Cain the kin-slayer, to the evil humanity punished by the Flood, to the cursed descendants of Ham, and finally to the foundation of Babylon the Great, later ruled most famously by Nebuchadnezzar, the scourge of Israel and despoiler of the Temple. Through this conduit, medieval traditions saw the sin of Adam's fall passed down from Cain to Babylon, residing in a particular lineage of humanity.

Cain and the Two Cities

The bare bones of the biblical narrative outlined above were, in typical late antique and medieval fashion, adapted, augmented and transformed in a variety of imaginative ways, endowing the story with a firmer racial logic and filling in the gaps of the spare biblical narrative with apocryphal lore that would emphasize the degenerate sexuality of Babylon's line. In Josephus's version of the Cain and Abel story, for example, he describes Cain as "thoroughly depraved."[27] Cain's exile and God's mark upon him "only served to increase his vice"; after his exile he "indulged in every bodily pleasure," like his Babylonian descendants.[28] Cain builds the first city in human history after the expulsion from Paradise (Genesis 4:17), foreshadowing the later post-flood founding of Babylon by his descendent Nimrod.[29] Josephus explains that in this way Cain corrupted the simple agrarian life of humanity with urban living: "He was the first to fix boundaries and to build a city, fortifying it with walls and constraining his clan to congregate in one place."[30] Josephus sums up the corruption of the line of Cain: "Thus, within Adam's lifetime, the descendants of Cain went to depths of depravity, and, inheriting and imitating one another's vices, each ended worse than the last."[31] There is nothing said about Cain's sexual morality in the Bible, but later authors were quick to make him a degenerate forefather of Babylon, progenitor of a depraved race.

For Augustine, as we saw in chapter 1, Cain's narrative of murder and city-building represents the historical manifestation of the metaphorical, transhistorical Babylon: Cain's turning away from God as the object of

---

27 *Jewish Antiquities*, I.53: Greek *πονηρότατος*; the Latin translation of Josephus reads *malignissimus*.

28 *Jewish Antiquities*, I.60.

29 Cain builds the first city: Augustine, *De civitate dei*, XV.17; Isidore, *Etymologiae*, XV.3. Luther envisions this first city as the spot where Babel/Babylon itself would rise after the flood: "He [Moses] related that Cain's son Enoch was the first before the Flood to strive for sovereignty and to build a city, which he wanted to call by his own name. I believe that it was located at the place where Babel stood after the Flood; for as the historical accounts of the heathen testify, the plain of that region was very beautiful" (*Works*, II.196). Luther also makes more explicit the connection between Cain and Nimrod: "For us it is enough to know that Babylon was built by Nimrod, perhaps at the same place where Cain had built the city of Enoch" (Luther, *Works*, II.200).

30 *Jewish Antiquities*, I.62.

31 *Jewish Antiquities*, I.66.

his love is a natural consequence of Adam's fall from the righteous way of life, the City of God. Augustine thus explains that the strife between Cain and Abel "demonstrated the hostility between the two cities themselves, the City of God and the city of men."[32] In his reading of this section of Genesis, Augustine observes that the lines of Seth and the lines of Cain are kept separate, yet brought together just before the Flood: "There are, then, two lines of descent, the one from Seth and the other from Cain; and, as we have said, these two distinct orders of mankind [*istae duae series generationum*] reflect the two cities: the one Heavenly, which is a pilgrim in this world, and the other earthly, which longs for earthly things and clings to them as its only joys."[33] He explains that the two lines "became afterwards so mingled and mixed together [*commixta atque confusa*] that the whole human race, except for eight persons, deserved to perish in the Flood."[34]

Bede similarly notes that Adam "engendered the corrupt family of the human race"; by this he means that the Fall gave birth to postlapsarian humanity, the human race as we know it.[35] Cain's line is thus the result of a process of human degeneration. The corruption of Cain and his line proceeds from Adam's sin, after which "the human race degenerated (*degenerante*) from the purity of its first manner of life."[36] Bede follows Augustine in clearly defining the antediluvian world as a symbolic struggle between the line of Cain – a race that "would fix their hearts upon the pleasures of this life" and establish a terrestrial city – and the opposition: "that branch of the human race which descends from Seth to Noah," which represents

32 Augustine, *De civitate Dei*, XV.5: quod autem inter Cain et Abel, inter duas ipsas ciuitates, Dei et hominum, inimicitias demonstrauit.

33 Augustine, *De civitate Dei*, XV.15: Cum itaque istae duae series generationum, una de Seth, altera de Cain, has duas, de quibus agimus, distinctis ordinibus insinuent ciuitates, unam caelestem in terris peregrinantem, alteram terrenam terrenis tamquam sola sint gaudiis inhiantem uel inhaerentem. Cf. also XV.8, 21.

34 Augustine, *De civitate Dei*, XV.20: quo modo postea sic commixta fuerit atque confusa, ut uniuersum genus humanum exceptis octo hominibus diluuio perire meretur. See also XV.22. Note the use of *confusa* here, nodding to the tradition that *Babylon est confusio.*

35 Bede, *In Genesim*, I.1.26; trans. 90: corruptamque ex se prosapiam generis humani procreauit.

36 Bede, *In Genesim*, II.4.20–2; trans. 156: degenerante humano genere a castitate prime conuersationis. Bede also notes that the line of Cain was not only cursed by his murder, but was also "polluted by the adultery of Lamech" (*adulterio Lamech polluta est*): *In Genesim*, II.4.18–20; trans. 155.

the elect who walk with the Lord in this life and are, in fact "his city and temple."[37] According to Bede, the primeval city Cain builds symbolizes the faith the wicked put in things of this earth, rather than on the just rewards of heaven.[38] In Bede's exegesis of Genesis these two divisions of humanity designate the "race of the wicked" that would be destroyed in the flood and the "race of the faithful" that would be saved by Noah.[39] In Augustine and Bede's conception, the dichotomous thinking encouraged by the Two Cities metaphor implies a similar binary understanding of the human race as divided into the line of Seth (good) and the kin of Cain (evil).

Josephus, Augustine, and Bede represent a traditional medieval understanding of Cain and his line in Genesis, and that understanding is binary: good and evil, the pure and the corrupt, humanity dividing into "us" and "them" – the human and the degenerate, less-than-human. Of the three, of course, Augustine was the most sophisticated thinker, but Augustine's system itself degenerates in its reception and tends to inform a more simplistic binary understanding of race in Western culture; this dichotomous or binary thinking about "the human family" would be unmoored from its Augustinian foundation to serve as a template for "lines" of humanity, i.e., races.

The Corruption of the Antediluvian World

And so, leading up to the Flood, the cursed line of Cain is set against the righteous line of Seth. The two divisions of humanity presumably meet in the enigmatic story of Genesis 6, in which the "sons of God" consort with "the daughters of men" and give birth to "giants, the men of renown" – a famously cryptic passage in the Bible.[40] Who are the sons of God and the daughters of men? Are these figurative expressions, and are we to understand "the sons of God" as the righteous line of

37 Bede, *In Genesim*, II.4.17; trans. 154–5: in huius uitae delectatione corda fundarent ... in illa generis humani prosapia quae per Seth ad Noe descendit ... Ipsi enim sunt ciuitas eius et templum. Luther reads this section of Genesis in a similar fashion: see *Works*, II.10.

38 Bede, *In Genesim*, II.4.17; trans. 154–5.

39 Bede, *In Genesim*, II.5.25–9; trans. 167: quodque in diebus eius [i.e., Lamech's] impiorum natio exterminanda, et per ipsum esset transacto diluuio generatio restauranda fidelium.

40 See Lewis, *Study of the Interpretation of Noah and the Flood.*

Seth, and the "daughters of men" as the tainted line of Cain? Medieval Christian commentators in the mainstream generally interpreted the passage in this fashion, including Augustine and Bede.[41] The Old English poem *Genesis A* also follows this tradition in its adaptation of the Genesis narrative:

At that time, the kin of Seth,
(the beloved lord of his people)
still remained in the Lord's love,
very dear to him and renowned,
until the sons of God began to seek brides
from the tribe of Cain, a cursed folk,
and the sons of men chose wives for themselves
from among that people, the fair and beautiful daughters
of that sinful race, against the will of God.[42]

The great crime here is that the two distinct lines of humanity have begun to intermarry, interbreed, and intermingle against the will of God (*metodes est*). The sin apparently is one of miscegenation – two "races" interbreeding, against divine law.[43] Bede, moreover, clearly identifies the nature of this sin as sexual contamination of two lines: "It seems, therefore, that as long as the offspring of the race of Seth were not commingled [*non commixta*] with the offspring of Cain,

41 Augustine, *De civitate Dei*, 15.23; Bede, *In Genesim*, II.6.1–2; trans. 168–9. See Stephens, *Giants in Those Days*, 78–9.

42 *Genesis A*, 1245b–52:

Ða giet wæs Sethes cynn,
leofes leodfruman on lufan swiðe
drihtne dyre and domeadig,
oðþæt bearn godes bryda ongunnon
on Caines cynne secan,
wergum folce, and him þær wif curon
ofer metodes est monna eaforan
scyldfulra mægð scyne and fægere.

43 Stephens calls this standard Christian interpretation of the sons of God and daughters of men as two lines of humanity a "racial equation" (*Giants in Those Days*, 79). James Kugel notes that even the earliest readers of Genesis interpreted this as a sexual transgression (*Bible as It Was*, 142).

they preserved the standard of their chastity unimpaired. But after slipping into lust they united themselves to the cursed offspring of wicked women, and then, when the grace of their chaste minds had been corrupted, they began to be sharers [*consors*] of his [i.e., Cain's] curse."[44] Their libidinal desire is their downfall – as soon as they have sex they share in the curse. And, of course, the offspring of that sexual act transmits the sin to the next generation. Bede emphasizes that "the race of Cain," "the whole race that was descended from him" was cursed in several ways: by Adam's fall, Abel's murder, Lamech's killing of Cain, and the adultery of Lamech, and therefore the line was "defiled" [*foedata*].[45] Moreover, in the Bible, Cain's direct descendants end with Tubal-Cain's sister, Naamah; Bede explains that this is appropriate since Naamah means "pleasure" (*voluptas*), signifying the "satisfying of carnal pleasures."[46] He adds that "not long after the birth of this woman, the whole cursed race [*progenies maledicta*] was destroyed by the flood."[47] In summary, Bede clearly explains that the "sons of God" in Genesis 6 refers to the race of Seth while the "daughters of men" refers to the offspring of Cain, and the nature of their sin is sexual. As the pure race of Seth pollutes itself with the infectious seed of Cain, the entire "stock" is tainted and a primal sin is passed down to later generations in this line.

Later medieval culture continued to imaginatively adapt and transform this archetypal sexual miscegenation of pre-flood humanity. The thirteenth-century Middle English poem *Genesis and Exodus* explains that the sons of Seth "mixed with a cursed race" (*mengten wið waried kin*):[48]

The sons of Seth began to mis-marry,
Against which Adam forbade,

44 Bede, *In Genesim*, II.6.1–2; trans. 169: Videtur ergo quia generatio stirpis Seth, quamdiu cum progenie Cain non est commixta, inlibatam suae castitatis normam serauerit; at postquam in concupiscentiam lapsa nequam feminarum maledictae se soboli coniunxit, tunc et ipsa uitiato sobriae mentis decore, maledictionis eius coeperit existere consors.

45 Bede, *In Genesim*, II.4.18–20; trans. 155: Progenies Cain ... tota quae de illo nata erat soboles ... foedata.

46 Bede, *In Genesim*, II.4.22; trans. 157: in expletione uoluptatum carnalium.

47 Bede, *In Genesim*, II.4.22; trans. 157: Verum nata hac femina non multo post, uniuersa progenies maledicta diluuio consumpta est.

48 *Middle English* Genesis and Exodus, ed. Arngart, 544 (by line number).

and abandoned the fear of God.
They chose for themselves wives from [the line of] Cain
and mixed with a cursed race.
From them were born the giants,
mighty men and warlike, doomed.[49]

The poetic text dilates in an imaginative fashion, fascinated by the specific sexual degeneracy of the sinful antediluvian world. In the poem, Lamech commits the first degenerate sin of bigamy.[50] The children of Cain are also guilty of incest: "The sons of Cain broke the law, committed fornication with their brothers' wives."[51] The antediluvian women revel in "unnatural lusts" ([g]*olhed hunkinde*, 534). And rounding out the sexual sins of the antediluvian world is homosexuality:

Men began such business,
evil dalliance between themselves,
in a villainous fashion, against (natural) law.[52]

49 Mis-wiuen hem gunnen Seðes sunes
Agenes ðat Adam for-bead,
And leten Godes-frigti-hed.
He chosen hem wiwes of Caym
And mengten wið waried kin.
Of hem woren ðe getenes boren,
Migti men and figti, for-loren. (540–5)

50 Ðis Lamech was ðe firme man,
Ðe bigamie first bi-gan.
Bigamie is unkinde ðing,
On engleis tale twie-wifing. (447–51)

[This Lamech was the first man who engaged in bigamy. Bigamy is an unnatural thing. In English speech it is called "two-wifing."]

51 Caymes sunes wrogten vn-lage, / Wið breðere wife hore-plage (529–30).

52 Wapmen bi-gunnen quad mester,
Bi-twen hem-seluen hun-wreste plage,
A ðefis kinde, a-genes lage. (536–8)

The author of the fourteenth-century Middle English poem *Cleanness* sees similar corruption:

> And then in deeds of the flesh they invented filthy practices,
> and contrived against nature perverse works,
> and had sex with each other lustfully, in a perverted fashion.[53]

From its earliest understanding in the Middle Ages, the separation and classification of humanity in these linked narratives from Genesis were expressed in sexual terms, as unnatural copulation and miscegenation. Furthermore, it is an easy correlation between this dossier of sexual degeneracy in the antediluvian world of Genesis and the same complex of corrupt sexuality generally associated with Babylon that we detailed in the beginning of this chapter. Medieval authors were quick to spot such analogous traditions and connect them: We can begin to see here the glimmer of an idea of "race," a notion of human difference not deriving from climate-based theories or the principle of Noachid dispersion, but found rather in this "setting aside" of a particular dark strain of humanity.

---

53 And þenne founden þay fylþe in fleschlych dedez,
And controeued again kynde contraré werkez,
And vsed hem vnþryftyly vchon on oþer,
And als with oþer, wylsfully, upon a wrange wyse (265–8)

Poems of the Pearl Manuscript, ed. Andrew and Waldron, by line numbers.
The Southern Version of the *Cursor Mundi* also tells the story of "Cain's kin" (*kaymes kynne*, 1496), and his "brood" (1507), including Lamech the first bigamist (*þe firste on lyue / Þat bigan to double wyue*, 1527–8), and then finally details the sexual corruption of the men and women in this line before the flood, doing the Middle English *Genesis and Exodus* one better by explaining that *both* men *and* women of Cain's kin engaged in homosexual acts:

> Euer þei ʒaf her lyf to lust
> Þat shende her soulis al to dust
> Wymmen as we hit fynde
> Wente togider aʒeyne kynde
> And men also þe same wyse. (1567–71)

> [They always gave their lives over to lust, which destroyed their souls all to dust. Women, we find, came together with women, against the laws of nature, and men did as well.]

(*Southern Version of Cursor Mundi*, vol. I, ed. Horrall, by line numbers).

But there is another complementary tradition of understanding the enigmatic story of Genesis 6, one that contains the same fear of miscegenation, but does not equate the sons of God with Seth's children and the daughters of men with Cain's line. Rather than two lines of humanity commingling (one pure and one evil), the miscegenation in this alternate tradition mixes the terrestrial and the extraterrestrial, the human and the non-human. According to modern biblical scholarship, what is present in this chapter of Genesis appears to be a vestigial tradition of divine or semi-divine non-human beings ("the sons of God," the *Nephilim*, in Hebrew) mingling with humanity ("the daughters of men") and producing awe-inspiring semi-divine offspring – giants, mighty ones, the men of renown.[54] Our alternative tradition in late antiquity and the Middle Ages read the story on this basis. For example, in the apocryphal *Book of Enoch* (second century BCE), we learn that the "sons of God" are the inhuman Watchers, fallen angels who desire to copulate with humanity, the "daughters of men."[55] The Watchers take these women and "began to cohabit with them and to defile themselves with them"; giants are born of this unnatural union, creatures who grow too powerful, turn against humanity, and "began to devour their flesh, and [to drink their] blood" (28). The Flood therefore is a direct result of a crime against the natural order of things: the divine non-human beings mate with humanity and produce monstrous, misshapen, dangerous offspring.[56] The sexual mixing has dire consequences in the *Book of Enoch*: "and there arose much impiety on the earth and they committed fornication and went astray and corrupted their ways ... Then the giants began to devour the flesh of men, and mankind began to become few upon the earth" (29).

54 See Alter, *Genesis*, 26; on this tradition of interpretation see Stephens, *Giants in Those Days*, 76–8.

55 The apocryphal Book of Enoch was originally composed in Hebrew or Aramaic in the second century BCE, then translated into Greek, Ethiopian, and other languages and found its way into Latin and vernacular textual traditions in the Middle Ages. Citations are from *Book of Enoch*, ed. Black, VanderKam, and Neugebauer, by page numbers.

56 See *Book of Enoch*, ed. Black et al., 34–5: "As for celestial spirits, heaven shall be their dwelling-place: but for terrestrial spirits, born upon the earth, on the earth shall be their dwelling-place. But the vicious spirits (issuing) from the giants, the Nephilim – they inflict harm, they destroy, they attack, they wrestle and dash to the ground, causing injuries; they eat nothing, but fast and thirst and produce hallucinations, and they collapse. And these spirits will rise against the sons of men and women, from whom they came forth. From the day of the time of the slaughter, destruction and death of the giants, the Nephilim, the spirits which came forth from their bodies will go on destroying, uncondemned. In such ways they will destroy until the day of the end, until the great judgement, in which the great aeon will be completed."

With the birth of the semi-human giants, God levels his judgment upon the Watchers, initiating the genesis of a new line of creation, a dark offshoot of the human family tree, generated through unnatural miscegenation: "And now the giants, who have been produced from spirits and flesh, shall be called mighty spirits upon the earth, and on the earth shall be their dwelling-place. Evil spirits shall come forth from their bodies, for from men have they come, and from the holy watchers is the beginning of their creation and 'the beginning' of their origins. Evil spirits shall they be called upon the earth" (34). Josephus follows a slight variant of this tradition; he asserts that the line of Seth endured as righteous men for seven generations, but "in course of time, they abandoned the customs of their fathers for a life of depravity."[57] The "angels of God" (Greek *ἄγγελοι θεοῦ*; Latin, *angeli Dei*) then slept with the women of Seth's line and "begat sons who were overbearing and disdainful of every virtue, such confidence had they in their strength."[58] Thus, in Josephus the miscegenation is not directly attributed to the line of Cain; it is the line of Seth that falls into sin.[59] Seeing the degeneration of his creation, God resolves to destroy humanity and "create another race pure of vice."[60] In this tradition, the divine sons of God and the earthly daughters of men produce the race of giants and other monstrous, inhuman creatures that may or may not survive the Flood.[61]

But whether the transgressive antediluvian miscegenation occurs between a cursed line of humanity and a pure strain, or between human and inhuman "races," the central dynamic of miscegenation remains the same: the unnatural mingling of "types" brings on a corruption and degeneracy of the original vital stock of humanity, producing hybrids and monstrous category errors – a human lineage set apart and marked by its transgression.[62] The basic elements of this archetype reconstitute themselves after the Flood.

---

57 *Jewish Antiquities*, I.72.

58 *Jewish Antiquities*, I.73.

59 Also, the offspring are not literally giants or monsters: they are *like* giants. Bede follows a similar non-fantastical reading: *In Genesim*, II.6.3–4; trans. 169–70.

60 *Jewish Antiquities*, I.75.

61 On the medieval understanding and representation of monsters, see Friedman, *Monstrous Races*; Williams, *Deformed Discourse*; Cohen, *Of Giants*.

62 Friedman explain that if Adam were perfect and his descendants were not, this corruption "was often seen as the consequences not only of the Fall, but also of alien strains entering a tribal line of descent, so that the resulting people were less than fully human" (*Monstrous Races*, 89).

Evil after the Flood and the Curse of Ham

In theory, no matter the origin of antediluvian humanity's taint, such corruption should have died out beneath the waters of the Flood; however, the metaphorical City of Man, Babylon, does not die out – earthly desires and their attendant evils continued to fester. Medieval commentators were thus faced with a problem: if God destroys humanity because it has become corrupt, saving only the righteous Noah and his family to start over with a "pure race" (as Josephus expressed it), then why does evil reappear after the Deluge, apparently *contra* God's intentions? Did not all evil humanity perish in the Flood? Medieval authors addressed the conundrum in a number of ways.[63] According to mainstream Augustinian traditions, the answer once again lay in the familiar Two Cities metaphor – "Babylon" denotes an inherent ethical tendency of humanity (a love of self and earthy things rather than a love of God) that no flood can fully extinguish; corruption is therefore the essential trajectory of the world and humanity after the Fall, whether before the flood or after. All things decline and degenerate, even the "unblemished" human stock that survived the flood. Although the flood wipes out everyone except Noah and his family, the sinful taint of Cain and his line inevitably re-emerges: in this sense, the City of Man, "Babylon," always resides within humanity.

But other medieval traditions craved a more literal explanation for the survival of evil after the Flood. They deployed various ingenious strategies, but found their main answer in the story of the so-called Curse of Ham. Of Noah's three sons, Shem and Japheth are honourable, but Ham is marked for evil. After the Flood, Noah plants a vineyard and makes wine:

> And [Noah] drinking of the wine was made drunk, and was uncovered in his tent. Which when Cham [Ham] the father of Canaan had seen, to wit, that his father's nakedness was uncovered, he told it to his two brethren without. But Sem [Shem] and Japheth put a cloak upon their shoulders, and going backward, covered the nakedness of their father: and their faces were turned away, and they saw not their father's nakedness. And Noah awaking from the wine, when he had learned what his younger son had done to him, he said: "Cursed be Canaan [i.e., Ham's son], a servant of servants shall he be unto his brethren." (Genesis 9:21–5)

63 See Friedman, *Monstrous Races*, 99–103; Stephens, *Giants in Those Days*, 84–92; Mellinkoff, "Cain's Monstrous Progeny, Part II."

Later generations, down through the centuries, would know this transgression and resulting malediction as the Curse of Ham.[64] Used to explain the post-flood reappearance of evil, Ham's curse constituted a latter-day mark of Cain, the genesis of another cursed, tainted branch of humanity. Ham begets the cursed Canaan; from Canaan comes Cush (progenitor of the Kushites, the African races according to medieval tradition); and then finally the same line gives birth to Nimrod the giant, the grandson of Ham and the first human tyrant, the founder of Babylon.

The Curse of Ham fired the imagination of medieval writers in various ways and his post-flood transgression was soon linked to the similar corruption of the pre-flood world; Ham's taint was seen as a throwback to the sins of Cain's line, the "daughters of men." Although the Bible tells us essentially nothing about Ham, late antique and medieval authors expanded his character, giving him a colourful pre-flood history and marking him as a "bad seed" even before the flood. Ham comes to bear a physical mark of his curse – black skin (like Cain in some traditions).[65] Some commentators assumed he had always been black; others thought he turned black when Noah cursed his descendants; still others argued that Ham married a surviving descendant of cursed, black Cain.[66] John Cassian (d. ca. 435), for example, explains that Ham engraved secret evil inscriptions of magic and demon worship on metal and stone before the flood, so that they might not be ruined by the waters and lost; thus afterwards he found these preserved traces of the earlier corrupt world and "transmitted the seeds of perpetual wickedness to later generations" (*perpetuae nequitiae seminarium transmisit in posteros*).[67] These "seeds" of Cassian are important – they are metaphorical, used to describe the transmission of a trait across generations and define a group of related descendants according to that trait. Likewise, according to a variety of medieval Irish texts, the descendants of Cain inscribed their history on

---

64 For the Curse of Ham see Friedman, *Monstrous Races*, 100–3; Evans, "From the Land of Canaan to the Land of Guinea"; Braude, "Sons of Noah"; Haynes, *Noah's Curse*; Goldenberg's exhaustive study, *Curse of Ham*; and Whitford, *Curse of Ham in the Early Modern Era*.

65 On black Cain see Mellinkoff, *Mark of Cain*, 76–7; Goldenberg, *Curse of Ham*, 178–82; Kidd, *Forging of Races*, 33–5.

66 See Goldenberg, *Curse of Ham*, 141–56, and the many references in his notes.

67 *Iohannis Cassiani Conlationes*, ed. Petchenig, *Conlatio* VIII.xxi.7–8; John Cassian, *The Conferences*, trans. Ramsey, 305–7. See also *Conlatio* VIII.xxi.3. On Cassian's "racial" interpretation of the sons of God and daughters of Men, see Stephens, *Giants in Those Days*, 79–82.

stone columns that survived the flood.[68] In some traditions Naamah, the last woman of Cain's line, marries Noah before the flood, thus allowing the Cain-seed to survive the cataclysm, as she passes on her evil proclivities to Ham; in other texts, Ham's wife herself is from the line of Cain. It was even thought that Ham committed some sort of sexual sin on the ark, polluting himself, and thus bearing the foul seed of the pre-Flood world over the waters.[69] All of this tells us that if Cain is the first villain in human history, Ham is closely connected to him by analogy as the first villain of the new world after the rushing flood. Both are patriarchs of Babylon, so to speak: Cain is associated with murder, exile and depravity; Ham is defined by sexual transgression, whether that is breaking a taboo by seeing his father's genitalia (and laughing), or through later legends of his sexual escapades.

What is important here for our purposes is that Cain and Ham are linked in premodern Christian tradition; they are analogical progenitors of tainted human lineages on either side of the great Flood. Ham is a displaced Cain; he is Cain's "postdiluvian analogue."[70] Linking the two characters in this way is also a widespread medieval tradition, followed by Augustine, Bede, the eleventh-century Middle Irish *Lebor Gabála Érenn* (*The Book of the Taking of Ireland* – a large pseudo-history blending biblical and native mythology), Mandeville's *Travels* and many others. The tradition of connecting the two extends into the early modern world with Martin Luther:

> The deed as well as the lot of Ham and of Cain are almost alike. Cain kills his brother. This deed is proof enough that there was no respect for his parent in his heart. He is excommunicated by his father, secedes from the church that had the true God and the true worship, builds the city of Enoch, and devotes himself completely to civil concerns. Ham likewise sins against his father by his disrespect. When he later hears the verdict of the curse, by which he is excluded from the promise of the Seed and from the church, he smugly withdraws from God and from the church; for he is cursed, not in his own person but only in his son, and he goes to Babylon and there builds a royal city.[71]

68 See Orchard, *Pride and Prodigies*, 68.

69 See Goldenberg, *Curse of Ham*, 290–2, notes 62–5.

70 The phrase is from Friedman, *Monstrous Races*, 100. See also Claeske, "Children of Adam and Eve," 5–6.

71 Luther, *Lectures on Genesis* in *Works*, II.180; cf. also 210: "Similarly, when two sons had been born to Adam, two kinds of people took their origin from them. Cain left

Luther's explication of Genesis further specifies that the descendants of Ham built Babylon (213) and that at the Tower of Babel's destruction "the ungodly descendants of Ham were wretchedly scattered" (221).[72] We perhaps do not reflexively think of Cain and Ham as a similar pair or as part of the Matter of Babylon and the Tower of Babel, but several mutually reinforcing traditions in the premodern world connected both figures to Babylon: Cain as the founder of the City of Man and Ham as both the conduit of Cain's evil and as the progenitor of Nimrod, founder of the actual city.[73]

Cain, Ham, and the Lineage of Monstrosity

Another compelling link between Cain and Ham in the medieval tradition was that each of them was thought to have spawned a line

---

his father, established a special church without God's command, and held the true church in contempt. The same thing happens here among the sons of Noah. From Ham, as from an ungodly and wicked source, the false and lying church takes its origin." See Haynes, *Noah's Curse*, 50–1 for Luther's association of Cain with Ham.

72 See also 204: "And so *the descendants of the ungodly Ham*, even though they were cursed, drove the descendants of blessed Shem out of their own territory and took possession of Palestine, Syria, and the adjoining areas, as far as *Babylon*"; and 364: "Now it is known from the sacred record that the first kingdom after the Flood or after the division of languages was *Babylon*, a most fertile place. *This kingdom was established by Nimrod, Ham's grandson*, to whom Africa was assigned. His son Cush had possession of Egypt. But Ham's grandson Nimrod was dissatisfied with the paternal boundaries. He attacked the holy generation in the east, and through tyranny he took possession of the land of Shinar and built Babylon, as Moses related previously, in the eleventh chapter." Emphasis mine in both quotations, showing Luther's association of Ham with Babylon. For more examples of Ham's connection to Babylon see Luther, *Works*, II.175 and II.213; on Luther and Ham see Haynes, *Noah's Curse*, 32–3; Whitford, *Curse of Ham*, 81–4. See also John Calvin (1509–64), *Commentaries on the First Book of Moses Called Genesis*, trans. King, 1:302, passim, who treats the story of Ham, Nimrod, and Babylon much like Luther.

73 A third figure allows us to connect this complex of characters even closer to Babylon – Jonitus, the legendary fourth son of Noah. A curious widespread medieval tradition gave Noah a fourth son, born after the flood, named Jonitus. According to the legend, Jonitus received great wisdom from God, invented the science of astronomy and became the tutor of Nimrod, our founder of Babylon. The source for the legend of Jonitus is Pseudo-Methodius's *Apocalypse* (ed. and trans. Garstad, 3.2–6), and the story was widely replicated in influential later texts such as Peter Comestor's *Historia Scholastica* and Vincent of Beauvais's *Speculum Historiale.* On Jonitus, see further Akbari, *Idols in the East*, 82–8; see Anlezark, *Water and Fire*, 254–7 on Jonitus, and on Sceaf, the Anglo-Saxon legend of another ark-born son of Noah (245–73).

of monsters.[74] One of the most famous representations of this latter-day tainted line of Cain is, of course, the monster Grendel in *Beowulf*.[75] The poet describes Grendel as something between man and monster, incorporating aspects of the human and the non-human, much like the half-supernatural/half-human hybrid Genesis offspring of the Book of Enoch.[76] The Grendel-kin live in the isolated margins of the world, out beyond the light of civilization. A border-crosser (*mearcstapa* 103a) and eater of men, Grendel lives in isolation because God had condemned him "as the kin of Cain" (*in Caines cynne*, 107a); he is "battered by sins" (or "crimes") (*synnum geswenced*, 975a); he is a *wiht unhælo* (120b) a "creature of evil," or, perhaps a better translation, a "degenerate thing."[77] As he gives us Grendel's ancestry, the *Beowulf*-poet explains that God avenged the slaying of Abel by driving Cain far from mankind; and beyond the fields we know, the cursed line produced new forms of life:

> From there were born all the deformed races:
> ogres and elves and evil monsters,
> and also the giants who fought against God
> for a long time – he repaid them for that.[78]

Ham has a parallel reputation as the originator of monsters; for example, in the eleventh-century Middle Irish treatise known as *The Six Ages of the World* (*Sex Aetates Mundi*):

> And so Cham (Ham) is the first person that was cursed after the Flood, and he is the heir of Cain after the Flood, and from him there sprang

74 On the monstrous races descending from Cain and Ham see Friedman, *Monstrous Races*, 87–107 and 99–105, respectively; Hannaford, *Race*, 127–46.

75 On *Beowulf* and the kin of Cain see Friedman, *Monstrous Races*, 103–7, in which he shows "how the idea of a cursed line is carried out in a literary treatment of one of Cain's progeny" (103). See also Melinkoff, "Cain's Progeny, Part I" and "Cain's Progeny, Part II"; Quinones, *Changes of Cain*, 41–61; Orchard, *Pride and Prodigies*, 58–85.

76 On the Book of Enoch in Anglo-Saxon England and its possible connection to *Beowulf*, see Kaske, "*Beowulf* and the Book of Enoch" and Melinkoff, "Cain's Progeny, Part I."

77 Citations from *Klaeber's Beowulf*, ed. Fulk et al.

78 *Beowulf*, 111–14:

> Þanon untydras ealle onwocon
> eotenas ond ylfe ond orcneas
> swylce gigantas þa wið Gode wunnon
> lange þrage; he him ðæs lean forgeald.

the Luchorpaín ("leprechauns"), and Fomoraig (giants/Fomorians), and horse-heads (or "goat-heads"), and in general every unshapely form that there is in men.[79]

This Irish tradition clearly links Cain and Ham (the "heir of Cain after the Flood") and Ham, rather than Cain, produced "every unshapely form" (Old Irish *archena*) known to man. The link between Cain and Ham (or, as he is spelled often in medieval texts "Cam" or "Cham"), is nicely encapsulated in the *Beowulf* scribe's difficulty in rendering Cain's name both times it appears in the manuscript. At line 107a, the scribe first wrote *cames cynne* ("the kin of Cam" [Ham]) but then changed it to *caines cynne*, ("the kin of Cain"). A similar mix-up happens in the second occurrence of Cain's name, at line 1261b of the poem, when the scribe wrote *camp*, again a confusion for *cain/cam*.

The late antique/medieval reception and adaptation of Genesis led to an inexorable logic: that the human race was bifurcated, the pure set against the impure. Any sexual mixing of the two led to monstrosity through the unnatural union of different orders of nature. As Sulpicius Severus (c. 360–c. 430) concludes: "From their alliance [i.e., sons of God and the daughters of men] giants are said to have sprung. For the mixture with them of beings of a different nature, as a matter of course, gave birth to monsters."[80] Monsters, beings of a "mixed nature," inhabit the prehistory of Babylon: the degenerate "race"; semi-human creatures of uncertain categorization; a race defined by the anxieties of copulation, miscegenation and the blurring of ontological categories; a race that moved through history in the shadows out beyond the light, as the most visible sign of the abiding shadow of the City of Man.

---

79 Irish text from *The Irish Sex Aetates Mundi*, ed. and trans. Ó Cróinín, 34 (section number); translation is my own but based on Ó Cróinín: "Conid hé Cám de-side cét[d] uine ro-mallachad iar ndílinn 7 conid hé comarba Caín iar ndílinn 7 conid huad ro-génatar luchorpáin 7 fomoraig 7 goborchinn 7 cech écosc dodelba archena fil for doinib." On the Irish *Sex Aetates Mundi* and related texts, see Ó Cróinín's introduction and Friedman, *Monstrous Races*, 98–100. Cf. also the same material in the *Lebor Gabála Érenn*, which explains that "this Ham is the first man who was cursed after the flood" (Conad hé Cam cet duine ra mallaigedh iar ndilinn); a gloss on this sentence connects Ham to the monstrous races: "and thereafter there were born dwarfs and giants and horseheads and every unshapely form in general that there is among men" (Conad iarsin ra geinidar lupracanaig 7 fomoraig 7 gaburchind 7 cach egasg do-delba archena fil for dainib): Macalister, ed. and trans., *Lebor Gabála Érenn*, I.136–7.

80 Sulpicius Severus, *Chronicorum*, ed. Halm, 1.2; p. 5.

Nimrod the Giant

The lineage of the degenerate race runs from Cain to Ham and next to Nimrod – the great hunter before the Lord and yet another monstrous scion of Babylon. Any medieval reader would probably know three things about Nimrod: that he was the first tyrant, that he built the Tower of Babel and Babylon, and that he was a giant. Nimrod is not described as a giant in the Bible, but post-biblical Christian tradition made his gigantic monstrosity a commonplace.[81] Augustine explicates the Tower of Babel story by beginning with a blunt assertion that Nimrod himself founded the city of Babylon (*City of God*, XVI.4). Isidore concurs: "After the flood the giant Nimrod first founded the Mesopotamian city of Babylon."[82] Dante famously depicts Nimrod as a giant trapped in the ninth circle of Hell, who speaks an incomprehensible babbling language befitting the builder of the Tower of Babel: he is "Nimrod, through whose wicked thought / one single language cannot serve the world."[83] Almost any medieval text that mentions Nimrod depicts him as a giant.

Nimrod was also often specifically linked to Ham.[84] Josephus, for example, explains that it was "Nebrodes [Nimrod], grandson of Ham" who seized power after the Flood and "transform[ed] the state of affairs into a tyranny," forcing the people to depend on him rather than God; according to Josephus, Nimrod and his people threaten to build a tower higher than any flood waters in which he could reach the heavens "and avenge the destruction of their forefathers."[85] God then destroys the Tower of Babel, confounds human speech, and disperses humanity; Josephus concludes: "The place where they built the tower is now called Babylon from the confusion of that primitive speech once intelligible to all, for the Hebrews call confusion 'Babel'."[86]

81 On Nimrod as a giant see Stephens, *Giants in Those Days*, 67–70; Cohen, *Of Giants*, 22–4. For a fascinating survey of interpretations and representations of Nimrod from antiquity to the nineteenth century see Haynes, *Noah's Curse*, 41–61.

82 *Etymologiae*, XV.1.4: Primus post diluvium Nembroth gigans Babylonem urbem Mesopotamiae fundavit.

83 *Inferno*, trans. Mandelbaum, canto XXXI, lines 46–81, quotation at lines 77–8: questi è Nembrotto per lo cui mal coto / pur un linguaggio nel mondo non s'usa.

84 As Haynes notes, "Despite Nimrod's mythic prominence, medieval writers never lost sight of his blood relationship to Ham" (*Noah's Curse*, 49).

85 *Jewish Antiquities*, I.113–14.

86 *Jewish Antiquities*, I.117; cf. I.140–2.

Just as Josephus identifies Nimrod as a "grandson of Ham" (connecting the giant tyrant to a tradition of evil), Bede also connects the two, specifying Nimrod as a cursed son of Ham: "While the descendants of Shem and of Japheth remained in the innocence of a life of honesty, there arose from the cursed offspring (*de stirpe maledicta*) of Ham one [i.e., Nimrod] who corrupted the condition of the human way of life by a new kind of living."[87] The Old English poem *Genesis A* makes the same connection between the two. In a passage I cited in chapter 2, we first learn that Nimrod, firstborn son of Chus, became the mighty founder of famed Babylon (1628b–35a); as it continues, the passage then immediately associates Nimrod with Ham's line:

> At that time
> one speech was still common to all dwellers on earth.
> Also from Cam's [Ham's] stock sprang
> many descendants, and to these numerous people
> great families were born.[88]

All these texts construct a lineage for Babylon that stretches back from its monstrous giant founder Nimrod, to the cursed Ham and his depravity, and still further back to Cain's primal sin in the dawn of the world.[89]

---

87 Bede, *In Genesim*, III.10.8–9; trans. 218: Progenie Sem et Iafeth in uitae simplicitatis innocentia permanentibus, nascitur de stirpe Cham maledicta, qui statum humanae conuersationis nouo uiuendi genere peruerteret. See also Bede, *In Genesim*, III.10.30; trans. 226: "the sons of Ham have the beginning of their kingdom in Babylon, that is 'confusion,' which is in the land of Shinar, that is, 'the stench of them'" (filii Cham principium regni habent in Babylone, id est, "confusione," quae est in terra Sennaar, id est, "fetoris eorum").

88 Reord wæs þa gieta
eorðbuendum an gemæne.
Swilce of Cames cneorisse woc
wermægða fela; of þam widfolce
cneorim micel cenned wæron. (1635b–39)

89 The Old English translation of Boethius's *Consolation of Philosophy* also connects Ham and Nimrod in an imaginative way:

> They could have said what folly the giant Nimrod worked. Nimrod was the son of Chus; Chus was Ham's son, Ham Noah's. This Nimrod ordered the building of a tower on the field that was called Sennar, and in the nation that was called Deira, very near the city which is now called Babylon. They did that because they wished to know how high it was to heaven and how thick it was and how firm, or what was above it. But it came about, as was fitting, that the divine power scattered them

In the post-flood world, humanity after the Tower of Babel moved in different directions, dispersed by God's wrath. Included in the post-Babel dispersion were the descendants of Cain and Ham: outcasts from the human family, different in kind from the rest of their brethren.[90] Cain and Ham and their monstrous descendants are the ancestral line of Babylon; they are the patriarchs of Nimrod, Babylon's first imperial lord, and Nebuchadnezzar, its best-known latter-day tyrant and himself debased as an animal, like an echo of his half-human ancestors. Walter of Châtillon's *Alexandreis* even sees the Persians, lords of Babylon, as descendants of Nimrod: the ecphrasis on Darius's shield near the end of Book II depicts the "origin of Darius's sires, / and all the profane ranks of Giant race."[91] The pictorial lineage on the shield stretches from Nimrod and his giant antediluvian ancestors, to Nebuchadnezzar and Belshazzar, and on to Cyrus – all the evil rulers of Babylon.[92]

> before they were allowed to complete it, and cast down the tower, and killed many of them, and divided their speech into seventy-two languages.
>
> [Hi mihton secgan hwylc dysig Nefrod se gigant worhte. Nefrod wæs Chuses sunu; Chus wæs Chaames sunu, Chaam Noes. Se Nefrod het wyrcan anne tor on þam felda þe Sennar hatte, and on þære ðiode þe Deira hatte swiðe neah þære byrig þe mon nu hæt Babilonia. Þæt hi dydon for þam ðingum þæt hi woldon witon hu heah hit wære to þam hefone and hu þicke se hefon wære and hu fæst, oððe hwæt þær ofer wære. Ac hit gebyrede, swa hit cynn was, þæt se godcunda anweald hi tostente ær hi hit fullwyrcan moston, ond towearp þone torr, ond hiora manigne ofslog, ond hiora spræce todælde on twa and hundseofontig geþeoda.]

Old English Boethius, ed. Godden and Irvine; quotation from the B text (I.239–382), chp. 35, lines 129–38; translation from vol. II. 64. On this passage and its odd insertion of the Anglo-Saxon "Deira," see Orchard, *Pride and Prodigies*, 81–2.

90 Friedman, paraphrasing Hayden White, notes that the "concept of the decay of the species was natural to Judeo-Christian culture," because biblical narratives of the post-flood world were predicated upon the idea of "'better' and 'worse' races"; in the world presided over by the line of Ham and Nimrod, "tribal and racial differences become evidence of 'species corruption'" (*Monstrous Races*, 89; paraphrasing Hayden White in "Forms of Wildness," 14).

91 Trans. Townsend, II.579–80; *Alexandreis*, ed. Colker, II.498–9: origo patrum Darii gentisque prophanus / Ordo Gyganteae.

92 See also Darius's speech to his army in Book II, where he rallies the Persians, describing them as a race descended from Babylonian Belus:

> If ancient monuments remain, if memory
> still serves our fathers' record, who knows not
> that we trace back our lineage to the Giants?
> Who has heard nothing of our strife with gods,
> the bricks baked by our forebears, and the mortar

Nebuchadnezzar

Finally, the archetype of degenerate Babylonian monstrosity extends its line to the latter-day lord of Babylon, Nebuchadnezzar. Bede, for one, connects Nimrod directly to Nebuchadnezzar, describing him as a ruler of a great people descending from Nimrod's own lineage (*ex sua stirpe*).[93] In the bible God humbles this proud tyrant by debasing him, robbing him of human intellect, and driving him into the isolated wasteland as a bestial exile (as we saw in chapter 2).[94] The debasement of Nebuchadnezzar is retold in many medieval sources, and they tend to emphasize his monstrous, animal state. The Old English *Daniel* emphasizes Nebuchadnezzar's nakedness and the inhuman bestiality that sunders him from humanity: the Babylonian king becomes a "counselor to the

---

> with which they built the Tower? Who forgets
> the city whose eternal name derives
> from tongues' confusion [i.e., Babylon]. (Townsend trans. II.405–12)
> Si ueterum monimenta manent, si mente recordor
> Scripta patrum memori, quis nos a stirpe Gygantum
> Ignoret duxisse genus? quis bella deorum,
> Quis coctum laterem structamque bitumine turrim
> Nesciat a proauis, magnaeque quis immemor urbis
> Cui dedit aeternum labii confusio nomen? (Colker ed. II.348–53)

A medieval manuscript gloss to this passage reads:

> Note that in Babylon demons entered the bodies of women, whence Giants like Nimrod and many others were born. Of their stock were born Darius and Belus and Darius's other ancestors, which is why it says "from the lineage of the Giants," etc.
>
> [Notandum quod apud Babiloniam demones corpora mulierum intrauerunt, unde nati sunt Gigantes sicut Nemphrot et multi alii. De quorum genere fuit Darius et Belus et alii antecessores Darii, unde dicit "A STIRPE GYGANTVM, etc." (Colker ed. 382–3)]

93 Bede, *In Genesim*, III.11.8–9; trans. 231–2. The connection between Nimrod and Nebuchadnezzar can be seen even in early modern texts. See, for example, Bousset's *Discours sur l'Histoire universelle* (1681), in which he marvels at the power of Nebuchadnezzar: "Think of the works he erected in Babylon! What parapets, towers, gates, and city walls arose! It seemed as if the ancient Tower of Babel was to be recreated in the prodigious height of the Temple of Bel and as if Nebuchadrezzar wanted, again, to storm the heavens. His pride, though smitten by the hand of God, nevertheless revived in his successors ... pride became [Babylon's] downfall in the end" (*Discourse on Universal History*, 324).

94 In his debasement, Nebuchadnezzar was also a figure for bestial madness in the Middle Ages: see Doob, *Nebuchadnezzar's Children*, 54–94.

beasts" (*wilddeora gewita,* 623a) in the "wasteland of animals" (*wildeora westen,* 621a); he is a "miserable creature" (*earmsceapen,* 631a), a "naked wretched wanderer" (*nacod nydgenga,* 632a), and a "strange exile and deprived of clothing" (*wundorlic wræcca and wæda leas,* 633). Nebuchadnezzar's nakedness also provides an undercurrent of sexuality to his depiction and associates him with the Curse of Ham. He acts in opposition to God's will (*ofer metodes est,* 174b): the same exact half-line used to describe the sexual transgression of the antediluvian races of Noah's day in the Old English *Genesis A*. The Old English translation of Gregory the Great's *Pastoral Care* explains that God took away Nebuchadnezzar's kingdom and "turned him into an irrational beast and thus overturned his mind and placed him among the beasts of the field; and thus by that severe punishment he lost his humanity."[95] Walter of Châtillon describes him as a "king sustained by pasture and by stream, / who bellowed in a guise transformed by sin."[96] The Middle English poem *Cleanness* emphasizes his bestial transformation even further, presenting him as half-man, half-beast:

Hair, tangled and matted, flowed all around him,
so that it fell from his shoulders to his groin ...
Hollow were his eyes and under shaggy hairs,
and all was as grey as a buzzard, with very fierce talons
that were crooked and cruel like the claw of a kite.[97]

In other traditions, Nebuchadnezzar is also known for monstrous or aberrant sexuality. A Jewish tradition explains that Nebuchadnezzar

95 *Pastoral Care,* ed. Sweet, 38: hine gehwirfde to ungesceadwisum neatum, ond swæ awende mode he hine geðidde to feldgongendum deorum; ond swæ ðy ðearlan dome he forleas his mennisce.

96 Trans. Townsend, II.600–1; Colker ed. II.515–16: Agresti uictu pastum et fluuialibus undis / Turpe fuit regem uersa mugire figura.

97 *Cleanness,* in Andrew and Waldon, eds., *Poems of the Pearl Manuscript,* lines 1689–90, 1695–7:

Faxe, fyltered and felt, floȝed hym vmbe,
Þat schad fro his schulderes to his schere-wykes,
...
Holȝe were his yȝen and vnder campe hores,
And al watz gray as þe glede, with ful grymme clawres
Þat were croked and kene as þe kyte paune.

4.1. Blake's *Nebuchadnezzar* (1795). Tate Images. Used by permission.

sodomized the kings he conquered; when he tried to sodomize Zedekiah, God saved the king by enlarging Nebuchadnezzar's penis to gigantic proportions, punishing his sexual monstrosity in an ironically appropriate fashion.[98] To push us beyond the Middle Ages in anticipation of the next chapter, I have included William Blake's haunting illustration of the bestial Nebuchadnezzar (1795), with his long facial and body hair, his hollow eyes and vacant lips, his clawed and almost reptilian feet – a throwback to the monstrous ancestry of degenerate Babylon (see Figure 4.1).[99]

98 See Goldenberg, *Curse of Ham*, 190.

99 See also Boussuet's summary of Nebuchadnezzar's transformation: "While admiring his own greatness and the beauty of Babylon, he exalts himself above humanity. God strikes him, deprives him of his understanding, and degrades him to the rank of the beasts" (*Discourse on Universal History*, 160).

The Anglo-Saxon author Ælfric of Eynsham (c. 950–1010) called the Book of Genesis a *gecyndboc*, a book of creation or begetting – a book of origins.[100] For medieval authors, Genesis described not only the creation of the physical world, but also the origin of the various human races, the earliest generations of the human family. Within this constellation of origins, the archetype of the cursed race finds its first and greatest home in Babylon. Walking through the City of Man in prehistory was the cursed race, a vital element in the foundation of Christian history. In this regard "Babylon" serves as an index for a distinctive Western Christian way of thinking about race – one in which an aberrant, cursed strain was set apart and given the protean qualities of nightmare. As I noted at the outset, this idea of transmitted sin and its role in premodern racial thinking is not the sole, exclusive mode of racial thought in the Middle Ages: it is merely one powerful element in the mix, along with climate-based theories of race and the traditions of Noachid dispersion, among others theories no doubt yet to be fully limned by scholars; all of them overlapping, sometimes no doubt supplementing each other, at other times probably residing in contradiction. My aim is more modest here: to tell the story of one dimension of Babylon's allusive meaning in the Western tradition, a tale of degeneracy that gets caught up with the broader history of race in the West. This notion of an ancient past from which a "polluted race sprang forth" to threaten the present would become an important displaced component of racial thinking in widely dispersed contexts in later centuries.[101] With degenerate Babylon, the Middle Ages handed down to later centuries a powerful archetype for the classification of races and the expression and explanation of human difference.

---

100 Ælfric, *Preface to Genesis* in *Old English Heptateuch*, ed. Marsden, I.3–7, lines 47–8. See *DOE*, s.v. "gecyndbōc."

101 Quotation from Walter of Châtillon's *Alexandreis*, the inscription and ecphrasis on the tomb of Darius' wife, depicting the Genesis story:

> THENCE EXILED CAIN DOES NOT ESCAPE THE BOW
> OF TWICE WED LAMECH. A POLLUTED RACE
> SPRINGS FORTH. VIRTUE DEPARTS. VICE THRIVES. THEY CLING
> TO SHAMEFUL LUSTS. TRUE PIETY GROWS SLACK. (trans. Townsend, IV.243–6)
>
> Inde Cain profugus bigami non effugit arcum.
> Pullulat humanum genus et polluta propago.
> Decedit uirtus, uicium succedit, adherent
> Coniugio illicito, pietas rectumque recedunt. (Colker ed. IV.194–7)

Chapter Five

The Post-Medieval Genealogy of Babylonian Degeneracy and the Cursed Race Archetype

They are come from a far country, even from Babylon.

– 2 Kings 20:14 (AV)

It is absolutely necessary, for the peace and safety of mankind, that some of earth's dark, dead corners and unplumbed depths be let alone; lest sleeping abnormalities wake to resurgent life, and blasphemously surviving nightmares squirm and splash out of their black lairs to newer and wider conquests.

– H.P. Lovecraft, *At the Mountains of Madness* (1936), 339[1]

This chapter follows the afterlife of the Babylonian cursed race archetype – degenerate Babylon and its incipient racial logic – beyond the Middle Ages, observing its supplementary interaction with modern forms of racial thought and examining its expression in literature. I illuminate this peculiar strain of medieval racial logic's sublimation within the matrix of post-medieval racial discourse and, in doing so, highlight the malleability of the cursed race archetype, demonstrating the plasticity of its enduring tropes and their sometimes conflicted internal currents, as the archetype engages in cultural work through successive historical contexts. The concept of "race" that thus emerges in this chapter is one in which race is paradoxically both fixed and fluid; in these texts, "race" is seen as an enduring human attribute (implying a sense of fixity), but is also malleable and changeable.[2]

1 All citations from *At the Mountains of Madness* are to the edition in Lovecraft, *Thing on the Doorstep*, ed. Joshi, 246–340, by page number.

2 My language here about the mutability of racial logic draws from Buell's compelling view of race in *Why This New Race*, 6–10, 37–41.

A guide for what is to come: the following elements, in various combinations, comprise the Babylonian degenerate race archetype in its displaced, post-medieval form:

- a binary contrast between a "pure" racial line and a "degenerate" branch;
- placement of the degenerate race in an isolated location;
- a backdrop of deep time, often including a corresponding interest in atavism or primitivism;
- a curse or punishment of some sort – originating in a crime or transgression and authorized by a higher power;
- somatic monstrosity and grotesque transformation of the ideal or normative human form;
- frequent association with cannibalism and with taboo sexual transgression, often expressed as a miscegenation or mixing of races;
- all of these elements of the degenerate race are (or can be), under the proper conditions, contagious or infectious in nature, threatening "purer" humans.

Babylon itself may or may not be cited explicitly in the texts to follow, but nevertheless the works in this chapter often display distinctive, telling biblical echoes or allusions. But as displacements of degenerate Babylon and the cursed race archetype, what is important and evidential in this chapter's texts is the presence of the constituent elements delineated above and their ongoing revitalization in varied textual and historical environments. Through this process, the genealogy of degenerate Babylon establishes a firm place in the imaginative spaces of the Western tradition.

Thus I illuminate a continuity between a premodern idea of a cursed race (derived, as we saw in the last chapter, from medieval traditions of Babylon and its cursed, degenerate line) and modern forms of racial thought. But is "race" an anachronistic, invalid term when discussing premodern texts and cultures?[3] It has been well established that the modern understanding of race owes much to forms of scientific and pseudoscientific racial discourse situated in the eighteenth and nineteenth centuries.[4] While acknowledging the differences between premodern

---

3 See chapter 4, page 124, note 1.

4 See, e.g., Hannaford, *Race*; Banton, *Racial Theories*. More recently, early modern scholars have challenged this chronology, arguing for the importance of even earlier periods in the history of race: see, e.g., Kidd, *Forging of Races*; Goetz, *Baptism of Early*

and modern concepts of race, the evidence in this chapter argues for a thread of continuity between the two. The discrete dimension of medieval racial thought embodied in the Matter of Babylon and treated in the previous chapter runs both parallel to and discontinuous with more modern forms of racial thought.[5] That is to say, upon the template of medieval Babylonian degeneracy and its cursed race archetype, other racial discursive practices in later historical contexts would build varied models for understanding human identity and difference.

I proceed more or less chronologically in this chapter, pursuing the reception of Cain, Ham, and their cursed Babylonian progeny, first into the early modern world of European exploration. I then move to two parallel nineteenth-century traditions incorporating the cursed race archetype: the use of the Curse of Ham in the context of American slavery, and the mix of evolutionary and pseudo-evolutionary concepts of degeneration, atavism, and regression in nineteenth-century European racial thought. We find the archetype of degenerate Babylon in both of these nineteenth-century traditions, but adapted differently according to different historical and rhetorical contexts. Having established this potent mix, I then end with the reception of this racial complex in various late nineteenth- and early twentieth-century literary adaptations, working through select pulp fiction of H.G. Wells, Edgar Rice Burroughs, and H.P. Lovecraft.

Degeneracy and the Cursed Race in the World of Early Modern Exploration

The previous chapter established that the idea of a coherent degenerate lineage of Babylon – from Cain to Nebuchadnezzar – endured as a concept

---

Virginia, 9–11; Heng pushes the concept further back to the Middle Ages, and Isaacs, *Invention of Racism* places the origin of racism in the classical world, or more specifically, what he calls "proto-racism."

5 I paraphrase Hahn here: "A robust engagement that takes 'medieval race' – as constituted by religion, geopolitics, physiognomy, color – as *at once parallel and discontinuous with more recent racial discourses* will insure that the Middle Ages does not become (remain?) an excluded Other. Whatever the pitfalls of such a hybrid enterprise, it offers the promise of placing medieval studies at a rich and contested convergence point within modern intellectual and academic cultures, of making it a productive source for both models and minute particulars in the analysis of difference, and of creating a venue in which the shaping of identities and the motives of scholarship claim urgent notice" ("Difference the Middle Ages Makes," 26; emphasis mine).

into the early modern world. In his compendium of travel accounts, Samuel Purchas (1577–1626), for example, explicitly connects Cain, Ham, and Nimrod:

> For as *Cains* posteritie, before the Floud, were called *the Sonnes of Men,* as more sauouring the things of men then of God; more industrious in humane inuentions, then religious deuotions: so by *Noahs* Curse it may appeare, and by the Nations that descended of him, that *Cham* was the first Author, after the Floud, of irreligion ... From this *Cham* came *Nimrod, the mightie hunter before the Lord;* not of innocent beasts, but of men, compelling them to his subiection ... (45)[6]

By now this is a familiar genealogy: Cain to Ham to Nimrod, and with Nimrod, of course, we arrive at Babylon. Furthermore, whether it was Cain's mark or Ham's curse, the idea of a distinctive sinful tendency was seen as endemic to this line, the sign of crime inscribed on the body and passed down to posterity. Purchas sees Cain's mark not so much as a protection (as described in the Bible), but rather, following long Christian tradition, as an enduring mark of shame: Cain was "branded also by the Lord with some *sensible marke,* to exempt him, and terrifie others, from that bloudie crueltie" (28) and thus "his bodie [was] branded to contempt and shame till his death" (29).[7] Somatically marked by his crime, Cain passes his criminality down to his descendants: for Sir Walter Raleigh (1554–1616), Cain is the "Parent of an impious Race."[8] The curse upon Cain or Ham was clearly manifest in their descendants; as Purchas notes, in "*Cham* and his posteritie we see the authors of ruine" (46).

This notion of a cursed race defined by an "inherited," somatic trait is of key importance in the post-medieval fortunes of our medieval

6 Purchas, *Purchas his pilgrimage* (London, 1613), by page number.

7 On the mark of Cain tradition, see Mellinkoff, *Mark of Cain*, esp. 22–80. Physical blemishes (e.g., leprosy, beardlessness, horns, warts, black skin, a hairy body) were assigned to Cain: "Occasionally the idea of deformity or disfigurement was exaggerated to accentuate the beastlike nature of Cain. Cain was born entirely human. Not a demon, demihuman, or monster. But his rapid descent into evil, and his lack of natural feeling so grotesquely displayed in the brother-murder, provoked interpretations that emphasized the bestial quality of his character. Motifs or themes blurring the edges between Cain seen as a beastlike man, and Cain seen as a manlike beast, appeared among the many legends enlarging the biblical story" (Mellinkoff, *Mark of Cain*, 59).

8 Raleigh, *History of the World* (London, 1614), 63.

archetype.[9] The English traveller George Best (d. 1584) includes a well-known digression on the cause of Ethiopian blackness in his account of Martin Frobisher's journeys to find the Northwest Passage to the Far East (1576–8). In the debate over whether hot climate or some other inborn trait produced black skin in some races, Best argues that the Curse of Ham is the cause of Africans' blackness through their "lineall discent" from Ham.[10] According to Best, the sin behind the curse is disobedience and sexual transgression: Noah ordered his sons and wives on the ark to "vse continencie, and abstaine from carnall copulation with their wives" (XII.124–5). But Ham, however, hoping to produce the first child born after the flood (who would therefore inherit all the newly dry earth), chose "craftily" to try to "dis-inherite the off-spring of his other two brethren" (XII.125) by impregnating his wife on the ark.[11] As a punishment, the curse falls upon Ham's son Chus (Cush), "who not onely it selfe, but all his posteritie after him should bee so blacke and lothsome, that it might remaine a spectacle of disobedience to all the worlde" (XII.125). Subsequently, Japheth's kin inherit Europe, Shem and his posterity take Asia, and Ham and his black son are relegated to the isolated desolation of Africa, "a cursed, dry, sandy, and vnfruitfull ground, fit for such a generation to inhabite in" (XII.125). Best therefore concludes that "the cause of the Ethiopians blacknesse is the curse and naturall infection of blood" and not climate (XII.125). (Note here the clear intersection of a climate-based theory of race with our Babylonian racial logic.)

This "natural infection of the blood" present in the falling-off of Noah's son is also a process of degeneration mirroring or re-enacting the biblical entropy of fallen humanity: Purchas, for example, explains that, after the flood, Noah's family "degenerated in the wicked off-spring of cursed *Cham* whose posteritie peopled a great part [of Syria]" (67). Ham's line represents a degeneration of a once-pure stock, a taint passed down to his descendants. In a discussion of Saracens, Purchas explains that the

---

9 For select studies of race in the early modern period, see Banton, *Racial Theories*, 17–43; Hannaford, *Race*, 147–84; Kidd, *Forging of Races*, 54–78; Loomba, *Shakespeare, Race, and Colonialism*, 22–74; Iyengar, *Shades of Difference*; Feerick, *Strangers in Blood*.

10 Best, *A true discourse of the late voyages of discoverie* (1578); repr in Hakluyt, *Principall Navigations, Voyages, Traffiques & Discoveries of the English Nation* (1600), ed. Goldsmid, XII.124.

11 Purchas also explicates the transgression of Ham as sexual: "*Cham*, the sonne of *Noah*, was by his father banished for particular abuse of himselfe, and publique corruption of the world, teaching and practising those vices, which before had procured the Deluge, as sodomy, incest, buggery" (471).

religion of the Arabs cannot possibly be good "when as they had so bad an Author of their stocke, *accursed Cham*" (190). So we have evidence that in the early modern world the progeny of Cain and Ham constituted a lineage stained by a great crime (sexual or murderous or disobedient) and that the punishment for this primeval crime was inscribed as a visible mark upon the body, by divine authority.

In the mental maps of early modern Europeans, where, geographically speaking, did the various offshoots of this cursed branch of humanity reside? Cain, Ham, Nimrod and their kin were all associated, in different ways, with the principle of geographic dispersion.[12] Cain, for example, was understood both as a wandering exile and as the founder of the first city (Genesis 4:16–17), provoking dual traditions: that for his crimes he wandered as an exile forever, and that he founded the earthly prototype of Augustine's City of Man.[13] In the Vulgate Genesis 4:16, Cain "went out from the face of the Lord, and dwelt as a fugitive on the earth, at the east side of Eden." The Greek Septuagint Bible, rather than designating Cain a fugitive or wanderer (*profugus*), instead explains that Cain "dwelt in the land of Nod, on the east of Eden." Jerome (340–420 CE) offered a typical explication of this verse, refuting the idea that Nod [or Naid] was a specific location, and instead asserting a figural interpretation of this "place," bringing it in line with the idea of "wandering Cain":

> *And he dwelt in the land of Naid.* What the Septuagint translated as Naid is expressed in Hebrew as Nod, and is to be interpreted as *saleuomenos*, that is, unsteady, moving here and there like waves, and of unfixed abode. The reference is not, therefore, to a land called Naid, as the mass of our people think; but God's decision is discharged in that he wandered here and there as a wanderer and a fugitive.[14]

12 See also Evans, "From the Land of Canaan to the Land of Guinea" and Braude, "Sons of Noah." Haynes notes that "readers of Genesis have construed chapters 9–11 as a thematic whole, reflecting the themes of *dispersion* and *differentiation*" (*Noah's Curse*, 5; emphasis in original).

13 On the tradition of Cain as a city-dweller and citizen see Quinones, *Changes of Cain*, 23–42 and 255–6, n. 2.

14 Jerome, *Hebrew Questions on Genesis* (*Quaestiones Hebraicae in Genesim*): *Et habitavit in terra Naid.* Quod Septuaginta *Naid* transtulerunt, in Hebraeo NOD dicitur: et interpretatur σαλευόμενος, id est, instabilis et fluctuans, ac sedis incertae. Non est igitur terra *Naid,* ut vulgus nostrorum putat: sed expletur sententia Dei, quod huc atque illuc vagus et profugus oberravit (*PL* 23.col. 945).

Jerome's explanation notes competing interpretations of Nod/Naid, but the tradition of *Cain profugus*, wandering somewhere out in the undifferentiated geographical spaces of the world, had a long life. The *Beowulf* poet, for example, when explaining the ancestry of Grendel and his mother, tells us that after his crime, Cain was outlawed (*fag*), marked by murder (*morþre gemearcod*) and fled the pleasure of human society (*man-dream fleon*) to live in the wastelands (*westen warode*) (1261b–65a). Grendel and his mother, Cain's descendants, haunt the desolate moors (*moras*, 1348b), the hills of the wolves (*wulfhleoþu*, 1358a) and the terrible paths through the fens (*frecne fengelad*, 1359a), where they walk in the tracks of exile (*wræclastas*, 1352b) like their ancestor.[15] Likewise Purchas, in the same tradition (but several hundred years later), explains that God "cursed *Cain from the earth, to be a runnagate,* and wanderer thereon" (29), doomed by "that curse of his wandring to and fro on the earth" (29). Whether or not later commentators followed Jerome's specific suggestion, the idea that Cain was a wanderer in marginal lands, in places "inaccessible and unknown to mortals," as Bede puts it, was commonplace.[16]

Ham and Nimrod were similarly associated with geographic dispersion. We have already established that Ham served as a post-diluvian analogue of Cain; correspondingly, there was also a sense that Ham, after his curse, set off for distant lands like *Cain profugus*: in the geographic dispersion of the sons of Noah, Ham and his son Cush were traditionally assigned to exotic Africa and its unknown spaces, re-enacting the wanderings of Cain out beyond the boundaries of the civilized world.[17]

15 Friedman explains that "whether they were relegated to their own sinful cities or to a wild landscape without cities, the monstrous races were early seen as exiled from the society of mankind because of innately evil dispositions" (*Monstrous Races*, 31).

16 Bede, *In Genesim*, II.4.16; trans. 149: Habitauit ergo Cain non ad orientalem plagam paradisi. Alioquin ultra hunc mundum habitaret, sed in orientalibus mundi partibus quibus in proximo est paradisus, quamuis inaccessibilis et ignotus mortalibus. (Therefore Cain did not dwell in the east side of paradise, else he would dwell beyond this world, but in the eastern parts of the world to which paradise is close at hand, although inaccessible and unknown to mortals.) The main outlines of Bede's interpretation of Cain are followed by later influential medieval exegetes from Alcuin and Rabanus Maurus to Peter Comestor: see Mellinkoff, *Mark of Cain*, 46–51. Cain's wandering also provided the template for the legend of the Wandering Jew: see Mellinkoff, *Mark of Cain*, 38–40.

17 Although traditionally Ham is given Africa, his descendants build Babylon in Asia: Luther, for example, explains that after Ham's crime "He leaves his father haughtily and goes to Babylon; there, together with his descendants, he engages in building a city and a tower, and establishes himself as lord of all Asia" (*Works*, II.175).

And of course Nimrod's people are scattered at the Tower of Babel, sundered and dispersed linguistically as well as geographically.[18] In this regard, Luther combines the dispersion of Ham and Nimrod's tower: he saw the builders of Babel specifically as Ham's descendants and explains that after the destruction of the Tower of Babel "the ungodly descendants of Ham were wretchedly scattered" (*Works*, II.221). To summarize: all three significant figures in the primeval cursed lineage of Babylon – Cain, Ham, and Nimrod – are associated with geographic spatial dispersion driven by a curse or crime: Cain wanders because of filial murder; Ham's descendants inherit Noah's curse after their forefather's transgression; Nimrod and his people offend God at the Tower of Babel. What this means is that as Europeans entered the Age of Exploration and encountered new worlds and new indigenous populations, among the varied ways they were preconditioned to explain such "new races," one important hermeneutic was to see them as leftover remnants of Babylon's cursed and scattered founders – especially when these races differed somatically from a European norm.[19] Thus the notion of the degenerate Babylonian race was displaced and given an ambiguous geographic potential, becoming part of the mix of discourses that defined non-European indigenous populations.[20]

The Post-Medieval Curse of Ham

The Curse of Ham, in particular, moved around the world in the European Age of Exploration, finding black descendants of Noah in a variety of places.[21] Noah's curse specified that "cursed be Canaan; a servant of servants shall he be unto his brethren" (Genesis 9:25); this was interpreted

18 Bede postulates that one of the possible meanings of the name "Nimrod" is "exile" (*In Genesim*, III.10.10; trans. 220–1).

19 See Banton, *Racial Theories*, 23. For the influence of the medieval/premodern worldview on early modern explorers, see Flint, *Imaginative Landscape of Christopher Columbus*; Grafton, *New Worlds, Ancient Texts*; McCoskey, *Race*, 3–4.

20 Cf. Friedman, *Monstrous Races*, 197: "First, the monstrous men of antiquity were reduced to a single figure, the hairy wild man, and second, this figure became conflated with the aboriginal people found in the New World"; see also 197–207 for general discussion.

21 On the Curse of Ham in this period see Evans, "Strange Odyssey," 34–43; Braude, "Sons of Noah," 127–42; Freedman, *Images of the Medieval Peasant*, 94–6; Goldenberg, *Curse of Ham*, 175–7; Kidd, *Forging of Races*, 67–8, 75–6; Haynes, *Noah's Curse*, 32–40; Whitford, *Curse of Ham*; Glasson, *Mastering Christianity*, 41–72.

to mean that the racial descendants of Ham – wherever they might be found – were destined to be slaves to other races, i.e., the descendants of Ham's brothers Japheth and Shem. Increasingly throughout the sixteenth and seventeenth centuries, when confronted by new-found indigenous populations, Europeans applied the Curse of Ham to native races in Africa and elsewhere.[22]

For example, in his *Historie of Travell Into Virginia Britania* (1612), William Strachey speculates that the New World was peopled by the descendants of Ham. He notes that "Cham, and his famely, were the only far Travellors, and Straglers into divers and vnknowne countries."[23] He further thinks that Ham brought with him the practice of idolatry (a sinful practice traditionally originating in Babylon, as we have seen), and so Strachey deduces that the people of this New World have for many ages worshipped false gods, and thus ultimately there is little "difference ... betweene them and bruit beasts" since they at times worship "bruit beasts, nay things more vyle, and [abhor] the inbredd motions of Nature yt self, with such headlong, and bloudy Ceremonies, of Will, and Act" (55). There is, of course, a complex mix of discourses that meet in the early modern European apprehension of indigenous populations; but to think of the "savages" they found as Ham's long-ago dispersed children – monstrous, idol-worshipping, inbred beasts – was one traditional and powerful way Europeans processed the understanding of new cultures, by accessing the Matter of Babylon.

The dispersion of the cursed race to faraway lands is represented almost like a plague or infection, as the line of Ham multiplies in the dark margins of the world. In Johannes Boemus's *Omnium Gentium Mores Leges et Ritus* (1520), translated into English by William Watreman as *The Fardle of Facions* (1555), and collected in Richard Hakluyt's *Principall Navigations* (1598–1600), Boemus, deviating from the Noachid/African

22 As Haynes states, the "constitutive elements" of the Curse of Ham (slavery and blackness) were present in the tradition of understanding Genesis right from the beginning, but the specific rhetorical application of the curse to black races began in the Early Modern period and "by the early colonial period a racialized version of Noah's curse had arrived in America" (*Noah's Curse*, 8; see also 34–5). See also Peterson, *Ham and Japheth*, 44: "The use of the story of Noah and his three sons to legitimize the enslavement of blacks in America goes back to at least the beginning of the eighteenth century."

23 Strachey, *Historie of Travell into Virginia Britania (1612)*, ed. Wright and Freund, 54 (by page number). On Strachey and race in colonial America generally see Goetz, *Baptism of Early Virginia*, esp. 23–32.

tradition, explains that after Noah's curse, Ham first went to Arabia and his progeny then filled that land until they swarmed out and scattered to the rest of the world:

> For Cham, by the reason of his naughty demeanour towarde his father, beyng constrayned to departe with his wyfe and hys chyldren, planted him selfe in that parte of Arabia, that after was called by his name. And lefte no trade of religion to his posteritie, because he none had learned of his father. Whereof it came to passe, that when in processe of tyme they ware encreased to to many for that londe: beyng sent out as it ware, swarme aftre swarme into other habitations and skatered at length into sondrie partes of the worlde (for this banysshed progeny grewe aboue measure) some fel into errours wherout thei could neuer vnsnarle themselues.[24]

Ham's "naughty demeanour towarde his father" is Watreman's oblique reference to the sexually transgressive aspect of Ham's offence and Noah's curse. The passage also references the traditional idolatry of Ham's descendants: his "posteritie" has no real religion because he left Noah's side before his father could pass on proper godly worship to him. There is a note of monstrous fecundity here as the "banysshed progeny grewe aboue measure," swarms of them scattering "into sondrie partes of the worlde." Boemus continues in this manner, explaining that Ham's swarming descendants pushed into Egypt (Africa) and beyond:

> Neyther staied that darkenesse of iniquitie in Egipte alone, but where so euer the progeny of Cham stepte in from the begynnyng, there fell true godlines, all oute of minde and a bondage to the deuell entred his place. And there neuer was countrie, mother of moe swarmes of people, then that part of Arabia, that he, and his, chase to be theirs. So greate a mischief did the vntymely banishemente of one manne, bring to the whole.[25]

Geographic isolation, half-human monstrosity, criminal transgression, sexuality, disobedience, and parodic religious worship: these are common tropes of post-medieval Babylonian degeneracy in the early modern world, and even call to mind Shakespeare's Caliban in *The Tempest* (1611), described as an "abominable monster," a "man-monster," a "savage" endowed with a "vile race" [i.e., evil hereditary disposition]; he is a slave

24 In Hakluyt, *Principall Navigations*, ed. Goldsmid, VI.43–4.
25 Hakluyt, *Principall Navigations*, ed. Goldsmid, VI.44.

who desires to populate his isolated island with little Calibans through the sexual corruption of a pure daughter guarded by a most godlike figure, Prospero, who in the end must acknowledge the thing of darkness as his.[26]

I wish to stress again that Babylon's progeny and the Curse of Ham certainly did not serve as an uncontested master narrative for all aspects of early modern European encounters with indigenous populations. Many doubted the truth of the Curse of Ham or saw its effects differently. The sceptic Sir Thomas Browne, for example, dismisses the Curse of Ham as a cause of black skin in his *Pseudodoxia Epidemica* (1672), noting the "sundry improbabilities" of the theory and deploring the ignorant tendency to resort to "Miracles" or the "insearchable hands of God," rather than philosophical reason, as explanations of puzzling phenomena.[27] Nevertheless, early modern European encounters with indigenous populations were undoubtedly important in the modern construction of race as a conceptual category. And among the mix of ideologies and imaginative mediating strategies brought to bear upon the early scene of European encounter, the ancient archetype of the degenerate race – a preconception born in the Matter of Babylon – played a role, contributing a set of related tropes that would help structure the modern idea of race.

Even a later early modern text such as Defoe's *Robinson Crusoe* (1719) exhibits similar structuring tropes and language.[28] *Robinson Crusoe* does not mention Cain, Ham, Nimrod, or Babylon; yet in the novel's representation of indigenous encounter, we can detect – like a ghostly presence – the displaced archetype of the cursed race and its biblical trappings. *Robinson Crusoe* has a fairly overt Christian subtext: after his initial shock, Crusoe enjoys an Edenic existence on his isolated island. A latter-day Adam, Crusoe meditates upon his relationship to God and his state, and, like Adam, he is the terrestrial lord of his land:

> I was remov'd from all the Wickedness of the World here. I had neither the *Lust of the Flesh, the Lust of the Eye, or the Pride of Life* [John 2:16] ... I was Lord of the whole Mannor; or if I pleas'd, I might call my self King, or Emperor

26 Shakespeare, *The Tempest*, in *The Norton Shakespeare*, ed. Greenblatt, II.2.150–1; III.2.11; I.2.361. On the complex use of the word "race" in this passage, see Loomba, *Shakespeare*, 34–5.

27 Browne, *Pseudodoxia Epidemica*, ed. Robbins, I.518–23, at 518 and 523.

28 On race in the eighteenth century, see Marshall and Williams, *The Great Map of Mankind*; Hannaford, *Race*, 187–233; Hudson, "From 'Nation' to 'Race'"; Wheeler, *Complexion of Race*; Kidd, *Forging of Races*, 79–120; Two useful anthologies include Eze, ed., *Race and the Enlightenment* and Augstein, ed., *Race: The Origins of an Idea, 1760–1850*.

> over the whole Country which I had Possession of. There were no Rivals. I had no Competitor, none to dispute Sovereignty or Command with me. (128)[29]

Crusoe rules his Edenic "domain" in this fantasy of plenitude for nearly eighteen years before he discovers the existence of savage neighbouring cannibal tribes, who periodically descend on his island to engage in their feasts.[30] When he finds "the Shore spread with Skulls, Hands, Feet, and other Bones of humane Bodies" (164–5), he is shocked by the degeneracy of the cannibals and their distance from any sort of recognizable humanity: "All my Apprehensions were bury'd in the Thoughts of such a Pitch of inhuman, hellish Brutality, and the Horror of the Degeneracy of Humane Nature" (165). Crusoe sees himself as the antithesis of the cannibals and their degeneracy: after he vomits in revulsion and collects himself, he "gave God Thanks that had cast my first Lot in a Part of the World, where I was distinguish'd from such dreadful Creatures as these" (165). He believes that Nature has given him a particular "Aversion ... to these hellish Wretches" (166). In disgust, Crusoe distinguishes himself from the degenerate cannibals; his island world, like the dichotomous antediluvian world of Genesis before the flood, is a binary society, home to two races: the upright and godly (Crusoe) set against these degenerate "Monsters" and "their cruel bloody Entertainment" (168).

Furthermore, Crusoe is initially horrified to think that this savage race had been left alone to fester and degenerate in an unknown corner of the world for ages and ages. He explains that his Passions

> were at first fir'd by the Horror I conceiv'd at the unnatural Custom of that People of the Country, who it seems had been suffer'd by Providence in his wise Disposition of the World, to have no other Guide than that of their own abominable and vitiated Passions; and consequently were left, and perhaps had been so for some Ages, to act such horrid Things, and receive such dreadful Customs, as nothing but Nature entirely abandon'd of Heaven, and acted by some hellish Degeneracy, could have them run into (170).[31]

---

29 Defoe, *Robinson Crusoe*, ed. Crowley, by page number.

30 He then divides his time on the island into two distinct periods: the "happy Posture" of his initial Edenic years, and the fallen period, the "Life of Anxiety, Fear and Care" that he lives ever since he saw the footprint in the sand (196). On the connection between cannibalism and nineteenth-century ideas of race see Brantlinger, *Taming Cannibals*, 27–45.

31 Cf. the very similar language in Thomas Newton's *Dissertations on the Prophecies* (1754), a bestseller in Britain and America, here on the fulfillment of the Curse of Ham in the enslavement of Africans: "The whole continent of Africa was peopled principally

One of the keywords for us in this passage, as always, is *degeneracy*. Left alone in geographic isolation "for some Ages"; left without religion and instead guided only by their "abominable and vitiated Passions," this branch of the human race has degenerated from the common human stock into "unnatural Custom," much like Strachey and Boemus's vision of the children of Ham. All these traditional elements – basic tropes of the cursed race archetype – operate nevertheless under the rule of Providence and God's "wise Disposition of the World." In this telltale language we detect the sublimated Christian archetype of Babylonian degeneracy.[32] At its heart, the archetype of the cursed race is powerful because it is a doubled narrative pattern: a narrative of exile and return – the dark, menacing Other returned from the beyond; as well as a narrative of descent – a fall or degeneration from a pure state of plenitude.

In the next two sections of this chapter, I track the Babylon archetype of the cursed race in two later parallel traditions. The first concerns the role that the Curse of Ham played in nineteenth-century America, in the southern justification for American slavery. The second is the rise of criminal anthropology and related ideas (evolution, atavism, and degeneration, primarily) in nineteenth-century Europe. These are vast subjects, but the purpose here is not to provide comprehensive analysis, but rather to show the influence of degenerate Babylon within these discursive domains, to weave a new, very long thread into the conceptual understanding of these phenomena. In both cases, on either side of the Atlantic, the ancient archetype of the cursed race serves as a hermeneutic strategy to process ideas of race and human difference in

---

by the children of Ham: and for how many ages have the better parts of that country lain under the dominion of the Romans, and then of the Saracens, and now of the Turks? in what wickedness, ignorance, barbarity, slavery, misery live most of the inhabitants? and of the poor negroes how many hundreds every year are sold and bought like beasts in the market, and are conveyed from one quarter of the world to do the work of beasts in another?" (quoted in Glasson, *Mastering Christianity*, 66).

32 In a pattern we will see later, this degeneracy is infectious, as Crusoe begins to take on some savage characteristics and "go native." His time on the island begins to transform him: his skin has grown darker; he trims his long beard and mustache "into a large Pair of *Mahometan* Whiskers, such as I had seen worn by some *Turks*" (150); they "were of a Length and Shape monstrous enough, and such as in *England* would have pass'd for frightful" (150). He hides from the cannibals in a fortified cave, comparing himself to the giants of old: "I fancy'd my self now like one of the ancient Giants, which are said to live in Caves, and Holes, in the Rocks, where none could come at them" (179).

nineteenth-century contexts charged with new historical pressures and imperatives.[33]

Degeneracy and the Curse of Ham in Nineteenth-Century America

In *Blood Meridian, or The Evening Redness in the West,* McCarthy's baroque and bloody 1985 novel set in the nineteenth-century American Southwest – a novel as eloquent in its spare biblical diction as it is horrific in its depiction of racial Indian wars and massacres along the Texas-Mexico border – the Satanic character Judge Holden at one point mediates an encounter between a black character and a Mexican sergeant. The Judge, the narrator tells us, "hove up before the black":

> That dark vexed face. He studied it and he drew the sergeant forward the better for him to observe and then he began a laborious introduction in spanish. He sketched for the sergeant a problematic career of the man before them, his hands drafting with a marvelous dexterity the shapes of what varied paths conspired here in the ultimate authority of the extant – as he told them – like strings drawn together through the eye of a ring. He adduced for their consideration references to the children of Ham, the lost tribes of Israelites, certain passages from the Greek poets, anthropological speculations as to the propagation of the races in their dispersion and isolation through the agency of geological cataclysm and an assessment of racial traits with respect to climate and geographical influences.[34]

McCarthy's allusion to the Ham story and its role in "the propagation of the races in their dispersion and isolation" is historically accurate because Curse and its narrative of Babylonian degeneracy found a firm footing in nineteenth-century America.[35] The Curse of Ham was

---

33 For a selection of the vast scholarship on race in the nineteenth century, see Hannaford, *Race,* 235–76; Banton, *Racial Theories,* 44–97; Stepan, *Idea of Race in Science,* 1–110; Brantlinger, *Dark Vanishings,* 17–44, 164–88; Kidd, *Forging of Races,* 121–202; Brantlinger, *Taming Cannibals.*

34 McCarthy, *Blood Meridian,* 84–5.

35 See Wood, *Arrogance of Faith,* 84–111; Goldenberg, *Curse of Ham,* 142–4; Haynes, *Noah's Curse*; Peterson, *Ham and Japheth*; Kidd, *Forging of Races,* 138–41; Goetz, *Baptism of Early Virginia,* 21–30. Peterson's book is particularly rich in citing numerous primary nineteenth-century American sources that use the Curse of Ham. On the understanding of race in nineteenth-century America generally, see Hannaford, *Race,*

an important rhetorical justification for American slavery in the south, repeated and developed in a vast swath of texts.[36]

Using the Bible to justify slavery and unequal race relations was a common tactic in nineteenth-century America.[37] Both Ham and Nimrod figure prominently in biblical pro-slavery arguments. In southern eyes, the sins both figures held in common were rebellion and disobedience – Ham transgressing Noah's paternal authority, and Nimrod fomenting rebellion against God at the Tower of Babel; by analogy, the disobedient black slave was thus re-enacting the ancestral sin of his racial forbearers. For example, Ham was firmly connected to Babel, Babylon, and disobedience in popular American works such as Jerome Holgate's 1860 novel *Noachidae, or Noah and His Descendants.*[38] In this turgid retelling of Noah's posterity, it is the sons of Ham that build a tower and "the first great city after the flood: namely, Babylon" (265). The text places a great deal of emphasis on Ham's initial disobedience and the resulting rebelliousness of his offspring down to Nimrod. In the American context, the rebellious narratives of Ham and Nimrod were thus seen as a template for white owner/black slave relations, or white/black relations generally: the divinely sanctioned father and his intransigent, cursed, not-quite-human offspring – much like mighty Prospero and monstrous Caliban.[39] Moreover, for the American southerner Benjamin Palmer (as for Johannes Boemus in the sixteenth century), the disobedient race of Ham – in this case, black African slaves – resembles a plague: "The descendants of Ham, on the contrary, in whom the sensual and corporeal appetites predominate, are driven like an infected race beyond the deserts of Sahara, where under a glowing sky nature harmonizes with their brutal and savage disposition."[40] In the

---

270–2; Banton, *Racial Theories*, 48–62; Wood, *Arrogance of Faith*; Winthrop Jordan, *White Over Black*; Smedley and Smedley, *Race in North America*, 73–249.

36 Goldenberg explains that "[a]s the Black slave trade moved to England and then America, the Curse of Ham moved with it" (*Curse of Ham*, 175). He calls the Curse the "single greatest justification for Black slavery for more than a thousand years" (1).

37 Haynes, for example, notes the "perennial American tendency to apply stories from the postdiluvian chapters of Genesis to the problem of 'race' relations" (*Noah's Curse*, 4); this is also the central thesis of Kidd, *Forging of Races* and Wood, *Arrogance of Faith.*

38 Buffalo: Breed, Butler, 1860; by page numbers. On Holgate see Haynes, *Noah's Curse*, 107–11.

39 See Haynes, *Noah's Curse*, 99–101 on miscegenation as a form of disorder/rebellion associated with the Ham/Nimrod myth in the American south.

40 Benjamin Palmer, *Our Historic Mission, An Address Delivered before the Eunomian and Phi Mu Societies of La Grange Synodical College, July 7 1858* (New Orleans: True Witness

context of American southern pro-slavery ideology, it was the divine duty of the sons of Japheth – the white race – to curb such "sensual and corporeal appetites" and tend to this "infected race" through the divinely sanctioned institution of slavery.

The Curse of Ham was not a fringe idea or in any way obscure in this historical context. Pro-slavery advocates instead saw the story as one of *central* Christian importance; as one pro-slavery pamphlet puts it: "The fall, or defection of Ham, considered in all its results, is one of the most, if not the most, important event to [sic] the human race that has transpired since the flood; save, always, the advent and death of the Saviour, the great event of the universe."[41] In a typical formulation, the same pamphlet proclaims that black slaves, the "posterity of Ham," stand "lower in their position in the human family" than white races.[42] The pamphlet argues that if God sold even his beloved Israel into the "hands of wicked nations" for their transgressions, then

> Has He not the same right to dispose of the services of the degenerate children of a rebellious son [i.e., Africans] to their more righteous brethren [i.e., white Europeans and Americans]? If God in His wisdom sees fit to do this, as His Word declares He has done it, has He not both the power and grace to adapt these degenerate children to the condition He has prepared for them?[43]

In text after text, the Curse of Ham functions as a justification for the American enslavement of these "degenerate children." And once established as an element of slavery ideology, it of course merged with other elements of nineteenth-century racial discourse such as (pseudo)scientific thought.

The influential proslavery writer and physician Samuel Cartwright (1793–1863), for example, combined the biblical Curse of Ham with nineteenth-century biological science.[44] Cartwright cites the supposed

---

Office, 1859), 4–5; quoted in Haynes, *Noah's Curse*, 129; on Palmer see Haynes, *Noah's Curse*, 125–60.

41 Anonymous, *African Servitude: When, Why, and by Whom Instituted. By Whom, and How Long, Shall It Be Maintained* (NY: Davies & Kent, 1860), 1–18; excerpt repr. in Peterson, *Ham and Japheth*, "Appendix," 141–58, quotation at 147. On *African Servitude* see Haynes, *Noah's Curse*, 72–3.

42 *African Servitude*, in Peterson, *Ham and Japheth*, 152.

43 *African Servitude*, in Peterson, *Ham and Japheth*, 153.

44 On Cartwright, see Peterson, *Ham and Japheth*, 72.

physiological differences of African Americans to buttress his racist claims; among many examples, he argued that black people could work in the hot sun because they possessed a "cutilagenous membrane" that protected their eyes. And in the following remarkable passage from one of Cartwright's medical treatises, we see the terrible congruence between two sources of authority: nineteenth-century scientific concepts of race and the Bible:

> When the original Hebrew of the Bible is interrogated, we find, in the significant meaning of the original name of the negro [i.e., the name "Ham," in Genesis], the identical fact set forth, which the knife of the anatomist at the dissecting-table has made appear; as if the revelations of anatomy, physiology and history, were a mere re-writing of what Moses wrote.[45]

A chilling merger of scientific and religious language: the knife of the anatomist at the dissecting table and the Book of Genesis itself, each peeling back the flesh to find the same obvious truth beneath – the degenerate inhumanity of Ham's progeny.[46] According to Cartwright, the "revelations of anatomy, physiology and history" are a "mere re-writing" of Ham's story and the cursed race archetype. Here, in miniature, we see the incorporation of the biblical Babylonian archetype of degeneracy into a nascent modern "scientific" discourse of race.

An address from 1859 linking Cain and Ham gives us one final – and enduring – example of our archetype and its salient elements in the context of American race relations:

> You see some classes of the human family that are black, uncouth, uncomely, disagreeable and low in their habits, wild, and seemingly deprived of nearly all the blessings of the intelligence that is generally bestowed upon mankind. The first man that committed the odious crime of killing one of his brethren will be cursed the longest of any one of the children of Adam. Cain slew his brother. Cain might have been killed, and that would have put a termination to that line of human beings. This was not to be, and the Lord put a mark upon him, which is the flat nose and black skin. Trace mankind

45 Samuel A. Cartwright, "Diseases and Peculiarities of the Negro Race, Part 1," *De Bow's Review* 11 (July 1851): 64–9, at 68–9. On the merger of science and the Curse of Ham see Peterson, *Ham and Japheth*, 75–6, 134.

46 The phrase "what Moses wrote" refers to the traditional idea that Moses wrote the Pentateuch (including Genesis) through God's inspiration.

> down to after the flood, and then another curse is pronounced upon the same race – that they should be the "servant of servants"; and they will be, until that curse is removed; and the Abolitionists cannot help it, nor in the least alter that decree. How long is that race to endure the dreadful curse that is upon them? That curse will remain upon them, and they never can hold the Priesthood or share in it until all the other descendants of Adam have received the promises and enjoyed the blessings of the Priesthood and the keys thereof.[47]

These are the words of Brigham Young (1801–77), Mormon leader of the Church of Latter-Day Saints and founder of Salt Lake City. All of our ancient archetypal elements are here: a distinct wild class of the "human family" in a line stretching all the way back to Cain through Ham. This injunction against anyone of African descent holding the priesthood was a part of Mormon orthodoxy until the doctrine was changed by a church revelation in 1978. A long history, indeed.

The adaptive afterlife of the Curse of Ham in nineteenth-century America shows how the cursed race archetype could operate with devastating real-life effects in a specific historical context. The same archetype can be found in a very different historical context – the discourse of nineteenth-century European evolution, criminology, and degeneration.

Science and Degeneracy in the Nineteenth Century

Of the many pleasures to be found in Joseph Conrad's novel *The Secret Agent* (1907; set in 1886), not least is the doomed character of "poor Stevie" – the young mentally impaired brother-in-law of the fatuous and inept secret agent of the title – Adolf Verloc. Although Stevie is perhaps one of the few sympathetic characters in this dark and ironic work, nevertheless he is blown to bits in a botched attempt to detonate the Greenwich Observatory. Prior to his demise, Stevie – his impairment distinguished somatically by "the vacant droop of his lower lip" (7) – spends his days staying out of the way in the Verloc household.[48]

The ex-medical student and conspirator Alexander Ossipon looks Stevie over early in the novel and judges the boy's habits "perfectly typical ... Typical of this form of degeneracy" (34); when asked to elaborate what

---

47 Brigham Young, "Intelligence, etc." (1859), 290–1. On the Mormons and the Curse of Ham see Kidd, *Forging of Races*, 229–34.

48 Conrad, *Secret Agent*, ed. Lyon, by page numbers.

he means by a "degenerate," he explains "That's what he may be called scientifically. Very good type too, altogether, of that sort of degenerate. It's enough to glance at the lobes of his ears. If you read Lombroso – " (34). Ossipon here invokes Cesare Lombroso (1835–1909), the famed nineteenth-century Italian criminologist, a pioneer in the study of criminal psychology.[49] Lombroso was a highly influential physiognomist and phrenologist – he believed that the scientific observation and classification of physical details could reveal categories and types of criminal essence. Here he describes the revelation he had when examining the skull of a famous Italian criminal:

> This was not merely an idea, but a revelation. At the sight of that skull, I seemed to see all of a sudden, lighted up as a vast plain under a flaming sky, the problem of the nature of the criminal – an atavistic being who reproduces in his person the ferocious instincts of primitive humanity and the inferior animals. Thus were explained anatomically the enormous jaws, high cheek-bones, prominent superciliary arches, solitary lines in the palms, extreme size of the orbits, handle-shaped or sessile ears found in criminals, savages and apes, insensibility to pain, extremely acute sight, tattooing, excessive idleness, love of orgies, and the irresistible craving for evil for its own sake, the desire not only to extinguish life in the victim, but to mutilate the corpse, tear its flesh, and drink its blood.[50]

Regardless of Lombroso's rhetoric of new-found, original discovery here (but expressed, we should note, with at least a hint of religious language, as a "revelation"), we nevertheless see the familiar elements of our ancient archetype: crime, somatic deformity (and the corresponding contrast with a "normal," "pure" body); deep time (expressed through the concept of atavism); sexual transgression, and even cannibalism. Lombroso argued that such criminal degenerate traits were inborn, inherited, essential, and that such degeneracy was inscribed visibly on the body. Degenerate criminals were an evolutionary throwback to an

---

49 See Pick, *Faces of Degeneration* for a lucid history of criminal "degeneration" and related ideas (e.g., cretinism) in France, Italy and England, as well as analysis of key figures such as Lombroso, Bénédict Augustin Morel, Charles Féré, Havelock Ellis, Henry Maudsley, Max Nordau; on degeneration and Conrad's fiction see further Pick, *Faces of Degeneration*, 160–2.

50 "The Criminal," *Putnam's Magazine* 7 (1910): 793–6; repr. in Horton and Rich, eds. *Criminal Anthropological Writings of Cesare Lombroso*, 343–9, at 345.

earlier stage of human development; in his words above, the criminal is "an atavistic being who reproduces in his person the ferocious instincts of primitive humanity and the inferior animals." The criminal was, in effect, nothing less than a different species of humanity altogether, bearing the enduring marks of an earlier, primeval phase of creation. The influential *Encyclopedia Britannica* (11th ed., 1910–11) summarizes Lombroso's conclusions in a similar fashion: criminals display a "higher percentage of physical, nervous and mental anomalies" than the "non-criminal" population; this is "due partly to degeneration, partly to atavism. The criminal is a *special type of the human race*, standing midway between the lunatic and the savage" (emphasis added).[51] Max Nordau (1849–1923) asserts in his popular and influential German study *Degeneration* (*Entartung*, 1892; first English trans. 1895) – a book he dedicates to Lombroso – that "the cell of the degenerate is formed a little differently from that of sane men."[52] Such language represents a pseudoscientific, biological fumbling towards modern ideas of race and ethnicity, but it also, unknowingly, replicates and transmits the Babylonian cursed race archetype.

The atavistic criminality of this "special type of the human race" could be ameliorated and the savage impulses tamed, but they were always ready to break free. As Lombroso states in *Criminal Man* (*L'uomo delinquente*, 1876; first English trans. 1911):

> These facts clearly prove that the most horrendous and inhuman crimes have a biological, atavistic origin in those animalistic instincts that, although smoothed over by education, the family, and fear of punishment, resurface instantly under given circumstances. These immediate causes include illness, the weather, bad examples, and a sort of spermatic inebriation induced by excessive continence. This last factor explains why criminal behavior is common at the time of puberty in savage individuals or in those forced into a solitary or celibate life, such as priests, shepherds, and soldiers.[53]

Further, such criminal behaviour caused by the "resurfacing of animalistic instincts" was most often found in urban populations; the city itself, the Babylon of this world, was a bad influence. Criminality was an inherited

51 *Encyclopedia Britannica*, 11th ed. (1910–11), XVI.936, s.v. "Lombroso, Cesare." To be fair, this entry (and the entry on criminology) is also somewhat critical of Lombroso: see also s.v. "Criminology" (VII.464–5); Pick, *Faces of Degeneration*, 189.

52 Nordau, *Degeneration* (English trans. 1895; repr. 1993), 253.

53 Lombroso, *Criminal Man*, trans. Gibson and Rafter, 91.

disease, a pathology that revealed the mark of an earlier state of human development on the subject – a displaced curse of Ham or mark of Cain transposed to a new Babylon of the nascent world of modernity. Lombroso's atavism is a discourse of evolutionary classification; as such it asserts difference and continuity at the same time. The criminal atavistic human is different in a distinctive visible way; yet the difference itself finds its own place in an overall structure of temporal continuity. On the scale of human types, from noble and civilized to savage and primitive, the criminal fits here – validating the entire conceptual structure of classification and distinction, like a brick in a wall.

In the anthropological work of Lombroso and his contemporaries in Europe and England, we can see the origins of nineteenth-century racial ideologies. But as much as his ideas are situated synchronically in the worlds of nineteenth-century science and racial discourse, Lombroso's criminal anthropology still owes something to our Babylonian archetype and its diachronic genealogy. Lombroso would no doubt be appalled to hear a hypothesis that his ideas were structured by medieval concepts; he believed in scientific progress and looked upon the Middle Ages as a dark time of savage atavism. But one should remember that the scientists of the nineteenth century were also general men of letters and their intellectual backgrounds and methods included, as a matter of course, a deep grounding in the Bible, classical culture, and even medieval literature. Although Lombroso rejects the Middle Ages as an earlier stage of human development, he nonetheless, like other scientists of the period (such as Freud), makes frequent use of literary and historical examples from the medieval and classical worlds to enable his arguments. For example, in his collaborative book with Guglielmo Ferrero, *Criminal Woman, the Prostitute, and the Normal Woman* (*La donna delinquente, la prostituta e la donna normale*, 1893), he argues that female promiscuity was a feature of more primitive phases of human development, a defining element of earlier, more savage, and less advanced races and civilizations. Thus the modern prostitute is exhibiting atavistic behaviour, or is, in fact, herself a genetic throwback to an earlier era of human development:

> In the ancient days of civilized people, we find the same phenomena that we find today among savages: prostitution in all its forms. Prostitution was especially widespread in early times, which clearly confirms that modesty and matrimony are a late product of evolution.[54]

---

54 Lombroso and Ferrero, *Criminal Woman*, trans. Rafter and Gibson, 102.

It is no accident that Lombroso draws his first example of this atavistic prostitution from Herodotus's familiar description of Babylon: in Lombroso's words, "According to Herodotus, Babylonian women were obligated to go at least once to the temple of Venus and abandon themselves to a stranger; they were forbidden to return home until a foreigner had thrown coins in their laps and invited them to have intercourse outside the holy place" (102). Lombroso's use of Babylon here, via Herodotus, is a small but telling signal that, as much as his theories purport to be progressive, modern, and scientific, breaking away from the ignorance of the past, powerful premodern rhetorical traditions nevertheless still help structure his thought. Like the early modern encounter with the New World, nineteenth-century degeneration is a concept defined by a complex mix of ideologies, but we can nevertheless see the congruence between "native" nineteenth-century conceptions of degeneracy and our inherited paradigm of Babylonian degeneracy.

Fictive Adaptations of the Degenerate Race: Wells, Burroughs, Lovecraft

I turn now to three popular, influential authors and their adaptation of the entire genealogy we have constructed in this and in the previous chapter. At the end of the nineteenth and beginning of the twentieth centuries, H.G. Wells, Edgar Rice Burroughs, and H.P. Lovecraft inherited the rich blend of materials comprising the cursed race archetype, a model deriving from biblical and medieval texts, and then augmented by ingredients from the other traditions in this chapter. These authors, in turn, would pass down the transformed, adapted archetype to literature and popular cultural forms that endure to the present.

The fiction of H.G. Wells (1866–1946) gives us literary examples of the cursed race archetype, responding in complex ways to the discourse of nineteenth-century evolution, atavism, regression, and degeneracy.[55] In *The Island of Dr. Moreau* (1896), the shipwrecked protagonist, the naturalist Edward Prendick, discovers a horrific mongrelized community of

55 The scholarly literature on Darwin and evolution in nineteenth-century culture is enormous and I include here only selected studies that have guided my understanding: Bowler, *Evolution: The History of an Idea*; Young, *Darwin's Metaphor*; Levine, *Darwin and the Novelists*; Hannaford, *Race*, 272–6, 277–326; Banton, *Racial Theories*, 81–116; Beer, *Darwin's Plots*; Brantlinger, *Dark Vanishings*, 17–44, 164–88; Larson, *Evolution: The Remarkable History of a Scientific Theory*. See also above, notes 33 and 35.

"foul creatures" (80) on an isolated island – a marginal setting typical of the cursed race tradition.[56] These foul creatures are the experiments of the mad Dr. Moreau: animals that have been shaped, mixed, and transformed through surgery and vivisection, until they are something more than animal, but less than human. Moreau explains that he alters the "most intimate structure" of his creatures through his "art" (81).

In his isolated kingdom, Moreau very deliberately has been playing God and, like God, has created a new race – a race of unclassifiable beings.[57] Whatever the beast-men are, like Grendel and the kin of Cain they are monstrous ontological conundrums, not quite men, not fully monsters: as Moreau states: "The thing before you is no longer an animal, a fellow-creature, but a problem" (85). Although beasts in origin, they are clearly almost human; their community is, Moreau explains "a kind of travesty of humanity" (89). The beast-men live under the semblance of humanity, but there "is a kind of upward striving in them, part vanity, part waste sexual emotion, part waste curiosity" (90). Indeed, by the end of the story it is clear that there is not much separating human and animal, as Prendick concludes: "A strange persuasion came upon me that, save for the grossness of the line, the grotesqueness of the forms, I had here before me the whole balance of human life in miniature, the whole interplay of instinct, reason, and fate, in its simplest form" (109). As an adaptation of the cursed race archetype, Moreau's beast-people are monstrous beings created by a higher power, degenerating in both form and essence out beyond civilization, in an isolated corner of the world.

But regression from beast-men back to beasts is a problem: Moreau cannot keep his liminal creations from slipping back down the evolutionary ladder.[58] Attempting to maintain their pseudo-humanity, the beast-men

---

56 Wells, *Island of Dr. Moreau*, ed. Lightman, by page numbers.

57 Nineteenth-century ideas of race and evolution clearly inform the story in many ways: for example, as appropriate for a naturalist, Prendick refers in passing to the "negroid type" (86) of race and the "coarser Hebrew type" (98).

58 Cf. the twelfth-century Middle High German *Genesis*: "Adam had commanded his children, upon their lives to avoid certain herbs, that they [i.e., the descendants of Cain] might not thereby degenerate in their nature; his command disregarded, their nature they lost. The children which they bore were various; some had heads like a dog, some had mouths on their breasts, eyes on their shoulders, and had to live without heads. Some had one foot which was great and large, who straightaway ran into the woods like a beast; some brought forth children that walked on all fours like cattle. Some lost altogether their beautiful complexion; they became black and

establish a parodic religion and revere "the Law," a set of twisted religious precepts they chant in a famous "mad litany":

> Not to go on all-Fours; *that* is the Law. Are we not Men?
> Not to suck up Drink; *that* is the Law. Are we not Men?
> Not to eat Flesh or Fish; *that* is the Law. Are we not Men?
> Not to claw Bark of Trees; *that* is the Law. Are we not Men?
> Not to chase other Men; *that* is the law. Are we not Men? (65)

This mock-religious liturgy is a corrupted and parodic Christianity, a latter-day Babylonian idolatry practiced by the cursed race. The inhuman creatures here engage in the degenerate worship of a false God: namely Moreau himself, whom the monstrous race venerates as a dark God of pain and suffering presiding over a hellish domain of creation – Moreau's laboratory, the "House of Pain" where the beast-men are created.

We can see the fusion of premodern and modern traditions here. The beast-men resemble the premodern cursed children of Ham, following an idolatrous false religion in their monstrous rites. If Moreau's creatures lose even this tenuous connection to humanity, they will slide back into the atavism of bestial behaviour, like Lombroso's nineteenth-century criminals. Moreau explains that although the beast-men strive to keep their humanity, they continually regress: "As soon as my hand is taken from them the beast begins to creep back, begins to assert itself again" (89). Moreau's quest is to drive out the beast and, like God, create a new, pure race; but this doomed parody of creation is based on cruelty and the pain of vivisection: "Each time I dip a living creature into the bath of burning pain, I say: this time I will burn out all the animal, this time I will make a rational creature of my own. After all, what is ten years? Man has been a hundred thousand in the making" (89). As the creatures struggle to stay human, their repressed degeneracy manifests in various ways, for example transgressive sexuality: we are told the creatures habitually "attempted public outrages upon the institution of

---

terrible, there was nothing like them; their eyes were gleaming all the time, the teeth in their mouths were long; whenever they showed them they frightened the devil. Such life left the abandoned ones to all those who came after them; whatsoever inner nature the former had, such an outer nature the latter had to have" (quoted in Orchard, *Pride and Prodigies,* 72).

monogamy" (145).[59] Eventually one of his own creations kills Moreau, and subsequently Prendick escapes from the island after living alone with the beast-men for several months, during which time they finally revert all the way back to beasts.[60] Our genealogy of Babylonian degeneracy allows us to better understand the long traditions behind a work like *The Island of Dr. Moreau*: how the book speaks both to the active concerns of its immediate historical moment, but also how it fits in a longer story about the nature of the human race.

In *The Time Machine* (1895) Wells's time-travelling scientist/protagonist journeys forward from the nineteenth century to the year 802,701, only to find humanity has regressed and split into two distinct species under the pressure of evolution – the gentle, beautiful, and intellectually vacant Eloi, dwelling above ground; and the savage, monstrous, cunning Morlocks, dwelling below ground. While both races have regressed in their distinct ways, the Morlocks are an adaptation of our degenerate race archetype, analogous to Moreau's beast-men. The Morlocks are a "subterranean ... new race" (47), the "inhuman sons of men" (62) and "nauseatingly inhuman" (55).[61] In their underground domain they have evolved grotesque ape-like white bodies and large lidless eyes "like the white fish of the Kentucky caves" (47). The Morlocks are also cannibals, feeding off the Eloi in a grim parasitic social structure of the far future. The time-traveller muses upon the separation of the two new races and their social interdependence:

> But, clearly, the old order was already in part reversed. The Nemesis of the delicate ones was creeping on apace. Ages ago, thousands of generations ago, man had thrust his brother man out of the ease and sunshine. And now that

59 The novel's scene of the speaking of the Law also implies that there are further prohibitions, including one on animal sexuality: "And so from the prohibition of these acts of folly, on to the prohibition of what I thought then were the maddest, most impossible and most indecent things one could imagine" (65). The various film versions of the novel adapt these ideas in somewhat different ways. The classic 1932 film adaptation (*Island of Lost Souls*, dir. Erle C. Kenton) plays with the theme of sexual miscegenation, as Moreau plans to mate Parker (i.e., Prendick) with the panther-woman Lota and thus produce animal-human hybrids. Other film versions include *The Island of Dr. Moreau* (dir. Don Taylor, 1977) and *The Island of Dr. Moreau* (dir. John Frankenheimer, 1996).

60 In the film versions, the beast-men rise up against Moreau in the end and kill him by subjecting him to vivisection in his own lab.

61 Wells, *The Time Machine*, ed. Parrinder, by page number.

brother was coming back – changed! Already the Eloi had begun to learn one old lesson anew. They were becoming reacquainted with Fear. (58)[62]

Wells's novella is an influential classic of early science fiction. Yet in a passage such as this – with its fearful return of the evil brother, long ago separated from the "family of man," exiled to the dark places of the world, and now returning as a Nemesis – we see the archetype of Babylonian degeneracy, operating imaginatively within the nineteenth-century discourse of evolution.

Although the nineteenth-century discourse of race generally saw such degenerate traits as inherited and essential characteristics, literary adaptations often suggest that the racial degeneracy is (or could be) catching and infectious.[63] For example, Wells clearly intended *The Island of Dr. Moreau* in part as a moral fable about inherent human savagery and the latent bestiality within all human beings. Accordingly, Prendick, of pure human stock, has not escaped his encounter with the degenerate race unscathed. As the beast-people slowly revert to animals after Moreau's death, Prendick himself takes on bestial qualities, undergoing "strange changes" as he describes it: tan skin beneath his tattered clothes, long and matted hair; he notes that even after his rescue: "I am told that even now my eyes have strange brightness, a swift alertness of movement" (146). When Prendick returns to civilization, he finds himself seeing "the Beast" in all the civilized passers-by; and he no longer quite belongs to the human community: "I was almost as queer to men as I had been to the Beast People. I may have caught something of the natural wildness of my companions" (154).[64]

Using Wells's influential narratives as typical examples, we can abstract certain elements of the cursed race archetype in its late nineteenth-century form as it moves into twentieth-century popular literature and culture. The basic shape of this abstracted narrative runs as follows.

---

62 Quinones connects the Morlocks and Eloi to the Cain and Abel tradition (*Changes of Cain*, 201–5).

63 See Brantlinger, *Taming Cannibals*, 65–85 (chapter 3: "Going Native in Nineteenth-Century History and Literature") for background to the common anxiety that whites would "go native" and be infected with savage traits in a native context. On atavism in late Victorian Gothic literature see Mighall, *Geography of Victorian Gothic Fiction*, 130–65 (chapter 4: "Atavism: A Darwinian Nightmare").

64 When Prendick is forced to say the Words of the Law, he explains that "[s]uperficially the *contagion* of these brute men was upon me, but deep down within me laughter and disgust struggled together" (65–6; emphasis added).

A representative of civilized humanity, usually male and often in some way an embodiment of science and rationality, travels to a marginal or hidden place. This place may be any relatively unexplored, occluded or enclosed geographic location: an island, a mountain range, a rural locale, a city's "underworld," subterranean spaces, even outer space. What is essential, however, is the location's spatial separation from mainstream human civilization.[65] In this marginal zone the protagonist encounters the degenerate cursed race – often represented as ancient or old, with ties to the deep past and thus isolated or hidden from the rest of the world, left to fester/degenerate/evolve with hideous results. Further, the cursed race is usually defined by somatic mutation, often a mark of divine punishment, or (in a displacement of such divine power) the work of a (pseudo)scientific evolutionary processes. Their degenerate monstrosity is an inherited trait, and the race is usually defined by sexual deviance, as well as cannibalism and other taboo somatic practices. The degenerate race horrifies and fascinates the civilized protagonist, who falls into danger and then escapes, but not before running the risk of infection by their tainted degeneracy, even if (*contra* logic), the protagonist is not of the same racial "stock." The protagonist then generally returns to mainstream civilization, a changed man or woman. A host of authors in early twentieth-century adventure, fantasy, science fiction and horror literature use this narrative template for their work; among the most influential for later twentieth- and twenty-first century cultural forms were Edgar Rice Burroughs and H.P. Lovecraft.

The fame of Edgar Rice Burroughs (1875–1950) rests on his creation of Tarzan and a large, influential corpus of work in adventure, fantasy, and science fiction. In his various fictional worlds, each the subject of many novels – the Tarzan books, the Pellucidar series, the John Carter of Mars saga, and others – Burroughs often dramatizes the contrast between civilization and savagery. In his series of novellas that comprise *The Land that Time Forgot* (1924) he creates an isolated setting for an exploration of the dynamics of evolution adapted to early twentieth-century popular adventure fiction.[66] In the novel, the lost island continent of Caprona (or,

65 In Farah Mendlesohn's taxonomy, this pattern resembles a "portal-quest fantasy" (*Rhetorics of Fantasy*, 1–58).

66 *The Land That Time Forgot, The People That Time Forgot, Out of Time's Abyss*, published first as serial fiction in *Blue Book Magazine* in 1918; published together as a collected trilogy under the title *The Land That Time Forgot* in 1924. All references are to this collected trilogy: Edgar Rice Burroughs, *The Land That Time Forgot*, by page numbers.

as the inhabitants call it, Caspak) teems with deadly races and creatures representing every stage of the primordial past, up and down the "scale of evolution" (130) – from ape-men bereft of language to advanced stone-age cultures; from dinosaurs to saber-tooth tigers. Familiar nineteenth-century racial language defines the island's primitive proto-humans by their "negroid" features (80; see also 88): flat noses, "prognathous faces" (a technical term from nineteen-century craniology), and hairy bodies (92).[67]

The strange island is apparently an organized cross-section of earth's evolutionary history: in its southern sphere, the earlier ages of the deep past dominate, and as one travels north, the later ages of antiquity and evolution prevail. Nowhere, however, do our protagonists see any children or young among the humanoid inhabitants. The highest evolutionary level of humans on the island, the Galu, possess the strange secret of Caspak: rather than give birth normally, the Galu women bathe in special pools and release eggs which flow down the water currents of the island, back to the southernmost portion. There the eggs "evolve" into the most primitive forms of life and begin their slow climb up the evolutionary ladder; each individual egg passes through the various stages of evolution, from amphibian all the way to the most primitive form of human, and then up the seven-stage human evolutionary scale of the island, until the cycle begins anew. It is a fantasy of ontogeny recapitulating phylogeny outside the womb.[68]

Caspak is thus an image of an utterly self-sufficient, perfectly ordered evolutionary system; the island's hermetically sealed, cyclical evolutionary scheme is a popularized reception of Darwinian ideas, bent to serve the need of science/adventure fiction. But, as should be familiar by now in our long cursed race tradition, any classification of human races seemingly cannot be complete without an outcast, deformed, tainted line distinguished from the dominant lineage that supplements the order of the pure system. Therefore, one more race inhabits Caspak: the Wieroo, a swarm of deformed humanoid winged creatures (see Figure 5.1) who live in a haunted isolated city decorated with millions of human skulls and surrounded by deadly wilderness.

Our civilized protagonist marvels at the number of skulls, with a telling biblical allusion: "The City of Human Skulls ... They must have been

67 On the pseudoscientific racial term "prognathous" see Banton, *Racial Theories*, 38–40.

68 On the nineteenth century concept encapsulated in the phrase "ontogeny recapitulates phylogeny," see Banton, *Racial Theories*, 34, 40–2.

5.1. Wieroo. Cover art by Roy G. Krenkel for Edgar Rice Burroughs, *Out of Time's Abyss* (vol. 3 of *The Land That Time Forgot*), Ace Books, 1963.

collectin' 'em since Adam" (235). The Wieroo are only male; they reproduce by capturing and impregnating human females from the most advanced tribe on Caspak, like the fallen angels of the *Book of Enoch* impregnating the "daughters of men." These hapless captive women give birth to the next generation of monstrous Wieroo, bearing only male offspring. Early in their evolution, the Weiroo were distinguished from other races of the island by their proclivity for warfare and conflict; they have also evolved wings and live in isolation in Caspak, away from the other humanoid races. Like Ham's progeny or Crusoe's savages, the Weiroo live in a degenerate social system based on uncontrolled passions left to ferment in their isolation, existing in a perpetual state of self-defeating and irrational homicidal chaos:

> So cruel had they become and so bloodthirsty that they no longer had hearts that beat with love or sympathy; but their very cruelty and wickedness kept them from conquering the other races, since they were also cruel and wicked to one another, so that no Wieroo trusted another. (278)

While the Weiroo consider themselves the pinnacle of evolution in Caspak, we learn that they are a corrupt offshoot and dead-end, standing outside the ordered evolutionary scale and progression of the island.

Lost in this antediluvian world, our civilized male protagonists strive against atavistic cave-men and the savage Wieroo. As in Prendick's contamination by Moreau's beast-men, exposure to all this savage degeneracy brings out the latent savagery of Burroughs's protagonists. For example, our hero, Bowen Tyler duels with a savage cave-man rival for the life of a fair cave-maiden, both men filled with "primal passions":

> Two abysmal beasts sprang at each other's throats that day beneath the shadow of earth's oldest cliffs – the man of now and the man-thing of the earliest, forgotten then, imbued by the same deathless passion that has come down unchanged through all the epochs, periods and eras of time from the beginning, and which shall continue to the incalculable end – woman, the imperishable Alpha and Omega of life. (98)

If there is a particular distinguishing characteristic of these modern literary appropriations of Babylonian degeneracy, it might be this narrative formula, whereby a protagonist of civilized character finds himself infected by the savagery and degeneracy of the tainted race and place and begins to lose himself.

The immensely influential H.P. Lovecraft's (1890–1937) forays into horror, science fiction, and the weird tale take the corrupting influence of the degenerate race even further, adapting the cursed race archetype to his own personal brand of racial intolerance, which owes much to nineteenth- and early twentieth-century precursors. Lovecraft's lamentable racism is a well-documented fact, expressed in stories such as "The Doom That Came to Sarnath," "The Dream-Quest of Unknown Kadath, "The Shadow Out Of Time," "The Dunwich Horror," "He," "The Call of

Cthulu," and "The Lurking Fear."[69] Two stories in particular illustrate well Lovecraft's adaptation of the cursed race archetype in the conventions of horror fiction: "The Horror at Red Hook" and "The Shadow over Innsmouth."

Lovecraft's 1925 trip to New York City and his disgust at its urban immigrant squalor inspired "The Horror at Red Hook" (1927).[70] Once again, the narrative follows a typical "scientific" outsider, this time detective Thomas Malone and his forensic investigations into an epidemic of child-kidnapping and wealthy recluse Robert Suydam's strange death. To his relatives' dismay, Suydam – a Kabbalah scholar and "profound authority on mediaeval superstition" (122) – has begun to associate with the disreputable criminal underworld of Red Hook. As Suydam's appearance grows disheveled, "prowl[ing] about like a veritable mendicant" (122), his relatives attempt to have him committed. To throw off the investigation, Suydam marries a respectable society woman; however, after the wedding, onboard a ship at the Cunard Pier, the couple is found murdered, their bodies drained of all blood and the word "LILITH" scrawled on the stateroom wall in "fearsome Chaldee letters" (129). This bit of Babylonian oriental atmosphere continues when an "Arab with a hatefully negroid mouth" (129) arrives to claim Suydam's body, bearing a written injunction previously signed by Suydam himself.

Lovecraft's detective is a "scientist" in the Lombroso tradition, conversant with nineteenth-century criminal anthropology: Malone "was conscious, as one who united imagination with scientific knowledge, that modern people under lawless conditions tend uncannily to repeat the darkest instinctive patterns of primitive half-ape savagery in their daily life and ritual observances" (120). We have seen from Lombroso that lawless urban conditions can induce atavism, and the dangerous setting of Red Hook is Lovecraft's racist nightmare of New York immigration and urban corruption: the Brooklyn neighbourhood is "the polyglot abyss of New York's underworld" (118), where the "population is a hopeless tangle and enigma" (119); it is characterized by "a babel of sound and filth" (119), in which "the blasphemies of an hundred dialects assail

69 On the pervasive topic of Lovecraft's racism see Joshi, *H.P. Lovecraft: The Decline of the West*, 74–80, 127–9 for initial orientation.

70 "The Horror at Red Hook" in *Dreams in the Witch House*, ed. Joshi, 116–37, by page numbers.

the sky" (120).[71] The police have tried to barricade the district, in a futile attempt at "protecting the outside world from the contagion" (120).

Malone senses some ancient evil trait lurking beneath the degenerate sub-human criminals of Red Hook:

> [H]e seemed to see in them some monstrous thread of secret continuity; some fiendish, cryptical, and ancient pattern utterly beyond and below the sordid mass of facts and habits and haunts listed with such conscientious technical care by the police. They must be, he felt inwardly, the heirs of some shocking and primordial tradition; the sharers of debased and broken scraps from cults and ceremonies older than mankind. (120–1)

We shall see that the source of this "monstrous thread of secret continuity" is ultimately a great non-human evil, part of Lovecraft's mythos of ancient inhuman forces that predate humanity. Yet this monstrous "thread" or "pattern" stretching back into the past, and leading all the way down to the current "heirs of some shocking and primordial tradition" clearly is our ancient cursed race archetype, adapted to and infused by a blatant early twentieth-century American racism.

Lovecraft casts the horror at Red Hook as Oriental in character. We have already noted the mysterious "Chaldee letters" and the sinister negroid Arab bearing Suydam's post-mortem message, but Lovecraft paints a broader picture of Oriental degeneracy. Malone wonders whether he is dealing with the "hellish vestiges of old Turanian-Asiatic magic and fertility-cults" (121). In Red Hook, we learn, Suydam lives among "certain nameless and unclassified Asian dregs" (123), in the midst of a "very unusual colony of unclassified slant-eyed folk who used the Arabic alphabet" (123). These degenerates are "squat figures" with "squinting physiognomies" (124), hailing from somewhere in Kurdistan and speaking a "dialect obscure and puzzling to exact philology" (124). Disgusted by these "squinting Orientals" (128), Malone pursues his investigation into the kidnappings through "unbelievable throngs of mixed foreigners in figured robes, mitres, and other inexplicable devices" (130). The Oriental atmosphere in this case is a clear indicator of the Babylon myth's influence.

The detective's search leads beneath the basement of Suydam's house, where a door gives way to a pit filled with "nighted crypts [and]

71 For other uses of "babel/babble" (which obviously call to mind the Tower of Babel), see 119, 122, 133.

titan arcades" (131). This horrible place is not much different from Boemus's sixteenth-century vision of Asia and Africa overflowing with the burgeoning, monstrous swarms of Ham's children and their degenerate idolatry:

> Avenues of limitless night seemed to radiate in every direction, till one might fancy that here lay the root of a contagion destined to sicken and swallow cities, and engulf nations in the foetor of hybrid pestilence. Here cosmic sin had entered, and festered by unhallowed rites had commenced the grinning march of death that was to rot us all to fungous abnormalities too hideous for the grave's holdings. Satan here held his Babylonish court, and in the blood of stainless childhood the leprous limbs of phosphorescent Lilith were laved. (132)

"Babylon" itself signs this passage, allusively capping a familiar concatenation of elements: a "root of a contagion," a "hybrid pestilence," a "cosmic sin" that had long "festered by unhallowed rites" (note the religious language: "sin" and "rites"). Malone sees (or thinks he sees?) incubi and succubi praying to Hecate, the dancing of fauns and demons – a entire "Walpurgis-riot of horror" bubbling up from the "unsealed wells of night" (132). In this "Babylonish court," Suydam's reanimated corpse resists being sacrificed to Lilith in a blasphemous rite and dramatically crumbles to "decay and bone" (134) as the house collapses around Malone.

After the detective is rescued, beneath the ruins of the church the authorities find cells with "solitary prisoners in a state of complete idiocy ... found chained, including four mothers with infants of disturbingly strange appearance" who die soon after exposure to light (135). As we have seen, the cursed race always has its appetite for procreation and miscegenation – its hunger to reproduce and thereby taint the "pure" line. And, as usual, the cursed race only temporarily withdraws to the shadows after its supposed defeat, always ready to erupt again: "the evil spirit of darkness and squalor broods on amongst the mongrels in the old brick houses" (136). The degenerate masses of Red Hook "still chant and curse and howl as they file from abyss to abyss, none knows whence or whither, pushed on by blind laws of biology which they may never understand" (136). The narrator asks: "Who are we to combat poisons older than history and mankind?" (136).

We find Lovecraft's "weird tale" version of the degenerate archetype adapted in a somewhat different fashion in his classic story "The Shadow over Innsmouth" (1931).[72] Innsmouth is an old and crumbling town, dying in isolation on the New England coast. Our first-person narrator embarks on what he hopes will be a quaint antiquarian tour, but he finds that Innsmouth and its strange population have fallen on bad days over the past few generations, shunned by neighbouring towns. Before he even arrives in Innsmouth, he learns it is a "dismal, decadent place" (275), an "exaggerated case of civic degeneration" (275); it is a "community slipping far down the cultural scale" (277). A librarian tells him that a century ago a "peculiar secret cult ... had gained force there and engulfed all the orthodox churches"; it was "The Esoteric Order of Dagon," and "was undoubtedly a debased, quasi-pagan thing imported from the East" (277).[73] Our undaunted narrator, however, eagerly arrives in town only to be repulsed by the locals' appearance. The Innsmouth inhabitants have more than a touch of nineteenth-century criminal monstrosity about them, with their receding foreheads, bulging watery eyes and flat noses, thick lips and diseased skin, blue-grey hands, immense feet and odd creases along the sides of their necks (279). The scientifically curious narrator speculates as to the race of one shambling specimen, the narrator's interest in physiognomy calling to our mind Lombroso and the discourse of criminal degeneracy:

> Just what foreign blood was in him I could not even guess. His oddities certainly did not look Asiatic, Polynesian, Levantine, or negroid, yet I could see why the people found him alien. I myself would have thought of biological degeneration rather than alienage. (279)[74]

The secret of Innsmouth slowly emerges as the narrator finds himself trapped in the town. The community experienced a terrible economic crisis a century ago when the fishing stock dried up; the town struck an evil bargain with an ancient race of demonic undersea beings based in a lost city beneath the ocean waves. The creatures have bred with the human inhabitants of Innsmouth, and these half-breed miscegenated offspring mutate slowly to their inhuman amphibian form over the course of their lives until they finally take to the water for good, to live the life eternal in their ancient, cursed, undersea city. Our narrator learns much from the

72 "The Shadow over Innsmouth," in *Call of Cthulhu*, ed. Joshi, 268–335.

73 We might remember the Order of Dagon and the papal mitre in Hislop's charge that Catholicism was really Babylonian paganism; see chapter 3, pp. 115–16).

74 The narrator also calls the Innsmouth inhabitants "degenerate creatures" (326).

crazed old man Zadok Allen, one of the few normal Innsmouth residents left, who explains in his New England dialect that the creatures "brung us fish an' treasure, an' shud hev what they hankered arter" (303). What they "hankered arter" was sex, procreation, a desire to create a terrible offshoot species of humanity and eventually take over the world.

Before Zadok Allen flees the scene in a burst of frenzied terror, he tells our narrator, in his final mad words near the end of the story that the town had turned away from the Christian faith and embraced the worship of the degenerate Ancient Gods – the idolatry of Ham and Babylon:

> I was a mighty little critter, but I heard what I heerd an' seen what I seen – Dagon an' Ashtoreth – Belial an' Beëlzebub – Golden Caff an' the idols o' Canaan an' the Philistines – Babylonish abominations – *Mene, mene, tekel, upharsin* – (300–1).

With these final Hebrew words hanging in the air (they are, of course, the famed "writing on the wall" of Belshazzar's Babylon in chapter 5 of the biblical Book of Daniel), Zadok Allen leaves our young man to be hunted down by the Innsmouth folk. The narrator narrowly escapes, but later, back in the civilized world, we learn he has been "infected": he begins to apprehend a certain "terror of [his] own ancestry" as he slowly realizes that he himself is of the Innsmouth line (332).[75] In his tortured dreams he walks beneath the ocean waves, wandering through a typical Lovecraftian city of "titanic sunken porticoes and labyrinths of weedy Cyclopean walls" (333). He starts to acquire the "Innsmouth look," and in the end joins his monstrous race beneath the oceanic city, to "dwell amidst wonder and glory for ever."[76]

One could further multiply similar adaptations of the cursed race archetype almost indefinitely across the traditions of late nineteenth- and twentieth-century popular fiction in authors as varied as Rudyard Kipling and H. Rider Haggard, Arthur Machen and Robert E. Howard. But perhaps the most obvious current descendants of degenerate Babylon

75 On Lovecraft's notion of inherited evil see Lévy, *Lovecraft: A Study in the Fantastic*, trans. Joshi, 73–8.

76 This last phrase of the story encodes a biblical allusion: the words are a parody of the 23rd Psalm (see Burleson, *H.P. Lovecraft: A Critical Study*, 176).

5.2. A degenerate "crawler" from *The Descent* (dir. Neil Marshall, 2005)

and its narrative of the cursed race lurk in the traditions of modern horror, across fiction, film, and television. For example, *The Descent* (2005; dir. Neil Marshall), already a cult-classic modern horror film, sends a group of female friends cave spelunking "out in the middle of nowhere" (as one of the characters puts it) in the American Appalachian mountains – a setting calling to mind incest and backward, inbred country folk in American popular culture.[77] A cave-in traps the women in an extensive network of deep underground chambers where they are attacked by blind cannibal semi-human monsters (strongly reminiscent of Wells's Morlocks). A Neanderthal-style cave-painting in the caverns leads to the revelation of an ancient evil: the cannibal creatures are the malformed descendants of cave-men who (as one of the women puts it) "have evolved perfectly to live ... in the dark." The women must fight these "crawlers" and escape. *The Descent* perhaps sounds silly and simplistic in plot summary, but it is an extremely effective horror film. But note the presence of our archetypal elements: geographic isolation; somatic transformation: the crawlers have misshapen bodies, pointed ears, no hair, pointed teeth (see Figure 5.2); sexuality: the crawlers are naked and their attacks on the female party carry suggestive overtones of

77 All quotations from the Blu-ray disc: *The Descent: Original Unrated Cut* (Lionsgate Films, 2005).

sexual violence; graphically depicted cannibalism; a debased, popularized notion of evolution explaining the generation of an ancient, separate line of debased humanity. And there is even a certain sense of infectious contagion in the film: in several instances, the female protagonists must "descend" (or degenerate) to the level of the crawlers and their violence in order to survive.[78]

I wish to conclude with a few summary reflections about the internal logic of this long tradition, the archetypal elements that adapt under the pressure of changing historical and generic circumstances. There are many aspects to the inner dynamics of this tradition that merit further exploration – the place of the body and its organic functions; the role of geographical isolation, space and place; the complex interplay between essentialist definitions of race or difference and performative, mobile or transferable conceptions; the changing role of technology, and much else. But I do wish to pause over two defining characteristics: the curious resonance of time in this tradition and the discourse of classification.

The concept of degeneracy in the Matter of Babylon is bound to the workings of time itself, particularly as expressed in lineage and reproduction. As I have noted before, the Book of Genesis is the book of origins for the Christian West, a way to understand the beginning of Time and all created things, and to place the present in relation to that origin. It seems to me not a coincidence that the concept of degeneracy incorporates and thematizes Time and its narrative expression. De-generation is entropic; it is a falling-away or a falling-from, a descent *through* time. Degeneracy, de-evolution, atavism, corruption – all these words presuppose a narrative form unspooling across linear time. As a concept, degeneracy is partially bound to the narrative representation of time and the way time connects past and present in a seamless, if vast, continuity. Moreover, as revealed in our tradition of degeneracy, there appears to be something potentially fearful in that, in Prospero's "dark and backward abysm" of time and its eruption into the present – from the sudden appearance of Grendel, after his kind had walked the blank spaces of the map for eons, to Lovecraft's long-sleeping primeval Gods,

78 A partial list of interesting films with analogous narratives would include science fiction/horror blends such as *Altered States* (1980; dir. Ken Russell), *Nightbreed* (1990; dir. Clive Barker), and *Pandorum* (2009; dir. Christian Alvart), as well as backwoods incest films such as *Deliverance* (1972; dir. John Boorman), the various *The Hills Have Eyes* productions (1977 and 1985, dir. Wes Craven; 2006, dir. Aleandre Aja), and the infamous *The X-Files* episode "Home" (1996; dir. Kim Manners).

representatives of a past so immense and lost that the human mind cracks at the strain of trying to encompass it.

Furthermore, the discourse of classification stands behind the hermeneutic imperatives of this tradition. Sorting and classifying human communities as pure or degenerate, as a straight branch of the human tree or a crooked one, animates the process of understanding human difference both temporally and spatially – that is, in the acknowledging of human difference in history and in the world at large. Foucault notes that natural history is "a way of generalizing the principle of continuity and the law that requires that all beings form an uninterrupted expanse."[79] The discourse of species (and I would say, of race as well), in other words, is the prior condition that enables classification itself: the simultaneous employment of both distinction and continuity in any scheme of classification. For Foucault, structure in natural history provides the a priori conceptual framework for categorical naming, classifying, designating, and ultimately, understanding. A consequence of this discourse of structural continuity, he further notes, is the generation of monsters: "On the basis of the power of the continuum held by nature, the monster ensures the emergence of difference ... against the background of the continuum, the monster provides an account, as though in caricature, of the genesis of differences."[80] What Foucault posits as a defining element of seventeenth-century discourse, I, however, would say is a characteristic of the long tradition of Babylonian degeneracy and its representation of time and race, time's monstrous abyss and its lengthening shadows.

79 Foucault, *Order of Things*, 152.
80 Foucault, *Order of Things*, 156–7; see also Williams, *Deformed Discourse*, 107–11.

PART III

Babylon as Sublime Topos

Babylon the wonder of all tongues

– Milton, *Paradise Regained*, III.280

Babylon,
Learned and wise, hath perished utterly,
Nor leaves her speech wherewith to clothe a sigh
That would lament her ...

– from Wordsworth, *Ecclesiastical Sketches*, XXV ("Missions and Travels")[1]

1 Wordsworth, *Sonnet Series and Itinerary Poems, 1820–1845*, ed. Jackson, 153, lines 9–12.

Chapter Six

City of Ruins

Babylon is fallen, she is fallen, and all the graven gods thereof are broken unto the ground.

– Isaiah 21:9

Thus, when traveling in the territory of Ersilia, you come upon the ruins of the abandoned cities, without the walls which do not last, without the bones of the dead which the wind rolls away: spider-webs of intricate relationships seeking a form.

– Italo Calvino, *Invisible Cities*, trans. Weaver, 76

For Calvino, Babylon is one of the cities that "menace in nightmares and maledictions."[2] This chapter examines the inception and afterlife of nightmare Babylon in the West. We have already seen various ways the name of Babylon is a potential word of menace: Babylon as a metaphor for the tyranny of Empire; Babylon as a figure for Hell and the vagrant City of Man; Babylon as the origin and archetype of degenerate humanity. But, as I turn in the following chapters to visions of Babylon as a sublime place, I first excavate in this chapter an enduring image of nightmare Babylon: the ruined city.

A few words first about my use of the term "topos" in this chapter and the next. The *OED* defines a "topos" as a "traditional motif or theme (in a literary composition); a rhetorical commonplace, a literary convention or formula." Ernst R. Curtius's influential discussion of medieval *topoi* identified these motifs or conventions as a feature of classical rhetoric

2 Calvino, *Invisible Cities*, trans. Weaver, 164.

and education – they were "topics" (topoi) to be used in literary composition.[3] In the original Greek, a topos (τόπος) is a "place." The etymon lurks behind modern English "topic" (i.e., a subject, as in the rhetorical tradition) and "topography" (i.e., mapping "places"). My use of topos here in Part III draws together the sense of topos as both a rhetorical topic or subject in literature and as a place. These chapters focus on the literary motif or convention (topos) of Babylon as a specific *place* (topos) – a sublime place.

What I shall call in this chapter the "Babylon ruin topos" functions as a sublime complement to Babylon's other imaginative genealogies. Babylon-as-ruin is the foundational image for Western depictions of lost cities, dead and belated civilizations, haunted and cursed ruins. Babylon and Babel are the first cities thrown down to ruin in the Western tradition. In this genealogy, Babylon menaces the dreams of the West as a place of belated doom and haunted remains. As we saw in chapter 1, images of Babylon's power and greatness move in tandem with images of her wreck and passing. In the Western imagination Babylon has always been both an agent of destruction and a figure for self-destruction: Babylon breaks the walls of Jerusalem and is then herself devastated by the Persians, agents of God's wrath. Babylon creates ruins; Babylon is a ruin. In turning to images of ruin, this chapter argues that Babylon is the forerunner of the ruin topos in Western culture, more influential than the smoldering remains of Troy, Rome, or any other ruined cities of myth and legend. From ancient writings to medieval topoi, from romanticism and the nineteenth-century excavations of the Near East to later displaced Babylons, dark images of the ruined, cursed city haunt the arts and letters of the West.

Ruins have always provoked and fascinated the imagination; humanity is, in Rose Macaulay's words, "ruin-minded."[4] But the significance of ruins goes beyond simple fetish. The fascination with ruins points to an important fact about human perception and understanding. The enduring interest in ruined, imperfect, incomplete structures models the

3 Curtius, *European Literature and the Latin Middle Ages*, trans. Trask.

4 Macaulay, *Pleasure of Ruins*, 20: "The human race is, and has always been, ruin-minded. The literature of all ages has found beauty in the dark and violent forces, physical and spiritual, of which ruin is one symbol." For discussions of ruins in art, architecture, and the imagination, the classic study is Macaulay's; see also Mortier, *La Poétique des ruines en France*; Goldstein, *Ruins and Empire*; Janowitz, *England's Ruins*; Woodward, *In Ruins*; Fagan, *From Stonehenge to Samarkand*.

nature of human perception; as Thomas McFarland argues, "The phenomenology of the fragment is the phenomenology of human awareness."[5] An ever-present sense of insufficiency or lack drives human understanding; our knowledge is always partial, always insufficient, and as we move through the world of experience the hermeneutic circle turns, providing new experiences that remake our sense of pre-understanding even as new interpretive opportunities open up before us. In other words, "Incompleteness, fragmentation, and ruin ... are at the very center of life."[6] The partiality of ruins – the way we see both the present fragment and the absent whole – represents the partiality of human understanding and its dialectic of presence and absence.

Moreover, this interplay of presence and absence is a fundamental aspect of the sublime. The apprehension of ruins implies the perception of a still greater, absent grandeur: the perception of this grandeur informs the sublime.[7] As they tantalizingly provoke the imagination with their incomplete presence, ruins suggest a larger, ghostly absence. Vita Sackville-West gives us an example of this in *Twelve Days* (1924), a memoir of her travels in Persia. In an eloquent passage she describes the ruins of Persepolis:

> Now you are in the midst of the ruins ... A little further, and you are in the Hall of the Hundred Columns, a wilderness of tumbled ruins, but ruins which in their broken detail testify to the richness of the order that once was here: fallen capitals; fragments of carving small enough to go into a pocket, but whorled with the curls of an Assyrian beard; wars and dynasties roll their forgotten drums, as the fragment is balanced for a moment in the palm of the hand.[8]

---

5 McFarland, *Romanticism and the Forms of Ruin*, 3. Cf. Macauley, who explains that "Ruin is always over-stated; it is part of the ruin-drama staged perpetually in the human imagination, half of whose desire is to build up, while the other half smashes and levels to earth" (*Pleasure in Ruins*, 100).

6 McFarland, *Romanticism and the Forms of Ruin*, 5.

7 See McFarland, *Romanticism and the Forms of Ruin*, 29–30: "The sublime ... is the perception of very large fragments, such as mountains, with the accompanying awareness that this largeness implies still larger conceptions that can have no such objectivization and therefore cannot be compared. The sublime is, so to speak, an implied comparison in which only the diasparactive object exists." See Shaw, *Sublime* for a good general introduction to the sublime.

8 Sackville-West, *Twelve Days: An Account of a Journey across the Bakhtiari Mountains in South-western Persia*, 133. Cf. also 134: "Ruined cities. Ranging away from Persepolis, I remember other wrecks of pride, splendour, and majesty: the ziggurat of Ur against the sunset, the undulating mounds that were Babylon, the gay broken colonnades of Palmyra."

The wilderness of broken details and the fragment poised in the hand conjure up the structure's former order. In a similar fashion, Babylon-as-ruin points to greater, absent immensities, including (as we shall see) the absent burden of history itself. Part of this chapter's agenda is to show that the sublime is not exclusive to the eighteenth and nineteenth centuries, as commonly thought, but rather, in the fascination of ruins we see a vital aspect of the sublime over the full course of Western culture.

In its sublime dimensions, the Babylon ruin topos therefore allows us to examine a powerful and changing way of thinking about time and the past in the Western tradition. The relationship between Babylon and future apocalypse was, we saw in chapter 1, part of Babylon's use as a political metaphor. But something else fascinating comes to light when we examine the notion of Babylon as ruin, especially in its later, post-medieval displacements. In this chapter and the next we shall see that the history of Babylon-as-ruin gives us something else: not a myth of future destruction, but a myth of destruction in the deepest past; not a fall from Paradise or from the Golden Age, but rather a lingering anxiety over the abyss of (pre)history. The Babylon ruin topos stands for the past as enemy; the past as dark father; the *past* as apocalyptic ruin, rather than the future. Half-shrouded in myth and defined by an absent presence, Babylon-as-ruin has always been fallen or diminished from the perspective of the Western tradition; as such, Babylon stands for what we might call a historical anxiety of influence: in the domain of the Babylon ruin topos the weight of past history is a burden, a dark paternity overhanging action in the present.

As I examine what one scholar calls the "strange death-dance of thought occasioned by ruins,"[9] and unfold the genealogy of the Babylon ruin topos, I will attend to the slow interaction of several long-standing Western cultural motifs around the name of Babylon, a dossier of sublime elements:

- the twinned tradition of the *encomium urbis* ("praise of a city") and the *excidio urbis* ("destruction of a city") motifs;
- the fall and destruction of an evil, culturally advanced and powerful city through transgression (usually pride);
- punishment and destruction of the city through divine or otherwise non-human and, ultimately, impersonal forces;

9 Goldsten, *Ruins and Empire*, 10.

- the *transitus mundi* ("passing of the world") motif, particularly in its medieval formation, in which the ruined city serves as an occasion for existential speculation;
- the changing mix of sublime emotions provoked by the leftover ruins of the city: awe, nostalgia, sadness, terror.

The Ancient City: Glory and Destruction

Cities enthralled the ancient imagination, both in their abiding glory and in their dramatic destruction. The *encomium urbis* motif ("praise of a city") has a long history as a set trope of classical rhetoric: Dionysius of Halicarnassus, Menander the Rhetorician, Hermogenes, Rutilius Namantius and others all wrote in praise of an abstract ideal City even as they wrote about particular cities.[10] Ausonius's *The Order of Famous Cities* (Latin, early fourth century CE), for example, presents a series of poems praising a ranked list of cities beginning with golden Rome "[f]irst among cities, the home of the gods."[11] Praise for the glory of the city, the height of human achievement, is a perennial motif in Western thought, the opposite, one might say, of the pastoral mode that exalts the non-urban experience. But the dark converse of the *encomium urbis* motif, however, was the *excidio urbis* tradition: the destruction and desolation of the City. Antipater of Sidon's Greek poem on the destruction of Corinth (latter half of second century BCE), gives us the familiar stock images and emotions of the *excidio urbis* tradition, here in the translation by modern American poet Kenneth Rexroth:

> Where is your famous beauty,
> Corinth of the Dorians?
> Where is your crown of towers?
> Where are your ancient treasures?

10 For an overview, see *Classical Tradition*, ed. Grafton et al., s.v. "Cities, Praise of"; Curtius, *European Literature*, 157. On the classical tradition of city eulogies and its background to similar Old English poems such as *Durham* and *The Ruin*, see Schlauch, "An Old English 'encomium urbis'"; A. Lee, "*The Ruin*: Bath or Babylon?." For an example from the Byzantine tradition see Nicetas Choniates, *O City of Byzantium*, trans. Magoulias, 317–19 and the general survey in Alexiou, *Ritual Lament*, 83–101.

11 *Ordo nobilium urbium* in *Ausonius*, trans. White, I.268–85 (volume and page numbers), at 268 (*Prima urbes inter, divum domus, aurea Roma*); translation by White, on facing pages.

Where are the temples of the
Immortals, and where are the
Houses and the wives of the
Lineage of Sisyphos,
All your myriad people?
Most unhappy city, not
A trace is left of you. War
Has seized and eaten it all.
Only the inviolate sea nymphs, the daughters of the
Ocean, remain, crying like
Sea birds over your sorrows.[12]

It is as if the potential entropy of destruction and decay must always underwrite the human striving and growth and fecundity represented by the healthy *communitas* of the City: life and death, comedy and tragedy, the *encomium* of the city paired with its inevitable *excidio.*

As we saw in chapter 1, this duality of power and weakness was a central element in the Babylon mythos from the very beginning: Babylon's might and her passing were mutually reinforcing images. This polarity was based, of course, on a historical reality: Babylon's elder civilization *was* more or less forgotten and dispersed, essentially lost to Western history until it was rediscovered in the nineteenth century. From the West's perspective, ancient Babylonian and Assyrian civilization were more myth and rumor than fact. A variety of authors note Babylon's belated nature. Strabo tells us that in his time the greater part of Babylon has been deserted; in the *Politics,* Aristotle uses the Babylonians as an example of a fallen people brooding upon past glories, explaining that "the Persian king has repeatedly crushed the Medes, Babylonians, and other nations, when their spirit has been stirred by the recollection of their former greatness."[13] In the fourth century the Roman emperor Constantine notes (in a disapproving discussion of pagan human sacrifice) that "Memphis and Babylon have received the fruit that was proper to such worship, having been laid waste and left uninhabited along with their ancestral gods. And I say this not from report, but I myself have been present to behold it, and have been an eyewitness of the miserable fortune of the cities."[14] Mandeville's fourteenth-century description is probably equal parts fact and

12 *Poems from the Greek Anthology,* trans. Rexroth, 19.
13 Strabo, *Geography,* XVI.1.5; Aristotle, *Politics,* III.13.1284b.

fiction, but also summarizes the basic Western understanding of Babylon as presently a belated ruin; he describes the site of ancient Babylon as a "wretched place ... so full of serpents and dragons and other venomous beasts that no man can come there"; he explains that the once-mighty and beautiful place is now a ruin: "there were within that circle many fair buildings that are now destroyed and now the entire place is a wilderness."[15] For most of the Western tradition, Babylon has been and always will be fallen, left in ruins.

The Ruin of Biblical Babylon

These tangible facts of Babylon's fall were, however, equally conditioned by the image of Babylon's fall in the Bible. The Western idea of Babylon's passing derived mainly from the Bible's images of prophetic destruction. The desolation of cities is a common trope in the Bible: Sodom and Gomorrah, Jerusalem, Nineveh, Tyre and Sidon, and Edom all share with Babylon the powerful image of the sublime city brought low and reduced to desolation. The biblical language of civic desolation is powerful and poetic: see, for example, Zephaniah's prophecy of God's judgment upon Nineveh:

> And he will stretch out his hand upon the north, and will destroy Assyria: and he will make the beautiful city a wilderness and as a place not passable, and as a desert. And flocks shall lie down in the midst thereof, all the beasts of the nations: and the bittern and the urchin shall lodge in the threshold thereof: the voice of the singing bird in the window, the raven on the upper post, for I will consume her strength. This is the glorious city that dwelt in security: that said in her heart: I am, and there is none beside me: how is she become a desert, a place for beasts to lie down in! Every one that passeth by her, shall hiss and wag his hand. (Zephaniah [Vulgate Sophonias] 2.13–15)[16]

---

14 Translation from *Constantine and Christendom*, trans. Edwards, 37. Latin edition: *Konstantins Rede an die Hilge Versammlung*, ed. Heikel, *Eusebius Werke* I.149–92. For similar citations of deserted Babylon see Pausanias, *Description of Greece*, VIII.33.3; Pliny, *Natural History*, VI.30.122.

15 M.C. Seymour, ed. *Bodley Version of Mandeville's Travels*, 31, lines 22–32: "wreched place ... so ful of nederis and of dragonys and othere venym bestis that no man may come thedyr ... ther were in the cerkele manye fayre edificis that now arn distroyed and now is al wildyrnesse."

16 Cf. the judgment against Edom: Isaiah 34.5–15; see also Isaiah 1:1–10; Jeremiah 50–1.

Negative views of cities generally outweigh positive images in the Bible. In their rich imagery of destruction, what biblical writings add to the classical *excidio urbis* tradition is the machinery of divine causation and the repossession of the natural world after the city's fall. An expression of God's power, the natural world reclaims the proud city for the wilderness. As in the Tower of Babel tradition, the city is a tainted invention of fallen man, an expression of pride and the Fall. For later Christian-derived traditions, all the destroyed cities of the Bible would coalesce into one evil City, in the same way that Augustine would conflate earthly existence into the City of Man, and name it "Babylon."

Babylon herself is singled out for special prophecies of destruction in both the prophets and Revelation. God's righteous judgment will destroy the city and its ruins will be forever cursed:

> Because of the wrath of the Lord [Babylon] shall not be inhabited, but shall be wholly desolate: every one that shall pass by Babylon, shall be astonished, and hiss at all her plagues ... And Babylon shall be reduced to heaps, a dwelling place for dragons, an astonishment and a hissing, because there is no inhabitant ... Thus saith the Lord of hosts: That broad wall of Babylon shall be utterly broken down, and her high gates shall be burnt with fire, and the labours of the people shall come to nothing, and of the nations shall go to the fire, and shall perish. (Jeremiah 50:13; 51:37; 51:58)

Babylon's destruction will be sudden and total: as Revelation laments, "Alas! Alas! That great city, Babylon, that mighty city; for in one hour is thy judgement come."[17] Revelation implies that the city will disappear utterly:

> And a mighty angel took up a stone, as it were a great millstone, and cast it into the sea, saying: With such violence as this shall Babylon, that great city, be thrown down, and shall be found no more at all. (Revelation 18:21)

Babylon will be consumed as the sea swallows a great millstone cast into its depths. In such rich metaphoric language one detects something more than the "vindictive pleasure" in the overthrow of an oppressor.[18]

---

17 Revelation 18:9–10; cf. Revelation 18:2 and 14:8: "That great Babylon is fallen, is fallen; which made all nations to drink of the wine of the wrath of her fornication."

18 The phrase "vindictive pleasure" is from Macauley, who notes that some of the earliest depictions of ruins derived from a vindictive pleasure that "was inextricably

The biblical image of ruined Babylon implies an aesthetic, a sense of awe at the sudden passing of that which seemed likely to endure forever.

We find the rich dialectic of praise and destruction, *encomium* and *excidio*, in the most famous and influential passage on Babylon's destruction, from Isaiah:

> And that Babylon, glorious among kingdoms, the famous pride of the Chaldeans, shall be even as the Lord destroyed Sodom and Gomorrha. It shall no more be inhabited for ever, and it shall not be founded unto generation and generation: neither shall the Arabian pitch his tents there, nor shall shepherds rest there. But wild beasts shall rest there, and their houses shall be filled with serpents: and ostriches shall dwell there, and the hairy ones shall dance there. And owls shall answer one another there, in the houses thereof, and sirens in the temples of pleasure. (Isaiah 13:19–22)[19]

The biblical prophecies of Babylon's fall introduce rich imagery into the overarching Babylon ruin topos. There is a complex aesthetic dimension to Isaiah's ruins here, with their simultaneous images of energy and desuetude: the staccato negations (no inhabitants, no more tents, no shepherds, no human activity) held against the contrary energy of the natural world, as the animals move about and dance among the static urban remnants.[20] It is no surprise that the fall of Babylon caught the imagination of nineteenth-century painters and illustrators in the romantic tradition such as John Martin and Gustave Doré (see Figures 6.1 and 6.2).

---

mixed with triumph over enemies, with moral judgment and vengeance, and with the violent excitements of war"; such ruins are the "haunts of the catastrophic imagination of man" (*Pleasure of Ruins*, 1).

19 Frye notes, concerning this passage, that "[t]he animals of the manifest demonic include the jackals and hyenas, which are associated with destroyed and abandoned kingdoms, many of them on the border of a shadow world in which it is difficult to know where animals stop and evil spirits begin" (*Great Code*, 151); he made a similar point in *Fearful Symmetry*, 221: "As the chill of old age comes over the historical cycle, its life dries up in huge tumorous cities, Nineveh, Babylon, Rome, Tyre, which thereupon become the symbols of the tyranny denounced by the prophet. Eventually the cities themselves are abandoned to nature, which creeps back over their stony skeletons as men move elsewhere to build more cites."

20 In a discussion of this same passage from Isaiah, Macaulay notes that the animal-inhabitants of ruins is a pervasive motif: "The vengeance of the Lord, the fall of the proud, the desolation of the rich and powerful: but, beyond all these, surely a profound, passionate, poetic pleasure in ruins as such. Out come the screech-owls, the dragons, the satyrs, the bitterns, the serpents, the jackals, the bats, even the moles, all the familiar creatures of ruin that haunt demolished cities and glooming fancy" (*Pleasure of Ruins*, 1).

6.1. John Martin, *The Fall of Babylon* (1831). The British Museum. Used by permission.

6.2. Gustave Doré, *Fallen Babylon* (1866).

Troy and Rome, Jerusalem, Sodom and Gomorrah: Babylon is only one of the rich variety of cities famed for both glory and destruction in the ancient traditions of Western culture. Yet Babylon can claim priority over them all: Babylon was the first of these great cities to fall, its Tower of Babel the first vaunting human structure to be thrown down overnight by the Divine. It is this priority that Babylon contributes to the history of ruins in the West, along with a rich array of images deriving from the classical and biblical traditions. The ancient world was fascinated by cities, but such places always had a dual signification: an image of human achievement, the best of humanity, but also an image of overreaching, tyranny, and pride. The twin poles of the *encomium* and the *excidio* give us life and death – the past of vivacity and the present of desolation. As this complex of traditions moved into the Christian Middle Ages, cities thus invited speculation on existential issues: what does this cycle of urban growth and decay say about the world and humanity's place in it?

Babylon and the Medieval *Excidio Urbis* Tradition

In Christian traditions, ruins come to serve as a metaphor for aging, the decay of the body, and mortality – all the varied manifestations of the *transitus mundi* motif, the passing of all things on this earthly world.[21] In the medieval tradition ruins likewise became an occasion to meditate upon any number of existential concerns such as the cycle of human birth, life, and death; the permutations of human history; chance and accident, and Fortune. The cycle of glory and decay spoke deeply to the Christian cultures of the Middle Ages, and corresponding laments for destroyed cities are common in medieval literature. The famed poem of Venantius Fortunatus (c. 530–c. 600) on the destruction of Thuringia begins with a lament over the "sad condition" (*condicio tristis*) brought on by war and the swift changes of fortune: "How suddenly proud kingdoms fall to their ruin!" (*quam subito lapsu regna superba cadunt!*).[22] As an *encomium*, the poem contrasts the age-old former beauty of the city with its current destruction (3–11), and focuses on the vivid images of once-vibrant people now dead and gone (11–30). Through this contrast the poet tells us that Thuringia's proud glory has been humbled (*decidit in humili gloria celsa loco*, 10).

Likewise the Anglo-Saxon man of letters Alcuin (c. 735–804) uses the *excidio urbis* motif in his poem commemorating the sack of the monastery of Lindisfarne on the English coast in 794 at the hands of Viking raiders; he develops an analogy between the sacking and despoiling of the monastery and the great destruction endured by great cities of history.

21 Woodward, *In Ruins*, 89; Fagan, *From Stonehenge to Samarkand*, xxii: "Ruins have long been a metaphor for death and resurrection, a reminder that the faithful will decay before achieving eternal life." See also Macaulay, *Pleasure of Ruins*, 11: "The acceptance of ruin as a natural doom was heightened by the sense of God's judgments and of the transient values of this world."

22 Venantius Fortunatus, *De excidio Thoringiae*, MGH, AA. 4.1. 271–5; lines 1–2.

The poem begins by dispassionately noting the vicissitudes of the world: seasons turn, day follows night, and

> Under the heavens' high pole nothing remains everlasting;
> All things change at various times.[23]

In this giddy world, the greatest of things will fall – unexpectedly, yes, but somehow inevitably – to utter ruin (25–6). All earthly things decay and are ultimately lost in the Christian medieval tradition, no matter how permanent and substantial they appear to human eyes. Alcuin cites examples of kingdoms and rulers throughout history subject to the same inevitable alteration: Persia, Macedonia, Rome, Jerusalem. But his first example is Babylon:

> O mighty Babylon and the Chaldean provinces, the kingdom's capital and its kings' chief source of power, you have fallen![24]

Babylon's priority is both temporal and one of magnitude: it was the first city and the greatest of cities, yet it also fell, as inexorably as day turns to night. In the poem, Alcuin eventually turns to the consolation that comes from meditating on the contrasting permanence of God and the eternal: the reward for steadfast faith in turbulent times will be eternal happiness in heaven.

In this regard, Babylon's fall was clearly an *exemplum* of the inevitable ruin of earthly glory. For example, the Old English poem *Daniel* tells us that "the city of Babylon was the most famous / of the strongholds known to men, the greatest and most glorious / of the ones men inhabit."[25] However, the mighty city is, in the end, only an exemplum of pride and overwrought earthly glory, as the poet's depiction of Nebuchadnezzar's boasting makes clear, in a passage I quoted previously:

> Then the Chaldean king continued to declaim
> with great boasting when he ruled the fortress,

---

23 *Versus de clade Lindisfarensis monsterii*, MGH, Poet. Lat. I, 229–35; lines 11–12: Nil manet aeternum, celso sub cardine caeli, / Omnia vertuntur temporibus variis.

24 *Versus de clade Lindisfarensis monsterii*, 31–2: Nobilis urbs regno et prima potentia regum / Perdidit, o, Babilon Caldea regna potens.

25 *Daniel*, ed. Krapp, 691–3a: Þæt wæs þara fæstna folcum cuðost, / mæst and mærost þara þe men bun, / Babilon burga.

and in his glory he looked upon the city of Babylon,
towering high and extending far over the plain of Shinar,
that he, the war-king built as a great marvel for his host.
Then he became resolute and arrogant beyond all men
because of the distinguished gift God had given him:
a kingdom of men and a world as a possession,
in the days of mankind: "You are my great and famed city
which I wrought for my glory with my vast power.
I wish to possess a resting-place, a dwelling and home, in you."[26]

As the Persians gather to destroy the Babylonian kingdom, the poet comments that God "allowed the glory of Babylon to fade / which heroic men ought to have preserved."[27] And yet although Babylon was an exemplum of human pride and tyranny, the Anglo-Saxons could still muster a note of sublime awe at her passing. The Old English translation of Orosius's *Seven Books of History Against the Pagans* expands upon its Latin source in a description of the city, ending on an elegiac note by personifying Babylon and giving her a wistful speech in response to ruin and desolation:

This same city of Babylon, which was the first and greatest of all cities, is now diminished and most desolate. Such is the city now, which previously was the most secure and wondrous and greatest of all works, and as such she

26 *Daniel*, ed. Krapp, 598–611:

Ongan ða gyddigan þurh gylp micel
Caldea cyning þa he ceastre weold,
Babilone burh, on his blæde geseah,
Sennera feld sidne bewindan,
heah hlifigan, þæt se heretyma
werede geweorhte þurh wundor micel;
wearð ða anhydig ofer ealle men,
swiðmod in sefan, for ðære sundorgife
þe him god sealde, gumena rice,
world to gewealde in wera life:
"Ðu eart seo micle and min seo mære burh
þe ic geworhte to wurðmyndum,
rume rice. Ic reste on þe,
eard and eðel, agan wille."

I restore the manuscript reading *ceastre weold*, following Farrell.

27 *Daniel*, ed. Krapp, 682–3: let Babilone blæd swiðrian / þone þa hæleð healdan sceoldon.

was set as an example to all middle-earth; and thus it is as if Babylon herself may speak to all mankind and say: "And so now I am fallen and have passed away; mark well: you can look upon me and know that you cannot possess anything of strength or security that may endure."[28]

Here Babylon is an example (*bysen*) of the *transitus mundi* theme. In this expansion one can sense here both the Anglo-Saxon reverence for mighty urban works and an inevitable, attendant note of transience. The sentiments expressed in these Old English texts represent the medieval formulation of the Babylon ruin topos.

One of the most famous images of ruin in the corpus of Old English poetry is the enigmatic and fragmentary Old English poem *The Ruin*, which describes a nameless, lost, once-proud city left destroyed by the impersonal forces of war and plague. Some scholars have asserted that the city depicted in *The Ruin* literally is Babylon, an argument not generally accepted.[29] However, I would argue that the stock situation depicted in *The Ruin*, namely, the interplay of the *encomium urbis* and *excidio urbis* traditions is indeed part of the wider Babylon ruin topos.[30] As an *encomium*, the poem tells us that the city had been a wondrous creation until it was brought low by the impersonal forces of fate:

Bright were the city-buildings, many a bathing-hall,
an abundance of high gables, the great sound of an army,

28 *Old English Orosius*, ed. Bately, II.iiii.43–4: Seo ilce burg Babylonia, seo ðe mæst wæs and ærest ealra burga, seo is nu læst and westast. Nu seo burg swelc is, þe ær wæs ealra weorca fæstast and wunderlecast and mærast, gelice and heo wære to bisene asteald eallum middangearde, and eac swelce heo self sprecende sie to eallum moncynne and cweþe: "Nu ic þuss gehroren eam and aweg gewiten, hwæt, ge magan on me ongietan and oncnawan þæt ge nanuht mid eow nabbað fæstes ne stronges þætte þurhwunigean mæge."

29 In his short article "*The Ruin* as Babylon," Keenan argues against the poem depicting any specific location and instead argues that the city in the poem is Babylon, basing his argument on a few quotations from Revelation and some general inferences drawn from Augustine's Jerusalem/Babylon dichotomy. This line of argument has not been accepted, and the usual assumption now is that the poem, to the extent that it is drawing upon real life, depicts a ruined Romano-British city, perhaps Bath. For a conspectus of the scholarship on "The Ruin," along with a reconstruction, interpretation, and translation of the damaged manuscript text, see Orchard, "Reconstructing *The Ruin*." A recent discussion of the architecture depicted by the poem can be found in Garner, *Structuring Spaces*, 155–62.

30 Hume argues against the existence of a special native English interest in ruins in "The 'ruin-motif,'" but see the more nuanced analysis of Liuzza in "The Tower of Babel."

many a mead-hall full of the joys of men –
until fate the mighty changed all that.[31]

In the heyday of the city's glory many a glittering, proud warrior marvelled at the city's treasure, on all its prosperity, and "on this bright city of a broad kingdom" (*on þas beorhtan burg bradan rices*, 37); but mighty fate (*wyrd seo swiþe*, 24b) has left all that only a memory. Old English *wyrd* or fate is a notoriously slippery word, its meaning landing on a spectrum between simply "events that have transpired," all the way to a more concrete personified concept (e.g. as a translation of Latin *Fortuna*).[32] Regardless of the specific meaning of *wyrd* in this context, what is important for our purposes is that the force of *wyrd* is impersonal: the poem leaves the exact initiating cause of the city's ruin (whether divine or human) unknown. The poem's attention, rather, is on the sustained contrast between the glittering past and the dead present.

Images of the city's decay and destruction dominate the poem:

Fallen roofs, ruined towers,
destroyed ring-gates, rime on lime,
the protection from storms sheared away, collapsed,
eaten away by age. Earth's grasp holds
the master builders, perished, lost,
the earth's hard grip, until a hundred
generations of men have passed away.[33]

---

31 *The Ruin*, ed. Krapp and Dobbie, ASPR III.227–8, lines 21–4:

Beorht wæron burgræced, burnsele monige,
heah horngestreon, heresweg micel,
meodoheall monig ᛗ dreama full,
oþþæt þæt onwende wyrd seo swiþe.

32 See Fell, "Perceptions of transience."

33 *The Ruin*, 3–9a:

Hrofas sind gehrorene, hreorge torras,
hrungeat berofen, hrim on lime,
scearde scurbeorge scorene, gedrorene,
ældo undereotone. Eorðgrap hafað
waldend wyrhtan forweorone, geleorene,
heardgripe hrusan, oþ hund cnea
werþeoda gewitan.

The natural world – the "earth's hard grip" – has taken over the ruined city, much like the encroachment of the desert and its creatures on the ruins of Babylon. Note also the emphasis on time: there is a sense of awful grandeur in the notion of human light extinguished and almost forgotten in the expanse of the ages. All human endeavours therefore seem small and puny in the face of impersonal desolation:

> The slain fell everywhere, days of plague came,
> death carried off all of these sword-brave men;
> their place of war became wasted foundations,
> the city decayed.[34]

The interplay of presence and absence generates the haunting poetic beauty of *The Ruin*: the fragmented remains conjure up their former wholeness and amplitude in a spectral trace. The wasted and destroyed remains of the city, the ruins themselves, haunted by their former glory, induce a sense of wonder, as the first two lines of the poem declares:

> Wondrous is this stone wall, broken by fate;
> The city buildings crumble, the work of giants decays.[35]

Wrætlic (here translated as "wondrous"), like *wyrd*, is a polysemous word, falling into two main camps of meaning: the adjective can describe something wondrous, marvellous, strange or curious; the word can also be a term for beauty: it can describe something artfully made, something

---

34 *The Ruin*, 25–8a:

> Crungon walo wide, cwoman woldagas,
> swylt eall fornom secgrofra wera;
> wurdon hyra wigsteal westen staþolas,
> brosnade burgsteall.

Cf. Nahum 3:1–3, on the destruction of Nineveh: "Woe to thee, O city of blood, all full of lies and violence: rapine shall not depart from thee. The noise of the whip and the noise of the rattling wheels and of the neighing horse and of the running chariot and of the horsemen coming up, and of the shining sword and of the glittering spear and of a multitude slain and of a grievous destruction: and there is no end of carcasses, and they shall fall down on their dead bodies."

35 *The Ruin*, 1–2: Wrætlic is þes wealstan, wyrde gebræcon; / burgstede burston, brosnað enta geweorc.

beautiful, splendid, and elegant.[36] Whatever the precise meaning, *wrætlic* in this context surely denotes a medieval sense of the sublime, as does the phrase *enta geweorc*, the "work of giants." This resonant phrase only appears a few times in Old English, and only in poetry. In each occurrence it signifies the wonder inspired by great works of the past, awe-inspiring monuments of an elder age wrought by human hands. The phrase is found in the gnomic poem *Maxims II*, where it helps sum up the essential nature of cities as wondrous creations:

> Cities can be seen from far away,
> the skilful work of giants, which remains in this world,
> the splendid stone-walled creation. [37]

In the Old English poem *The Wanderer*, the phrase is part of the poet's vision of desolation; similar to *The Ruin*, *The Wanderer* laments that each day the world of men "declines and falls" (*dreoseð ond feallep*, 63b).[38] The eponymous narrator has a vision of a time of apocalyptic desolation when "all the riches of the world stand waste," a world in which the ruins of once-great buildings decay (*woriað*, 78a), while all their inhabitants have been taken by death. Although *The Wanderer*'s sense of desolation and its use of the *transitus mundi* motif as it marvels over the ruined *enta geweorc* is much like *The Ruin*, in *The Wanderer*, by contrast, the agent of destruction is specified, not left impersonal. God destroys the *enta geweorc*:

> Thus the creator of men destroyed this world,
> until the ancient works of giants stood idle,
> without the revelry of city-dwellers.[39]

36 Bosworth-Toller, s.v. "wrætlic."

37 *Maxims II*, ed. Dobbie, ASPR VI.55–7; lines 1b–3a: Ceastra beoð feorran gesyne, / orðanc enta geweorc, þa þe on þysse eorðan syndon, / wrætlic weallstana geweorc.

38 *The Wanderer*, ed. Krapp and Dobbie, ASPR III.134–7, by line number.

39 *The Wanderer*, ed. Krapp and Dobbie, 85–7: Yþde swa þisne eardgeard ælda scyppend / oþþæt burgwara breahtma lease / eald enta geweorc idlu stodon. *Enta geweorc* is even more evocative in *Beowulf*, where it appears three times: the hilt of the giant sword Beowulf uses to decapitate Grendel is the "ancient work of giants" (*enta aergeweorc*, 1679a); the dragon's hoard is the "old work of giants" (*eald enta geweorc*, 2774a); and the vaulted chamber of the dragon's barrow is also "the work of giants" (*enta geweorc*, 2717b).

The Babylon ruin topos stands behind these ruined cities; moreover, the separate instantiations of the topos also participate in the creation of a broader, ever-evolving ruin tradition. For these poets, ruined cities evoke a mythic past in comparison to which the present seems small and mean. *The Ruin* is most likely not a literal depiction of Babylon, but the poem's vision of civic ruin and desolation, and its attitude towards the past, do concur with the Babylon ruin topos's similar dynamics.

What the medieval instantiations of Babylon ruin topos capture, then, is the typical medieval sense of the world grown old, the notion that the diminutive present is overshadowed by a greater, more awe-inspiring past.[40] It is a sublime experience, as Rose Macaulay eloquently summarizes:

> The ascendancy over men's minds of the ruins of the stupendous past, the past of history, legend and myth, at once factual and fantastic, stretching back and back into ages that can but be surmised, is half-mystical in basis. The intoxication, at once so heady and so devout, is not the romantic melancholy engendered by broken towers and mouldered stones; it is the soaring of the imagination into the high empyrean where huge episodes are tangled with myths and dreams; it is the stunning impact of world history on its amazed heirs. Such ascendancy has been swayed down the ages by the ruins of Troy, of Crete, Mycenae, Tyre, Nineveh, Babylon, Thebes, Rome, Byzantium, Carthage, and every temple, theatre and broken column of classical Greece; it is less ruin-worship than the worship of a tremendous past.[41]

If the fascination with ruins, ruined cities, and the "tremendous past" is a constant of Western thought, if this fascination is powered by the twin impulses of the *encomium urbis* and *excidio urbis* traditions, then Babylon – by virtue of its position as the primal model of the exulting city, rising up around the Tower of Babel itself and then falling to wrack, doom, and ruin – stands behind *The Ruin* and all other medieval depictions of the ruined city.

---

40 See Dean, *World Grown Old in Later Medieval Literature*. Cf. Macaulay, *Pleasure in Ruins*, 254: "[W]e link the stupendous past with our smothering, runagate, unlovely present, appeasing our eternally nostalgic appetite with its desperate reaches beyond the horizon to where stretch the limitless, only partly charted, dimly seen and largely obliviated civilities and deserts of time."

41 *Pleasure of Ruins*, 40.

The powerful medieval synthesis of these elements persists through the early modern period and indeed extends to the present. The use of ruins as a figure for the passing of the world is a familiar early modern motif; perhaps the best examples are by the poets Petrarch (1304–74), Joachim du Bellay (1525–60), and Edmund Spenser (1552–99).[42] Spenser's *Ruins of Time*, an elegy for Sir Phillip Sidney, constructs a lament for the ancient ruined city of Roman Britain, Verulamium.[43] The personified Verulamium decries the "unstedfast state / Of all that lives, on face of sinfull earth" (43–4), lamenting that "all that in this world is great or gaie, / Doth as a vapour vanish, and decaie" (55–6). All the fine towers, walls and palaces of the city "now are turned to dust, / And overgrowen with blacke oblivions rust" (97–8). The "spoyle of time" (119) has brought Verulamium to destruction. Spenser draws on the rich imagery of the prophets and the *encomium / excidio urbis* tradition when he places the screech owl beneath the heap of ruins where the lordly falcon used to stand. Like Alcuin's poem on Lindisfarne, the only consolation Spenser's poem draws from this desolation is the steadfast promise of eternal salvation in heaven (582–8).

In the fashion exemplified by Spenser's poem, Babylon as symbol of the *transitus mundi* endures to the present. In most respects, modern iterations of the Babylon ruin topos feel very medieval. A typical example

---

42 Three of Spenser's 1591 poetic *Complaints* – *The Ruins of Time*, *Visions of Bellay*, and *The Ruins of Rome* – treat ruins and are all indebted to Du Bellay: *The Ruins of Rome* is in fact a translation of Du Bellay's *The Antiquities of Rome* (*Les Antiquitez de Rome*, 1558). Du Bellay's poem expresses the classic *transitus mundi* theme in a traditional way:

> Voy quel orgueil, quelle ruine: et comme
> Celle qui mist le monde sous ses loix
> Pour donter tout, se donta quelquefois,
> Et devint proye au temps, qui tout consomme.
> ...
> Reste de Rome. O mondaine inconstance!
> ce qui est ferme, est part le temps destruit ...

[See what pride, what ruin, and how she who brought the world under her laws, in vanquishing all, at last vanquished herself and became the prey of time, which devours all ... Remains of Rome. O worldly inconstancy! Whatever stands firm is destroyed by time.] (*The Antiquities of Rome* 3.5–8, 12–13; cf. also sonnets 7, 27, 31.) Texts and translation from Joachim du Bellay, *The Regrets, with The Antiquities of Rome*, ed. and trans. Helgerson, by sonnet and line numbers.

43 *The Ruines of Time* in *The Yale Edition of the Shorter Poems of Edmund Spenser*, ed. Oram, et al., 225–61, citation by line numbers. On Spenser's poem see Goldstein, *Ruin and Empire*, 11–24.

is Siegfried Sassoon's (1886–1967) poem "Babylon," which has a nostalgic and monitory depiction of ruined Babylon:

> Babylon that was beautiful is Nothing now.
> Once to the world it tolled a golden bell:
> Belshazzar wore its blaze upon his brow;
> Ruled; and to ruin fell.
> Babylon – a blurred and blinded face of stone –
> At dumb Oblivion bragged with trumpets blown;
> Teemed, and while merchants throve and prophets dreamed,
> Bowed before idols, and was overthrown.
> Babylon the merciless, now a name of doom,
> Built towers in time, as we today, for whom
> Auguries of self-annihilation loom.[44]

As a World War I poet, Sassoon adapts the plangent Babylonian sublime to the awful visions of ruin in his own day, when "[a]guries of self-annihilation" loomed for European civilization. However, the medieval ruin topos, even with its elements of the sublime, does not extend to modernity completely unchanged. The Babylon ruin topos transforms under a number of subsequent influences: romanticism, the gothic, the scientific excavation of historical Babylon. These influences add new elements to the Babylon ruin topos: the city as emblem of fate and fortune and the passing of earthly glory becomes the dead, haunted, cursed city of the gothic and its derived traditions: pulp adventure, science fiction, fantasy, and horror.

Ruined Babylon in the Nineteenth Century: Romanticism, the Gothic, and Excavation

Interest in ruins was intense in the eighteenth and nineteenth centuries,[45] and it is a commonplace that ruins spoke powerfully to the arts and literature of the period.[46] From the "chaos of ruins" scattered throughout

44 Sassoon, *Collected Poems*, 223. Reprinted by permission of the Sassoon estate.
45 See note 4, above, esp. Goldstein, *Ruins and Empire* and Janowitz, *England's Ruins.*
46 McFarland argues that "Incompleteness, fragmentation, and ruin – *ständige Unganzheit* – not only receive a special emphasis in Romanticism but also in a certain perspective seems actually to define that phenomenon" (*Romanticism and the Forms of Ruin*, 7). See also Alexandra Warwick, "Lost Cities: London's Apocalypse" and Mighall, "Gothic Cities."

Byron's *Childe Harold's Pilgrimage*, to Wordsworth's *Tintern Abbey*, to Shelley's "Ozymandias," to paintings such as Thomas Cole's *The Course of Empire* (1833–6), the romantic uses of ruins were varied and sublime.[47] The "Invocation" of Constantin-François Volney's *The Ruins* (French, 1791; English trans. 1796) stands as a representative romantic attitude towards ruins:

> Hail solitary ruins, holy sepulchres, and silent walls! You I invoke; to you I address my prayer. While your aspect averts, with secret terror, the vulgar regard, it excites in my heart the charm of delicious sentiments – sublime contemplations.[48]

Volney's "sublime contemplations" were also in turn touched by the gothic tradition, with its distinctive geography of haunted castles, ruins, and other foreboding enclosed spaces.[49]

But even as Shelley wrote of Ozymandias's shattered visage, a steady stream of publications reported on the unearthing of buried civilizations and lost histories of the East. Romanticism and the gothic coincided with the first European scientific excavations of important Near Eastern sites in the eighteenth and nineteenth centuries.[50] Excavations and exploration drove an interest in lost cities and lost civilizations, under certitude that there were as yet unexplored spaces waiting to be found and, moreover, anatomized and understood scientifically and rationally. Western European travellers' accounts and bestselling archaeological books then produced a widespread mania for the Orient.[51] These writings also touched off a flood of corresponding manifestations in literature and the arts, from well-known works to many now-obscure poems, plays, and historical fictions set in and around the ancient East. A European vision of the ancient Near East was becoming a fully assimilated part of

47 For Cole's five-part series of paintings, held by the New York Historical Society, see http://explorethomascole.org/tour/items/69/series.

48 Volney, *Les ruines, ou Méditations sur les révolutions des empires* (1791); English translation, *The Ruins; or, Meditation on the Revolution of Empires and the Law of Nature* (1796).

49 On the relationship between romanticism and the gothic see Punter, *Literature of Terror*, 87–113; Gamer, *Romanticism and the Gothic*. On the Gothic and its relationship to the sublime see Boting, *Gothic*, 3–4, 38–43; Voller, *Supernatural Sublime*, 31–88.

50 For the history of European excavation in the Near East see Lloyd, *Foundations in the Dust*; Larsen, *Conquest of Assyria*; Damrosch, *Buried Book*; Seymour, *Babylon*, esp. 138–61, 185–223. See also McGeough, *Ancient Near East in the Nineteenth Century*.

51 The seminal study is Said, *Orientalism*.

everyday life and reference. To allow the ridiculous to exemplify this cultural obsession: by the time of Gilbert and Sullivan's *Pirates of Penzance* (1879), the bumbling modern Major General Stanley could boast, in his patter song, of his ability to "write a washing bill in Babylonic cuneiform" just as well as he knows "every detail of Caractacus's uniform."[52] Artistic representations and real-world excavations were reciprocal; nineteenth-century archaeology, romanticism, and the gothic were overlapping phenomena, each reinforcing the other.

Under these influences – the shifting aesthetics of romanticism and the gothic – the premodern understanding of Babylon-as-ruin underwent a certain transformation; or, perhaps it is better to say that certain latent elements in the Babylon ruin topos were enhanced, augmented, and extended. The ruined city as a sublime expression of the medieval *transitus mundi* theme endured as a cultural topos more or less unchanged; but in other contexts a distinctive gothic element was added to the mix. Horror, fear, terror, and dread were integral parts of the gothic landscape: its haunted castles and abbeys, its subterranean caves and labyrinths.[53] The discourse of archaeology with its exploration of unknown spaces and ancient ruins merged with the gothic emphasis on enclosed spaces.

The excavations at Babylon and Nineveh and other near eastern sites in the 1840s and 1850s clearly helped develop the incipient strain of gothic romanticism associated with Babylon as a ruin. The written accounts by men such as A.H. Layard (1817–94), George Smith (1840–76), and Henry Rawlinson (1810–95) form a corpus of writing that at times feels to be perhaps fifty per cent archaeological/scientific discovery, twenty per cent travel memoir, twenty per cent adventure fiction and ten per cent romantic reverie.[54] A detailed examination of selected texts shows their influence on the Babylon ruin topos: continuity with premodern discourse and the new influence of gothic romanticism.

The Bible certainly guided and preconditioned Layard and others in their understanding of the ruins of Babylon and Assyria.[55] For example, Layard describes the ruins at Kalah Sherghat in a sublime biblical idiom;

52 *Pirates of Penzance* in *Annotated Gilbert and Sullivan*, ed. Bradley, I.84–195; Act I, lines 476–7.

53 See Aguirre, *Closed Space*, 91–114.

54 On archaeological travel writing see Fagan, *Stonehenge to Samarkand*.

55 See Larsen, *Conquest of Assyria*, 277–9.

after a dramatic nocturnal storm, the great mound of ruins is barely illuminated by the party's campfire:

> The great mound could be distinguished through the gloom, rising like a distant mountain against the dark sky. From all sides came the melancholy wail of the jackals, who had issued from their subterranean dwellings in the ruins, as soon as the last gleam of twilight was fading in the western horizon. The owl, perched on the old masonry, occasionally sent forth its mournful note. The shrill laugh of the Arabs would sometimes rise above the cry of the jackal. Then all earthly noises were buried in the deep roll of the distant thunder. It was desolation such as those alone who have witnessed such scenes, can know – desolation greater than the desolation of the sandy wastes of Africa: for there was the wreck of man, as well as that of nature. (274)[56]

Layard and other archaeologists cite the Bible frequently, and in this passage the jackals, the owls, the atmosphere of desolation all seem straight out of our famed passage from the Book of Isaiah already cited. It is, of course, possible that Layard did see all these animals among the ruins; more likely, however, is that the biblical topos of ruined Babylon – infused with an undeniable sublime romantic gloom – informs this passage.

While most of the time Layard's prose is factual and more or less objective, at times he allows his emotions to shine through in a kind of romantic reverie. For example, in the preface to his *Popular Account of Discoveries at Nineveh,* Layard explores the feelings conjured up by the ruins of Babylon:

> There is, at the same time, a vague mystery attaching to remains like these, which induces travellers to examine them with more than ordinary interest, and even with some degree of awe. A great vitrified mass of brick-work, surrounded by the accumulated rubbish of ages, was believed to represent the identical tower, which called down the divine vengeance, and was overthrown, according to an universal tradition, by the fires of heaven. The mystery and dread, which attached to the place, were kept up by exaggerated accounts of wild beasts, who haunted the subterraneous passages, and of the no less savage tribes who wandered amongst the ruins. (vii–viii)

---

56 Layard, *Popular Account of Discoveries at Nineveh* (1851), by page number. This book was a popular abridgement of Layard's *Nineveh and its Remains,* 2 vols. (London, 1849).

Within the context of a biblical template (the reference to the Tower of Babel and divine vengeance), Layard here explains that when confronted by the ruins of Babylon, the traveller feels awe, mystery, and dread – a perception of the sublime that is of "[m]ore than ordinary interest." These are the tropes of romanticism and the gothic, provoked by the biblical Babylon topos of wild beasts dancing amid ruins.

And thus we can see this synthesis of traditions most clearly in Layard's dramatic extended formal summary of the ruin and decay of once-glorious Babylon, worth quoting here at length:

> It is not difficult to account for the rapid decay of the country around Babylon. As the inhabitants deserted the city the canals were neglected. When once those great sources of fertility were choked up, the plains became a wilderness. Upon the waters conveyed by their channels to the innermost parts of Mespotamia depended not only the harvests, the gardens, and the palm groves, but the very existence of the numerous towns and villages far removed from the river banks. They soon turned to mere heaps of earth and rubbish. Vegetation ceased, and the plains, parched by the burning heat of the sun, were ere long once again a vast arid waste.
>
> Such has been the history of Babylon. Her career was equally short and splendid; and although she has thus perished from the face of the earth, her ruins are still classic, indeed sacred, ground. The traveller visits, with no common emotion, those shapeless heaps, the scene of so many great and solemn events. In this plain, according to tradition, the primitive families of our race first found a resting-place. Here Nebuchadnezzar boasted of the glories of his city, and was punished for his pride. To these deserted halls were brought the captives of Judaea. In them Daniel, undazzled by the glories around him, remained steadfast to his faith, rose to be a governor amongst his rulers, and prophesied the downfall of his kingdom. There was held Belshazzar's feast, and was seen the writing upon the wall. Between those crumbling mounds Cyrus entered the neglected gates. Those massive ruins cover the spot where Alexander died. (539–40)[57]

The passage begins with the objective discourse of science and archaeology, as Layard explains the role of canals in the arid fate of Babylon. Yet the Babylon myth's tropes are present as well as absent presences – the short and splendid history of the city, Nebuchadnezzar's pride, Daniel,

57 Layard, *Discoveries in the Ruins of Nineveh and Babylon* (1853).

and Belshazzar's feast, Cyrus and Alexander. And then finally the sublime romantic view of history: the ruins are "classic," "sacred ground"; one contemplates this sacred ground "[w]ith no common emotion," as the ruins communicate the awesome weight of the past to posterity.[58]

By the end of the nineteenth and the beginning the twentieth century, this ruined Babylon of gothic romanticism begins to appear in displaced form as a consequence of full cultural assimilation. This is especially clear in the nascent genres of fantasy, horror, science fiction, and pulp adventures. In these genres, displaced Babylons abound in the ubiquitous trope of the lost, dead, haunted city. An influential example is the work of Lord Dunsany (Edward Plunkett, 18th Lord of Dunsany, 1878–1957), one of the founding fathers of modern fantasy literature.[59] Dunsany is quite fond of the desolate city topos; in all cases, the Babylon mythos is his clear influence. Take, for example the city of Sardathrion in Dunsany's story "Time and the Gods" (1906).[60] The tale is part of Dunsany's idiosyncratic personal mythology, the action set in a nameless land whose gods conjure the city of Sardathrion into existence through the power of their "marble dreams" (49). The city is hidden to all men except a chosen few. Like Babylon, Sardathrion is set in a faraway place, concealed in a lush valley surrounded by the barrier of a great desert:

> For round the valley a great desert lies through which no common traveller may come, but those whom the gods have chosen feel suddenly a great longing at heart, and crossing the mountains that divide the desert from the world, set out across it driven by the gods, till hidden in the desert's midst they find the valley at last and look with eyes upon Sardathrion. (49–50)

In this semi-allegorical story, Time is the slave of the gods, sent forth into the world from Sardathrion "to heal or overwhelm" humanity (50). Time will eventually return to destroy the gods, but they are oblivious to this in their pride. One day, when Time had been dispatched by them "to nimbly smite some city whereof the gods were weary" (50–1), the gods

58 A feature of the Gothic tradition from its inception is the impingement of the past on the present, a sort of historical return of the repressed: see Boting, *Gothic*, 1; Mighall, *Geography of Victorian Gothic Fiction.*

59 See Joshi's introduction to Lord Dunsany, *In the Land of Time*, ed. Joshi, ix–xxiii.

60 All citations to Dunsany's fiction are from Dunsany, *In the Land of Time*, ed. Joshi; "Time and the Gods," 49–52.

speak to each other in their arrogance, glorying in their power "above the twilight":

> "Surely we are the lords of Time and the gods of the worlds besides. See how our city Sardathrion lifts over other cities. Others arise and perish but Sardathrion standeth yet, the first and the last of cities. Rivers are lost in the sea and streams forsake the hills, but ever Sardathrion's fountains arise in our dream city. As was Sardathrion when the gods were young, so are her streets to-day as a sign that we are the gods." (51)

Much in this passage recalls the medieval tradition we have already examined: Sardathrion, like Babylon, glories in her power and might at a sublime moment before her inevitable fall; Dunsany's gods, like Nebuchadnezzar and Belshazzar in the Old English *Daniel*, foolishly exult in the power of their mighty city, which, like Babylon in the medieval tradition, is the first and last of cities.

Of course, as if on cue, Time suddenly appears with a bloody sword to declare: "Sardathrion is gone! I have overthrown it!" (51). The gods raise a lament in Dunsany's distinctive biblical idiom, language clearly influenced by Revelation and the prophets on Babylon:[61]

> "Sardathrion? Sardathrion, the marble city? Thou, thou hast overthrown it? Thou, the slave of the gods?" ... And a new cry went wailing through the Twilight, the lament of the gods for Their dream city, crying: "Tears may not bring again Sardathrion." ... "How oft when Night came suddenly on Morning playing in the fields of Twilight did we watch thy pinnacles emerging from the darkness, Sardathrion, Sardathrion, dream city of the gods, and thine onyx lions looming limb by limb from the dusk." (51)

Sardathrion's onyx lions call to mind the great statues unearthed by Layard at Nineveh. The brief narrative ends with a voiced lament, offering a vivid image of biblical ruin:

> "Let one fragment of thy marbles stand up above the dust for thine old gods to caress, as a man when all else is lost treasures one lock of the hair of his beloved.

61 On the stylistic influence of the AV on Dunsany see Joshi, *Lord Dunsany*, 203–9.

> "Sardathrion, the gods must kiss once more the place where thy streets were once.
> "There were wonderful marbles in thy streets, Sardathrion.
> "Sardathrion, Sardathrion, the gods weep for thee." (52)

Sardathrion's destruction is very much like the vision of doom in Dunsany's prose poem "The City" (1913)[62] in which the speaker's fancy sees a vision of a desert city and an exodus of its unwanted poets and artists; the people are leaving because "some doom ... is going to fall on the city," abandoning the metropolis to face the "ominous look on the face of the sky" (216). The poem concludes on an Ozymandian note: "And only a thousand years later I passed that way, and there was nothing, even among the weeds, of what had been that city" (216).

We see the same dissolute and doomed city of the desert in "Idle Days on the Yann" (1908),[63] in which Dunsany's narrator journeys down the river Yann in a fantastical land of dreams. Along the river of dreamland they encounter a series of fantastic cities, a running catalogue much like Calvino's *Invisible Cities.* The narrator explains to his shipmates that he is from a desert surrounding "a beautiful blue city called Golthoth the Damned, which was sentinelled all round by wolves and their shadows, and had been utterly desolate for years and years, because of a curse which the gods once spoke in anger and could never since recall" (146). Astahahn, another city on the Yann, is of vaguely oriental design, calling to mind the glories unearthed by nineteenth- and early twentieth-century excavation:

> All in that city was of ancient device; the carving on the houses, which, when age had broken it, remained unrepaired, was of the remotest times, and everywhere were represented in stone beasts that have long since passed away from Earth – the dragon, the griffin, and the hippogriffin, and the different species of gargoyle. Nothing was to be found, whether material or custom, that was new in Astahahn. (151)

Further down the Yann, the famed Perdóndaris is "a powerful city ... encompassed by a wall of great strength and altitude" (155). When the narrator departs down the river, he never sees the city again, for he has

62 Dunsany, *In the Land of Time,* 216.
63 Dunsany, *In the Land of Time,* 146–62.

heard "that something swift and wonderful has suddenly wrecked Perdóndaris in a day – towers, and walls, and people" (156). Tropes of the Babylon ruin topos recur here, scattered among these three cities: cities of sublime beauty and wonder; prodigious walls and the marvels of immense antiquity; oriental exoticism; a curse and divine judgment (in response to some sort of implied transgression); biblical desolation and the animals of the wasteland. Golthoth, Astahahn, Perdóndaris: these are the cities of fantasy and products of Dunsany's lush imagination, but they display the distinctive features of the Babylon ruin topos.

Babylon itself makes an appearance. In his prose poem "The Raft-Builders" (1909),[64] Dunsany compares writers to "sailors hastily making rafts upon doomed ships" (198). Oblivion, like the sea, is all around humanity waiting to destroy its history, but writings and memories are the rafts that attempt to defeat Oblivion and Time itself:

> See now the wreckage of Babylon floating idly, and something there that once was Nineveh; already their kings and queens are in the deeps among the weedy masses of old centuries that hide the sodden bulk of sunken Tyre and make a darkness round Persepolis. (198)[65]

We might fruitfully compare this aquatic motif to Layard's speculation on the meaning of the ruins at the Babylonian site of Tel Jemal, in which he uses a similar oceanic conceit:

> As the evening crept on, I watched from the highest mound the sun as it gradually sank in unclouded splendor below the sea-like expanse before me. On all sides, as far as the eye could reach, rose the grass-covered heaps marking the site of ancient habitations. The great tide of civilisation had long since ebbed, leaving these scattered wrecks on the solitary shore. Are those waters to flow again, bearing back the seeds of knowledge and of wealth that they have wafted to the West? We wanderers were seeking

64 Dunsany, *In the Land of Time*, 198.

65 Cf. Emerson's essay "History": "The instinct of the mind, the purpose of nature, betrays itself in the use we make of the signal narrations of history. Time dissipates to shining ether the solid angularity of facts. No anchor, no cable, no fences avail to keep a fact a fact. Babylon, Troy, Tyre, Palestine, and even early Rome are passing already into fiction. The Garden of Eden, the sun standing still in Gibeon, is poetry thenceforward to all nations. Who cares what the fact was, when we have made a constellation of it to hang in heaven an immortal sign?" (*Essential Writings*, ed. Atkinson, 116).

> what they had left behind, as children gather up the colored shells on the deserted sands. At my feet there was a busy scene, making more lonely the unbroken solitude which reigned in the vast plain around, where the only thing having life or motion were the shadows of the lofty mounds as they lengthened before the declining sun.[66]

Both Dunsany and Layard address similar issues in a shared register: the ruined city as a sublime mode of understanding the nature of time and the workings of the past.

However, the clearest evidence for direct influence of the Babylon-ruin topos in its gothic/romantic inflection is Dunsany's story "The Fall of Babbulkund" (1907).[67] This tale is also an Ozymandian/Orientalist pastiche refracted through Dunsany's baroque imagination. Like much of Dunsany's work, "The Fall of Babbulkund" deliberately blurs the line between fantasy and reality; the story's action is, and is not, set in the real world. The story begins with a simple declaration of the city's name and central image: "I said: 'I will arise now and see Babbulkund, City of Marvel'" (73). The name "Babbulkund" itself, of course, recalls the Tower of Babel, and Babbulkund is a displaced Babylon. Babbulkund was founded long ago, in a vaguely oriental setting:

> She [Babbulkund] is of one age with the earth; the stars are her sisters. Pharaohs of the old time coming conquering from Araby first saw her, a solitary mountain in the desert, and cut the mountain into towers and terraces. They destroyed one of the hills of God, but they made Babbulkund. She is carven, not built; her palaces are one with her terraces, there is neither joint nor cleft. Hers is the beauty of the youth of the world. She deemeth herself to be the middle of Earth, and hath four gates facing outward to the Nations. (73)

Dunsany places Babbulkund beyond a mythic, Joycean "Araby"; the city is a sacred *omphalos* in the middle of the earth, facing out to all the nations. The solitary hill of God, out of which Babbulkund is carved, is a displaced Tower of Babel, which was also raised up to rival the heavens in the "beauty of the youth of the world."

The tale's narrator gathers three companions for a pilgrimage to this sublime city. They seek a wonder at the numinous centre of the world and

---

66 Layard, *Discoveries in the Ruins of Nineveh and Babylon* (245); see also the illustrations on 344–5; 350–1; 359–60; 363.

67 Dunsany, *In the Land of Time*, 73–85.

journey to "the land of which Babbulkund is the abiding glory" (74). The men hire "camels and Arab guides" (74) and journey through the heat of a great desert. As they cross the wasteland on their quest to Babbulkund, they encounter mysterious solitary travellers; at their campfire the first of these prophet-figures declares: "'Hearken and I will tell you of Babbulkund, City of Marvel'" (74). He explains that the city (like Babylon) resides at the meeting place of the "River of Myth [and] the Waters of Fable" (74). The rivers flow through the desert wasteland until meeting in marvellous fecundity at Babbulkund: "Sterile and desolate they float far through the desert each in the appointed cleft, with life upon neither bank, but give birth in Babbulkund to the sacred purple garden whereof all nations sing" (74). Like mythic Babylon and its Hanging Gardens, Babbulkund also boasts wondrous gardens in the midst of a vast, sterile desert.

The party then encounters a second traveller/prophet, who relates further wonders of the city and its pseudo-Egyptian ruler Nehemoth. Babbulkund, the traveller tells them, has seven wonders (recalling Babylon and the Seven Wonders of the World): three in the middle of the city and four at the gates. The city has been enriched by plunder and tribute from around the world, from all points of the compass. The prophet's description wraps the speaker and his company in a scene of sublime wonder:

> The traveller ceased to speak. For a long time the clear stars, sisters of Babbulkund, had shone upon him speaking, the desert wind had arisen and whispered to the sand, and the sand had long gone secretly to and fro; none of us had moved, none of us had fallen asleep, not so much from wonder at his tale as from the thought that we ourselves in two days' time should see that wondrous city. Then we wrapped our blankets around us and lay down with our feet towards the embers of our fire and instantly were asleep, and in our dreams we multiplied the fame of the City of Marvel. (80)

In their fragmentation, ruins suggest the absent glory of plenitude; likewise, the spectral glory of the provoked imagination is always greater than any reality: the unheard melodies more sweet than real music. In this same fashion, the dreams and tales of Babbulkund conjure up a sublime image for the travellers that will not answer to any reality.

Finally, a third traveler, weary and dressed in tattered rags, overtakes them the next evening; he carries a message of prophetic doom to Babbulkund, speaking once again in a biblical idiom that recalls the prophecies of Babylon's fall. He proclaims: "I am the servant of the Lord the God of my people, and I go to do his work on Babbulkund" (81). He praises Babbulkund, "the most beautiful city in the world," (81), a city sprung from the beauty of artists' dreams. But a discordant note of transgression creeps into his *encomium urbis*: "Oh! Very beautiful is white Babbulkund, very beautiful she is, but proud; and the Lord the God of my people hath seen her in her pride" (82). Babbulkund, like Babylon of old, worships false gods in her pride: in this case, the "abomination Annolith" and the dog-god Voth (82). The reluctant prophet laments: "'Alas for thee, Babbulkund, alas that I may not even now turn back, for to-morrow I must prophecy against thee and cry out against thee, Babbulkund'" (82). He warns the pilgrims to see the beauty of Babbulkund before sudden doom overtakes the city.

The next day the company draws near Babbulkund, but cross a group of refugees fleeing the city, people "not of the race of the people of Babbulkund," but rather slaves "captured in youth and taken away from the hills that are to the northward" (83). These enslaved people, obviously recalling the captive Jews of Babylon, tell how Nehemoth had been troubled by "dreams of doom" (83) of the destruction and desolation of Babbulkund, like Nebuchadnezzar and Belshazzar in medieval traditions of Babylon's fall. Nehemoth and his people consult their false idols, but no one can interpret the portents; there is no Daniel-figure here for them. The slave refugees move on, leaving the party uncertain as a great desert storm builds. At the end and climax of the story, the pilgrims perceive a great wailing wind from the direction of Babbulkund, a blast in which "hundreds of sandy shapes went towering by, and there were little cries among them and sounds of a passing away" (85). When they arrive at the junction of the rivers, Babbulkund is gone, and rather than discover the enthralling city of their dreams, they confront a vision of desolation, in biblical tableau:

> All round us lay the sand and rocks of the unchanging desert, save to the southwards where the jungle stood with its orchids facing skywards. Then we perceived that we had arrived too late, and that her doom had come to Babbulkund; and by the river in the empty desert on the sand the man in rags was seated, with his face hidden in his hands, weeping bitterly. (85)

The story's coda adopts the pseudo-biblical voice of historical chronicle:

> Thus passed away in the hour of her iniquities before Annolith, in the two thousand and thirty-second year of her being, in the six thousand and fiftieth

> year of the building of the World, Babbulkund, City of Marvel, sometime called by those that hated her City of the Dog, but hourly mourned in Araby and Ind and wide through jungle and desert; leaving no memorial in stone to show that she had been, but remembered with an abiding love, in spite of the anger of God, by all that knew her beauty, whereof still they sing. (85)

"The Fall of Babbulkund" nicely encapsulates most of the elements of the Babylon-ruin topos as influenced by nineteenth-century gothic romanticism and the discourse of archaeology. In the twinned expression of the *encomium urbis* and *excidio urbis* in this passage, and in the blasphemous idolatry punished by a divine vengeance, it is easy to see the Matter of Babylon moving beneath the surface of this story, animating its various tropes and motifs to construct a displaced Babylon ruin. Dunsany's twist here is that there are no physical ruins left of Babbulkund: the destruction of the city has been total and it is only in story and song, imagination and dream – as absent presence – that Babbulkund may endure. The shattered visage of Ozymandias remains to provoke the mind in Shelley's poem; but of Dunsany's city there is no trace.

Ruined Babylon and Modernity

And what of later, more distant displacements of the Babylon ruin topos? The dead, cursed, ruined city endures as a standard trope of pulp adventure, science fiction, horror, and fantasy literature. The Babylon ruin topos in this displaced form can be found in the work of authors as varied as H. Rider Haggard, Arthur Machen, M.R. James, Clark Ashton Smith, Robert E. Howard, Edgar Rice Burroughs, Michael Moorcock, J.R.R. Tolkien, and C.S. Lewis.

The city has always been a central subject of science fiction, not only in pulp/popular form, but also in the work of more ambitious authors such as Clifford D. Simak, Arthur C. Clarke, Samuel Delany, Greg Bear, and China Miéville.[68] Science fiction often envisions the rise of the mega-city on earth – enormous decadent metropolises, some of them planet-spanning: examples include Trantor in Asimov's classic *Foundation* series

---

68 See Clifford D. Simak, *City* (1952); Arthur C. Clarke, *The City and the Stars* (1956); Samuel Delany, *Dhalgren* (1975); Greg Bear, *Strength of Stones* (1981) and *City at the End of Time* (2008); China Miéville, *The City and the City* (2009), and many others. For a good discussion of the city as image and setting in science fiction, see Wolfe, *Known and Unknown*, 86–124.

6.3. The Tower of Babel from *Metropolis* (dir. Fritz Lang, 1927).

(1951–3), Mega City-1 in the long-running British comic book institution *Judge Dredd*, and Terminus in Dan Simmons's *Hyperion Cantos* (1989–97). The dystopic future megacity produces the corresponding striking iconic visuals of overcrowded cities in films such as Fritz Lang's *Metropolis* (1927), Michael Anderson's *Logan's Run* (1976), Ridley Scott's *Bladerunner* (1982), and all their myriad offshoots and imitations. *Metropolis* has an active biblical subtext, adapting the Tower of Babel and the Whore of Babylon for its expressionist critique of class in Weimar Germany (see Figure 6.3).

These vast cities of the future often tend towards totalitarianism and oppression, as in the dystopic vision of *Metropolis*, *Brazil* (1985, dir. Terry Gilliam), and *The Matrix* (1999, dir. Andy and Lana Wachowski). Such corruption and gigantic decadence often result in destruction and ruin. The ruined city of course appears in post-apocalyptic fiction as early as Richard Jeffries's *After London* (1885) and has a healthy life in the clichés of contemporary post-apocalyptic film and television: the striking desolate visions of abandoned London and New York in *28 Days Later* (2002, dir. Danny Boyle) and *I Am Legend* (2007, dir. Francis Lawrence), for example. In science fiction set off-planet, enigmatic ruins and relics left behind by lost, dead advanced races are standard plot devices (an innovation traceable to Lovecraft, as we shall see): the monolith in *2001: A Space Odyssey* (1968, dir. Stanley Kubrick); Jack McDevitt's novels, especially *The Engines of God* (1995); the cult television series *Babylon 5* with its cursed planet and city of Za-ha-dum (1994–8); and the galaxy-spanning lost civilization of the "Ancients" in the *Stargate* universe (various series, 1994–2010). Thus we find ruined, displaced Babylons in science fiction from the sublime to the ridiculous, from Cormac McCarthy's *The Road* to the 1970s *Planet of the Apes* films.[69]

Displaced Babylons also abound in seminal fantasy literature: Tolkien's evil or corrupted fortress-cities: Utumno, Angband, Moria, Barad-dûr ("The Dark Tower"), and Minas Morgul ("Tower of Dark Sorcery"), a corrupt and degraded shadow of its former beautiful incarnation as Minas Ithil ("Tower of the Moon").[70] In the first book of C.S. Lewis's Narnia series, *The Magician's Nephew* (1955), the children Polly and Digory accidentally reanimate the evil Queen Jadis of Charn, a ruined city that had been "deserted for hundreds, perhaps thousands, of years" (48) on a dying ancient planet.[71] In the eerie Hall of Images they find a long line of royal statues, images of the rulers of Charn, many of them cruel of aspect, and "even despairing ... as if the people they belonged to had done dreadful things and also suffered dreadful things" (52–3). The children, to their eventual regret, awaken one of these figures: Queen Jadis, the last ruler of Charn, who had put herself under a spell of suspended animation, and who will later enter Narnia as the White Witch, origin of evil. The children tour the ruined city with Jadis:

> And on the earth, in every direction, as far as the eye could reach, there spread a vast city in which there was no living thing to be seen. And all the temples, towers, palaces, pyramids, and bridges cast long, disastrous-looking shadows in the light of that withered sun. Once a great river had flowed through the city, but the water had long since vanished, and it was now only a wide ditch of gray dust. (65; see Figure 6.4)

As a professor of medieval literature and devout Anglican, Lewis was no doubt influenced here by the Babylon ruin topos, which would have been part of his basic intellectual apparatus. As the children look at this image of desolation, the Queen expostulates in a familiar biblical idiom:

> "Look well on that which no eyes will ever see again," said the Queen. "Such was Charn, that great city, the city of the King of Kings, the wonder of the world, perhaps of all worlds." (65)

69 As with most science fiction, the select citations here represent a vast, wider range of materials: novels, short stories, periodicals and internet fan sites, films, television series, graphic novels, video games, parodies of all types. Contemporary science fiction tends to metastasize into various multimedia forms.

70 On the city in fantasy literature, with examples, see *Encyclopedia of Fantasy*, ed. Clute and Grant, s.v. "city" and Irvine, "Urban Fantasy."

71 Lewis, *The Magician's Nephew* (1955), by page numbers.

6.4. The ruined city of Charn. Illustration by Pauline Baynes, from C.S. Lewis, *The Magician's Nephew* [1955], 46. Used by permission of the estate of C.S. Lewis.

Jadis herself descends from Lilith, the demonic daughter of Adam and Eve, and has both Jinn and giant blood in her veins; we learn she had destroyed Charn with the terrible magic of The Deplorable Word in a war of pride with her sister. Once spoken, the Word destroyed all life on the planet, except the speaker. Charn, like Dunsany's Babbulkund, is a displaced Babylon, embodying its familiar images and tropes.

The list of displaced Babylons could be extended almost indefinitely in genre fiction and popular culture of all sorts, but I wish to pause to explicate one final influential author at greater length: H.P. Lovecraft, who was fascinated, perhaps even obsessed, by the haunted city motif.[72] Lovecraft's influence adds an important element to the Babylon ruin topos in the twentieth century: a new bleak sense of time and history distinctive to early twentieth-century modernity.[73]

Lovecraft inherits all the tropes of the Babylon ruin topos active through the nineteenth century; Lovecraft himself was an amateur antiquarian and scientist, and based his fiction on eighteenth and nineteenth century models, especially Edgar Allen Poe's work. A few of Poe's gothic writings about cities obviously caught Lovecraft's imagination.[74] Poe's poem "The City in the Sea" (1845), for example, reads like an early sketch of Lovecraft's story "The Call of Cthulu" (1928):

Lo! Death has reared himself a throne
In a strange city lying alone
Far down within the dim West,
Where the good and the bad and the worst and the best
Have gone to their eternal rest.
There shrines and palaces and towers
(Time-eaten towers that tremble not!)
Resemble nothing that is ours.
Around, by lifting winds forgot,
Resignedly beneath the sky
The melancholy waters lie.

No rays from the holy heaven come down
On the long night-time of that town;
But light from out the lurid sea
Streams up the turrets silently –

72 On Lovecraft and the city see Menegaldo, "City in H.P. Lovecraft's Work" and Lévy, *Lovecraft*, 46–9.

73 On the relationship between fantasy/horror literature and modernism see Casey, "Modernism and Postmodernism."

74 On Lovecraft's debt to Poe, see Burleson, *H.P. Lovecraft: A Critical Study*, 213–17; see also note 84, below.

Gleams up the pinnacles far and free –
Up domes – up spires – up kingly halls –
Up fanes – up Babylon-like walls –
Up shadowy long-forgotten bowers
Of sculptured ivy and stone flowers –
Up many and many a marvellous shrine
Whose wreathéd friezes intertwine
The viol, the violet, and the vine.

Resignedly beneath the sky
The melancholy waters lie.
So blend the turrets and shadows there
That all seem pendulous in air,
While from a proud tower in the town
Death looks gigantically down.

There open fanes and gaping graves
Yawn level with the luminous waves;
But not the riches there that lie
In each idol's diamond eye –
Not the gaily-jewelled dead
Tempt the waters from their bed;
For no ripples curl, alas!
Along that wilderness of glass –
No swellings tell that winds may be
Upon some far-off happier sea –
No heavings hint that winds have been
On seas less hideously serene.

But lo, a stir is in the air!
The wave – there is a movement there!
As if the towers had thrust aside,
In slightly sinking, the dull tide –
As if their tops had feebly given
A void within the filmy Heaven.
The waves have now a redder glow –
The hours are breathing faint and low –
And when, amid no earthly moans,
Down, down that town shall settle hence,

Hell, rising from a thousand thrones,
Shall do it reverence.[75]

This "strange city" with its "[t]ime eaten towers" broods amid "melancholy waters"; it is a place of "open fanes and gaping graves" with no heavenly illumination, but instead a light from the "lurid sea" climbs up its domes and shrines, and up its "Babylon-like walls." Death looks "gigantically" down from a "proud tower" in the midst of the city. All these elements derive from our now-familiar Babylon ruin dossier, including a proud Tower rising amid the "Babylon-like walls."

In a stroke of imagination that would deeply influence Lovecraft, Poe displaces another abandoned Babylon to a new uncharted wasteland of the nineteenth century: the Antarctic. Poe's strange, perhaps unfinished, novella *The Narrative of Arthur Gordon Pym of Nantucket* (1837) features a phantasmagoric journey to the Antarctic, where the eponymous narrator encounters a series of adversaries in episodic adventures; in a climactic voyage, Pym journeys to the depths of the South Pole, on the run from natives across the mysterious island of Tsalal. Pym and his companion find strange glyphs carved into the labyrinthine hills of the island mountains, suggesting the presence of a lost civilization. They descend into an even deeper abyss with a distinct Babylonian cast:

> The place was one of singular wildness, and its aspect brought to my mind the descriptions given by travellers of those dreary regions marking the site of degraded Babylon. Not to speak of the ruins of the disruptured cliff, which formed a chaotic barrier in the vista to the northward, the surface of the ground in every other direction was strewn with huge tumuli, apparently the wreck of some gigantic structures of art; although, in detail, no semblance of art could be detected. Scoria were abundant, and large shapeless blocks of the black granite, intermingled with others of marl, and both granulated with metal. Of vegetation there were no traces whatsoever throughout the whole of the desolate area within sight. Several immense scorpions were seen, and various reptiles not elsewhere to be found in the high latitudes.[76]

By now, the elements of the Babylon ruin topos are familiar: an ancient or lost civilization; sublime ruins and remnants found in the midst of a

75 Poe, *Poetry and Tales*, 67–8.
76 *The Narrative of Arthur Gordon Pym of Nantucket* in Poe, *Poetry and Tales*, 1003–1182, at 1171.

wasteland; even the presence of evil fauna – here scorpions and reptiles – inhabiting the ruins. All of these motifs are signed, as it were, by a direct reference to "degraded Babylon" itself.

Following these images of the city in Poe, the cursed city is a central element in Lovecraft's work. His poems such as "The City" "The Eidolon," "The Nightmare Lake," "The Outpost," "The Courtyard," and "The Dweller" seek to recreate the atmosphere of dread and gloom in Poe's "The City in the Sea."[77] "The Dweller" gives us a primordial evil haunting a ruined city, again signed by a direct Babylon reference:

> [The city] had been old when Babylon was new;
> None knows how long it slept beneath that mound;
> Where in the end our questing shovels found
> Its granite blocks and brought it back to view.
> There were vast pavements and foundation walls,
> And crumbling slabs and statues, carved to shew
> Fantastic beings of some long ago
> Past anything the world of man recalls.
>
> And then we saw those stone steps leading down
> Through a choked gate of graven dolomite
> To some black haven of eternal night
> Where elder signs and primal secrets frown.
> We cleared a path – but raced in mad retreat
> When from below we heard those clumping feet. (1–14)

Lovecraft's fiction (far better-known and more effective than his fumbling poetry) returns again and again to the Babylon ruin topos. Visionary, gothic cities inspire both wonder and terror in tales such as "Polaris," "Dagon," "Facts Concerning the Late Arthur Jermyn and His Family," "Celephaïs," "Nyarlathotep," "The Dream-Quest of Unknown Kadath," "The Shadow Out of Time," and "The Call of Cthulhu," with its sunken city of R'lyeh.[78] In "The Doom That Came to Sarnath" (1920) men found the city of Sarnath near a vast lake in the land of Mnar, near

77 All citations from Lovecraft's poetry are from *Ancient Track: Complete Poetical Works,* ed. Joshi, by line numbers.

78 In "The Call of Cthulhu" the sculptor Henry Wilcox carves out a figure of the god Cthulhu based on his psychic dreams, complete with indecipherable hieroglyphics. When asked by an archaeologist whether he had made the object or found it, the

an older city called Ib, an evil place "peopled with beings not pleasing to behold" (5).[79] The men of Sarnath destroy the inhuman creatures of Ib and cast their remnants into the great lake. The city of Sarnath grows to Babylonian proportions: "So Sarnath waxed mighty and learned and beautiful, and sent forth conquering armies to subdue the neighboring cities ... The wonder of the world and the pride of all mankind was Sarnath the magnificent. Of polished desert-quarried marble were its walls, in height 300 cubits and breadth 75, so that chariots might pass each other as men drave them along the top" (6–7).[80] The detail of walls broad enough for chariots to pass each other is drawn directly from stock descriptions of Babylon we examined in chapter 1. For a thousand years Sarnath exults in its power until finally the ghastly descendants of Ib rise up out of the lake and destroy Sarnath. Only haunted ruins remain after that: "Through all the land of Mnar and the lands adjacent spread the tales of those who had fled from Sarnath, and caravans sought that accursed city and its precious metals no more" (10).

"The Nameless City" is a very similar story, also with a vaguely Middle Eastern setting. The tale opens with an archaeologist (much like Layard) discovering a crumbling city "[r]emote in the desert of Araby":

> When I drew nigh the nameless city I knew it was accursed. I was travelling in a parched and terrible valley under the moon, and afar I saw it protruding uncannily above the sands as parts of a corpse may protrude from an ill-made grave. Fear spoke from the age-worn stones of this hoary survivor of the deluge, this great-grandmother of the eldest pyramid; and a viewless aura repelled me and bade me retreat from antique and sinister secrets that no man should see, and no man else had ever dared to see. (30)

One can sense the general influence of Dunsany here (an author Lovecraft revered); the city and general structure of the tale recall Sardathrion

---

sculptor replies: "It is new, indeed, for I made it last night in a dream of strange cities; and dreams are older than brooding Tyre, or the contemplative Sphinx, or garden-girdled Babylon" (in Lovecraft, *Call of Cthulhu*, ed. Joshi, 139–69, at 143).

79 Citations from "The Doom That Came to Sarnath" and "The Nameless City" are from Lovecraft, *Dreams in the Witch House*, ed. Joshi, 5–11 and 30–41, respectively.

80 The hyperbolic description continues, including gardens, lion statues and "tower-like temples" (8), upon which the men of Sarnath, like the ancient Chaldeans, observe and study the stars.

or "The Fall of Babbulkund."[81] Lovecraft's narrator tells us that the city, hidden by the "sands of uncounted ages," must have been in ruin "before the first stones of Memphis were laid, and while the bricks of Babylon were yet unbaked" (30). The narrator enters these "brooding ruins" and searches for "relics of the forgotten race" (31). His emotion is sublime awe: "I saw that the city had been mighty indeed, and wondered at the sources of its greatness. To myself I pictured the splendours of an age so distant that Chaldaea could not recall it" (31). The narrator believes that the "primeval ruins" hold the traces of "antediluvian people" (32), and encounters an inhuman evil lingering in the ruins: a howling wind emanating from the city depths chases him away in fear as a "hell-born babel of the howling wind-wraiths" (40) almost drives him insane.[82]

We might compare Lovecraft's "The Nameless City" to an anecdote in Layard's *Popular Account of Discoveries at Nineveh*, a book Lovecraft might well have read. At Birs Nimroud, Layard's men excavate a giant winged lion statue with a human head (now in the British Museum). The night before the discovery, Layard cannot sleep, sounding here much like a typical Lovecraftian narrator:

> I had slept little during the night ... Hopes, long cherished, were now to be realised, or were to end in disappointment. Visions of palaces under-ground, of gigantic monsters, of sculptured figures and endless inscriptions, floated before me ... I fancied myself wandering in a maze of chambers from which I could find no outlet. Then, again, all was reburied, and I was standing on the grass-covered mound. (15)

The next morning they discover the huge monstrous stone head, terrifying the Arab workmen. Layard comments:

> I was not surprised that the Arabs had been amazed and terrified at this apparition. It required no stretch of the imagination to conjure up the most strange fancies. This gigantic head, blanched with age, thus rising from the bowels of the earth, might well have belonged to one of those fearful beings which are pictured in the traditions of the country, as appearing to mortals, slowly ascending from the regions below. (49)

---

81 On Lovecraft's debt to Dunsany see Schweitzer, "Lovecraft and Lord Dunsany"; Joshi, *H.P. Lovecraft*, 20–4; Burleson, *H.P. Lovecraft: A Critical Study*, 221–5; Joshi, *H.P. Lovecraft: The Decline of the West*, 115–19.

82 Cf. a similar howling "babel" in "The Shadow out of Time," 393.

6.5. Discovery of giant head in Nimrud Palace, Iraq; from Layard, *Popular Account of Discoveries at Nineveh* [1851], 48. Courtesy of the O. Meredith Wilson Library at the University of Minnesota.

In Lovecraft's fiction, of course, the monsters really do exist; for Layard, this is just the superstition of the local Arabs (see Figure 6.5).

Layard is moved, rather, by the sublime depth of history as he contemplates these monstrous figures that long ago guarded the temple entrance in the ancient city:

> I used to contemplate for hours these mysterious emblems, and muse over their intent and history. What more noble forms could have ushered the people into the temple of their gods? What more sublime images could have been borrowed from nature, by men who sought, unaided by the light of revealed religion, to embody their conception of the wisdom, power, and ubiquity of a Supreme Being? ... They had awed and instructed races which flourished 3000 years ago ... For twenty-five centuries they had been hidden from the eye of man, and they now stood forth once more in their ancient majesty. But how changed was the scene around them! The luxury and

> civilisation of a mighty nation had given place to the wretchedness and ignorance of a few half-barbarous tribes. The wealth of temples, and the riches of great cities, had been succeeded by ruins and shapeless heaps of earth. (52)

The immense age of the earth was gradually understood scientifically in the nineteenth century, in terms of geology, evolutionary biology, and archaeology, leading to the representation of time here in Layard's account. This changing sense of time in turn transformed the Babylon ruin topos in response to modernity. The linked sense of deep time and history within modernity, hinted at here by Layard, was by the time Lovecraft wrote in the 1930s – during the heyday of modernism – a fully assimilated commonplace fact: time was infinitely more vast than humanity had ever dreamed. Lovecraft incorporates this understanding of time as a vast abyss – and the corresponding conclusion that the universe is an infinite, impersonal place – into his fiction, creating a new inflection of the Babylon ruin topos.

Lovecraft's "The Nameless City" would serve as an outline for his most extensive, successful, and influential adaptation of the Babylon-ruin topos: his superb novella *At the Mountains of Madness* (1936).[83] This late work is in many ways the culmination of Lovecraft's artistic ambitions and the most representative expression of his adaptation of the Babylon ruin topos.[84] *At the Mountains of Madness* tells the tale of William Dyer, professor of geology at fictional Miskatonic University and his harrowing scientific expedition to the Antarctic. Dyer relates the retrospective narrative of his disastrous journey because a new expedition to the same terrible place has been announced, and he wishes to dissuade anyone from disturbing the secret horror found there. In many ways a reimagining or adaptation of Poe's *Narrative of Arthur Gordon Pym*, *At the Mountains of Madness* likewise places the Babylon-ruin topos not in the near East, nor in deserts of some fantastic Dunsanian dreamland, but in the unknown waste of the Antarctic, one of the last truly unknown spaces on the map in the 1930s.[85]

83 All citations from *At the Mountains of Madness* are from Lovecraft, *Thing on the Doorstep*, ed. Joshi, 246–340, by page numbers.

84 On *Madness* as one of Lovecraft's finest, most ambitious works, see Burleson, *H.P. Lovecraft: A Critical Study*, 165–71; Cannon, *Lovecraft*, 105; Joshi, *Dreamer and a Visionary*, 300; Miéville, "Introduction," xii.

85 See Eckhardt, "Behind the Mountains of Madness," 31. Critics sometimes refer to *Madness* as a "sequel" to *Arthur Gordon Pym*, but this is not quite correct: see Joshi,

Dyer and his team sail from Boston in September of 1930, entering a sublime polar region coloured by Lovecraft's imagination, a place "vivid and fancy-stirring" (249), journeying into "regions never trodden by human foot or penetrated by human imagination" (254). After arriving at their Antarctic base, the expedition proceeds by plane to the unexplored inland. As they move into the frigid wasteland, Dyer sees what he believes are fantastic mirages generated by the polar climate: "Distant mountains floated in the sky as enchanted cities, and often the whole white world would dissolve into a gold, silver, and scarlet land of Dunsanian dreams and adventurous expectancy under the magic of the low midnight sun" (253).[86] It is a "land of mystery in a dream or gateway to forbidden world of untrodden wonder" (256); an "ineffable majesty" (257) characterizes the landscape around them.[87] In the distance they see a massive mountain range of unimaginable sublime height, a

---

H.P. Lovecraft, 37; *Thing on the Doorstep*, ed. Joshi, 420. In *Madness* a character directly cites Poe's story (250, 331), and Lovecraft also incorporates a few of Poe's details, including Poe's enigmatic refrain "Tekeli-li"; it is perhaps more accurate to say that Lovecraft's story adapts the same imaginative world of Poe's story, reworking some of Poe's concepts into something new: see Zanger, "Poe's Endless Voyage," 282–3. On the relationship of *Madness* to Poe's *Arthur Gordon Pym* see Cannon, *Lovecraft*, 101–2; Indick, "Lovecraft's POElar Adventure"; Cerasini, "Thematic Links."

86 Cf. Layard's account of the "remarkable effect of mirage" he encounters near the ruins of Ctesiphon: "As the quivering sun rose in unclouded splendor, the palace was transformed into a vast arcade of enormous arches resting upon columns and masses of masonry" (572). In a note to this passage, he relates another incredible mirage: "I witnessed another very remarkable effect of mirage in the early spring of 1840, when riding one morning over the plains near Bir, on the Euphrates. Suddenly, as if by enchantment, a magnificent city, standing on the borders of a lake, rose before me. Palaces, domes, towers, and the spires of Gothic cathedrals were reflected in the blue waters. The deception was so complete, the appearance so real, that I could scarcely believe some mighty capital had not been by magic transported into the Desert. There was scarcely a stone or bush to account for this singular phenomenon" (*Discoveries in the Ruins of Nineveh and Babylon*, 572–3).

87 Again, cf. Layard, *A Popular Account of Discoveries at Nineveh*, in which he describes what it is like for a Western traveler who comes to the ruins of Babylon and Nineveh, expecting to behold more dramatic remains (such as ruins in Greece and Rome), but instead confronts huge shapeless mounds and must then imagine the buildings left behind in the past: "The more he conjectures, the more vague the results appear. The scene around is worthy of the ruin he is contemplating; desolation meets desolation: a feeling of awe succeeds to wonder; for there is nothing to relieve the mind, to lead to hope, or to tell of what has gone by. These huge mounds of Assyria made a deeper impression upon me, gave rise to more serious thoughts and more earnest reflection, than the temples of Balbec and the theatres of Ionia" (5).

6.6. Nicholas Roerich, *The Dead City* (1918). Used by permission of the Nicholas Roerich Museum, New York, NY

"titanic mountain rampart" that inspired their "deepest sense of adventure" (255).

Lake, the team biologist, leads a sub-expedition to these mountains; his subsequent radio communications with the main party ominously speak of "[o]dd formations" on the mountain slopes: "Great low square blocks with exactly vertical sides, and rectangular lines of low vertical ramparts, like the old Asian castles clinging to steep mountains in Roerich's paintings" (256; see Figure 6.6).[88]

Lake and his party begin drilling and exploring at the base of the inland mountain site, finding a cave and extensive subterranean caverns at the base of the mountains, a "new-found gateway to secrets of inner earth and vanished aeons" (259). They discover the inert, intact remains

88 The work of Russian painter Nicholas Roerich (1874–1947) is mentioned several times in *Madness* as an analog to what the characters are seeing: 249, 270, 279, 280, 337.

of an inhuman species immeasurably more ancient than any human civilization, buried in extensive fossil deposits. At this point the main party ominously loses contact with Lake's sub-expedition; Dyer and the rest of the party launch a rescue.

As Dyer and his fellow scientists approach the mountain site by plane, the landscape resonates with the visionary power of the dark sublime:

> The sailor Larsen was first to spy the jagged line of witch-like cones and pinnacles ahead ... Little by little, however, they rose grimly into the western sky; allowing us to distinguish various bare, bleak, blackish summits, and to catch the curious sense of phantasy which they inspired ... In the whole spectacle there was a persistent, pervasive hint of stupendous secrecy and potential revelation; as if these stark, nightmare spires marked the pylons of a frightful gateway into forbidden spheres of dreams, and complex gulfs of remote time, space, and ultra-dimensionality. I could not help feeling that they were evil things – mountains of madness whose farther slopes looked out over some accursed ultimate abyss. That seething, half-luminous cloud-background held ineffable suggestions of a vague, ethereal *beyondness* far more than terrestrially spatial; and gave appalling reminders of the utter remoteness, separateness, desolation, and aeon-long death of this untrodden and unfathomed austral world. (269–70; emphasis in original)

Dyer's premonitions will turn out to be true – stupendous secrets and horrific revelations await the expedition, terrors that will reveal the insignificant place of humanity in the universe. The scientific discourse of modernity infuses this passage; Lovecraft took pains to make his story accurate by the standards of 1930s science, and the "complex gulfs of remote time, space, and ultra-dimensionality" will be Lovecraft's enduring modernist contribution to the Babylon ruin topos.[89]

They find Lake's camp destroyed, the men and dogs slaughtered – dissected in a coldly scientific fashion. One team member, Gedney, and one dog are gone; the fossilized creatures are missing. Dyer and the graduate student Danforth decide to cross the mountain range at its lowest point in search of further information, journeying into a "hidden

89 On Lovecraft's knowledge of science and exploration in *Madness* see Eckhardt, "Behind the Mountains of Madness"; Cannon, *Lovecraft*, 103; *Thing on the Doorstep*, ed. Joshi, 420; Miéville, "Introduction," xv. On Lovecraft's relationship to science fiction see Lévy, *Lovecraft*, 79–81; Leiber, "A Literary Copernicus"; Joshi, *H.P. Lovecraft*, 59.

trans-montane world" (280). On the verge of flying over the mountains to the secrets beyond, they feel a "tense expectancy":

> The touch of evil mystery in these barrier mountains, and in the beckoning sea of opalescent sky glimpsed betwixt their summits, was a highly subtle and attenuated matter not to be explained in literal words. Rather it was an affair of vague psychological symbolism and aesthetic association – a thing mixed up with exotic poetry and paintings, and with archaic myths lurking in shunned and forbidden volumes. (282)

Here their tense expectancy gives way to a sublime encounter. They perceive the evil mystery through a mixture of psychological affect and aesthetic perception, feeling both terror and wonder.[90] Indeed, as they cross the mountains they cry out "in mixed awe, wonder, terror, and disbelief" (283) as they discover an enormous ruined prehistoric city, a "blasphemous city" (284), a "palaeogean megalopolis" (286), an "unhallowed place" (291), a "monstrous city ... many million years old" (294), a place of "appalling antiquity and lethal desolation" (296) stretching off for a hundred miles in all directions. This is Lovecraft's ultimate Babylon, an awe-inspiring, alien city of menace and nightmare.

Eventually Dyer and Danforth learn the truth in their investigation of the city's ancient hieroglyphics: the dead primeval city is one of many built eons ago by the "Great Old Ones," a race of alien beings who arrived on earth before the beginning of terrestrial life. Moreover, the Old Ones "were the makers and enslavers" (297) of life on earth. They built cities under the sea and created terrestrial life "at first for food and later for other purposes" (299), having done the same thing on other planets, using their most powerful slaves, "shoggoths" – shifting, huge, horrific blobs of semi-sentient protoplasm able to mimic other life forms. Humans, as well, were the creation of the Old Ones, who used them sometimes for food and sometimes for amusement. Over the eons, other extraterrestrial races arrived on earth and fought wars with the Old Ones in the long eons before the dawn of human history. The shoggoths as well grew too powerful and revolted against their creators and masters. The Antarctic had been the Old Ones' original place of colonization and the abandoned Antarctic city was both their last stronghold and oldest settlement.

---

90 Cf. Macaulay, *Pleasure of Ruins*, 9: the "basic element in ruin-sensibility" in the Western tradition is its "blend of pleasure and romantic gloom."

But in Lovecraft's world of sublime horror – a terror inflected by the discourse of modernity – ever deeper depths always open up beneath the abyss, in the same way that the modern science of Lovecraft's day had opened up the infinite, ever-receding depths of interstellar space and time.[91] As terrible and alien as the primeval Old Ones were, they themselves feared yet another even more ancient and inhuman evil beyond their city, over an even higher mountain range set deeper into the hidden continent three hundred miles away: "It seems that there was one part of the ancient land – the first part that ever rose from the waters after the earth had flung off the moon and the Old Ones had seeped down from the stars – which had come to be shunned as vaguely and namelessly evil" (307–8). A subterranean river flowed from that shunned place to a "Stygian sunless sea that lurked at earth's bowels" under the Old Ones' city (308). The Old Ones built a city at the bottom of that sea, growing in decadence and worshipping that nameless evil in their very last outpost, facing extinction as the advancing ice destroyed the terrible city now lying in ruins around Dyer and Danforth. The final reason for their extinction and the ruin of their city is more hinted at than explained.

Lovecraft's primeval city has all the details of a displaced Babylon. As Dyer and Danforth descend into the ruins, they discover the remains of a tower at the city centre, a "monstrous cylindrical tower figuring in the very earliest carvings" they had examined (319). A displaced Tower of Babel, this structure was the very first to be built in the city, as Dyer explains: "Perhaps it embodied architectural marvels as yet unencountered by us. It was certainly of incredible age according to the sculptures in which it figured – being indeed among the first things built in the city" (319). If this tower's description is not enough to call to mind the Tower of Babel – it is a "prodigious round space"; its walls are "boldly sculptured into a spiral band of heroic proportions"; it is fifty million years old and covered with "bizarre and disturbing cosmic sculptures" (320) – Lovecraft then makes the Babylon connection explicit:

> But the salient object of the place was the titanic stone ramp which, eluding the archways by a sharp turn outward into the open floor, wound spirally up the stupendous cylindrical wall like an inside counterpart of those once climbing outside the monstrous towers or ziggurats of antique Babylon. (320)

91 Levy notes that Lovecraft's notion of the Beyond or the Otherworld is "almost always situated *in the depths*" in "a place situated under the reassuring surface of things downward from 'the edge of the world'" (*Lovecraft*, 63; see also 63–71 for full discussion).

This displaced, ruined Tower of Babel sits atop the entrance to a Lovecraftian abyss, a Babylonian hell-pit. Lovecraft's ruined city clearly hearkens back to the Babylon ruin topos, in both its vivid images and through direct allusion.

Beneath the tower they find the bodies of Gedney and the missing dog; they also find the reanimated Old Ones – now freshly dead, presumably killed by shoggoths in the depths beneath the city. Below the tower they find the entrance to the great abyss and the "unfathomed regions of earth's core" (325) leading to the dark underground sea and the nameless evil beyond the further mountains. Their descent is interrupted when they encounter a shoggoth (voicing the same enigmatic closing cry of Poe's *Narrative of Arthur Gordon Pym*: *Tekeli-li*! *Tekeli-li*!) and narrowly escape. As they flee the city in their plane, Danforth looks back and glimpses some final, unnamed horror that drives him insane: it is a vision of what lay *beyond* the distant "terrible mountains of the forbidden land" (336), a hideous undescribed sight reflected in the clouds like a mirage: "a single fantastic, daemoniac glimpse, among the churning zenith-clouds, of what lay back of those other violet westward mountains which the Old Ones had shunned and feared" (339). Danforth's final vision is itself a ruin, or an absent presence: it is a trace, a fragment, only a glimpse, leaving the full outline of the sublime terror to the imagination.

For Lovecraft, there is always a deeper past, and the deeper you go into the past, the greater the terror, in a process of infinite regression. Lovecraft inherits the medieval Babylon ruin topos with its lineage stretching from the ancient world to the nineteenth century. Under the further influence of nineteenth-century scientific and archaeological discourse, Lovecraft contributes a distinct sense of modernity to the topos: namely, his idea of "cosmic terror," that humanity is an insignificant phenomenon in an infinitely ancient, infinitely hostile universe.[92] Thus we can see both continuity and change as Lovecraft adapts the Babylon ruin topos

92 This notion of "cosmic terror," depends on a new understanding of time, namely that "our much vaunted historical, linear time is itself bound, fore and aft, by a much vaster, cosmic time of Elder Things and divine blueprints ... it is human history that looks like a parenthesis in a much larger, and evil, design" (Aguirre, *Closed Space*, 174–5). On this central theme of cosmic indifference in Lovecraft's fiction, see Joshi, *H.P. Lovecraft*, 59–60; Mariconda, "Lovecraft's Cosmic Imagery"; Schultz, "From Microcosm to Macrocosm"; Robert M. Price, "Lovecraft's 'Artificial Mythology,'" the latter three all in *An Epicure in the Terrible*, ed. Schultz and Joshi, 188–98, 199–219, and 247–56 (at 247–41), respectively. On Lovecraft's nihilism and philosophical worldview see Joshi, *Decline of the West* and Airaksinen, *Philosophy of H.P. Lovecraft*.

in his seminal and influential work. Just as the Anglo-Saxons felt a sublime awe when confronted by the *enta geweorc* and marveled at the great fall of Babylon, the first and most powerful of empires founded when giants walked the earth, so too Lovecraft sets all of human civilization in opposition to an even elder civilization, a civilization in turn dwarfed by an even greater, more ancient evil, and on and on.

Lovecraft, standing in as representative of the ruined city motif in pulp and weird fiction of the early twentieth century, provided the pervasive template for the lost civilization/haunted city topos in modern and contemporary iterations of science fiction, fantasy, and horror.[93] *At the Mountains of Madness* alone has proved to be quite influential: it inspired the renowned John W. Campbell sci-fi/horror story "Who Goes There?" (1938), which in turn led to a film adaptation, *The Thing from Another World* (dir. Howard Hawks and Christian Nyby, 1951). Campbell's story was then remade by director John Carpenter as the cult classic *The Thing* (1982), a film that also generated a recent remake/prequel, *The Thing* (dir. Matthijs van Heijningen, 2011). *Madness* was adapted as a graphic novel in the *ligne clair* style by I.N.J. Culbard (2010); and several spin-offs/sequels have been written by authors such as Charles Stross, Tim Curran, and Peter Watts. And finally, Ridley Scott's recent film *Prometheus*

93 For Lovecraft's influence see Cannon, *Lovecraft*, 123–6; Joshi, "Lovecraft Criticism: A Study," 25; Miéville, "Introduction," xi. In the past decade or so, Lovecraft's star has risen even further: in 2005 a collection of his fiction was published in the prestigious Library of America series, and *At the Mountains of Madness* was published in a Modern Library edition with an introduction by China Miéville. A long line of writers after Lovecraft continued to adapt and extend his "Cthulhu Mythos," including August Dereleth, Clark Ashton Smith, Robert Bloch, Robert E. Howard, Fritz Leiber, Henry Kuttner, and Ramsey Campbell (all of them very successful and influential authors in their own right). Aside from an ever-growing body of scholarship and adaptation of Lovecraft's fiction into film, television, and graphic novels, a measure of Lovecraft's current interest can be seen in the number of recent anthologies of new Lovecraft-inspired short fiction: *Tales of the Lovecraft Mythos*, ed. Robert M. Price (Minneapolis: Fedogan and Bremer, 1992); *Weird Shadows Over Innsmouth*, ed. Stephen Jones (Minneapolis: Fedogan and Bremer, 1994); *The New Lovecraft Circle* (Minneapolis: Fedogan and Bremer, 1996); *Acolytes of Cthulhu* (Minneapolis: Fedogan and Bremer, 2001); *Weird Shadows Over Innsmouth*, ed. Stephen Jones (Minneapolis: Fedogan and Bremer, 2005); *Lovecraft Unbound*, ed. Ellen Datlow (Milwaukee: Dark Horse, 2009); *Black Wings: New Tales of Lovecraftian Horror*, ed. S.T. Joshi (Hornsea, East Yorkshire: PS Publishing, 2010); *New Cthuhlu: The Recent Weird*, ed. Paula Guran (Gaithersburg, MD: Prime Books, 2011); *Worlds of Cthulhu*, ed. Robert M. Price (Minneapolis: Fedogan and Bremer, 2012). An incomplete but representative guide to Lovecraft's pop-culture influence is Smith, *H.P. Lovecraft in Popular Culture.*

6.7. Alien temple complex on moon LV-223; concept art from *Prometheus* (dir. Ridley Scott, 2012).

(2012) is essentially *At the Mountains of Madness* with the setting moved from the Antarctic to outer space, Lovecraft's ruined city of the Old Ones giving way to the mysterious temple complex of the Engineers on the distant moon LV-223 (see Figure 6.7).

Given the enduring Western fascination with ruins, it is no accident that Babylon figures as the quintessential ruin writ large. We can see the striated elements of that genealogy – the classical *encomium urbis/excidio urbis* tradition; the scriptural ruin of the prophets' Babylon; and then, as always, the important medieval synthesis: the merger of classical and biblical strands with the *transitus mundi* theme, in which Babylon's ruins become an existential statement about life, death, and the universe. In the nineteenth century the topos takes on new characteristics under the

94 Macaulay, *Pleasure in Ruins,* 104.

influence of romanticism, the gothic, and western European excavations in the Near East. Finally, in the twentieth century a distinctive note of modernity creeps into the tradition through pulp genres and popular culture.

Seen as a whole, across this broad sweep of centuries, the ongoing adaptation of the Babylon ruin topos embodies a way of knowing, a mode of apprehending the past that incorporates the dynamics of background and foreground, priority and belatedness, absence and presence. The long history of the Babylon ruin topos shows us a way of understanding history in which the overarching shadow of a grim past, a belated, compelling chapter in human prehistory that is always already only a rumor and a myth, waits in dark lucidity, helping to give the present potential shape and form. Macauley sensed this in her great study of ruins:

> The ghosts of Nineveh and Babylon, those mighty cities gone down into the immensities of the desert, have haunted men's minds with a sense of fearful hugeness, with their winged man-headed bulls guarding majestic gates, their improbable Assyrian grandeur. Vanished Assyria is no part of our western heritage; its ruins, uncovered, speak of an alien world in alien tongues; they stun us with aloof astonishment; Sennacherib and Sargon, Nebuchadnezzar and his court, seem as strange and as remote as the winged bulls themselves. Not there, as in Greece, do we meet the legends and the myths we know; the ghosts that haunt those deserts are not the familiars of our childhood tales.[94]

On a final note, it is my sense that the enduring appeal of the Babylon ruin topos resides in the sublime emotional affect evoked through the interplay of presence and absence, in the image of the city cast down to ruin. Absence, in that Babylon is always belated, always lost, always gone, always a ruin – the very emblem of the faded glories, both proud and terrible, of human history. Presence, in that, though lost, Babylon always remains on the horizon of the possible as a ruin, as the trace left behind and a remnant signifying the burden and weight of the past.

Chapter Seven

Babylon and the Coordinates of Romance

And I will carry you away beyond Babylon.

– *Acts of the Apostles* 7:43

"To Babylon, my lords, to Babylon!"

– Tamburlaine in Marlowe, *Tamburlaine the Great, Part II* (1590), IV.iv.133

Prends ton chemin vers Babylone.
[Take your road to Babylon.]

– Voltaire, *Zadig, or Destiny: A Tale of the Orient* (1757) in *Romans et contes*, 114

According to the previous chapter, one side of Babylon's sublime nature lies in ruins – the awe-inspiring topos of the dead city. Yet Babylon is also a place of beauty as well as terror. In this, our final allusive genealogy, "Babylon" signifies a place of sublime beauty and endures as a topos of Eastern wonders, a fairy tale land of enchantment and adventure. A well-known nursery rhyme gives us a signature of this tradition:

How many miles to Babylon?
Three score miles and ten.
Can I get there by candle-light?
Yes, and back again.
If your heels are nimble and light,
You may get there by candle-light.[1]

1 P. Opie and I. Opie, *Oxford Dictionary of Nursery Rhymes*, 73–4. The editors note the "inherent mystery" of these lines and explain that the general phrasing structure of the

How, when, and where does this sublime Babylon of romance arise? How does "Babylon" evolve into a byword for great distance, adventure, and the far-off reaches of the imagination, as in our nursery rhyme? "How many miles to Babylon"; "as far as Babylon"; "from here to Babylon"; "beyond Babylon": among the many valences Babylon possesses in Western thought, this proverbial equation of Babylon with fantastic distance (almost as one would say in the English-speaking world, "from here to Timbuktu," or "over the rainbow") displays an extensive history. This final chapter discovers the history of this topos – the distant, exotic and sublime Babylon of adventure – and argues for the genesis of this topos within the symbolic geography of romance.[2]

In this romance tradition, Babylon functions as a metonymic figure for "the East" or "the Orient"; the part (Babylon) stands in for the whole (the East). As each term in that equation mutually reinforces the other down the *longue durée* of history, Babylon as "the East" constitutes an important dimension of Western Orientalism.[3] In this chapter I argue that this Babylon topos enters Western culture, and endures, through romance – a mode always closely related to travel and travel's attendant construction of space and distance.[4] From the Middle Ages to the present,

---

rhyme (but not necessarily the specific citation of Babylon) can be traced back to at least the late thirteenth century; "Babylon" they suggest, is here the "far-away luxurious city of early seventeenth-century usage." Many poets have incorporated allusions to this evocative nursery rhyme into their own poetry, e.g., Robert Louis Stevenson in *A Child's Garden of Verses* ("To Minnie") and Robert Graves in "A Song for Two Children."

2 Although I devote substantial space to medieval romance in this chapter, my argument generally concerns the broader history of romance as a literary mode. In this regard, my understanding of romance has been shaped by Auerbach, *Mimesis*, trans. Trask, 123–42; Frye, *Anatomy of Criticism*, 186–203 and *Secular Scripture*); Beer, *Romance*; Parker, *Inescapable Romance*; McDermott, *Novel and Romance*, 12–23; Fuchs, *Romance*; Cooper, *English Romance in Time*, 7–15.

3 The seminal study is Said, *Orientalism*. It has long been acknowledged that Said's study (focused on the eighteenth and nineteenth centuries), is weak on the complex representation of the East in Western premodern cultures (see, e.g., Akbari, *Idols in the East*, below). This chapter therefore contributes to our understanding of "medieval Orientalism" (as inaccurate as that term might be). The literature on the subject is enormous and I provide here only selected basic references on the representation of the East or "the Orient" in medieval literature: Campbell, *Witness and the Other World*, 1–161; Heng, *Empire of Magic*; Heffernan, *Orient in Chaucer and Medieval Romance*; Akbari, *Idols in the East*. For the East in the classical world, see Romm, *Edges of the Earth in Ancient Thought*, 82–120.

4 See Heng, *Empire of Magic*, 239–305; Goodman, *Chivalry and Exploration*, 45–82; Linton, *Romance of the New World*, 2. See also Romm, *Edges of the Earth*, 3–8 on geography as a literary tradition in the ancient world. On the connection between geography and

Babylon is a fundamental topos of romance, as a place and as a subject: a stylized figure for distance and adventure out in the great Beyond. Mary Helms notes that cultures charge distant spaces with "cosmologically symbolic significance"; this chapter demonstrates the sublime symbolic significance of Babylon as a distant place or space.[5] If the inspired and directed path of pilgrimage leads to Jerusalem, the errant wandering of romance leads to Babylon.[6]

The Romance Babylon: Classical Backgrounds

Although Babylon enters the world of romance most profoundly in the Middle Ages, classical culture contributed important precursors to the topos. As we saw in chapter 1, classical cosmographers and historians from Strabo to Solinus and Herodotus to Orosius located the city definitively in the east.[7] Babylon was, like other important cities, an imaginative coordinate, a way to construct a symbolic geography of civilization, with cities such as Troy and Rome, Jerusalem and Babylon demarcating the outline or shape of the Western *oikumene.* This classical inheritance lies directly behind the world of medieval cartography and cosmography, in which Babylon always held a special place in the Christian geographic imagination. Medieval world maps in all periods generally give Babylon a central place, usually contiguous with Jerusalem (see Figure 7.1).[8]

---

adventure tales in the eighteenth and nineteenth centuries see Phillips, *Mapping Men and Empire.*

5 Helms, *Ulysses' Sail,* 18.

6 On the wandering, "errant" mode of romance see Parker, *Inescapable Romance.*

7 E.g., Pliny, *Naturalis Historia,* VI.121–2, 428; Solinus, *Collectanea Rerum Memorabilium,* 227; Martianus Capella, *De Nuptiis Philologiae et Mercurii,* VI.701; Orosius, *Historiarum Contra Paganos Libri VII* (who places Assyria, Mesopotamia, Babylonia, and Chaldea – all overlapping terms – in his geographical survey [I.2.17, 20–1]); in Book VI he refers to Babylon as being "in the middle of the east" (*in medio Oriente;* VI.21.20); Isidore of Seville, *Etymologiae,* XIV.iii.13; Aethicus Ister, *Cosmographia,* 108.3–6. See also the basic citations from Herodotus, Strabo, Diodorus Siculus et al., in chapter 1.

8 The enormous thirteenth-century English "Hereford Map" gives us Babylon in its center/top quadrant in Asia, on the river Euphrates, above a crucified Jesus and Jerusalem at the center of the map. In this small close-up detail of Babylon (Figure 7.1), we see the typical blurring of Babylon and the Tower of Babel. The legend *Turris babel* ("Tower of Babel") appears above the top of the large city/tower at the left of the image. Westrem notes that this is the "largest, most elaborate architectural device on the map" (*Hereford Map,* 84). The faint image of a serpent with horns, breathing fire, rises from the second tier of the tower, off to the right. Another brief legend, just to the left of a

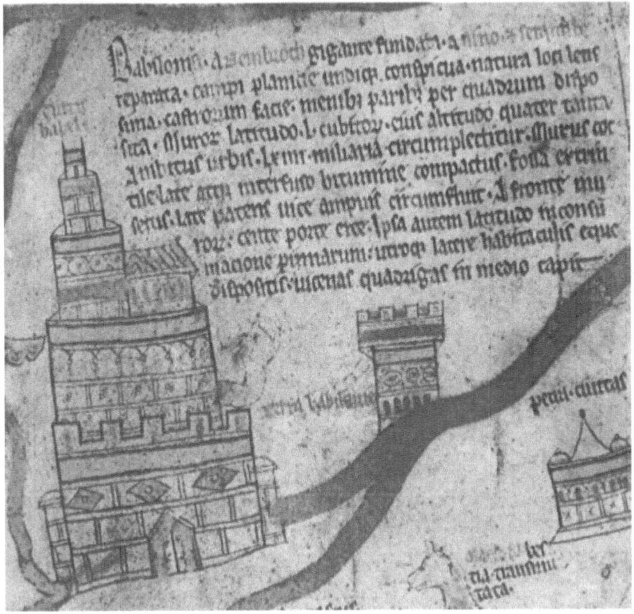

7.1. Babylon on the Hereford *Mappa Mundi* (ca. 1285). © The Hereford Mappa Mundi Trust and the Dean and Chapter of Hereford Cathedral. Used by permission.

---

second, smaller tower on the river, reads *terra babilonie* ("the land of Babylon"). Westrem explains that each of these architectural images could represent the city of Babylon or the Tower of Babel or both at the same time.

A third, more extensive legend sits between and above the two architectural images; at seventy-three words, it is the lengthiest legend on the entire map. The legend is drawn from Orosius's description of the city of Babylon (*History*, II.6.7–10):

> Babylon was founded by the giant Nimrod, and restored by Ninus and Semiramis, easily seen from all directions because of the plain's level surface, and most fortunate in the nature of its location. It was designed like a military encampment, with walls of equal height in the shape of a square, the width of the walls being 50 cubits and their height four times that. The distance around the city was altogether 64 miles. The wall was built with baked bricks on the outside and black pitch packed in between. Outside the wall stretched a broad channel, flowing around it in place of a river. One hundred bronze gates were on the outside of the walls. The latter were in fact wide enough – atop the ramparts – to accommodate small guard stations at regular intervals on either side with 20 four-horse chariots [running] down the middle.

Translation of this legend and all other information about the Hereford Map images and legends is drawn from Westrem, *Hereford Map,* 84–7.

The ancient world saw Babylon as a place of wonders (*mirabilia*): the city gloried in marvels of sublime beauty – such as the famed Hanging Gardens of Babylon, one of antiquity's Seven Wonders of the World.[9] Aethicus Ister's eighth-century pseudo-travel account, the *Cosmographia,* gives us the basic classical vision of Babylon's beauty: "we discovered the most celebrated city of Babylon, its power excelling that of all cities, and more famous; we judged it to be the alpha and omega of all in the entirety of its strength and elegance and beauty."[10]

But the sublime incorporates terror and awe as well as beauty: other elements of the classical tradition saw Babylon as a place of prodigious exoticism. *The Wonders of the East,* a popular medieval Latin geographical catalogue, circulated in late antiquity in epistolary form as the *Letter of Pharasmanes (or Fermes) to Hadrian*; subsequently in the Middle Ages it lost its epistolary framework and was transmitted and translated into the vernacular, often with illustrations, as a catalogue of marvels to be found in the Eastern regions of the world: monstrous races and fantastic places.[11] Like much of "the Orient" depicted in the text, Babylon in *Wonders of the East* is a place of sublime oversized marvels and outlandish things: the "the biggest and highest of all mountains" looms over "the lands of Babylon."[12] Deadly serpents and monstrous donkeys with horns as big as oxen, inhabit the "very great wasteland which is in the southern part of Babylonia."[13] A related early medieval collection of *mirabilia,* the *Book of Monsters* (*Liber Monstrorum*) describes the vast two-headed serpents of the Assyrian desert, whose eyes "shine ... through the nocturnal shadows like lanterns" (*per umbras nocturnas ... in modum lucernae lucent*).[14] Beauty and

9 On the "Hanging Gardens of Babylon," a complex mythic subject in its own right, see Dalley, *Mystery of the Hanging Garden* and Seymour, *Babylon,* 55–6, 72–5.

10 *Aethicus Ister,* ed. and trans. Herren, 108.3–6: "famosissimam urbem repperimus Babylloniam, extollente uirtute cunctarum urbium caeleberior; quam omnium primam ac nouissimam arbitrati sumus omnem roborem et decorem et pulchritudinem."

11 I use the editions published as appendices Ia (Latin text), Ib (Old English text), Ic (translation) by Orchard in *Pride and Prodigies,* 175–203, citations by section number (§).

12 "Đonne is oðer rice on Babilonia landum þær is seo mæste dun betweoh Media dune 7 Armenia. Seo is ealra duna mæst 7 higest" (§ 25).

13 "On sumon lande assan beoð akende þa habbað swa micle hornas swa oxan. Þa syndon on ðam mæstan westene þæt is on ða suð healfe fram Babilonia" (§ 6).

14 *Liber Monstrorum,* ed. Orchard in *Pride and Prodigies* as Appendix IIIa (Latin text) and IIIb (translation), 254–317, III.2, citations by book and section number. The snakes and venomous creatures in the desert around Babylon appear in many other sources: e.g., Mandeville's *Travels,* and the J2 recension of the *Historia de Preliis*: "From there he [Alexander] went with his army to the land of Babylonia, where they encountered

horror: the West fears and desires Babylon as the exotic East, a place of monsters and marvels on the edges of the world.[15] For classical civilization and, to some extent, its medieval inheritors, the East was a frontier, a peripheral zone where the "normal rules" do not apply, as Ranulf Higden explains in his *Polychronicon* (early 14th c.): "Among these things it should be noted that the far reaches of the world often thrive with new marvels, as if nature plays more freely in secret and remote places than she does openly and nearer to us."[16]

Babylon also functions as a stable reference point or coordinate in the undifferentiated plenitude of eastern *mirabilia. Wonders of the East* begins with the description of an unnamed "colony" (Old English *landbunes*, Latin *colonia*), imparting essential information: the colony's dimensions and its distance to Babylon:

> The colony is at the beginning of the land Antimolima, which land is 500 in the tally of the lesser measurement, which are called *stadia*, and 368 of the greater, which are called *leuuae*. On that island there is a great multitude of sheep, and from there to Babylon it is 168 of the lesser measurement called *stadia*, and 115 in the greater measurement called *leuuae*.[17]

Such data are not as gripping for the reader as giant serpents, but this pedestrian use of Babylon nevertheless indicates its role as a coordinating point in an imaginative map of the East. *Wonders of the East* often designates

---

snakes of incredible size that were disgusting and extremely vicious. They had two heads whose eyes shone like lanterns" (*Romances of Alexander*, trans. Kratz, 87). Benjamin of Tudela also notes the "serpents and scorpions" that infest the ruins of Nebuchadnezzar's palace at Babylon and Babel, making people afraid to enter the ruins (*Itinerary of Benjamin of Tudela*, trans. Adler, 54).

15 As Akbari notes: "In the medieval imagination, the Orient was the place of origins and of mankind's beginning; it was also, however, a place of enigma and mystery, including strange marvels and monstrous chimeras, peculiarities generated by the extraordinary climate ... It was both beginning and end, charged with potentiality and danger" (*Idols in the East*, 3).

16 *Polychronicon Ranulphi Higden*, ed. Babington, 1.34.360: Inter haec hujusmodi advertendum est, quod mundi extremitates novis semper quibusdam prodigiis pollent; ac si natura licentius ludat in privato et remoto, quam in propatulo et propinquo.

17 "Seo landbunes in on fruman from Antimolima þam lande; ðæt land is on rime þæs læssan milgetæles ðe stadia hatte fif hund, 7 þæs micclan milgetæles þe leuua hatte ðreo hund 7 eahta 7 syxtig. On ðam ealande byð micel menigeo sceapa. 7 þanon is to Babilonia þæs læssan milgetæles stadia hundteonig 7 eahta 7 syxtig, 7 ðæs micclan þe leuua hatte fiftyne7 hundteonig" (§ 1).

locations by using Babylon as a reference point in this fashion: "Hascellentia is the name of the land on the way to Babylon"; it is eight hundred *stadia* "from Babylon to the city of Persia"; it is three hundred *stadia* from Babylon to the city of Archemedon, which is "the biggest city after Babylon."[18] Babylon serves as a stable reference point or coordinate in the text, working to focus and present the plenitude of eastern marvels.

Beyond this outline of the classical geographical tradition, the large and influential body of Alexander the Great materials also shaped the understanding of Babylon's eastern location in antiquity. The texts of the Alexander romance tradition also played a key role in the genesis of European romance in the Middle Ages.[19] In the Greek *Alexander Romance* of Pseudo-Callisthenes (third century), the ultimate source of innumerable medieval European Alexander materials, Babylon serves as an important coordinate point in time and space – the city is the centre of Alexander's conquered empire, his unification of West and East; it is also the place of his death.[20] All the world meets in Alexander's Babylon. At the centre of history's greatest empire, Babylon faces both West and East; vast geographical coordinates traverse and radiate from the city. In the *Alexander Romance*, Darius, the "king of kings," rules the Persian empire from Babylon, a sovereign power stretching over a multitude of Eastern peoples.[21] When Alexander defeats Darius and the heritage of imperial power moves from Persia to Macedon (the *translatio imperii* tradition), Alexander's Babylon becomes a crossroads of history and geography, a nexus of imperial power at the juncture of East and West. In an edict Alexander establishes the broad reach of his imperial power with his subjects:

> I wish your lands to be established in prosperity, and the roads of Persia to remain peaceful for trade and travel, so that merchants may come from Greece to you, and you to them. I shall build roads and erect signposts from the Euphrates and the crossing to the Tigris, as far as Babylon.[22]

---

18 *Wonders of the East*, §5, §6, §2.

19 See Cary, *Medieval Alexander*, ed. Ross.

20 For Alexander's death in Babylon see Pseudo-Callisthenes, *Greek Alexander Romance*, trans. Stoneman, 148, 157–8. See also *Historia de Preliis*, J1 recension, in *Romances of Alexander*, trans. Kratz, 1–82, at 78–82; the Old English translation of the *Letter of Alexander to Aristotle*, in Orchard, *Pride and Prodigies*, Appendix IIa, IIb, (§ 38, also § 40).

21 Pseudo-Callisthenes, *Alexander Romance*, "king of kings": 72, 73, 74; see also 73, 95 on Alexander's rule.

22 *Alexander Romance*, 111.

In Alexander's reign all the world's eyes turn to Babylon: "Then Alexander entered the great city called Babylon, where he found waiting for him emissaries from provinces throughout the world."[23] Alexander's death in Babylon (a commonplace of classical and medieval historiography) therefore sends reverberations across the world. Orosius, for example, records that at the height of his power, Alexander returns to Babylon from India, where the terrified representatives of the whole world (*totius orbis*) wait for him; but the Macedonian dies at Babylon, poisoned.[24] The association of Babylon with Alexander's empire and death would make any shortlist of basic facts about the Macedonian in the Middle Ages. Alexander the Great would in fact become one of the Nine Worthies of medieval legendary chivalry and romance, along with Hector, Charlemagne, King Arthur and others. The "Matter of Alexander" comprised a significant strand in the DNA of medieval romance, carrying Babylon – the place of Alexander's greatest triumph and his famous demise – along with it.

From this mix of influences designating Babylon's location, we see that classical culture saw Babylon as the gateway to the East and to the nameless, marvellous frontier beyond. One example from classical romance shows Babylon as a liminal place separating known and unknown, West and East. In Chariton's *Chaereas and Callirhoe* (mid-first century CE) the heroine Callirhoe, separated from her lover by a number of romance misfortunes, must plunge into the unknown as she crosses into Babylonian territory: "But when she reached the Euphrates, beyond which there is a vast stretch of unending land – it is the threshold of the King's great empire – then longing for her country and family welled up in her, and she despaired of ever returning."[25] In her lament to "Malicious Fortune" before crossing into Babylon, she exclaims: "Now you are hurling me from my familiar world – I am at the other end of the earth from my own country ... I am being taken beyond the Euphrates, shut up in the depths of barbarian lands where the sea is far away."[26] The classical East beyond the Euphrates and Babylon is presented as an unbounded space, a frontier of distant space without end and a stage for the wandering adventures of romance.[27] The classical world put Babylon on the map; once there, this coordinate marked out a zone of romance and wonder for the Middle Ages.

---

23 The "J2 recension" of the *Historia de Preliis* (*Romances of Alexander*, trans. Kratz, 87).

24 Orosius, *History*, III.20.1–4.

25 *Collected Ancient Greek Novels*, ed. Reardon, 76.

26 *Collected Ancient Greek Novels*, ed. Reardon, 76.

27 See Romm, *Edges of the Earth*, 82–3.

Babylon, Cairo, and the Crusades

Building upon such classical precedents, the crucial development of Babylon as a metonymic figure for the East begins in the high and late Middle Ages (i.e., after c. 1000), in the intersection of crusade romance and historiography. In these texts we have a coalescence of two distinct places: ancient biblical Babylon (or "Babylon the Great") of Mesopotamia and Egyptian Cairo, also referred to as "Babylon" in the Middle Ages. It is a commonplace that a wide variety of medieval Western authors writing in various languages refer to Cairo simply as "Babylon" (or sometimes "lesser Babylon" or "New Babylon" or "Babylon-in-Egypt").[28] The Egyptian location is the town or fortress of Bāb-al-yūn (Arabic: "the city of On," derived from the earlier "Pi-Hapi-n-On" of the Pharaohs) or al-Fustāt, founded by Cambyses in 525 BCE just south of Cairo; Cairo itself was founded in 969 CE and the two places eventually merged and today are part of Old Cairo.[29] Understandably, Arabic "Bab-al-yun" was rendered as "Babylon" early in the Western tradition; thus in a wide variety of medieval texts – particularly beginning with the crusades – Cairo, Alexandria, Memphis, or Egypt could all be called "Babylon" and their lord the "Sultan of Babylon."[30]

The following representative survey of crusade texts illustrates the pervasive use of "Babylon" as "Cairo": Fulcher of Chartres (b. 1059; First Crusade) refers many times to "Babylon" or the "king of Babylon"; most of the

28 On the Babylon and Babylon-in-Egypt (Cairo) confusion see Wolff, *How Many Miles to Babylon?*, 1–2, 138. Many scholars routinely note this confusion; see for example Westrem, *Broader Horizons*, 235: "Many medieval Europeans referred to the entire metropolitan area as Babylon or New Babylon (Babylonia [Nova]). The analogy between the sultan of Egypt's capital and that of Nebuchadnezzar became a cliché in medieval Europe, although some writers were discriminating."

29 For historical Cairo in the Middle Ages see Raymond, *Cairo*, trans. Wood, 7–190. For the Western medieval understanding of Egypt see Wolff, *How Many Miles to Babylon*, 40–60.

30 This is truly a medieval commonplace. For example, in addition to the texts discussed in this chapter, Babylon also denotes "Cairo/Egypt" in William of Malmesbury; the *Alliterative Morte Darthur*; the Breton lay *Emaré*; Peter Comestor, *Historia Scholastica*; Boccaccio, *Decameron* (Day 2, story 7); also Boccaccio, *Il Filocolo*; Wolfram von Eschenbach, *Parzival*; Malory, *Morte Darthur*. Although the undifferentiated naming of Cairo as Babylon becomes much more common in the later Middle Ages, Babylon-in-Egypt is nevertheless mentioned very early in classical and early medieval sources: e.g., Diodorus Siculus, *Library of History*, I.56.3; Strabo, *Geography*, XVII.1.30; Josephus, *Jewish Antiquities*, II.315; Bede, *De temporum ratione* (*Chronica maiora*), 484; Wallis, trans. *Bede: The Reckoning of Time*, 182. The crusader city/fortress of Acre could also be called "Babylon" as well: see Schein, "Babylon and Jerusalem: The Fall of Acre."

time he means Cairo and the Sultan of Egypt, yet he also sometimes refers to the biblical Babylon, sometimes without clear distinction between the two.[31] William of Tyre (c. 1130–86) does the same thing in his *History of Jerusalem* (First Crusade),[32] as do Guibert of Nogent (c. 1055–1154) and Anna Comnena (1083–1153).[33] The anonymous chronicle of the Third Crusade, the *Itinerarium Peregrinorum et Gesta Regis Ricardi*, also refers many times to Babylon-in-Egypt as "Babylon" and the Egyptians as "Babylonians."[34] We find the same usage in Robert of Clari's *Conquest of Constantinople* (Fourth Crusade);[35] Oliver of Paderborn's *Capture of Damietta* (Fifth Crusade), who also refers to both Babylons;[36] and Joinville's *Life of St. Louis* (Seventh Crusade), and on and on.[37] In texts such as these, "Babylon," almost always without further qualification or explanation, refers to Cairo or Egypt. The medieval appellation is sometimes obscured in modern translations where authors translate "Babylon" as "Cairo" or "Egypt," often without comment.[38]

From the early tenth century to the late twelfth century Egyptian Cairo was the centre of the Fatimid caliphate after the shift of power from Baghdad in the tenth century. Thus, the early Western *chansons de geste* (dating from the same period) placed the centre of Saracen power with the emir of "Babylon": this was *Babylon Aegyptiaca* or "Egyptian Babylon." Once established as a literary trope, however, Babylon/Cairo found its way into the later "Saracen romances" derived from the *chansons de geste* even though historical circumstances had changed. Literary tradition thus preserved a historical anachronism; as a result, "Babylon" remained the centre of Saracen power in the imaginary world of later medieval romance

31 Fulcher of Chartres, *History of the Expedition to Jerusalem*, trans. Ryan: "Babylon" for Babylon-in-Egypt, 125, 155, 159, 182, 237, 283, etc.; "Babylon" for the biblical Babylon, 134, 260.

32 William of Tyre, *A History of Deeds Done Beyond the Sea*, trans. Babcock and Krey: "Babylon" for Cairo or Egypt (I:419, 553; II:315–16); biblical Babylon (I:199, 344; II:7).

33 Levine, trans., *Deeds of God through the Franks*; *The Alexiad of Anna Comnena*, trans. Sewter: "Babylon/Babylonians" for Cairo/Egyptians, 352, 352, 370; biblical Babylon, 416, 440, 504.

34 *Chronicle of the Third Crusade: A Translation of the Itinerarium Peregrinorum et Gesta Regis Ricardi*, trans. Nicholson, 272, 283, 289, 290, 337, 338.

35 Robert of Clari, *Conquest of Constantinople*, trans. McNeal, 36, 37, 45, 59.

36 Oliver of Paderborn, *Capture of Damietta*, trans. Gavigan: Cairo as "Babylon" and the Egyptians as "Babylonians" (66, 68, 73, 81, 85, 116, 117, 118); their ruler as the "Sultan of Babylon" (74, 97, 105, 107, 114, 123, 129, 131, 132); biblical Babylon (98).

37 Jean de Joinville, *Life of St. Louis*, trans. Hague: Cairo as "Babylon," 59, 60, 69, 90, 96, etc.

38 For example, in his translation of Marco Polo, Latham always translates the original text's "Babylon" as "Cairo" or "Egypt," depending on context: see 39, 142, 232–3, 308, 326. Cf. Marco Polo, *Il Milione*, ed. Benedetto, XIII.11: "soldan de Babelonie."

(and beyond), although Cairo was no longer the centre of Saracen power in the real world.

One word for two famed cities: this accident of history has, of course, been duly noted by editors and scholars, but I do not think the implications of the two Babylons have quite been explored. Did medieval authors always keep the two Babylons separate, not allowing elements of the pervasive biblical Babylon tradition to influence their representation of Babylon-in-Egypt or vice versa? Was there no imaginative traffic between the two, no cross-fertilization? It seems unlikely and part of my argument is that, indeed there was such transference; through such a synthesis Babylon becomes a standard topos of romance. Mandeville takes care to distinguish the biblical Babylon of Nimrod and Nebuchadnezzar from the Egyptian city:

> And understand well that this Babylon that I speak of now, where the Sultan dwells, is not Babylon the great where the confusion of tongues happened, which is in the great desert of Arabia. But now it has been a long time since any man has dared to visit that same wretched place, because it is so full of serpents and dragons and other venomous beasts that no man can come there. The ambit of that tower, within the compass of the city that had been there, at one time ran for twenty-five miles in circumference. And although it is called a "tower," yet there were within that circle many fair buildings that are now destroyed and now the entire place is a wilderness. Nimrod the king, who was king of that land, founded that same tower, mighty and enormous; and he was the first earthly king that ever existed. That same city of Babylon was set on a fair plain upon the river Euphrates that ran through the city at that time ... From Babylon, where the Sultan dwells, to get to Babylon the great is a forty-day journey through the desert, and it is not under the rule of the Sultan, but is within the lordship of the king of Persia.[39]

If Mandeville tries to distinguish the two Babylons in order to avoid a confusing error, it stands to reason that other authors were not as

---

39 M.C. Seymour, ed. *Bodley Version of Mandeville's Travels*, 31.22–33 to 33.1–16:

> And wete ye wel that this Babylonye that I speke of is now where the Soudon is dwellynge, nys not the grete Babilonye where that the confusioun of tongis [was made], the whech that is in the grete desertys of Arabye. But now it is long tyme sithe that ony man durste go for to visite that eche wreched place, for it is so ful of nederis and of dragonys and othere venym bestis that no man may come thedyr. The serkel of that tour, with the compas of that cete that there was, sumtyme contynuede xxv. myle aboute. And thow it be callid a tour, yit ther were in

discriminating and did in fact mistake one for the other, intentionally or unintentionally. In fact, in the world of romance, where all places tend to have a blurry dream-like sense of unreality, one can see the synthesis at work whereby the two Babylons slowly merge into one imaginative Babylon, a metonymic figure for the East, a coordinate in the "fantastic geography of travel to the Orient," to use Lynn Ramey's phrase, and part of the symbolic geography of romance as it constructs the "place" of Heathendom.[40]

In the *chansons de geste* (e.g., the *Song of Roland*) and then in later derived medieval "Saracen romances" such as *Floris and Blancheflour*, the *Sowdene of Babylon, Richard Coer de Lyon, Bevis of Hamptoun, Sir Ferumbras, Huon of Bordeaux, Daurel et Beton*, and the "Pseudo-Turpin Chronicle," a reified Heathenness or Pagandom opposes the world of Christendom. In these texts the most important coordinating point for the non-Christian Saracen world of the East beyond the Western frontier is referred to as "Babylon."[41] Recent scholarship has stressed the importance of the Crusades and the encounter of East and West in the genesis of romance as a literary form.[42]

> the cerkele manye fayre edifcis that now arn distroyed and now is al wildyrnesse. That eche tour mechil and heuge foundede the kyng Nembrok that was kyng of that lond, and he was the fyrste erthely kyng that euere was. That eche cete of Babilonye was set in a fayr pleyne vpon the reuer of Eufrates that ran thour the cete that tyme ... Fro Babylonye, where that the Soudon dwellyth, for to pase to the grete Babylonye arn xl. iurneis thour desert, and it is not vndyr the subieccioun of the Soudon but withinne the lordshepe of the kyng of Pers ...

Cf. also 27.22–3, in which the text explains that there is now but one sultan, the one "of Egipt, that we holdyn the Soudon of Babylonye." The *Metrical Version of Mandeville's Travels*, ed. M.C. Seymour, distinguishes between the two Babylons even more explicitly, designating the Egyptian city as "Lesser Babylon" and "Cairo":

> For in Babiloine þe Lesse
> There þe Sawdones dwellinge es
> In the cite of Cair [Cairo]
> That stant vppon a fair riuer,
> And Nile þat ryuer cleped it ys,
> Oone of þe stremes of paradys. (36.1289–94)

On Mandeville and the East see Campbell, *Witness*, 122–61; Higgins, *Writing East*; Heng, *Empire of Magic*, 238–305.

40 Ramey, *Christian, Saracen and Genre*, 71.

41 For a useful survey of these romances see Daniel, *Heroes and Saracens*.

42 See Heng, *Empire of Magic*, 16–61. Benedict Robinson notes that "crusading violence" is a "part of the narrative inheritance of romance" and that "a crusading ethos has shaped the genre from within, through its relationship to a violence that it both suspends and solicits" (*Islam and Early Modern English Literature*, 36).

In crusade romance "Babylon" is an important focal point in the negotiation of Occidental and Oriental identity. The imaginative unreality of Babylon lends itself in a flexible fashion to this process. As Norman Daniel notes, in the Saracen romances Babylon/Cairo "tends to mean a (or the) principal place of the Saracens without being precisely sited anywhere."[43] Literally speaking, "Babylon" means Egypt or Cairo in this context, but as an imaginative place in the developing symbolic geography of romance, this Babylon is more than just the city of Cairo, drawing as it does, by virtue of the word's allusive power, upon the entire tradition of Babylon in medieval thought.

When we consider the broader traditions of Babylon in the Middle Ages – the ancient city's biblical association with pagan threat; its connection to ideas of empire, conquest, power, exile, and return; its apocalyptic associations; its connection (through Nimrod) to tyranny, pride, and the entire Tower of Babel tradition; its dyadic relationship to Jerusalem and its metaphoric dimension in the Augustinian contrast between the City of Man and the City of God – given all these associations developed in our preceding chapters, it is not difficult to see the easy congruence between Babylon the Great and Babylon-in-Egypt, as the two meet and merge in the world of romance.[44] As we have seen, the word "Babylon" has a richly allusive dimension in Western thought; it is as much a metaphor as it is a simple place name and that metaphoric potential of the word enabled "Babylon" to transcend its status as an Egyptian city or region in romance and establish itself instead as a Western sign of exotic adventure and almost unimaginable, even sublime, distance.

Babylon in Medieval Romance

These various Babylon traditions combine in medieval romances that dramatize the encounter between Christianity and Islam. Two case studies will

---

43 *Heroes and Saracens*, 67. Babylon in this regard is what Akbari would call a "shifting center" of the Orient (*Idols in the East*, 65).

44 See for example, the biblical tradition of "proud Babylon" infusing Oliver of Paderborn's apostrophe to Damietta: "Damietta! renowned among kingdoms, very famous in the pride of Babylon, ruler of the sea" (88). We also find the tradition of Babylonian corruption and sexual decadence in the same text: Oliver laments that after the capture of Damietta, the Christians were infected with the corrupt mores of the native Egyptians/Babylonians: "No one can describe the corruption of our army after Damietta was given us by God, and the fortress of Tanis was added. Lazy and effeminate, the people were contaminated with chambering and drunkenness, fornications and adulteries, thefts and wicked gains" (106). On these traditions see, respectively, chapters 1 and 4.

illustrate this development: the relatively early Middle English romances *Floris and Blancheflour* and *Richard Coeur de Lyon*.[45] *Floris and Blanchflour* was a popular story, extant in versions across medieval Europe.[46] The original Old French *Floire et Blanchefleur* was composed in the twelfth century (c. 1160–70); Middle English translations of the Old French narrative were produced by the mid-thirteenth century, making the tale one of the oldest extant Middle English romances. The narrator explains that in his tale of separated young lovers, he will show "Hou after bale hem com bote" (1224) [how for them relief came after misery] – a typical romance pattern. The banished heroine Blancheflour has been enslaved by Babylonian merchants who in turn sell her to the Emir of Babylon's harem. Our hero Floris must find and rescue her. "Babylon" in this text is certainly the Egyptian city (variously called Babylon, Cairo, and Alexandria in other medieval versions of the romance). But at times the biblical Babylon tradition influences the narrative. For example, one character describes the power and size of the city:

> To go around Babylon it is,
> without a doubt, seventy miles,
> and at the walls
> there are seven times twenty gates.
> Within there are twenty towers
> in which every day there is trading;
> every day throughout the year
> there is trading in full progress.
> And there are more than a hundred towers

---

45 For a representative selection of the large scholarly literature on the representation of Saracens and Islam in medieval literature and thought see Daniel, *Islam and the West* and *Heroes and Saracens*; Southern, *Western Views of Islam*; Metlitzki, *Matter of Araby*, 117–219, 240–50; Flori, "La caricature de l'Islam dans l'occident médiéval"; Ramey, *Christian, Saracen and Genre*; Cohen, "On Saracen Enjoyment"; Tolan, *Saracens*; Beckett, *Anglo-Saxon Perceptions of the Islamic World*; Calkin, *Saracens and the Making of English Identity*; Kinoshita, *Medieval Boundaries*; Akbari, *Idols in the East*, esp. 155–99.

46 I use the Middle English version in *Sentimental and Humorous Romances*, ed. Kooper, by line numbers in the text. For a comparative study of *Floire and Blanchefleur* and its European versions (which includes Boccaccio's *Il Filocolo*) see Grieve, *Floire and Blancheflor and the European Romance*. In this work Grieve notes that Babylon = Cairo (48), but then later cites the "tower and garden in Babylon/Alexandria" (135) and then explains that Blancheflour's "moral and spiritual death" occurs in "Alexandria, Cairo or Babylon, as the various texts name the location of the Emir and his tower" (136, 137).

in the outer precincts.
The least of these towers
would be able to withstand
the entrance of an emperor,
whether by might or stratagem.
And even if all the men
that have ever been born
were to swear to do so upon their deaths,
they would be as likely
to catch the sun or moon
as to get the maid.[47]

Although this passage presumably describes Cairo, it reads very much like historiographic descriptions of ancient Babylon from Herodotus through the entire derived tradition of medieval universal history: e.g., the precise mathematical depiction of the walls, the city's fecund wealth, and the general hyperbole – all common tropes of ancient Babylon.[48]

---

47 Lines 587–604:

> Abouten Babiloine, withouten wene,
> Sexti longe milen and tene
> And ate walle thar beth ate
> Seven sithe twente gate.
> Twente toures ther beth inne,
> That everich dai cheping is inne;
> Nis no dai thourg the yer
> That scheping nis therinne plener.
> An hondred toures also therto
> Beth in the borewe, and somdel mo.
> That alderest feblest tour
> Wolde kepe an emperour
> To comen al ther withinne,
> Noither with strengthe ne with ginne.
> And thei alle the men that beth ibore
> Adden hit up here deth iswore,
> Thai scholde winne the mai so sone
> As fram the hevene hegh the sonne and mone.

48 Ramey, however, argues that "Babylon" in *Floire et Blanchefleur* refers more generally to the region or kingdom of Babylon in Egypt, rather than the specific city of Babylon (*Christian, Saracen and Genre*, 74–5).

Similarly, a description of Babylon's tower within the city (Blancheflour's prison) calls to mind the Tower of Babel tradition:

And in the city in the middle,
there stands a wondrous tower, I tell you.
Whoever sees it, from near or far,
reckons that it is a thousand fathoms tall
and a hundred fathoms wide,
and it is made with great pride
of limestone and marble;
there is nothing like it in the Christian world.
The mortar is so well made
that no man can break it with steel.
And the globe on the roof
is made with such skill
than men have no need
to burn torch or lantern at night;
such an ornament was never made
that shines at night like the sun during the day.[49]

Although this is not the literal Tower of Babel cast down by God, this latter-day wondrous tower soaring above an idolatrous heathen city

49 Lines 605–20:

And in the bourh, amide the right,
Ther stant a riche tour, I thee aplight.
A thousand taisen he his heighe,
Woso it bihalt, wid, fer, and neghe.
And an hondred taises he is wid,
And imaked with mochel prid
Of lim and of marbelston;
In Cristienté nis swich non.
And the morter is maked so wel,
Ne mai no man hit breke with no stel.
And the pomel above the led
Is iwrout with so moche red,
That men ne dorfen anight berne
Neither torche ne lanterne;
Swich a pomel was never bigonne,
Hit schineth anight so adai doth the sonne.

named "Babylon" would inevitably summon the biblical archetype to medieval minds. Like Nimrod's Tower of Babel, this tower is made "with great pride" (*mochel prid*); it pushes aloft to hyperbolic heights almost beyond human comprehension; and even the tower's surmounting globe that imitates the sun suggests humanity's rivalry of God's power in the Tower of Babel tradition. Further, the French version of the romance describes a river of paradise – the "Eufrates" – flowing around the city.[50] What is the Euphrates doing here if Babylon is Cairo/Egypt?[51]

This merging of Babylon traditions, coupled with the indeterminate symbolic geography of romance, results in a sublime "Babylon," an exotic Babylon of the imagination and romance in which the distant East stands for the endless distant spaces of romance. In *Floris and Blanche-flour* the Babylonian merchants sail "over the sea to their country" (*over the see ... to her contree*); and thus after so "longe" journey "to Babyloyn they ben coom" (187–8, 189–90). Much like the mournful separation of Callirhoe from her lover when she goes beyond Babylon, a great distance here separates our medieval romance heroine from her beloved. The distraught Floris vows to pursue her "[t]haugh it were to the worldes ende" (330), the implication being that Babylon itself is at (or beyond) the world's end. In its repetition, "to Babylon" becomes almost a set phrase in the romance: a woman tells Floris that his love has been carried "over the se ... To Babiloyne" (414, 417); another informant tells him that "to Babiloyne she is ibrought" (505); Floris pledges to find her "at Babiloine" (434). One can find similar phrases equating Babylon and distance in texts such as *Richard Coer de Lyon*, the *Sowdene of Babylon*,

50 Examining the French version of the romance in *Medieval Boundaries*, 77–104, Kinoshita sees *Floire et Blanchefleur* as a subversive text that reflects the complex historical contact between Islam and the West in the Mediterranean, a "world of cross-confessional contact and long-distance trade," "a site of possibility and transformation" (78, 87). To this end, she generally treats the representation of Babylon in the poem as a more or less accurate reflection of medieval Cairo, but nevertheless acknowledges that the depiction of Babylon is "[h]ighly conventionalized" (92) and that the Tower of Babylon is an "eastern version of the enchanted castles of romance" (93). My focus is on the literary influence and fabrication at work in the romance's depiction of Babylon.

51 As Grieve notes, geography is "rather muddled" in *Floris and Blanchefleur* and this is "not unusual for romance" (*Floire and Blancheflor*, 134). Even Mandeville, normally careful to distinguish the two Babylons (as we saw earlier), nevertheless places the story of Nebuchadnezzar and the three youths at the Egyptian Babylon: *Defective Version of Mandeville's Travels*, ed. M.C. Seymour, 21.3–28.

The Three Kings of Cologne, and many others.[52] The world of medieval romance associates "Babylon" with distance, travel, and adventure.

In another very early Middle English romance, *Richard Coer de Lyon*, notable for its flamboyant imaginary response to the historical crusades and for its corresponding fantastic depiction of a Saracen alterity,[53] the signifier "Babylon" is clearly a synthesis of biblical tradition and romance. After the defeat of Arsuf, Saladin, pursued by King Richard, retreats to his chief city, centre of the heathen world, "Babylon":

The supreme Sultan of Heathenness
had indeed fled to Babylon.
He then sent forth his decree
and many a bold pagan gathered there.[54]

As in biblical tradition, Babylon represents a centre of imperial power: at the city the Sultan "gathered many a bold pagan" (*semblyd many a bold paynyme*, 5386) to fight the West. When Richard besieges the city (5405ff.), he faces Babylon's legendary walls: "Þe cyte was so strong wiþjnne, / Þat no man myȝte vnto hem wynne" (5415–16). The city is the centre of the imperial pagan world: when Babylon falls, Saladin laments: "Allas, allas! / Þe prys off heþenesse is done!" (5830–1). The "prys" of Heathenness falls, like the Babylon of old, despite its mighty defenses. Richard's capture of Babylon is completely fictitious; Heng notes that the city is "presumably Cairo" (though essentially imaginary) and argues that Richard's victory is a literary/ideological displacement of Saladin's historical recapture of Jerusalem.[55] In the romance world of *Richard Coer de Lyon*, Babylon presides

52 In the *Sowdone of Babylon*, for example, the enemy Saracens come "[f]ro Babyloyne" (69), and when Charlemagne learns of the Saracens' depredations, he resolves to "chase them out of Christendom" (*him oute of Cristendome chace*, 586). Charlemagne swears that unless their sultan Laban converts, "Babyloyne shal he never see / For alle his grete aray" (765–6). I use the edition of this Middle English text in *Three Middle English Charlemagne Romances*, ed. Lupack, 1–103, by line number.

53 See, e.g., Heng, *Empire of Magic*, 62–113.

54 *Der Mittelenglische Versroman über Richard Löwenherz*, ed. Brunner, by line numbers:

The cheff Sawdon of Heþenysse
To Babyloyne was flowen jwysse.
His counseyl he offsente þat tyme,
Þere semblyd many a bold paynyme. (5383–6)

55 Heng, *Empire of Magic*, 77.

over a vast imperial power encompassing distant lands – Saladin tempts Richard by offering him powerful kingdoms in a sublime catalogue that includes Babylon:

> And if he would forsake Jesus,
> And take Mohammed as his lord,
> Of Syria he would make him king,
> And of Egypt, that rich place,
> Of Darras, and of Babylon,
> Of Araby, and of Cessoyne,
> Of Africa, and of Bogye
> And of the land of Alexandria,
> Of Greater Greece, and of Tyre,
> And of many a rich empire;
> And he would make him the Sultan,
> Of all India, all the way to Prester John's kingdom.[56]

Such a listing of exotic places is part of the spatial world of romance; in that symbolic geography Babylon is a coordinate in the epic list of exotic places.[57] These sublime catalogues function in two ways. They emphasize

---

56 Lines 3703–14:

> And ȝyff he wolde Jhesu forsake,
> And Mahowne to his lorde take,
> Of Surrye he wolde make hym kyng,
> And off Egipte, þat ryche þyng,
> Off Darras, and off Babyloyne,
> Off Arabye, and off Cessoyne,
> Off Affryk, and of Bogye,
> And off þe lond off Alysaundrye,
> Off Grete-Grece, and off Tyre,
> And off many a ryche empyre;
> And make hym he wolde Sawdoun anon
> Off al Ynde, vnto Preter Jhon.

57 Such catalogs (no doubt derived in part from epic) are deployed elsewhere in the romance. For example, when Saladin assembles his armies at the battle of Arsuf he draws upon a plenitude of fabulous kingdoms:

> Many was þe heþene man
> Wiþ Saladyn þat come þan:
> Off Inde, off Perse, off Babyloyne,

Saladin's vast imperial power (analogous to the Babylonian imperial tradition) and they also represent the plenitude and variety of Eastern spaces, the vast lands of "Heathennesse."

The East of *Richard Coer de Lyon* is part of the immense, boundless world of romance. When Richard and his two companions set sail for the East, disguised as pilgrims, they travel "through many lands far and near" (*Þorwȝ manye londes, fer and nere,* 622). They raise sail and "were at sea for a long time" (*in þe see þey were long,* 628). The distances and lands push at the limits of human comprehension as the Saracens come from "more lands than anyone can speak of / Except he that created heaven and hell" (*moo landes þan ony can telle, / Saue he þat made heuene and helle,* 4975–6). As in *Floris and Blancheflour,* the figure of "Babylon" here constructs formulaic phrases denoting distance. At the beginning of the romance, Richard and his knights travel on the sea "to þe cyte off Babylone" (636); Saladin will make Richard king "off Babyloyne" (3707); Saracens come to fight Richard "off Babyloyne" (4969) [from Babylon;

Off Arabye, and off Cessoyne,
Off Aufryk, and off Bogye,
Off al þe lond off Alysaundrye,
Off Grete Grece, and off Tyre,
And off man another empyre;
Off moo landes þan ony can telle,
Saue he þat made heuene and helle.
(4967–76; see 6600–10 for a very similar catalogue)

See also the similar epic catalog in the *Sowdone of Babylon,* where Laban, the "powerful sultan of Babylon" (*[o]f Babiloyne the riche Sowdon*), the "mightiest man on earth" (*[m]oost myghty man ... of moolde,* 135–6), dispatches a messenger "to Asia and Africa" (*to Assye and to Aufrike,* 102) to call up his levies:

He [Laban] sente oute his bassatoures
To realmes, provynces ferre and nere,
To townes, citeis, castels and tours,
To come to him there he were,
To Inde Major and to Assye,
To Ascoloyne, Venys, Frige and Ethiope,
To Nubye, Turkye and Barbarye,
To Macedoine, Bulgare and to Europe. (995–1002)

Cf. *Song of Roland,* laisses 189, 232–4 (the army of Baligant, Emir of Babylon); the catalogue of eastern kings (including "Micipsa, king of Babylon") in Geoffrey of Monmouth, *History of the Kings of Britain,* X.1–11; and the corresponding mustering in Laȝamon, *Brut,* 12657–66 ("Mæptisas of Babilone").

see the same phrase at 6606, 6914]; Saladin flees "To Babyloyne" (5384), and Richard urges the King of France to "wende to Babyloyne" (5196) in pursuit. And finally, the romance character of Babylon can be seen in the following catalogue, in which our usual roster of real Eastern places – Acre, Nineveh, Jerusalem – is joined by a place that sounds suspiciously like an allegorical or fairy tale location of romance, the "Castle Orgylous" ("the Castle of Pride"?):

> And afterwards they went by sea
> to Acre, that rich city.
> And thus set forth to Macedonia,
> and to the city of Babylon,
> and from there to Caesarea;
> they saw Nineveh
> and the city of Jerusalem;
> and went to the city of Bethlehem
> and to the city of Sidon-Tyre,
> and also went to Ebedy
> and to the Castle Orglyous,
> and to the city of Epiros,
> to Jaffa and to Safrane,
> to Mount Tabor and to Archas.[58]

The places of romance in *Richard Coer de Lyon* oscillate between fact and fiction. Norman Daniel explains that the representation of history

---

58 Lines 633–46:

> And seþen deden hem on þe see
> Toward Acres, þat riche cete;
> And so forþ to Massedoyne,
> And to þe cyte off Babyloyne,
> And fro þennes to Cesare;
> Off Nynyve þey were ware,
> And þe cyte off Ierusalem;
> And to þe cyte off Bedlem,
> And to þe cyte of Sudan Turry,
> And eke alsoo to Ebedy,
> And to þe Castel Orglyous,
> And to þe cyte of Aperyous,
> To Jaffe, and to Safrane,
> To Taboret, and to Archane.

and geography in the Saracen romances does not conform to any notion of "accuracy," and that these texts have a "taste for the exotic which has nothing to do with verisimilitude," with geography defined by "real names and imaginary ones mixed, high sounding and evil sounding syllables jumbled."[59] Both of the romances discussed here show the way elements of the broader biblical Babylon tradition merge with the representation of Babylon-in-Egypt. This ongoing synthesis occurs first during the early crusade centuries; the construction of the Babylon romance topos is thus part of the genesis of medieval romance in the historical contact between East and West in the eleventh and twelfth centuries. Once established as a typical place in romance, Babylon worked in tandem with the age-old tropes and structures of romance to create the mode's distinctive sense of errant and endless spatial wanderings.

The Western idea that the lands of the Saracens were vast and boundless was not a pure invention of the crusade romances. In her pilgrimage account, Egeria (late fourth/early fifth c.) surveys the "endless lands of the Saracens" (*fines Saracenorum infinitos*) as she looks out from Mount Sinai over Egypt, Palestine, and the East.[60] However, it was during the period from 1000 to 1300 that Babylon clearly became a metonymic figure for the unbounded East in romance. Although Babylon entered romance as part of a literary mode "intimately associated with the boundaries of Christendom and with the encounter of a world beyond Christendom,"[61] once established in romance, Babylon drifts further and further from any historical reality, essentially becoming a general symbol for great distance and adventure. Take, for example, Malory's narrative at the end of the Grail story:

> So when Sir Bors saw that he was in so far countries as in the parts of Babylon, he departed from city of Sarras, and armed him and came to the sea, and entered into a ship. And so it befell him by good adventure he came unto the realm of Logris; and he rode apace till he came to Camelot, where the King was.[62]

---

59 *Heroes and Saracens*, 65, 66. Goodman, *Chivalry and Exploration*, likewise notes that romances dealing with the east include "a mixture of real places and imaginary inventions" (47–8).

60 Egeria, *Diary of a Pilgrimage*, trans. Gingras, 53; Latin from *Itinerarium Egeriae* in *Itineraria et Alia Geographica*, ed. Franceschini and Weber, 27–90, III.62–6.

61 Robinson, *Islam and Early Modern English Literature*, 28.

62 Malory, *Le Morte Darthur*, ed. Cooper, XVII.401–2.

Although Malory's *Morte Darthur* is not a Saracen romance, in this late (fifteenth-century) example we can see how, by the end of the Middle Ages, Babylon is ensconced as an imaginary location in the fabulous errant geography of romance, a point of reference structuring the space between Home and Away.

Babylon in Early Modern Romance

The growing establishment of this topos becomes clear when we turn to popular early modern romances of the fifteenth and sixteenth centuries. The encounter with Islam is typical of early modern romance: in this encounter there is a firm continuity between the medieval and early modern depictions of Babylon.[63] In works such as Pulci's *Il Morgante Maggiore* (1483), Boiardo's *Orlando Innamorato* (1487), Joanot Martorell and Martí Joan de Galba's *Tirant Lo Blanc* (Catalan, 1490), Ariosto's *Orlando Furioso* (1516), and Tasso's *Gerusalemme Liberata* (1581) we see many of the elements of the romance Babylon in the "scene of cross-cultural encounter."[64] The authors of these enormously influential romances use "Babylon" as a mobile, all-purpose name that can refer to Cairo, Damascus, Baghdad, the biblical Babylon – or, as I have been arguing, essentially an amalgam of them all: the undifferentiated centre of the Heathen East infused by the spirit of romance.[65]

63 See Robinson, *Islam and Early Modern English Literature*, 5: "If romance evokes the space of contact and encounter, late medieval and early modern romance takes as paradigmatic the encounter with Islam." For further studies of romance and the encounter with Islam in the context of New World exploration see Linton, *Romance of the New World*; Barbara Fuchs, *Mimesis and Empire*, esp. 13–23, passim.

64 Robinson, *Islam and Early Modern English Literature*, 2. Luigi Pulci (1432–84), *Morgante*, trans. Tusiani; Matteo Boiardo (1441–94), *Orlando Innamorato*, trans. Ross; Joanot Martorell (1413–68) and Martí Joan de Galba (d. 1490), *Tirant Lo Blanc*, trans. Rosenthal; Ludovico Ariosto (1474–1535), *Orlando Furioso*, trans. Reynolds; Torquato Tasso (1544–95), *Jerusalem Delivered*, trans. Esolen.

65 "Babylon" is also an alternate name for Baghdad in the early modern period. John Cartwright's *The Preacher's Travels* (1611) includes a "description of New Babylon, now called Baghdad." Baghdad, he notes, "by some is called New Babylon; and may well be, because it rose out of the ruins of Old Babylon, not far distant; being nothing so great, nor so fair, for it contains, in circuit, but 3 English miles ..." (*Early Modern Tales of Orient*, ed. Parker, 123). Babylon also appears to be an alternate name for Baghdad in William Biddulph's *The travels of çertaine Englishmen into Africa, Asia, Troy, Bythinia, Thracia, and to the Blacke Sea* (1609) and Anthony Sherley's *Travels into Persia* (1613): see *Early Modern Tales of Orient*, ed. Parker, 90, 97 and 66. For a survey of early modern

In each of these texts, Babylon designates an important city of the heathen East, the centre of Saracen power. Here East faces West, both as reified categories, and "Babylon" serves as a convenient shorthand for the East. The great enemy is the "Sultan of Babylon" in *Tirant Lo Blanc.* In *Orlando Furioso* Charlemagne beseeches God to aid his army against the Saracens lest "the false and evil laws / Of Babylon (*la legge falsa di Babelle*) will flourish and bring low" all of God's people (XIV.71).[66] In Tasso's *Gerusalemme liberata* "Babylon" seems to generally refer to Baghdad, but similarly, the Saracen forces can be thought of collectively as "Babylon": Raymond exhorts Godfrey of Bouilon: "You will be victor over Babylon" (VII.62).[67] Left somewhat vague (again, no doubt in part due to the formless, itinerant geography of romance) is whether "Babylon" in any of these texts refers specifically to a "real" city.[68] Of course, changing historical circumstances – in particular, the West's ongoing relationship with the Islamic world during the period 1500–1700 – influence the reception and contours of this complex of ideas, but the underlying pattern remains much the same. Even more clearly than in the medieval romances, then, in early modern romances a reified East acts as

---

travel accounts to the Near East see Hachicho, "English Travel Books," (also provides some coverage of the sixteenth and seventeenth centuries); see also Seymour, *Babylon,* 86–97. On the influence of medieval romance on early modern travel/exploration literature see Goodman, *Chivalry and Exploration*; Robinson, *Islam and Early Modern English Literature.*

66 Italian text from Ludovico Ariosto, *Orlando Furioso,* ed. Debenedetti and Segre; trans. Reynolds.

67 *Per te fia il regno dei Babel distrutto.* Italian text from Torquato Tasso, *Gerusalemme Liberata,* ed. Caretti; trans. Esolen. Esolen's translation here is a bit free; more literally: "By you the kingdom of Babel will be destroyed." Note that Esolen, like many translators, renders "Babel" as "Babylon." In this use of "Babel" there is a clear influence from the biblical Babylon tradition: Godfrey in turn replies to Raymond's stirring words, saying that if he had in his army even ten men as valiant as Raymond, he "would burn to put down Babel's pride, / from Bactria to Thule unfurl the Cross!" (*ardirei vincer Babèl superba / e la Croce spiegar da Battro a Tile,* VII.69).

68 In Pulci's enormous Charlemagne romance *Morgante,* we have both the Egyptian Babylon and the biblical Babylon. He merges both: see Canto XV, stanza 90 (*Bambillona*); Canto XVII, stanza 13 (classical Babylon); Canto XXIV, stanza 8 (see 841, note to XVII.6, on this confusion). Boiardo's *Orlando Innamorato* seems to call Baghdad "Babylon," but he also refers to ancient/biblical Babylon at least once. (Perhaps at II.i.6 there is also some confusion with Babylon-in-Egypt.). In *Tirant lo Blanc* the Sultan of Babylon is an Egyptian ruler, but there are also several references to the biblical Babylon: [Babylon-in-Egypt, 185, 316, 228, 265, 284, 502; biblical Babylon, 463, 502(?), 509].

an antagonist to a reified "West"; and "Babylon" serves as a convenient shorthand or metonymic marker for this reified East.[69]

Given their popularity and subsequent influence, these early modern romances complete the process of securing Babylon as a sublime, fairy tale location; Babylon becomes a place "beyond the fields we know," to use one of Dunsany's favoured expressions. In the often playful world of early modern continental romance (a mode far from the tone of the *chansons de geste*) it becomes easier to ask "How many miles to Babylon?" and expect the answer to point only towards the realm of imagination rather than to a specific place. In Pulci's *Morgante*, as in many early modern romances, a vast number of characters engage in complex interwoven adventures set against a broad backdrop of space, moving easily over great distances. In the *Morgante* Orlando travels through the eastern lands of Egypt and Persia with his giant companion (and Christian convert) Morgante. Arriving at Babylon (*Bambillona*) "through many a winding way" (*per molte contrade*, XVI.112), the enemy captures and imprisons Orlando in the city; he later escapes, conquers the kingdom, and rules the city, for a time, as the Sultan of Babylon.[70] Likewise in Boiardo's romance, Babylon is the setting for the inset love-triangle romance tale of Tisbina, Iroldo, and Prasildo told by Fiordelisa to Ranaldo. In this story, Babylon and its characters are not Saracen enemies; the story is a tale of noble lovers, suffused with the escapist, Eastern exoticism of distant lands. Iroldo introduces Babylon:

A trip of twenty days from here
A great and noble city stands,
Once Queen of all the orient;
The city's name is Babylon. (I.xvii.2)[71]

The lovesick Prasildo journeys to Medusa's Garden to win Tisbina's love; he travels great distances across romance landscapes and finally returns to Babylon:

each day seems a hundred as
He passes Nubia (to save time)

69 See Goodman, *Chivalry and Exploration*, 47: "Where the Greek prose romances depict the heterogeneous religious landscape of the ancient Mediterranean, the later medieval and Renaissance texts focus almost exclusively on the confrontation of Christianity and Islam."

70 Italian text from Luigi Pulci, *Morgante*, ed. Ageno; trans. Tusiani.

71 Vinte giornate de quindi vicina

And sails the sea of Araby
With good winds, rushing day and night
Until he reaches Babylon. (I.xii.42)[72]

Mary Campbell notes that in the Middle Ages "'The East' is a concept separable from any purely geographical area. It is essentially 'Elsewhere.'"[73] The East as "Elsewhere" is an enduring topos of the long romance tradition in Western culture. "Babylon" played a key "anchoring role" in both the original construction of that sense of "Elsewhere" and in its promulgation to the present day.[74] Having established this new "Babylon of the Imagination," born of a merging of Babylon traditions in a specific historical circumstance, the remainder of this chapter will examine later examples of this sublime Babylon romance topos in order to demonstrate both its longevity and its important malleable nature as the Babylon romance topos, in displaced form, powered the construction of the fantastic East in later literary traditions.

Babylon and Romance after 1700: Satire, Adventure, Fantasy

The medieval and early modern Babylon romance topos thus had an important role in establishing "the East" as a flexible, productive system of imaginative discourse, a "space of special freedom and fantasy."[75]

Sta una gran terra de alta nobiltade,
Che già de l'Orïente fo regina;
Babilonia se appella la citade.

(Italian text from Ross's facing-page translation.)

72 Passa per Nubia, per tempo avanzare,
E varcò il mar de Arabia con bon vento;
Sì giorno e notte con fretta camina,
Che a Babilonia gionse una matina.

73 *Witness*, 48; she also notes the "European suspicion of distance in general" (68).

74 The phrase "anchoring role" derives from *Idols in the East*, 285 where Akbari briefly examines the "the role of the city in anchoring Orientalist discourse." In this regard she cites Jerusalem, but notes that "Jerusalem also had other parodic opposites in medieval Orientalism: the degenerate site of Mecca, identified by the author of the *Roman de Mahomet* as the seat of all perversion and iniquity, and the ancient city of Babylon, ruled over by 'Sultans' who figure as important characters in *Fierabras*, the *King of Tars*, and *The Book of John Mandeville*" (286).

75 Phrase from Geraldine Heng: "By virtue of its geographical distance and its mythological proximity ... the East represents a space of special freedom and fantasy

The modern (post-1700) fortunes of the Babylon romance topos proceed in tandem with the fortunes of modern Orientalism. The vogue for "things Oriental" in western European literature and culture during the eighteenth and nineteenth centuries is well-trodden scholarly territory. In what follows I show only how the Babylon romance topos was part of this obsession: where went the Orient, there went Babylon and its displaced adaptations.

In the literary world, *The Thousand and One Nights* entered Western literary history in the eighteenth century through various European translations, influencing a wide range of authors and touching off a vogue for "oriental tales" and related genres from the eighteenth century through at least the first half of the nineteenth.[76] Orientalist literature in prose and verse flowed from the pens of both canonical and now-forgotten authors: Thomas Gueullette, *Mogul Tales* (French, 1723; English trans. 1736); J.P. Bignon, *Adventures of Abdalla, son of Hanif* (English trans. 1729); Johnson's *Rasselas, Prince of Abissinia* (1759); William Collins, *Oriental Eclogues* (1759); John Hawkesworth, *Almoran and Hamet* (1761); James Ridley, *Tales of the Genii* (1764); Clara Reeve's critical work *The Progress of Romance* (1785) and the tale "The History of Charoba, Queen of Egypt"; William Beckford, *Vathek, An Arabian Tale* (1786); Walter Savage Landor, *Gebir* (1798), and many others. The eighteenth century also saw the rise of the pseudo-oriental letter: fake letters (often satiric) written by "Persians" and "Arabs" and purportedly sent back to the East to report on Western values and cultures: Giovanni Paolo Marana's *L'Espion turc* (*Letters Written by a Turkish Spy*) (1684–6), translated into English 1687–93; Montesquieu's *Lettres persanes* (1721); Lyttleton's *Persian Letters* (1735); Oliver Goldsmith's *Citizen of the World* (1762).[77] The orientalist mode in literature continued in English literature of the early nineteenth century with examples such as Robert Southey, *Thalaba the Destroyer* (1800)

---

within the Western imaginary: an exotic locale, safely elsewhere, through which the European here-and-now may transact a variety of imagined relations" (*Empire of Magic*, 193).

76 See Ballaster, *Fabulous Orients*; Warner, *Stranger Magic*. For introductions to the European reception of *The Thousand and One Nights* see Caracciolo, *Arabian Nights in English Literature*; Irwin, *Arabian Nights: A Companion*; Sallis, *Sheherazade Through the Looking Glass*.

77 For introductions to the eighteenth-century oriental tale, see the still useful study by Martha Pike Conant, *Oriental Tale in England in the Eighteenth Century*; *Oriental Tales*, ed. Mack; Ballaster, *Fabulous Orients* and her edited collection of tales *Fables of the East: Selected Tales 1662–1785*.

and *The Curse of Kehama* (1810); Byron's "Eastern Tales"; Shelley, *The Assassins* (1814), *Alastor: or the Spirit of Solitude* (1815), *The Revolt of Islam* (1818), *Prometheus Unbound* (1820); Thomas Moore, *Lalla Rookh* (1817), and more. As Said and others have established, such literary texts and a host of other materials constituted the Western discourse of Orientalism, a Romantic and fictitious vision of the East tied to imperialist politics.[78]

The Babylon romance topos helped structure this Orientalist vision. The equation of Babylon and romance becomes a commonplace by the later nineteenth century. For example, Theron B. Appell's very justly neglected melodrama *Belshazzar, or the Fall of Babylon: A Tale of the Orient* (1861) is a novella set at the time of the biblical fall of Babylon; yet the preface speaks for itself, in its designation of Babylon as a place and subject of romance:

> READER, let your imagination wander back to that period of time, when Babylon the Great, then Queen of the earth, reigned over the Eastern world, the most beautiful and powerful city of the Orient. Its mighty walls spanned the Euphrates, and encompassed within their limits an area fifteen miles square. But, 'tis useless for me to describe its hundred gates of brass, its hundreds of squares and towers, its statues and palaces, its hanging gardens laden with rich fruit and filling the air with the fragrance of their blossoming flowers. The terraces that overhung, and the splendid barges that floated upon the waters of the Euphrates, as it meandered through the city, – these are familiar to every reader of history. 'Tis enough that *there* were fit scenes for *the enactment of those deeds which romancers love to chronicle*, and but few of which have been handed down to us by history.[79]

Likewise, in a very typical nineteenth-century travel account, American Sullivan Holman M'Collester describes Baghdad with a similar romance flavor in *Babylon and Nineveh through American Eyes* (1892):

> The city of Baghdad stands upon both sides of the Tigris ... The minarets over-topping the city are numerous, unmistakably publishing the fact that Mahomet is greatly honored here. As the sunlight glints tower, dome, grove, and water, a fairy-like picture is presented. Surely a glamour of romance broods over it in the present and all the more from the past, because in the

78 On Romantic Orientalism see Leask, *British Romantic Writers and the East.*
79 Appell, *Belshazzar, or the Fall of Babylon: A Tale of the Orient* (1861), 1 (emphasis added).

> imagination I see it ruled over by so many different nationalities. The 'Arabian Nights' represent it under many a fascinating word-picture.[80]

And finally we can add A.H. Layard's musings upon the collected excavations at Nineveh in 1845, as he wanders through the galleries "for an hour or two, examining the marvellous sculptures." When he emerges, the experience is one of dream and romance: "We look around in vain for any traces of the wonderful remains we have just seen, and are half inclined to believe that we have dreamed a dream, or have been listening to some tale of Eastern romance."[81] In these passages we can see many of the elements that echo the tradition I have been detailing, especially linked to the specific word "romance." These representative travel passages give us the wandering imagination, the Eastern world, a beautiful city of the Orient, fairy tales, and the glamour of romance. By the mid-nineteenth century the Babylon of medieval romance, Babylon-in-Egypt, has merged with Babylon-the-Great of antiquity to create a new place: a Babylon of the imagination, moving further and further from any empirical reality to inhabit a space solely defined by the coordinates of romance.

In her study of the impact of *The Thousand and One Nights* on Western literary culture, Ros Ballaster argues that by reading such tales eighteenth-century "readers in the West came to draw their mental maps of oriental territories and distinctions between them from their experience of reading tales 'from' the Orient."[82] As successive generations of readers consumed these texts and fashioned a symbolic geography of the Orient, the idea of distant (Eastern) space endemic to the Babylon tradition became a productive "artistic resource" for the creation of fiction.[83] We will see in the following pages how displacements of the Babylon romance topos moved into various literary genres and modes: satire, fantasy, historical fiction, pulp adventure, and science fiction. In these works, Babylon and its displaced avatars represent a space of distant lands and imagined exotic adventure. As medieval/early modern romance became *conte oriental*, fairy tale, novel, mystery, historical fiction, children's literature, fantasy literature, and science fiction, the image of the faraway

80 M'Collester, *Babylon and Nineveh through American Eyes* (1892), 36–7.

81 A.H. Layard, *Nineveh* (1849); quoted in Macaulay, *Pleasure in Ruins*, 96.

82 Ballaster, *Fabulous Orients*, 8.

83 Quoted phrase from Romm, *Edges of the Earth*, 173 (see generally 172–214).

place – the exotic world of the displaced imagination coordinated by a fabulous cityscape – remained.

Voltaire, Babylon, and Satire

In his *contes philosophiques* Voltaire (1694–1778) provides two examples of the Babylon romance topos in his parody of the pervasive genre of the European "oriental tale" (*conte oriental*), a form deeply influenced by *The Thousand and One Nights.* He sets the action of *Zadig, or Destiny: A Tale of the Orient* (*Zadig, ou La Destinée: Histoire Orientale*; 1757) in ancient Babylon and follows the romance adventures, the exile and return, of the young hero-protagonist, Zadig.[84] Voltaire also places *The Princess of Babylon* (*La Princesse de Babylone*, 1768) in the exotic romance world of ancient Babylon and environs. *The Princess of Babylon* is a literary parody of both the oriental tale and of romance; it is also a philosophical satire of European customs and mores.[85] Voltaire's Babylon is not a misnamed Cairo; it is literally ancient Babylon the Great. Nevertheless, the depiction of the city draws upon the synthetic Babylon romance topos developed over the preceding centuries. The tale begins with a rich description of opulent Babylon, set on the "enchanted banks" (*rivages enchantés*, 349) of the Tigris and Euphrates. Ringed by gorgeous gardens and groves, King Belus's Babylonian palace stretches towards the clouds like the Tower of Babel. The gardens of Semiramis, which, the narrator tells us, "astonished Asia several ages afterwards" (*étonnèrent l'Asie plusieurs siècles après*, 350) were nevertheless only a "feeble imitation of these ancient marvels" (*faible imitation de ces antiques merveilles*, 350) in Belus's city. Babylon is "superb" (*superbe*, 356); defined by "magnificence" (*magnificence*, 359): it is the "immense, proud, voluptuous city of Babylon" (*l'immense, l'orgueilleuse, la voluptueuse ville de Babylone*, 411).

A typical romance plot ensues: an ancient oracle decrees that Princess Formosanta of Babylon, daughter of king Belus, may only marry the man able to bend the bow of Nimrod (*l'arc de Nembrod*, 350) and kill a ferocious lion in combat. Suitor-kings from Egypt, India, and Scythia attempt this Odyssean task at a lavish tournament. But Amazan, a young shepherd

84 All quotations from Voltaire's tales are from Voltaire, *Romans et contes*, ed. Deloffre and van den Heuvel, by page numbers in the text. Translations from *Complete Romances of Voltaire*, with my own modifications. On Voltaire and Babylon see also Seymour, *Babylon*, 165–7.

85 See Pearson, *Fables of Reason*, 6, 194–203, passim.

in disguise, triumphs at the contest. Mounted on a unicorn and bearing a phoenix on his wrist, Amazan is a rather over-the-top romance hero/knight-errant who has travelled to Babylon from a distant country; his striking features shine with a mixture of beauty unknown at Babylon (*mélange de beauté inconnue à Babylone*, 352). Having triumphed over his fellow suitors, the unknown knight abruptly and mysteriously departs, leaving poor Princess Formosanta to pursue him through the world – an innocent abroad – for the remainder of the narrative. The Babylonians consider the knight's mysterious arrival and sudden departure to be a "strange adventure" (*aventure étrange*, 358); Formosanta's quest to find Amazan will involve all sorts of wild adventures and marvels.

In terms of structure, *The Princess of Babylon* is a classic romance, but it is also a parody of romance: the knight does not search for the damsel; instead, the damsel pursues the fleeing knight. Fully in line with our Babylon romance topos, this world of adventure presents Babylon as an important spatial coordinate, one of the centers of a vast and distant world of wandering romance. Amazan confesses that he has made a solemn vow "to roam about the world" (*courir le monde*, 392), and indeed he "roams about the world, without knowing where he is destined" (*il court le monde sans savoir où il va*, 383). The action takes our characters on a grand tour: Arabia, China, Scythia, the (ancient/proto-) countries of Europe (e.g., Albion = England; Gaul = France). The magic of romance – unicorns, griffins, phoenixes – permeates the tale, but Voltaire uses the romance form to scrutinize and satirize contemporary Europe as well. This parodic appropriation of romance can be seen in a self-reflexive moment when, detained in Albion (England) by bad weather, the melancholy Formosanta lifts her spirits by ordering her maid to read romances (*romans*) to her; such tales, she notes, are "the factors of the universe" (*les facteurs de l'univers*, 388). Formosanta purchases these tales (*contes*) to read and "expected to find in those histories some adventure similar to her own, which might alleviate her grief" (*elle espérait qu'elle trouverait dans ces histoires quelque aventure qui ressemblerait à la sienne, et qui charmerait sa douleur*, 388). Eventually Voltaire reunites and reconciles our separated lovers in typical romance fashion: Amazan marries Formosanta and rules Babylon happily ever after. The knight sets forth, and in the end, returns triumphant; the basic tropes of romance prophesied by an oracle at the beginning of the tale come true: "A mixture of everything – life and death, infidelity and constancy, loss and gain, calamities and good fortune" (*Mélange de tout; mort vivant, infidélité et constance, perte et gain, calamité et bonheur*, 368). *The Princess of Babylon* is by turns light-hearted confection and rather biting satire: the *conte* demonstrates the adaptability and mobility of the Babylon romance topos in a turn to a more ironic mode of literary expression.

Dunsany and the Fantastic

Other displaced versions of the Babylon romance topos are not so lighthearted. The sublime exotic city of the East, the beautiful and seductively dangerous city Elsewhere, is an important topos in the literature and arts of the fantastic. Dunsany, like almost all the later fantasy authors he influenced, from Robert E. Howard to George R.R. Martin, constructs an alternate fantastic reality – an Elsewhere – as the basis for his fiction. One story in particular illustrates the afterlife of the Babylon romance topos in literature of the fantastic.

In "The Wonderful Window" (1911) an old man in an "Oriental-looking robe" suddenly intrudes on the shop of one Mr. Sladden, an ordinary businessman who dreams of romance; in fact, the narrator tells us that for our excessively ordinary protagonist "a touch of romance – a mere suggestion of it – would send his eyes gazing away as though the walls of the emporium were of gossamer and London itself a myth, instead of attending to customers."[86] Trapped in the mundane world, Mr. Sladden (his Dickensian name an amalgam of "slack" and "sodden") longs for romance, fantasy, and exotic adventure. The old man in his Oriental clothes bears a parcel wrapped in dirty paper; the fact that it "was covered with Arabic writing was enough to give Mr. Sladden the idea of romance" (219). Inside the package is a magic window that the man obtained in "the streets of Baghdad" (219); with little prompting, he wondrously and seamlessly installs the window in Mr. Sladden's home after the shopkeeper purchases it. But now, when Mr. Sladden looks out the window he sees not dismal modern London, but rather "a mediaeval city set with towers" (221); the window is a portal to some other time and place. Regularly gazing out his magic window, he comes to love the distant vision of the city "as an exile in some desert might love the lilies of his home" (221): he names the city "Gold Dragon City" (222). But one day his vision turns dark as he observes the capture and destruction of

86 "The Wonderful Window" in Dunsany, *In the Land of Time*, ed. Joshi, 219–23, at 219. "The Wonderful Window" was later adapted by Dunsany as a radio play, *Golden Dragon City* (broadcast on BBC radio September 17, 1934): see Joshi, ed., *Land of Time*, 396.

the city; horrified by the violence and by his helpless spectatorship in the face of his vision's desecration, he breaks the window in frustration and his dream disappears forever.

"Gold Dragon City" is Babylon, the Babylon romance topos, reanimated in displaced form. All the elements are there: romance, an Eastern city (Baghdad), a medieval connection, the enchanted atmosphere of the Orient, a magical city living under the shadow of destruction and armed conflict, a Western observer or outsider, the fabulous distance of fantasy and magic. Dunsany's tale represents for us the use of the Babylon romance topos in the pervasive mode of the fantastic and its derived forms – not just literature, but in later forms such as film, television, and the graphic novel.

Harold Lamb and Robert E. Howard: Historical Fiction and Pulp Adventure

Dunsany's tale is also notable for its use of medieval tropes – it is, in its own way, a manifestation of medievalism, the reimagining of the Middle Ages in a later period. The neo-medieval reception of Babylon romance continues with two highly influential pulp authors of the early twentieth century whose work combines historical fiction and the adventure story: Harold Lamb (1892–1962) and Robert E. Howard (1906–36). Lamb was a well-published popular historian, particularly of the Crusades and the Mongols; he was in many ways the Barbara Tuchman of his day. He was also a prolific writer of very popular adventure fiction set in the Middle Ages.[87] Publishing much of his work in *Adventure* magazine during the 1920s and 1930s, Lamb also deeply influenced Robert E. Howard and later writers of adventure thrillers. Lamb's crusade fiction typically takes the following form: a Western protagonist (often a disgraced, disillusioned, or cast-off crusader) falls into a series of adventures among the

---

87 On Harold Lamb's biography and career see his official website (http://www.haroldlamb.com), as well as the introductions and supporting materials in the recent series reprinting his short fiction under the Bison Books imprint of the University of Nebraska Press: e.g., Harold Lamb, *Swords from the West* (2009); *Swords from the Desert* (2009); *Swords from the East* (2010); *Swords from the Sea* (2010). As a historian, Lamb wrote biographies of Genghis Khan, Tamerlane, and Alexander the Great, histories of the crusades, and juvenile fiction in addition to his historical/adventure fiction for adults. References to Lamb's fiction in this chapter are all drawn from *Swords from the West,* by page number.

Turks, Mongols, and Saracens of the medieval Near East. Lamb's tales owe an obvious debt to the romance tradition: they are episodic, often involve damsels in distress, travel, combat, and adventure. However, they do not typically include magic – Lamb strives to write realistic historical fiction, medieval re-creations in the tradition of Sir Walter Scott. Given Lamb's professional interest in the Crusades, the cultural encounter of East and West haunts his stories.

The East in Lamb's fiction is a sublime landscape beyond the frontier. The protagonists in "The Grand Cham" (1921), for example, journey to the East, "bound ... into unknown territory – into blank spaces on Venetian maps ... alone in a strange land" (255). In one of his best and most famous stories, "The Making of the Morning Star" (1924), the Western protagonist Sir Robert of Antioch rides into the East, into the land of Khar (Persia or Iran), "across a strange and barren land" (381). Although Lamb was a responsible historian and he took care to present an accurate, realistic understanding of the medieval world and a nuanced picture of both eastern and Western cultures, nevertheless, the Babylon romance topos guides his representation of eastern lands and cities. Khar, the "Land of the Throne of Gold," like Dunsany's "Golden Dragon City," is a displaced Babylon:

> They had heard that beyond the eastern mountain wall was a wide desert and beyond this a sea of salt water. Far to the east lay the greatest of the Moslem kingdoms, so it was said. This was known as Khar, or Khorassan, and many were the tales of its wealth. Like Cathay or the land of Prester John, the myth was voiced by wandering minstrels, and no man knew the truth of it, and no warrior of the Croises had penetrated farther to the east than the city of Damascus. (362)

In a footnote, Lamb himself glosses "Khar" as Persia or Iran. Yet our displaced Babylon romance elements are discernible: a land beyond boundaries ("beyond the eastern mountain wall"; "beyond ... a sea of salt water"); a sublime "wide desert" wasteland; formulas for hyperbolic distance ("far to the east"; "farther to the east"); sublime location ("greatest of kingdoms" and "the tales of its wealth"); a centre of Islam ("the greatest of Moslem kingdoms"). Lamb, a responsible and accurate historian, is nevertheless here influenced by the powerful syncretic Babylon romance tradition.

The adventurers end up in the city of Bokhara (modern Bukhara, Uzbekistan) – yet another displaced Babylon. Saracens control Bokhara, a wealthy city of the east surrounded by desert (403) and known as "the heart of Islam" (409). In fact, the narrative directly compares Bokhara to Babylon. Sir Robert and his companion the blind Father Evagrius enter Bokhara as captives:

> "Have we come to the prison, my son?" the gentle voice of Evagrius asked.
> "Nay, we are within the streets of a great city."
> "The sound of it is evil," nodded the priest. "And the smell is foul, both of dirt and incense. So must Babylon have been ere it was cast down." (404)

In response, Robert thinks to himself that "surely Babylon could not have been a greater place than this" (404).[88] Strategic command of Bokhara, heart of Islam, falls to the unlikely hand of Sir Robert against the imminent invasion of Genghis Khan (reminiscent of Orlando ruling as the Sultan of Babylon in Pulci's *Morgante*). In spite of Sir Robert's honourable help, the Mongols sack the city; as the narrator lingers over the rich Eastern plunder – "the riches of Islam, the spoil of Baghdad and Nineveh – the plunder of Balkh and India" (463) – one calls to mind the medieval descriptions of the wealth and plunder of Alexander's empire gathered at Babylon.

If these tropes were not enough to signal the affiliation of the East in this tale with our romance topos, there is a specific nod to medieval romance at the end of "The Morning Star." Like the self-reflexive reading of romances in Voltaire's *Princess of Babylon*, the end of Lamb's story self-consciously refers to the medieval romance tradition. The narrator tells us, in the final words of the story, that the legend of The Morning Star (i.e., Sir Robert's *nom de plume*) will live on as a "romaunt" that "came to be known even in the courts of Europe" (474):

> And when the fear of invasion had passed, the court of the king waxed merry. The minstrels and troubadours had a new song, made from the talk of the caravans that came over the border, and they sang of a crusader who adventured into paynimry itself and waged war upon the great cities. This they called the "Romaunt of the Longsword," and many a time in hall and woman's garden they related it for the pleasuring of the people of the castle who had ever an ear for something new. (473–4)

88 Cf. other Babylon-like details of Bokhara on 407, 411.

Voltaire's *conte* is satire; Dunsany's story is early fantasy; Lamb's story is historical fiction – yet all draw upon the same rich imaginative potential of the Babylon romance topos. Lamb's stories represent the process by which elements of the medieval Babylon romance tradition – including the imagined City at the heart of "paynimry itself" – passed into one of the mode's latter-day descendants: adventure fiction.[89]

Posterity knows Robert E. Howard best as the creator of "Conan the Cimmerian." Behind the pop culture clichés surrounding this flamboyant character, however, lies a complex and tortured author (Howard committed suicide in 1936 at age thirty) and a surprisingly large and varied body of fiction in several pulp genres: westerns, horror stories, humorous tall tales, regional Texas fiction, sports stories, historical fiction, and of course his immensely influential "sword and sorcery tales," the most famous set in an imaginary prehistoric "Hyborian Age" and featuring the barbaric Conan of Cimmeria. As an admirer, friend, and constant correspondent of H.P. Lovecraft, Howard was quite taken with the haunted, ruined city topos; he was similarly influenced by the exotic city of eastern delights, the sublime Babylon of romance.

We can clearly see this topos in Howard's non-Conan historical adventure fiction: stories heavily influenced by Lamb's work and published in magazines such as *Oriental Stories.* Howard's crusade stories follow a predictable pattern indebted to Lamb: a Western hero adventures in crusade lands and mingles (violently) with historical and fictional characters and events, offering much opportunity for Howard's rather unenlightened cross-cultural comparisons. Damsels are distressed and the heroic protagonists flex their muscles: all Howard's heroes seem to be proto-Conan figures, defined by immense physical strength, prowess, and mental endurance; his northern heroes are more barbaric (but also more honest, moral, and noble in a rough-hewn way) than the corrupt and degenerate ancient eastern cultures surrounding them.

Howard's crusade stories also depend on our familiar romance structures. The adventures typically move through a spacious romance

89 Romance is the ancestor of modern adventure fiction and the very concept of "adventure": see Nerlich's remarkable *Kritik der Abenteuer-Ideologie: Beitrag zur Erforschung der bürgerlichen Bewußtseinsbildung, 1100–1750* (1977), trans. by Crowley as *Ideology of Adventure: Studies in Modern Consciousness, 1100–1750*; Fraser, *Victorian Quest Romance*, 5–17. On the etymology of adventure (Old French *aventure*) see Nerlich, *Ideology of Adventure*, I.3. Nerlich notes that in the Middle Ages the concept of adventure (*aventure*) was closely connected to marvels or the miraculous (*mervoille*) (I.12).

geography. Asked where he will go, Godric de Villehard, a knight of Normandy and refugee from the Fourth Crusade replies:

> "Who knows? ... The world is before me – but not all the world with its shining leagues of sea or sand can quench the hunger that is in me. I must ride – that is all I know. I must ride till the ravens pluck my bones." ("Red Blades of Black Cathay" [1931], 14)[90]

Godric wanders into an East that is a "lost and nameless land," where he feels "strangely out of place in this setting of exotic luxury," among the "devious-minded peoples of Asia Minor" ("Red Blades of Black Cathay," 4, 11, 30). Similarly, in "The Sowers of the Thunder" (1932), Cahal Ruadh O'Donnel of Ireland ("Red Cahal"), a knight "newly come to the East" (90) sets out from a Damietta tavern; Cahal and his companion ride "into the unknown land" while "far in the east the vultures circled endlessly" (103). Fictive and semi-fictive cities punctuate this romance landscape. Cahal is on a quest to "a city called Shahazar, the treasure trove of the sultans" in "an unknown land of deserts and mountains" (101), a place ruled by "the lords of the East" (101), "a secret place of wealth and pleasure" (102). In "Lord of Samarcand" (1932) the protagonist Donald MacDeesa, a Celtic refugee from the battle of Nicopolis, "whose grim scarred visage was darkened by the suns of far deserts" (140), travels on his adventures to Samarcand, a city of enchantment and beauty, and a coordinating point in the Eastern wastelands and deserts.

Samarcand is, of course, not Babylon. However, like all of Howard's eastern cities (places he never visited except through books), Samarcand is a displaced romance Babylon. Consider the following description, an approach to the city in which the Western travellers "gaze upon the glory of Samarcand":

> They had covered that vast expanse of country in a time the Frank would have sworn impossible. He felt now the grinding wear of that terrible ride, but he gave no outward sign. The city shimmered to his gaze, mingling with the blue of the distance, so that it seemed part of the horizon, a city

90 Quotations from Howard's crusade stories in this chapter are from Robert E. Howard, *Lord of Samarcand*, ed. Burke. Quotations from the Afghanistan/El Borak stories are from Robert E. Howard, *El Borak*.

> of illusion and enchantment. Blue: the Tatars lived in a wide magnificent land, lavish with color schemes, where the prevailing motif was blue. In the spires and domes of Samarcand were mirrored the hues of the skies, the far mountains, and the dreaming lakes. (134)

This "city of illusion and enchantment," a part of the horizon beyond the "vast expanse of country" is a romance land of the unknown, a place no Westerner had ever beheld, a glorious city of spires and domes, ivory and marble. This Samarcand, like Babylon, is a crossroads of wealth and power: as MacDeesa's companion summarizes, "All the East rides the road to Samarcand" (135). The Westerners enter the city and marvel at "the goods and gauds of India and Cathay, of Persia and Arabia and Egypt"; as "[a]ll the Orient flowed in a broad river through the gates of Samarcand," MacDeesa himself is amazed by the eastern splendour: "The Frank's wonder grew; the cities of the West were hovels compared to this" (135).

Similar patterns obtain even when Howard shifts the time and place of his adventure fiction from the medieval Crusader Near East to modern (i.e., early twentieth century) Afghanistan. Some of Howard's best stories follow the exploits of Francis Xavier Gordon (known in eastern lands as "El Borak," "the Swift") and similar characters such as Kirby O'Donnell and Steve Clarney. El Borak's modern adventures are in Afghanistan and its contiguous regions, but the setting is really still the romance landscape of our Babylon tradition, coordinated by imagined cities.

Almost every El Borak story set in the wild Afghan terrain centers on a hidden, dangerous, opulent (or once opulent) city: Attalus (in "Sword of the Hills"); "forbidden Yolgan" (in "The Daughter of Erlik Khan," 35); Shaitan, "a city whose domes and towers glistened in the rosy dawn, like a magic city of sorcerers stolen from some fabled land and set down in this desert spot" (in "Three-Bladed Doom," 107); Shalizahr, a "fantastic city," a place El Borak "seemed to remember ... in some medieval historical connection" ("Three-Bladed Doom," 112), a "strange city" with "groves and gardens" hidden and guarded by high mountain peaks, with a "heterogenous population" of "Kurds, many Persians, and Yezidees ... Arabs, Mongols, Druses, Turks, Indians, even a few Egyptians" ("Three-Bladed Doom," 113); Rub el Harami, "a city of mystery and evil, which no white man had ever visited except as a captive, and from which none had ever escaped. A plague spot, sprawled in the high, bare hills, almost fabulous ... an outlaw city, whence the winds blew whispered tales too fantastic and hideous for credence" ("Sons of the Hawk," 282); in

"The Fire of Asshurbanipal," the setting is the nameless "silent dead city of black stone set in the drifting sands of the desert," a "mythical city," an "ancient City of Evil," a "city of the dead on which an ancient curse rested" (450–1). All of Howard's cities are displaced Babylons, usually an amalgam of our Babylonian themes of degeneracy, ruin, and romance.

El Borak and the other characters only find these displaced Babylons by progress through a vast romance landscape, a world of adventures beyond the Western frontier. El Borak is a native of El Paso, Texas, but "now for years soldier of fortune in the outlands of the world" ("Sword of the Hills," 7); he is an adventurer and rover "in the waste places of the East" ("Sons of the Hawk," 305). El Borak's adventures lead him, inevitably, to hidden cities through a fantastic desert wasteland. In "Blood of the Gods" the "shadowy desert stretched vast and mysterious" (236); pursued in this wasteland, Gordon becomes a "solitary figure, pitting an indomitable will against the merciless immensity of the thirst-haunted desert" ("Blood of the Gods," 248), a desert wasteland that, moreover, "was a breeding place of mysteries, a twilight realm of fantasy" ("Blood of the Gods," 251). In Steve Clarney's mind "The desert became not merely a material waste, but the greyness of the lost eons, in whose depths dreamed sunken things" ("The Fire of Asshurbanipal," 452–3). The familiar outlines of the Babylon romance topos are unmistakable: a vast eastern desert landscape punctuated by an exotic, fantastic City.

Other telltale allusions to the Babylon romance topos recur. Howard's characters self-consciously compare their modern predicaments to "a tale out of 'The Arabian Nights.'"[91] In the course of their adventures, characters often feel as if they have been drawn back in time to a medieval or ancient past, often with accompanying allusions to Babylon itself. Stuart Brent witnesses a fight in Rub el Harami; he watches in fascination, and the narrator explains that "But for modern weapons it might have been a riot in ancient Babylon, Cairo, or Nineveh" ("Sons of the Hawk," 299). El Borak feels much the same way in Shaitan: "Accustomed as he was to the furtiveness and subdued undertones of Eastern palaces, Gordon sensed here a more than ordinary atmosphere of mystery and secrecy ... Mystery and intangible menace lurked in those dim, gorgeous halls. He might have been traversing a palace of Nineveh or ancient Persia, but for the modern weapons of his escort" ("Three-Bladed

91 "Blood of the Gods," 265; see also "Sons of the Hawk," 280.

Doom," 114).[92] In the same story, Gordon is trapped in the nightmarish gulches and ravines outside Shalizahr, a place haunted by a half-human, half-ape man-eating monster who has countless victims: "The lights of Shalizahr glowed in the sky above the wall, and he could catch the weird melody of wining native citherns. A woman's voice was lifted in a plaintive song. He smiled grimly at the dark, skeleton-littered gorges about him. So might the lords of Nineveh and Babylon and Susa have revelled, heedless of the captives screaming and writhing and dying in the pits beneath their palaces – ignorant of the red destruction predestined at the maddened hands of those captives" ("Three-Bladed Doom," 148).[93]

It would be difficult to overestimate the influence of Robert E. Howard on twentieth century genre fiction, particularly adventure, thrillers, and sword-and-sorcery fantasy. Along with Victorian precursors such as Kipling, A. Conan Doyle, and H. Rider Haggard, Howard created an influential template for adventure fiction recognizable even in the Indiana Jones series of films. Howard, from early twentieth-century rural Texas and not much of a traveller, knew such "exotic" cities only from books; his imaginative twentieth-century versions of medieval romance operate through the Babylon textual tradition. Although he is famous today as an author in the fantasy tradition, what set Howard's fiction apart was its hard-edged, gritty realism: in his appropriation of the matter of Babylon we are a long way from the magical romances of the medieval and early modern worlds, or the parodic world of Voltaire's *contes*, yet the underlying narrative structures – the East, distance, travel deserts, ancient powerful cities, peril, Islam – remain the same.

---

92 El Borak even feels at times almost like a reincarnated warrior of the medieval or ancient past walking in Shaitan: "This was the most bizarre situation he [El Borak] had ever found himself in, in the course of a life packed with wild adventures and bloody episodes. He felt out of place in his boots and dusty khakis, in this mysterious city that turned the clock of Time back nearly a thousand years. There was a curious sensation of having strayed out of his own age into a lost and forgotten Past; a Past he had known before. It was almost like a flash of memory in which he saw himself, a black haired, black-eyed warrior from a far western isle, clad in chain mail of a Crusader, striding through the intrigue-veiled mazes of an Assassin city" ("Three-Bladed Doom," 122).

93 Cf. also "The Fire of Asshurbanipal," 456: the cursed city of the desert houses a demonic temple of devil worshippers, with an idol of Baal "on whose black altar in other ages many a screaming, writhing naked victim had offered up the quivering soul. The idol embodied in its utter, abysmal and sullen bestiality the whole soul of this demoniac city. Surely, thought Steve [Clarney], the builders of Nineveh and Kara-Shehr were cast in another mold than the people of today. Their art and culture were too ponderous, too grimly barren of the lighter aspects of humanity, to be wholly human."

Babylonian Romance in Twentieth-Century Fantasy and Science Fiction

Two final examples will illustrate the trajectory of the Babylon romance topos in the popular genres of fantasy and science fiction. Neil Gaiman's and Charles Vess's award-winning 1999 fantasy graphic novel *Stardust* (subtitled *Being a Romance Within the Realms of Faerie*) is a homage to medieval romance, to the fairy tale tradition, and to nineteenth-century neo-medieval fantasy authors such as William Morris, Arthur Machen, and Dunsany.[94] The young protagonist, Tristran Thorn, lives in the village of Wall in Victorian England; Wall takes its name from the ancient stone wall that separates the hamlet from the world of Faerie beyond. Tristran (a half-Faerie changeling himself) journeys beyond the wall to Faerie when he foolishly promises to retrieve a fallen star from the land beyond if his love Victoria will accept his advances. With a direct allusion to Dunsany's favourite phrase denoting romance travel, Tristran Thorn goes over the wall and passes "beyond the fields we know ... And into Faerie" (51).[95]

The fallen star takes terrestrial form as a beautiful maiden who becomes Tristran's true love interest. The star maiden falls "to the East" (47), which represents the land of Faerie in *Stardust*, the land of enchantment and adventure and not a mere compass direction. Tristran in fact tells his father he is going to the East on his quest: "*East.* His father nodded. There were two easts – east to the next county, through the forest, and East – the other side of the wall" (48). Gaiman envisions the East or Faerie as a place of unbounded distance, constructed by the imagination:

> A question like "How Big is Faerie?" does not admit of a simple answer. Faerie, after all, is not one land, one principality or dominion. Maps of Faerie are unreliable, and may not be depended upon. We talk of the Kings and Queens of Faerie as we would speak of the Kings and Queens of England. But Faerie is bigger than England, as it is bigger than the world (for, since the dawn of time, each land that has been forced off the map by explorers and the brave going out and proving it wasn't there has taken refuge in Faerie; so it is now, by the time we come to write of it, a most huge place

94 *Stardust* is clearly influenced by Dunsany's *The King of Elfland's Daughter* (1924) and *The Blessing of Pan* (1927).

95 Gaiman and Vess, *Stardust: Being a Romance Within the Realms of Faerie.* Gaiman adapted the graphic novel as a print-only novel later in 1999; it was also made into a Hollywood film, *Stardust* (dir. Matthew Vaughn), staring Claire Danes, Michelle Pfeiffer, and Robert De Niro, in 2007. Citations here are from the graphic novel, by page numbers.

> indeed, containing every manner of landscape and terrain). *Here*, truly, *there be Dragons.* (*Stardust*, 61; emphasis in original)

We see here the combination of at least two traditions: the medieval Celtic concept of Faery (including a hint of popularized medieval geography with the "Here there be Dragons" reference) and elements of our Babylon romance topos. The Celtic Otherworld (a staple inspiration of modern fantasy literature) here combines with a notion of the unbounded romance Orient like a tale out of *The Thousand and One Nights.*

But where is Babylon in this tale? *Stardust* does not centre on a city, but it does incorporate a Babylon allusion that brings us back to our numinous nursery rhyme from the beginning of this chapter and its evocation of sublime distance. Tristran wondrously travels great distances across Faerie on his quest through the magic of a "Babylon candle." Early in his journey, in a chance encounter, Tristan seeks aid from a diminutive old man (a dwarf or a gnome, really) named Charmed, a native inhabitant of Faerie who gives him a magic candle stub that will allow him to travel great distances. Tristan asks: "Do you think it will be far? ... To the star?" In response the little man asks, "rhetorically," "How many miles to Babylon?" Tristran then recites, in full, the poem "How Many Miles to Babylon," but dismisses it as "only a nursery rhyme" (75–6). Charmed does not agree that nursery rhymes are so inconsequential. He prods Tristran: "How many miles to Babylon? ... Can I get there by candlelight? There and back again" (94). Charmed gives Tristran the candle stub, remarking that "Most candles won't do it. This one took a lot of findin'" (94). Tristan puzzles over the unassuming lump, but Charmed explains that the boy should simply walk to the star with the lit candle in his right hand – and he should be quick about it ("Feet be nimble and light, yes?," 95; see Figure 7.2).

Charmed lights the unearthly candle, which does not flicker in the wind, and Tristran begins to walk forward as the "candlelight illuminated the world: every tree and bush and blade of grass" (95). A beautiful two-page sequence of six image-panels tracks Tristran's progress with the candle, as he magically travels great distances:

> With Tristran's next step he was standing beside a lake, and the candlelight shone brightly on the water ... and then he was walking through the mountains, through lonely crags, where the candlelight was reflected in the eyes of the creatures of the high snows ... and then he was walking through the clouds, which, while not entirely substantial, still supported his weight in comfort ... and then, holding tightly to his candle, he was underground,

7.2. The "Babylon Candle," from Gaiman and Vess, *Stardust* (1999), 97.

> and the candlelight glinted back at him from the wet cave walls ... now he was in the mountains once more; and then he was on a road through wild forest ... and another step, and he was in a leafy glen, and he could hear the chuckle of water as it splashed and sang its way into a small brook ... (96–7)

He has arrived at his destination via the magic "Babylon candle."[96] It is a clever little plot device, in keeping with Gaiman's typical creative (and renovative) interest in myth, folklore, and fairy tales. What is significant for us is the context: the Babylon allusion's place in a latter-day neo-medieval romance in which the city has transcended any urban referent and endures as a figure for pure imaginative distance.

We might extend the Babylon romance topos one final step further, transcending earth itself, by moving into the unbounded spaces of science fiction. J. Michael Straczynski's critically acclaimed television science fiction series *Babylon 5* (1994–8) follows the adventures of its eponymous

96 The exact phrase "Babylon candle" is never used in the graphic novel, but it is used on the internet by various Gaiman fan sites and on Wikipedia to designate the item.

7.3. Out on the Rim with the space station *Babylon 5*.

space station, "the last of the Babylon stations," in the twenty-third century (see Figure 7.3).

Modelled loosely on various science fiction television and film series, *Babylon 5* was a cut above the competition in its storytelling ambitions and literary influences, both in terms of its innovative five-year epic story arc as well as the individual episodes (the bulk written by Straczynski, but several were written by respected science fiction luminaries such as D.C. Fontana, Peter David, David Gerrold, Neil Gaiman, and Harlan Ellison, who also functioned as a creative consultant throughout the series).[97] But why name the station "Babylon 5," part of "the Babylon project"?

Straczynski explains that he chose Babylon due to his interest in Babylonian mythology and what he saw as its cosmic struggle between order and chaos, a theme he treated during the run of the show.[98] But I believe we can see the long shadow of our romance topos here as well. In this

97 All quotations and observations about the series are drawn from the collected DVDs (Warner Home Video, 2002–04).

98 Straczynski, DVD commentary on episode "Chrysalis" (season 1, disc 6).

Elsewhere universe, the Babylon stations were proposed and constructed in the aftermath of an interstellar war between humanity and the powerful alien Minbari civilization, a war that almost brought humanity to extinction. The Season One ("Signs and Portents") prologue, broadcast as a voiceover during each episode's opening credits, summarizes the role of the Babylon 5 station:

> It was the dawn of the third age of mankind, ten years after the Earth/Minbari war. The Babylon Project was a dream given form. Its goal, to prevent another war by creating a place where humans and aliens could work out their differences peacefully. It's a port of call – home away from home for diplomats, hustlers, entrepreneurs, and wanderers. Humans and aliens wrapped in two million, five hundred thousand tons of spinning metal, all alone in the night. It can be a dangerous place, but it's our last best hope for peace. This is the story of the last of the Babylon stations. The year is 2258. The name of the place is Babylon 5.

In some ways, then, Babylon 5 is a United Nations in space; but it is also a place of intersecting boundaries. Babylon 5 is a place where empires clash and good and evil struggle in starkly reified terms; it is a crossroads where human history takes significant turns. The station stands at the edge of known space, "all alone in the night," and facing the unknown; it is "out on the Rim," as the show puts it. The wild interstellar spaces beyond the Rim are like Borges's description of the East in Western thought: the Orient and unknown space are both "something vast, immobile, magnificent, incomprehensible."[99] This interstellar Babylon stands at a new frontier opposing a new vast, immobile, incomprehensible "East" under the sign of Babylon. It is somehow appropriate that Babylon as a topos of romance and adventure should leave the confines

---

99 Borges, "Thousand and One Nights," in *Seven Nights*, trans. Weinberger, 42.

100 Interestingly, Norman Daniel, in summarizing the world of the medieval Saracen romance, makes an analogy with science fiction and fantasy. He concludes that the medieval poems create a "closed and self-sufficient and wholly imaginary little world" (*Heroes and Saracens*, 267). He then cites a number of analogous modern literary worlds: such as the family saga (e.g., the Forsyte Saga) and soap operas; but he notes that "the parallel is even closer with the worlds created by science fiction" citing *Dune* and *The Lord of the Rings* and concluding: "We have to think of Mahon and Tervagant and the rest as anticipating the space invaders of twentieth century science fiction" (*Heroes and Saracens*, 268).

of terrestrial geography and take up a station-keeping coordinate, out on the Rim.[100]

In his introduction to *Orientalism*, Said, with ironic intent, quotes a French journalist who mourns the passing of "the Orient of Chateaubriand and Nerval" as he looks around the decrepit Beirut slums of the mid-1970s. Said notes that "The Orient was almost a European invention, and had been since antiquity a place of romance, exotic beings, haunting memories and landscapes, remarkable experiences."[101] The rest of Said's powerful seminal study deconstructs that fiction of the Orient as a place of romance, throwing into high relief the political realities underwritten by the Western discourse of "the Orient." For Said, the "romance of the Orient" is a pernicious ideology, no matter how beautiful or compelling its Western expressions.

There is undoubted truth in Said's perspective. Words and tales and images are put to real uses, of course, and I would not for wish to trivialize the historic political and social consequences of expressing Babylon as a metonymic figure for an entirely fictive Orient, existing only in the free play of Western imaginations. Yet there is also something sublime in these seemingly endless romance displacements of Babylon. "Go forth to Babylon!" exclaims Voltaire's angel in *Zadig* – a journey to both the known and the unknown of romance. As Patricia Parker notes, the narrative wanderings of romance, its dilation, delay, and open-endedness overturns or subverts narrative *telos*; romance form subverts resolution and endings.[102] The East that originates in the name of Babylon constitutes an exotic space of adventure beyond the borders of the known: all part of this endless dilation of romance. Romance seems to be a mode of endless regeneration, creating "a world where nothing remains, something older than history, younger than the present moment, always willing and able to descend again once more."[103] "How many miles to Babylon?" – our nursery rhyme poses the question as if awaiting a numerical answer, a simple arithmetic; but at the same time, the question is rhetorical, awaiting no "real" answer: this sublime Babylon of romance generates a sense of hope and a sense of an unbounded future that will always sit on the edge of the horizon.

101 *Orientalism*, 1.

102 Parker, *Inescapable Romance*.

103 Frye, *Secular Scripture*, 126.

Conclusion

Now concerning the wonders of Babylonia, let what has been said suffice.

– Diodorus Siculus, *Library of History*, II.12.3

The catalogue of forms is endless: until every shape has found its city, new cities will continue to be born.

– Italo Calvino, *Invisible Cities*, 139

In the ancient Akkadian narrative poem *Erra and Ishum* (8th c. BCE), Ishum quotes the chief Babylonian god Marduk's lament for the destruction of Babylon, Marduk's beloved city:

Alas for Babylon,
whose crown I fashioned luxuriant as a palm's,
but which the wind has scorched!
Alas for Babylon,
that I had laden with seeds, like an evergreen,
but of whose delights
I could not have what I hoped for!
Alas for Babylon,
that I tended like a thriving orchard,
but whose fruit I could not taste!
Alas for Babylon,
that I suspended like a gemstone seal
on the neck of the sky!

Alas for Babylon,
 that I clasped in my hand like the tablet of destinies,
 not handing it over to anyone else![1]

In these moving verses we hear a voice absent from this study: the authentic voice of the real ancient Babylon, rather than Babylon as seen under Western eyes. Of course, were we to turn our gaze to this Babylon, the resulting image would be much different from the imaginative adaptations we have seen in our long trek through Western traditions. There is perhaps some irony in the image of Marduk here, clasping Babylon in his hand like a tablet of destinies (much like the crumbling cuneiform tablets the poem itself was inscribed upon), refusing to hand it over to anyone else. Because of course Babylon did slip from the Babylonian grasp, in a sense, to take on a new life and become an essential element of Western imaginations. Although our focus has not been on the rich culture and literature of the real Babylon, nor on the surprising direct influence of ancient Babylon on the western Mediterranean cultures of antiquity, I think it nevertheless important to at least register here at the end, however briefly and imperfectly, the untold story of Babylon and its own voice, to draw attention to the partiality and artifice of Babylon under Western eyes.

In the West, to speak the three syllables of "Babylon" has been to engage with a complex immemorial tradition and to give it new sustaining life, no matter how far the distance from Marduk's Babylon. Babylon under Western eyes, in all its strange, disturbing and delightful transformations, is an example of "world literature," to use David Damrosch's compelling definition of the term: like a much-loved poem, Babylon long ago left its source culture and its original historical context to circulate, in ever-new forms and afterlives, out in the world, adapting to a seemingly endless variety of new host cultures.[2] And, as I have stressed, this receptive new life of Babylon in the overlapping genealogies I have presented does not reduce to a simple chronological history. When Babylon is used as a reference or allusion, any one or more aspects of the Matter of Babylon might be put into play, crossing time and place in complex ways. I do not believe I have even begun to exhaust the subject of Babylon's mythic life; and certainly any one of the many Babylon references I have used throughout this study could be more heavily historicized, its historical

1 Foster, ed., *Before the Muses*, I.780–1.

2 Damrosch, *What is World Literature?*; my language in this sentence draws from page 283.

context more fully explicated. But such a historicist project – so dominant in literary studies over the past thirty years, but now beginning to ebb – has not been my aim; rather, by taking several aerial views of the varied Western traditions of Babylon, the contours of its being come to light in a way that would not be possible at the level of fully synchronic cultural history as it is usually practiced. My concern here has been the sweep of aerial topography, not the context of each landmark. I am, nevertheless, reasonably confident that any one particular use of "Babylon" as a reference or citation or allusion can find a place in this study's genealogies. *Babylon Under Western Eyes* is not a key to all mythologies, but it does help us unlock and decode Babylon's myth.

Taken as a whole, then, what does this map of Babylon's strange *Nachleben* tell us as a case study in myth-making? Given what we have seen, what does Babylon's allusive power suggest about the workings of textual reference and allusion; the displacement, adaptation, and transformation of myths; and the formation of cultural traditions? Moreover, through such a case study, can we envision a new form of literary history?

Allusion and Tradition

We might begin with allusion's definitional problem. I stated in my introduction that I would have more to say about allusion once we had traversed Babylon's mythic genealogies. But should we even call the textual instantiations of Babylon scattered so thickly throughout this study "allusions"? Are they better described as "references"? "Citations"? To use "references" or "citations" does not do justice either to the richness of associations deployed by the city's invocation, or to the dynamism in its traditions of changing meaning. As for "allusion," "Babylon" does conjures up specific associations from a prior textual domain outside the text at hand; and therefore like an allusion, "Babylon" – one specific word – connects the moment of its textual instantiation to a prior archive of textual traditions, summoning up that prior text archive (whether individual or collective), and giving that prior extra-textual material new life within a new textual environment. That is, Babylon refers outside itself, dragging in associations from an extra-textual domain in the same way that an allusion connects the reader to a secondary text (and that text's hermeneutic traditions) outside or beyond the primary text at hand. And moreover, like allusion, allusive *intent* is usually (but not always) present in citations of Babylon: a writer often explicitly uses "Babylon" in order to generate a specific rhetorical effect. When Arthur

C. Clarke titles his 1951 anti-nuclear war short story "If I Forget Thee, O Earth," the "full-knowing reader" decodes this Babylon allusion by calling up the original, prior informing text (in this case, Psalm 136 and the exilic Babylonian political myth of the Captivity) and measures the "new" instantiation against its prior contextual meaning, each informing the other.[3]

So, "allusion," then: our tour through the Babylon myth demonstrates the important role allusion can play in creating a mythic tradition. The Babylon example shows that progressive iterative uses of allusion construct, or develop, or augment the very body of lore they depend on. That is, the more one refers to Babylon as (e.g.) a figure for moral corruption, and thus the more one uses the word and all it represents as a political or polemical metaphor, the more progressively rich (and commonplace) that tradition becomes and thus the more likely will it then subsequently be drawn upon by later authors as a source of further allusion.[4] In other words, based on the evidence assembled here, a theory of allusion should also account for the dynamics of *cumulative* effect and the progressive, incremental results of iterative allusion in forming a networked textual tradition. Allusion tends to be a term of discrete study, focusing on the specific delimited example, the discrete case of correspondence. However, the study of an ongoing vigorous tradition of allusion should recognize the different effects achieved when numerous allusions operate together and form an allusive tradition. The process of allusion progressively reifies that tradition; there is a dynamic, reciprocal relationship between an allusive tradition and its discrete textual instantiations: the more one alludes, the more the tradition reifies.

However it is also apparent that in tradition's *longue durée*, there can, in contrast, be a diminution or diffusion of the specific original inceptive context of an allusion. Not everyone is a full-knowing reader, and continued iterative displacement of a figure can render the original, specific context less and less available; the meaning conjured up may then have a more tenuous connection to the original context, thus opening it up for creative displacement. A reference to Babylon by Lovecraft, for example, might be perceived as no more than "exotic coloring," with little specific "Babylonian" meaning attached, the full and direct implications of the reference lost on most readers. That is to say, progressive displacement and adaptation can blur an archetype over time, as original forms bear

3 The term "full-knowing reader," is from Joseph Pucci's book of the same title.

4 On the generative potential of allusion, see Hollander, *Figure of Echo*.

less and less of their specific original meaning into new adaptations. In a strange way, then, one can "know" what Babylon means and "not know," in the same instance. Based upon our Babylon evidence, this process of potential diffusion tends to move in tandem with the secularization of originally biblical and/or Christian structures of meaning; we see this process in the way that my genealogies began in the midst of medieval Christian cultural materials and ended up displaced into secularized science fiction, fantasy, and horror.

Yet in the end, the term "allusion" does not quite suffice either as an explanation of the Babylon myth. Implicit in most discussions of allusion is the idea that the meaning signified by an allusion is itself veiled or at least partially obscure. Allusion is a sort of riddle or enigma, a species of literary play (hence its etymological connection to Latin *ludus*, "play" or "game") and solving the game (i.e., "getting" the allusion) is an essential part of the figure's effect. In contrast, to drop the word "Babylon" into a composition does not usually create a hidden or even partially hidden connection between two texts: Babylon often functions as a blunt citation or reference. Also, allusion is generally conceived as one text connecting to another singular discrete text; with Babylon, however, the source text is generally not one text but rather a complex of traditional associations. Thus, while "Babylon" displays some aspects of allusion, in other respects the term does not seem quite adequate.

"Allusion" therefore gives us a partial purchase on the problem, but we need a further supplement to better account for the dissemination of Babylon's myth across time and space. Aid comes from the scholarship on oral traditions, a longtime component of Anglo-Saxon literary studies; the late John Miles Foley, for example, devoted his career to understanding the persistence and dynamics of oral tradition from a comparative perspective. Adapting his findings allows us to supplement the working of allusion with another powerful way to understand the genesis and persistence of mythic traditions like Babylon.

Foley coins the terms "traditional referentiality" and "immanent art" to describe the complex aesthetic operations of oral "literature."[5] To briefly

5 I place "literature" in quotation marks here because, as Foley makes clear, "literature" is a text-based phenomenon and thus "oral literature" is something of a contradiction, even though the term is widely used; "verbal art" might be a better substitute. I use Foley's work here as representative scholarship on the field of oral tradition, even while drawing on his particular insights. On traditional referentiality and immanent art, see Foley, *Immanent Art*, esp. 6–8 and 38–60; *Singer of Tales in Performance*, 60–98; *How to Read an Oral Poem*, 109–24.

summarize: in the performance of traditional oral literature (e.g., the Homeric poems, South Slavic epic, etc.) words, phrases, and other traditional discreet oral building blocks or semantic units come trailing a host of unspoken, traditional meanings; according to Foley, these units employ a metonymic "traditional referentiality," the oral instantiation standing in for a broader traditional whole. They display an "immanent art": the explicit meaning of a word is only part of the aesthetic experience; a broader world of implicit, immanent meaning resides in that small utterance. In this system, traditional oral units such as words thus have an "idiomatic force" that summons up a "larger context"; words are "indexical" and metonymically key into a "traditional network" of unspoken meanings.[6] For Foley, the special linguistic register of words used in an oral poetic tradition allows for words to bear a rich concentration of implicit meanings and, moreover, enables that oral tradition both to persist over time and to interact with textual technologies:

> Because [oral poetic linguistic] registers are more highly coded than everyday language, because their "words" resonate with traditional implications beyond the scope of multipurpose street language, they convey enormously more than grammar and dictionaries (based as they are on the everyday language) can record. For this reason – because they offer ready access to meaning that otherwise lies just out of reach – registers can and do persist beyond live performance and into texts. Registers don't just get the composing job done; they connect oral poems to their oral traditions.[7]

Much of this seems applicable to the dynamics of the Babylon myth as I have explored it in this book. A single, semantically rich word potentially refers, through tradition, to a spectrum of immanent meanings. When exploring how Babylon's myth was transmitted over the generations, we can conclude that something like oral tradition, therefore, proceeds in tandem and in complex negotiation, with the equally pervasive text-based operation of allusion in order to generate and ever recreate the Matter of Babylon.

Generally speaking, cultural traditions of long-standing are often viewed suspiciously, either as hollow and corrupt relics, or as dangerous ideological illusions produced by a hegemonic voice. But I think

6 Foley, *How to Read an Oral Poem*, 113–14.
7 Foley, *How to Read an Oral Poem*, 116.

that *Babylon under Western Eyes* demonstrates the creative human dynamism of tradition, whether that tradition changes and endures on a textual basis through allusion, or within the oral domain of immanent art. This dynamism begins with an inceptive archetype, then grows through an ongoing creative process of displacement, adaptation and transformation – all terms that imply movement and change, the sort of mobile, recursive hermeneutic essential for the formation and maintenance of traditions.[8]

The Limits of Historicism

Given our view of the Babylon myth's complex dynamics, these brief concluding observations therefore suggest that certain cultural phenomena are not adequately understood in terms of simple narrative chronology or by means of a thoroughly synchronic historical contextualization. The historicist approach in literary studies has difficulty grappling with the problem of how texts transcend their historical moment: that is, how texts bear meaning and move readers across time, even when separated from their original historical context. In short, the historical approach to texts is very good at demonstrating how texts resonate in a synchronic fashion, but less adept in showing how texts carry meaning diachronically, particularly over large stretches of time, and particularly when the phenomenon under observation does not reduce to a simple notion of genetic linear time. This problem is perfectly illustrated in the complex temporality of the Matter of Babylon, its "polychronicity": one dynamic, mythic tradition; but comprised of several distinct genealogies within that tradition, genealogies that overlap, interact, crisscross, swell and deflate with meaning over the centuries in a complex resonant process, "enmeshing us in extended webs of influence."[9] The displacement, adaptation, and transformation of the Babylon myth across time, and the dynamic way, within that mythic tradition, the operation of allusion

8 Goldenberg, e.g., notes that "The Bible is not so much a framework, conceptual and structural, into which all subsequent thinking must fit (conform), as it is a grid upon which postbiblical thinking asserts itself, and in the process changes the biblical blueprint" (*Curse of Ham*, 8). On this importance of dynamic change in the construction and maintenance of traditions see, e.g., Shils, *Tradition*, esp. 44–6, 195–286; K.F. Morrison, *Mimetic Tradition*.

9 "Polychronicity" is Jonathan Gil Harris's term from "Four Exoskeletons and No Funeral"; the second quotation is from Felski, "Context," 578.

and referentiality defeats time, and confounds it by revivifying past traditions in the present: all these militate against the notion that literary understanding is reducible to historical contextualization.[10] What my trek through the Matter of Babylon suggests is that one might consider writing a new sort of literary history through rhetorical figures or other organizing modes that confound or cut across the usual temporalities implicit in traditional literary history. To write literary history by disjunction, by analogy, or by adaptation, gives us a quite different and original view of literary production.

In medieval thought, the city stood between the universe and the individual: the urban image was a microcosm of the universe and a macrocosm of the human body. The city as Neoplatonic form mirrored the structure of the universe, even as the urban community was represented as a body writ large.[11] In the medieval tradition, to represent the city was to speak of both the vast universe and the individual life, and all in between. And so we might extend that observation beyond the Middle Ages: Babylon is significant – as an idea, an image, an archetype – because the urban metaphor is one of humanity's longest-enduring modes of self-discovery and self-representation. Thus, to gather up the genealogies of imaginative Babylon is to assemble a partial picture of the human endeavour in the West, spread across worlds of dream and nightmare. Jerusalem is the shining city, the utopia of human community; Babylon, Jerusalem's shadow opposite, is something else entirely. But in the end Babylon is not simply a Hell opposed to Heaven; it is something more changeable, something more vitally interesting and human. Jerusalem is the unattainable vision: how the City might be; Babylon is the City as imagined in the shadows of that glory, abiding in the world of experience.

10 Felski makes much the same point in her summary of the power of literature to cut across time and historical context: "Their [i.e., texts from the past] temporality is dynamic, not fixed or frozen; they speak to, but also beyond, their own moment, anticipating future affinities and conjuring up not yet imaginable connections" ("Context," 579).

11 See Lilley, *City and Cosmos*, 7–12; Wheatley, *City as Symbol*, 9–10.

Bibliography

Primary Sources

Ælfric. *Grammar. Ælfrics Grammatik und Glossar.* Edited by Julius Zupitza. Berlin: Weidmann, 1880.

Ælfric. *Preface to Genesis.* In *The* Old English Heptateuch *and Ælfric's* Libellus de Veteri Testamento et Novo, edited by Richard Marsden. Vol. 1. EETS o.s. 330. Oxford: Oxford University Press, 2008.

Aethicus Ister. *The Cosmography of Aethicus Ister.* Edited and translated by Michael W. Herren. Turnhout: Brepols, 2011.

Alcuin. *Versus de clade Lindisfarensis monsterii.* Edited by Ernst Dümmler. MGH, Poet. Lat. Vol. 1. Berlin: Weidmann, 1881. 229–35.

Ammianus Marcellinus. *History.* Translated by John C. Rolfe. 3 vols. LCL. Cambridge, MA: Harvard University Press, 1935–9.

Andrew, Malcolm, and Ronald Waldron, eds. *The Poems of the Pearl Manuscript.* 5th ed. Liverpool: Liverpool University Press, 2008.

Appell, Theron B. *Belshazzar, or the Fall of Babylon: A Tale of the Orient.* New Haven: Tuttle, Morehouse, and Taylor, 1861.

Ariosto, Ludovico. *Orlando Furioso.* Edited by Santorre Debenedetti and Cesare Segre. Bologna: Commissione per i Testi di Lingua, 1960.

Ariosto, Ludovico. *Orlando Furioso.* Translated by Barbara Reynolds. 2 vols. New York: Penguin, 1973.

Aristotle. *The Basic Works of Aristotle.* Edited by Richard McKeon. New York: Random House, 1941. Reprint, New York: Modern Library, 2001.

Arngart, Olof, ed. *The Middle English* Genesis and Exodus. Lund: C.W.K. Gleerup, 1968.

Augustine. *De civitate Dei.* Edited by Bernhard Dombart and Alphonse Kalb. *Aurelii Augustini Opera* Vol. 14.1 and 14.2. CCSL 47, 48. Turnhout: Brepols, 1955.

Augustine. *The City of God against the Pagans.* Edited and translated by R.W. Dyson. Cambridge: Cambridge University Press, 1998.

Ausonius. *Ausonius.* Translated by Hugh C. Evelyn White. 2 vols. LCL. Cambridge, MA: Harvard University Press, 1919.

Ballaster, Ros, ed. *Fables of the East: Selected Tales 1662–1785.* Oxford: Oxford University Press, 2005.

Bately, Janet, ed. *The Old English Orosius.* EETS s.s. 6. London: Oxford University Press, 1980.

Bede. *A Biblical Miscellany.* Translated by W. Trent Foley and Arthur G. Holder. Liverpool: Liverpool University Press, 1999.

Bede. *De temporum ratione* (*Chronica maiora*). In Bede, *Opera Didascalica. Part II.* CCSL 123b. Turnhout: Brepols, 1977.

Bede. *Expositio Apocalypseos.* Edited by Roger Gryson. CCSL 121a. Turnhout: Brepols, 2001.

Bede. *In Ezram et Neemiam.* Edited by D. Hurst. CCSL 119a. Turnhout: Brepols, 1969.

Bede. *In Genesim.* Edited by C.W. Jones. CCSL 118a. Turnhout: Brepols, 1967.

Bede. *In Regum XXX Quaestiones.* Edited by D. Hurst. CCSL 119. Turnhout: Brepols, 1962.

Bede. *Commentary on Revelation.* Translated by Faith Wallis. Liverpool: Liverpool University Press, 2013.

Bede. *On Ezra and Nehemiah.* Translated by Scott DeGregorio. Liverpool: Liverpool University Press, 2006.

Bede. *On Genesis.* Translated by Calvin B. Kendall. Liverpool: Liverpool University Press, 2008.

Bede. *The Reckoning of Time.* Translated by Faith Wallis. Liverpool: Liverpool University Press, 1999.

Bellay, Joachim du. *The Regrets, with The Antiquities of Rome, Three Latin Elegies, and The Defense and Enrichment of the French Language.* Edited and translated by Richard Helgerson. Philadelphia: University of Pennsylvania Press, 2006.

Benjamin of Tudela. *The Itinerary of Benjamin of Tudela.* Translated by Marcus Nathan Adler. New York: Philipp Feldheim, 1907.

Beowulf. Klaeber's Beowulf and the Fight at Finnsburg. Edited by R.D. Fulk, Robert E. Bjork, and John D. Niles. 4th ed. Toronto: University of Toronto Press, 2008.

Best, George. *A true discourse of the late voyages of discoverie: for finding of a passage to Cathaya by the Northweast, vnder the conduct of Martin Frobisher, generall* (1578). Reprinted in Richard Hakluyt, *Principall Navigations, Voyages, Traffiques & Discoveries of the English Nation* (1600), edited by Edmund Goldsmid. 16 vols. Edinburgh, 1885–9.

Black, Matthew, James C. VanderKam, and Otto Neugebauer, eds. *The Book of Enoch, or, I Enoch: a New English Edition.* Leiden: Brill, 1985.

Blake, William. *The Complete Poems.* Edited by Alicia Ostriker. New York: Penguin, 1977.

Boiardo, Matteo. *Orlando Innamorato.* Translated by Charles Stanley Ross. Berkeley and Los Angeles: University of California Press, 1989.

Borges, Jorge Luis. "The Thousand and One Nights." In his *Seven Nights,* translated by Eliot Weinberger. New York: New Directions, 1984.

Boussuet, Jacques-Bénigne. *Discourse on Universal History.* Translated by Elborg Forster. Edited by Orest Ranum. Chicago: University of Chicago Press, 1976.

Brontë, Charlotte. *Villette.* Edited by Mark Lilly. New York: Penguin, 1979.

Browne, Sir Thomas. *Pseudodoxia Epidemica.* Edited by Robin Robbins. 2 vols. Oxford: Clarendon, 1981.

Brunner, Karl, ed. *Der Mittelenglische Versroman über Richard Löwenherz.* Leipzig: Wilhelm Braumüller, 1913.

Burroughs, Edgar Rice. *The Land That Time Forgot.* New York: Modern Library, 2002.

(Pseudo-) Callisthenes, *The Greek Alexander Romance.* Translated by Richard Stoneman. New York: Penguin, 1991.

Calvin, John. *Commentaries on the First Book of Moses Called Genesis.* Translated by John King. 2 vols. Grand Rapids, MI: Eerdmans, 1948.

Calvino, Italo. *Invisible Cities.* Translated by William Weaver. New York: Harcourt, Brace, Jovanovich, 1974.

Cartwright, Samuel A. "Diseases and Peculiarities of the Negro Race, Part 1." *De Bow's Review* 11 (July 1851): 64–9.

Cassian, John. *Iohannis Cassiani Conlationes.* Edited by Michael Petchenig. CSEL 13. Vienna, 1886.

Cassian, John. *The Conferences.* Translated by Boniface Ramsey. New York: Newman Press, 1997.

Cassiodorus. *Institutiones.* Edited by R.A.B. Mynors. Oxford: Oxford University Press, 1963.

Choniates, Nicetas. *O City of Byzantium: Annals of Niketas Choniates.* Transated by Harry J. Magoulias. Detroit: Wayne State University Press, 1984.

Claudian. *Claudian.* Translated by Maurice Platnauer. 2 vols. LCL. Cambridge, MA: Harvard University Press, 1922.

Comnena, Anna. *The Alexiad of Anna Comnena.* Translated by E.R.A. Sewter. New York: Penguin, 1969.

Conrad, Joseph. *The Secret Agent.* Edited by John Lyon. Oxford: Oxford University Press, 2004.

Curtius, Quintus. *History of Alexander.* Edited and translated by J.C. Rolfe. 2 vols. LCL. Cambridge, MA: Harvard University Press, 1946.

Dante. *Inferno*. Translated by Allen Mandelbaum. New York: Bantam, 1982.
Dante. *Letters. Dantis Alagherii Epistolae: The Letters of Dante.* Edited and translated by Paget Toynbee. 2nd ed. Oxford: Clarendon, 1966.
Defoe, Daniel. *Robinson Crusoe.* Edited by J. Donald Crowley. Oxford: Oxford University Press, 1972.
Dickens, Charles. *Bleak House.* Edited by Norman Page. London: Penguin, 1971.
Dickens, Charles. *David Copperfield.* Edited by Nina Burgis. Oxford: Clarendon, 1981.
Diodorus Siculus. *Library of History.* Translated by C.H. Oldfather et al. 10 vols. LCL. Cambridge, MA: Harvard University Press, 1933–67.
Disraeli, Benjamin. *Tancred.* Edited by Bernard N. Langdon-Davies. London: R. Brimley Johnson, 1904.
Donne, John. *The Sermons of John Donne.* Edited by Evelyn M. Simpson and George R. Potter. 10 vols. Berkeley and Los Angeles: University of California Press, 1953–62.
Douglass, Frederick. *What to the Slave is the Fourth of July?: An Address Delivered in Rochester, New York, on 5 July 1852.* In *The Frederick Douglass Papers*, edited by John W. Blassingame et al. Series 1. Vol. 2. New Haven: Yale University Press, 1982. 359–88.
Dronke, Peter, ed. and trans. *Semiramis.* In *Poetic Individuality in the Middle Ages: New Departures in Poetry 1100–1150*, edited by Peter Dronke. 2nd ed. 1970. Reprint, London: Committee for Medieval Studies, Westfield College, University of London, 1986. 66–75.
Dunsany, Lord. *In the Land of Time and Other Fantasy Tales.* Edited S.T. Joshi. New York: Penguin, 2004.
Edwards, Mark, trans. *Constantine and Christendom: The Oration to the Saints, The Greek and Latin Accounts of the Discovery of the Cross, The Edict of Constantine to Pope Silvester.* Liverpool: Liverpool University Press, 2003.
Egeria. *Itinerarium Egeriae.* In *Itineraria et Alia Geographica*, edited by E. Franceschini and R. Weber. CCSL 175. Turnhout: Brepols, 1965.
Egeria. *Diary of a Pilgrimage.* Translated by George E. Gingras. New York: Newman, 1970.
Eliot, George. *Daniel Deronda.* Edited by Graham Handley. Oxford: Clarendon, 1984.
Emerson, Ralph Waldo. *The Essential Writings of Ralph Waldo Emerson.* Edited by Brooks Atkinson. New York: Modern Library, 2000.
Encyclopedia Britannica. 11th ed. 1910–11.
Eusebius/Jerome. *Chronicon.* In *Eusebius Werke.* Vol. 7: *Die Chronik des Hieronymus*, edited by Rudolf Helm. Berlin: Akademie-Verlag, 1956.
Farrell, R.T. ed. *Daniel and Azarias.* London: Methuen, 1974.

Fortunatus, Venantius. *De excidio Thoringiae.* Edited by Frederic Leo. MGH, AA. Vol. 4.1. Berlin: Weidmann, 1881. 271–5.

Foster, Benjamin R., ed. and trans. *Before the Muses: An Anthology of Akkadian Literature.* 2nd ed. 2 vols. Bethesda, MD: CDL Press, 1996.

Fulcher of Chartres. *A History of the Expedition to Jerusalem, 1095–1127.* Translated by Francis Rita Ryan. Knoxville, TN: University of Tennessee Press, 1969.

Gaiman, Neil, and Charles Vess. *Stardust: Being a Romance Within the Realms of Faerie.* New York: DC Comics, 1998. Written by Gaiman, illustrated by Vess.

Gilbert, W.S., and Arthur Sullivan. *The Annotated Gilbert and Sullivan.* Edited by Ian Bradley. Vol. 1. New York: Penguin, 1982.

Godden, Malcolm, and Susan Irvine, eds. *The Old English Boethius.* 2 vols. Oxford: Oxford University Press, 2009.

Guibert de Nogent. *The Deeds of God through the Franks: A Translation of Guibert de Nogent's* Gesta Dei per Francos. Translated by R. Levine. Woodbridge, Suffolk: Boydell and Brewer, 1996.

Hakluyt, Richard. *Principall Navigations, Voyages, Traffiques & Discoveries of the English Nation.* Edited by Edmund Goldsmid. 16 vols. Edinburgh, 1885–9.

Heikel, I.A., ed. *Konstantins Rede an die Hilge Versammlung.* In *Eusebius Werke.* Vol. 1. Leipzig, 1902. 149–92.

Herodotus. *The Histories.* Translated by George Rawlinson. New York: Everyman, 1910.

Higden, Ranulph. *Polychronicon Ranulphi Higden.* Edited by Churchill Babington. RS 41. London, 1865. Reprint, 1964.

Hislop, Alexander. *The Two Babylons or Papal Worship Proved to be the Worship of Nimrod and His Wife* (1858). Reprint, Brooklyn, New York: A & B Publishers, 1999.

Holgate, Jerome. *Noachidae, or Noah and His Descendants.* Buffalo: Breed, Butler, 1860.

Horrall, Sarah M., ed. *The Southern Version of* Cursor Mundi. Vol.1. Ottawa: University of Ottawa Press, 1978.

Howard, Robert E. *El Borak and Other Desert Adventures.* New York: Del Rey, 2010.

Howard, Robert E. *Lord of Samarcand and Other Adventure Tales of the Old Orient.* Edited by Rusty Burke. Lincoln: University of Nebraska Press, 2005.

Isidore. *Etymologiae. Isidori Hispalensis Episcopi Etymologiarum sive Origium Libri XX.* Edited by W.M. Lindsay. 2 vols. Oxford: Oxford University Press, 1911.

James, Henry. *The Ambassadors.* Edited by Adrian Poole. New York: Penguin, 2008.

Jerome. *Hebrew Questions on Genesis* (*Quaestiones Hebraicae in Genesim*). *PL* 23.cols. 935–1009.

Joinville, Jean de. *Life of St. Louis.* Translated by René Hague. London: Sheed and Ward, 1955.

Josephus. *Jewish Antiquities.* Edited and translated by H. St. J. Thackeray et al. 9 vols. LCL. Cambridge, MA: Harvard University Press, 1927–65.

Josephus. *Jewish Antiquities. The Latin Josephus I. Introduction and Text, The Antiquities: Books I–V.* Edited by Franz Blatt. Acta Jutlandica 30. Copenhagen: Aarhus, 1958. 25–94.

Justin. *Epitoma Historiarum Philippicarum.* Edited by Francis Ruehl. Leipzig: Teubner, 1915.

Justin. *Epitome of the Philippic History of Pompeius Trogus, Books 11–12: Alexander the Great.* Translated by J.C. Yardley. Commentary by Waldemar Heckel. Oxford: Clarendon, 1997.

Juvenal. *Satires. Juvenal and Persius.* Edited and translated by Susanna Morton Braund. LCL. Cambridge, MA: Harvard University Press, 2004. 127–511.

Kingsley, Charles. *Alton Locke, Tailor and Poet: An Autobiography.* Edited by Elizabeth A. Cripps. Oxford: Oxford University Press, 1983.

Kooper, Erik, ed. *Sentimental and Humorous Romances: Floris and Blancheflour, Sir Degrevant, The Squire of Low Degree, The Tournament of Tottenham, and the Feast of Tottenham.* Kalamazoo, MI: TEAMS/Medieval Institute Publications, 2006.

Krapp, G.P., and E.V.K. Dobbie, eds. *The Anglo-Saxon Poetic Records.* 6 vols. New York: Columbia University Press, 1931–42.

Kratz, Dennis M., trans. *The Romances of Alexander.* New York: Garland Press, 1991.

LaHaye, Tim, and Jerry Jenkins. *Left Behind.* 13 vols. Wheaton, IL: Tyndale House, 1995–2007.

Lamb, Harold. *Swords from the West.* Lincoln: University of Nebraska Press, 2009.

Layard, Austen H. *A Popular Account of Discoveries at Nineveh.* London: John Murray, 1851.

Layard, Austen H. *Discoveries in the Ruins of Nineveh and Babylon; with Travels in Armenia, Kurdistan and the Desert: Being the Result of a Second Expedition Undertaken for the Trustees of the British Museum.* London: John Murray, 1853.

Lewis, C.S. *The Magician's Nephew* (1955). Reprint, New York: Scolastic, 1995.

Lombroso, Cesare, and Guglielmo Ferrero. *Criminal Woman, the Prostitute, and the Normal Woman.* Translated by Nicole Hahn Rafter and Mary Gibson. Durham: Duke University Press, 2004.

Lombroso, Cesare. "The Criminal." *Putnam's Magazine* 7 (1910): 793–6. Reprinted in *The Criminal Anthropological Writings of Cesare Lombroso Published in the English Language Periodical Literature During the Late 19th and Early 20th Centuries,* edited by David M. Horton and Katherine E. Rich. Lewiston, New York: Edwin Mellen, 2004. 343–9.

Lombroso, Cesare. *Criminal Man.* Translated by Mary Gibson and Nicole Hahn Rafter with Mark Seymour. Durham, NC: Duke University Press, 2006.

Lovecraft, H.P. *The Ancient Track: The Complete Poetical Works of H.P. Lovecraft.* Edited by S.T. Joshi. San Francisco: Night Shade Books, 2001.

Lovecraft, H.P. *The Call of Cthulhu and Other Weird Stories.* Edited by S.T. Joshi. New York: Penguin, 1999.

Lovecraft, H.P. *The Dreams in the Witch House and Other Weird Stories.* Edited by S.T. Joshi. New York: Penguin, 2004.

Lovecraft, H.P. *The Thing on the Doorstep and Other Weird Stories.* Edited by S.T. Joshi. New York: Penguin, 2001.

Lucan. *Civil War.* Edited and translated by J.A. Duff. 2 vols. LCL. Cambridge, MA: Harvard University Press, 1962.

Lupack, Alan, ed. *Three Middle English Charlemagne Romances.* Kalamazoo, MI: TEAMS/Medieval Institute Publications, 1990.

Luther, Martin. *Lectures on Genesis: Chapters 6–14.* Translated by George V. Schick. *Luther's Works.* Vol. 2. Edited by Jaroslav Pelikan. Saint Louis: Concordia Publishing House, 1960.

Luther, Martin. *The Babylonian Captivity of the Church.* Translated by A.T. W. Steinhäuser. Revised by Frederick C. Ahrens and Abdel Ross Wentz. *Luther's Works.* Vol. 36. Edited by Abdel Ross Wentz. Philadelphia: Muhlenberg Press, 1959. 3–126.

M'Collester, Sullivan Holman. *Babylon and Nineveh through American Eyes.* Boston: Universalist Publishing House, 1892.

Mack, Robert L., ed. *Oriental Tales.* Oxford: Oxford University Press, 1992.

Malory, Sir Thomas. *Le Morte Darthur: The Winchester Manuscript.* Edited by Helen Cooper. London: Oxford University Press, 1998.

Mandeville, John. *The Bodley Version of Mandeville's Travels.* Edited by M.C. Seymour. EETS o.s. 253. London: Oxford University Press, 1963.

Mandeville, John. *The Defective Version of Mandeville's Travels.* Edited by M.C. Seymour. EETS o.s. 319. London: Oxford University Press, 2002.

Mandeville, John. *The Metrical Version of Mandeville's Travels.* Edited by M.C. Seymour. EETS o.s. 269. London: Oxford University Press, 1973.

Map, Walter. *De nugis curialium: Courtiers' Trifles.* Edited and translated by M.R. James. Revised by by C.N.L. Brooke and R.A.B. Mynors. Oxford: Clarendon, 1983.

Marley, Bob, and the Wailers. "Babylon System." *Survival.* Island/Tuff Gong, 1979.

Martianus Capella. *De Nuptiis Philologiae et Mercurii.* Edited by F. Eyssenhardt. Leipzig: Teubner, 1866.

Martorell, Joanot, and Martí Joan de Galba. *Tirant Lo Blanc.* Translated by David H. Rosenthal. Baltimore: Johns Hopkins University Press, 1984.

McCarthy, Cormac. *Blood Meridian, or The Evening Redness in the West.* New York: Vintage, 1985.

Melville, Herman. *Mardi and A Voyage Thither.* Edited by Harrison Hayford et al. Evanston and Chicago: Northwestern University Press and The Newberry Library, 1970.

Melville, Herman. *Published Poems.* Edited by Robert C. Ryan et al. Evanston and Chicago: Northwestern University Press and The Newberry Library, 2009.

Methodius, Pseudo-. *Apocalypse* in *Pseudo-Methodius, Apocalpyse and An Alexandrian World Chronicle.* Edited and translated by Benjamin Garstad. Harvard: Harvard University Press, 2012.

Mézières, Philippe de. *Letter to King Richard II.* Edited and translated by G.W. Coopland. Liverpool: Liverpool University Press, 1975.

Milton, John. *The Complete Poetry and Essential Prose of John Milton.* Edited William Kerrigan, John Rumrich, and Stephen Fallon. New York: Modern Library, 2007.

Milton, John. *The Complete Prose Works of John Milton.* Edited by Don Wolfe et al. 8 vols. New Haven: Yale University Press, 1953–1982.

Nicholson, Helen J., trans. *Chronicle of the Third Crusade: A Translation of the* Itinerarium Peregrinorum et Gesta Regis Ricardi. Aldershot, Hampshire: Ashgate, 1997.

Nordau, Max. *Degeneration* (*Entartung*, 1892). First English trans. New York: D. Appleton, 1895. Reprint, Lincoln: University of Nebraska Press, 1993.

Ó Cróinín, Dáibhí, ed. and trans. *The Irish Sex Aetates Mundi.* Dublin: Dublin Institute for Advanced Studies, 1983.

Oliver of Paderborn. *The Capture of Damietta.* Translated by Joseph J. Gavigan in *Christian Society and the Crusades, 1198–1229*, edited by Edward Peters. Philadelphia: University of Pennsylvania Press, 1971.

Opie, Peter, and Iona Opie. *The Oxford Dictionary of Nursery Rhymes.* 2nd. ed. Oxford: Oxford University Press, 1997.

Orosius. *Pauli Orosii Historiarum adversum Paganos Libri VII.* Edited by C. Zangemeister. CSEL 5. Leipzig: Teubner, 1889.

Orosius. *Seven Books of History against the Pagans.* Translated by A.T. Fear. Liverpool: Liverpool University Press, 2010.

Ovid. *Metamorphoses.* Translated by Frank Justus Miller. 2 vols. LCL. Cambridge, MA: Harvard University Press, 1921–2.

Parker, Kenneth, ed. *Early Modern Tales of Orient: A Critical Anthology.* New York: Routledge, 1999.

Pausanias. *Description of Greece.* Translated by W.H.S. Jones and H.A. Omerod. 5 vols. LCL. Cambridge, MA: Harvard University Press, 1918–35.

Petrarch. *Liber sine Nomine. Petrarcas 'Buch Ohne Namen' und die Päpstliche Kurie.* Edited by Paul Piur. Halle/Saale: Max Niemeyer Verlag, 1925.

Petrarch. *De otio religioso.* In Francesco Petrarca, *Opere Latine.* Vol. 1. Edited by Antonietta Bufano et al. Turin: Unione Tipografico-Editrice Torinese, 1975.

Petrarch. *On Religious Leisure.* Edited and translated by Susan S. Schearer. New York: Italica Press, 2002.

Petrarch. *Petrarch's Book Without a Name: A Translation of the* Liber sine nomine. Translated by Norman P. Zacour. Toronto: Pontifical Institute of Mediaeval Studies, 1973.

Petrarch. *Petrarch's Lyric Poems.* Edited and translated by Robert M. Durling. Cambridge, MA: Harvard University Press, 1976.

Pliny. *Natural History.* Trans. H. Rackham et al. 10 vols. LCL. Cambridge, MA: Harvard University Press, 1938–63.

Poe, Edgar Allen. *Poetry and Tales.* New York: Library of America, 1984.

Polo, Marco. *Il Milione.* Edited by Luigi Benedetto. Florence: Olschki, 1928.

Polo, Marco. *The Travels.* Translated by R.E. Latham. New York: Penguin, 1958.

Pompeius Trogus. *Historiae Philippicae.* Latin text from the edition of Justin's *Epitome* by Ruehl.

Pompeius Trogus. *Philippic History. Justin: Epitome of the Philippic History of Pompeius Trogus.* Translated by J.C. Yardley. Introduction and notes by R. Develin. Atlanta, GA: Scholars Press, 1994.

Pomponius Mela. *De Chorographia libri tres.* Edited by Piergiorgio Parroni. Rome: Edizioni di Storia e Letteratura, 1984.

Pomponius Mela. *Pomponius Mela's Description of the World.* Translated by F.E. Romer. Ann Arbor, University of Michigan Press, 1998.

Pulci, Luigi. *Morgante.* Edited by Franca Ageno. Milan and Naples: Riccardi, 1955.

Pulci, Luigi. *Morgante: The Epic Adventures of Orlando and his Giant Friend Morgante.* Translated by Joseph Tusiani. Bloomington: Indiana University Press, 1998.

Purchas, Samuel. *Purchas his pilgrimage. Or Relations of the vvorld and the religions obserued in all ages and places discouered, from the Creation vnto this present In foure partes.* London: William Stansby, 1613.

R.A. Macalister, ed. and trans. *Lebor Gabála Érenn: The Book of the Taking of Ireland.* 5 vols. Dublin: Irish Texts Society, 1938–56.

Raleigh, Sir Walter. *History of the World.* London, 1614.

Reardon, B.P., ed. *Collected Ancient Greek Novels.* Berkeley and Los Angeles: University of California Press, 1989.

Rexroth, Kenneth, trans. *Poems from the Greek Anthology.* Ann Arbor: University of Michigan Press, 1962; rev. 1999.

Reynolds, George W.M. *The Mysteries of London.* 4 vols. London: George Vickers, 1846–8.

Robert of Clari. *The Conquest of Constantinople.* Translated by Edgar Holmes McNeal. New York: Columbia University Press, 1936. Reprint, Toronto: University of Toronto Press, 1996.

Sackville-West, Vita. *Twelve Days: An Account of a Journey across the Bakhtiari Mountains in South-western Persia.* Garden City, NY: Doubleday, 1928.

Sassoon, Siegfried. *Collected Poems.* London: Faber and Faber, 1947.

Scragg, D.G., ed. *The Vercelli Homilies and Related Texts.* EETS o.s. 300. Oxford: Oxford University Press, 1992.

Shakespeare, William. *The Norton Shakespeare.* Edited by Stephen Greenblatt et al. 2nd ed. New York: W.W. Norton, 2009.

Solinus, Gaius Iulius. *Collectanea Rerum Memorabilium.* Edited by Theodor Mommsen. Berlin: Weidmann, 1895.

Spenser, Edmund. *The Yale Edition of the Shorter Poems of Edmund Spenser.* Edited by William Oram et al. New Haven: Yale University Press, 1989.

Spenser, Edmund. *The Faerie Queene.* Edited by A.C. Hamilton et al. 2nd ed. New York: Longman, 2006.

Stoneman, Richard. *Legends of Alexander the Great.* London: J.M. Dent, 1994.

Strabo. *Geography.* Edited and translated by Horace Leonard Jones. 8 vols. LCL. Cambridge, MA: Harvard University Press, 1917–1932.

Strachey, William. *The Historie of Travell into Virginia Britania (1612).* Edited by Louis B. Wright and Virginia Freund. London: Hakluyt Society, 1953.

Sulpicius Severus. *Chronicorum.* Edited by C. Halm. CSEL 1. Vienna, 1866.

Sweet, Henry, ed. *King Alfred's West-Saxon Version of Gregory's Pastoral Care.* EETS o.s. 45, 50. London: N. Trübner, 1871–2.

Tasso, Torquato. *Gerusalemme Liberata.* Edited by Lanfranco Caretti. Milan: Arnoldo Mondadori, 1983.

Tasso, Torquato. *Jerusalem Delivered.* Translated by Anthony M. Esolen. Baltimore: Johns Hopkins University Press, 2000.

Thackeray, William Makepeace. *The History of Pendennis.* Edited by John Sutherland. Oxford: Oxford University Press, 1994.

Thackeray, William Makepeace. *The Newcomes.* Edited by Andrew Sanders. Oxford: Oxford University Press, 1995.

The Descent: Original Unrated Cut. Lionsgate Films, 2005.

Tolstoy, Leo. *Anna Karenina.* Translated by Richard Pevear and Larissa Volokhonsky. New York: Penguin, 2000.

Trollope, Anthony. *Can You Forgive Her?* Edited by Andrew Swarbrick. Oxford: Oxford University Press, 1982.

Vitruvius. *On Architecture.* Edited and translated by Frank Granger. 2 vols. LCL. Cambridge, MA: Harvard University Press, 1931, 1934.

Volney, Constantin-François. *Les ruines, ou Méditations sur les révolutions des empires.* Paris: Desenne, 1791. English translation: *The Ruins; or, Meditation on the Revolution of Empires and the Law of Nature.* New York: William A. Davis, 1796.

Voltaire. *Romans et contes.* Edited by Frédéric Deloffre and Jacques van den Heuvel. Paris: Gallimard, 1979.

Voltaire. *The Complete Romances of Voltaire.* 8 vols. in 1. New York: Walter J. Black, 1927.

Walter of Châtillon. *Galteri de Castellione Alexandreis.* Edited by Marvin L. Colker. Padua: Antenore, 1978.

Walter of Châtillon. *The Alexandreis: A Twelfth-Century Epic.* Translated by David Townsend. Peterborough, ON: Broadview, 2007.

Wells, H.G. *The Island of Dr. Moreau.* Edited by Alan Lightman. New York: Bantam, 1994.

Wells, H.G. *The Time Machine.* Edited by Patrick Parrinder. New York: Penguin, 2005.

White, Landeg, trans. *The Lusiads.* Oxford: Oxford University Press, 2002.

Whitfield, James Monroe. "America." In his *America and Other Poems.* Buffalo, NY: James S. Leavitt, 1853. 9–16.

William of Tyre. *A History of Deeds Done Beyond the Sea.* Translated by Emily Atwater Babcock and A.C. Krey. 2 vols. New York: Columbia University Press, 1943.

Wordsworth, William. *Sonnet Series and Itinerary Poems, 1820–1845.* Edited by Geoffrey Jackson. Ithaca: Cornell University Press, 2004.

Wright, John, trans. *The Play of Antichrist.* Toronto: Pontifical Institute of Mediaeval Studies, 1967.

Young, Brigham. "Intelligence, etc.: Remarks Delivered in the Tabernacle, Great Salt Lake City, October 9, 1859." *Journal of Discourses* 7 (1859): 282–91.

Secondary Sources

Abrams, M.H. *Natural Supernaturalism: Tradition and Revolution in Romantic Literature.* New York: W.W. Norton, 1971.

Aguirre, Manuel. *The Closed Space: Horror Literature and Western Symbolism.* Manchester: Manchester University Press, 1990.

Airaksinen, Timo. *The Philosophy of H.P. Lovecraft: The Route to Horror.* New York: Peter Lang, 1999.

Akbari, Suzanne Conklin. *Idols in the East: European Representations of Islam and the Orient, 1100–1450.* Ithaca: Cornell University Press, 2009.

Alexiou, Margaret. *The Ritual Lament in Greek Tradition.* Cambridge: Cambridge University Press, 1974.

Allen, Michael I. "Universal History 300–1000: Origins and Western Developments." In *Historiography in the Middle Ages*, edited by Deborah Mauskopf Deliyannis. Leiden: Brill, 2003. 17–42.

Alonso-Núñez, José Miguel. *La Historia Universal de Pompeyo Trogo*. Madrid: Ediciones Clásicas, 1992.

Alter, Robert and Frank Kermode, eds. *The Literary Guide to the Bible*. Cambridge, MA: Belknap Press of Harvard University Press, 1987.

Alter, Robert. *The Art of Biblical Narrative*. New York: Basic Books, 1981.

Alter, Robert. *The Art of Biblical Poetry*. 2nd ed. New York: Basic Books, 2011.

Alter, Robert. *Genesis: Translation and Commentary*. New York: W.W. Norton, 1996.

Alter, Robert. *Imagined Cities: Urban Experience and the Language of the Novel*. New Haven: Yale University Press, 2005.

Alter, Robert. *The Pleasures of Reading in an Ideological Age*. New York: Touchstone/Simon and Schuster, 1989.

Alter, Robert. *The World of Biblical Literature*. New York: Basic Books, 1992.

Anlezark, Daniel. *Water and Fire: The Myth of the Flood in Anglo-Saxon England*. Manchester, Manchester University Press, 2006.

Archibald, Elizabeth. *Incest and the Medieval Imagination*. Oxford: Clarendon, 2001.

Auerbach, Erich. *Mimesis: The Representation of Reality in Western Literature*. Translated by Willard Trask. Princeton: Princeton University Press, 1953.

Augstein, Hannah Franziska, ed. *Race: The Origins of an Idea, 1760–1850*. Bristol: Thoemmes Press, 1996.

Ballaster, Ros, ed. *Fables of the East: Selected Tales 1662–1785*. Oxford: Oxford University press, 2005.

Ballaster, Ros. *Fabulous Orients: Fictions of the East in England, 1662–1785*. Oxford: Oxford University Press, 2005.

Balsamo, Jean, ed. *Les Poètes Français de la Renaissance et Pétrarque*. Geneva: Droz, 2004.

Banton, Michael. *Racial Theories*. 2nd ed. Cambridge: Cambridge University Press, 1998.

Beckett, Katharine Scarfe. *Anglo-Saxon Perceptions of the Islamic World*. Cambridge: Cambridge University Press, 2003.

Beer, Gillian. *Darwin's Plots: Evolutionary Narrative in Darwin, George Eliot and Nineteenth-Century Fiction*. 2nd ed. Cambridge: Cambridge University Press, 2000.

Beer, Gillian. *The Romance*. London: Methuen, 1970.

Bellis, Alice Ogden. "The Changing Face of Babylon in Prophetic/Apocalyptic Literature: Seventh Century BCE to First Century CE and Beyond." In *Knowing the End from the Beginning: The Prophetic, the Apocalyptic and their Relationships*, edited by Lester L. Grabbe and Robert D. Haak. London: T&T Clark/ Continuum, 2003. 65–73.

Blumenfeld-Kosinski, Renate. *Poets, Saints, and Visionaries of the Great Schism, 1378–1417.* University Park, PA: Penn State University Press, 2006.

Boardman, John, et al., eds. *The Cambridge Ancient History.* Vol. 3, Part 2. 2nd ed. Cambridge: Cambridge University Press, 1992.

Borst, Arno. *Der Turmbau von Babel: Geschichte der Meinungen über Ursprung und Vielfalt der Sprachen und Völker.* 4 vols. in 6. Stuttgart: A. Hiersemann, 1957–63.

Boting, Fred. *Gothic.* New York: Routledge, 1995.

Bowler, Peter J. *Evolution: The History of an Idea.* Berkeley and Los Angeles: University of California Press, 1984.

Braden, Gordon. *Petrarchan Love and the Continental Renaissance.* New Haven: Yale University Press, 1999.

Brantlinger, Patrick. *Dark Vanishings: Discourse on the Extinction of Primitive Races, 1800–1930.* Ithaca: Cornell University Press, 2003.

Brantlinger, Patrick. *Taming Cannibals: Race and the Victorians.* Ithaca: Cornell University Press, 2011.

Braude, Benjamin. “The Sons of Noah and the Construction of Ethnic and Geographical Identities in the Medieval and Early Modern Periods.” *The William and Mary Quarterly* 54.1 (1997): 103–42.

Brower, Reuben A. *Alexander Pope: The Poetry of Allusion.* Oxford: Clarendon, 1959.

Brown, Peter. *Augustine of Hippo: a Biography.* 2nd ed. London: Faber and Faber, 2000.

Buell, Denise Kimber. *Why This New Race: Ethnic Reasoning in Early Christianity.* New York: Columbia University Press, 2005.

Burleson, Donald R. *H.P. Lovecraft: A Critical Study.* Westport, CT: Greenwood Press, 1983.

Burns, J.H., ed. *The Cambridge History of Medieval Political Thought, c. 350–c.1450.* Cambridge: Cambridge University Press, 1988.

Byrd, Max. *London Transformed: Images of the City in the Eighteenth Century.* New Haven: Yale University Press, 1978.

Caie, Graham D. “The Old English *Daniel*: a Warning against Pride.” *ES* 59 (1978): 1–9.

Calkin, Siobhain Bly. *Saracens and the Making of English Identity.* New York: Routledge, 2005.

Cameron, A., et al., eds. *Dictionary of Old English.* Toronto: Dictionary of Old English Project 1986–.

Campbell, Kofi Omoniyi Sylvanus. *Literature and Culture in the Black Atlantic: From Pre- to Postcolonial.* New York: Palgrave Macmillan, 2006.

Campbell, Mary B. *The Witness and the Other World: Exotic European Travel Writing, 400–1600.* Ithaca: Cornell University Press, 1988.

Cannon, Peter. *Lovecraft.* Boston: Twayne, 1989.

Caracciolo, Peter L. *The Arabian Nights in English Literature: Studies in the Reception of the Thousand and One Nights into British Culture.* London: Macmillan, 1988.

Cary, George. *The Medieval Alexander.* Edited by D.J.A. Ross. Cambridge: Cambridge University Press, 1956.

Casey, Jim. "Modernism and Postmodernism." In *The Cambridge Companion to Fantasy Literature,* edited by Edward James and Farah Mendlesohn. Cambridge: Cambridge University Press, 2012. 113–24.

Cerasini, Marc A. "Thematic Links in *Arthur Gordon Pym, At the Mountains of Madness,* and *Moby Dick.*" *Crypt of Cthulhu* 49 (1987): 3–20.

Chevannes, Barry. *Rastafari: Roots and Ideology.* Syracuse: Syracuse University Press, 1994.

Christianson, Paul. *Reformers and Babylon: English Apocalyptic Visions from the Reformation to the Eve of the Civil War.* Toronto: University of Toronto Press, 1978.

Claeske, Keith. "The Children of Adam and Eve in Medieval Irish Literature." *Ériu* 56 (2006): 1–11.

Clute, John and John Grant, eds. *The Encyclopedia of Fantasy.* New York: St. Martin's Press, 1997.

Cohen, Jeffrey Jerome. "On Saracen Enjoyment: Some Fantasies of Race in Late Medieval France and England." *JMEMS* 31.1 (2001): 113–46.

Cohen, Jeffrey Jerome. *Of Giants: Sex, Monsters, and the Middle Ages.* Minneapolis: University of Minnesota Press, 1999.

Collinson, Patrick. "Biblical Rhetoric: the English Nation and National Sentiment in the Prophetic Mode." In *Religion and Culture in Renaissance England,* edited by Claire McEachern and Debora Shuger. Cambridge: Cambridge University Press, 1997. 15–45.

Conant, Martha Pike. *The Oriental Tale in England in the Eighteenth Century.* New York: Columbia University Press, 1908. Reprint, New York: Octagon, 1966.

Cook, Albert. *The Burden of Prophecy: Poetic Utterance in the Prophets of the Old Testament.* Carbondale and Edwardsville: Southern Illinois University Press, 1996.

Cook, Eleanor. *Against Coercion: Games Poets Play.* Stanford: Stanford University Press, 1998.

Cooper, Helen. *The English Romance in Time: Transforming Motifs from Geoffrey of Monmouth to Shakespeare.* Oxford: Oxford University Press, 2004.

Coupe, Laurence. *Myth.* New York: Routledge, 1997.

Curtius, Ernst Robert. *European Literature and the Latin Middle Ages.* Translated by Willard Trask. New York: Bollingen, 1953.

Dahlberg, Charles. *The Literature of Unlikeness.* Hanover, NH: University Press of New England, 1988.

Dalley, Stephanie. *The Mystery of the Hanging Garden of Babylon: An Elusive World Wonder Traced.* Oxford: Oxford University Press, 2013.

Damon, S. Foster. *A Blake Dictionary: The Ideas and Symbols of William Blake.* Providence, RI: Brown University Press, 1965. Reprint, Boulder, CO: Shambhala, 1979.

Damrosch, David. *The Buried Book: The Loss and Recovery of the Great Epic of Gilgamesh.* New York: Henry Holt, 2006.

Damrosch, David. *What is World Literature?* Princeton: Princeton University Press, 2003.

Daniel, Norman. *Heroes and Saracens: An Interpretation of the* Chansons de Geste. Edinburgh: Edinburgh University Press, 1984.

Daniel, Norman. *Islam and the West: The Making of an Image.* Edinburgh: University of Edinburgh Press, 1960. Reprint, 1966.

Dean, James M. *The World Grown Old in Later Medieval Literature.* Cambridge, MA: Medieval Academy of America, 1997.

Dobbs-Allsopp, F.W. *Weep, O Daughter of Zion: A Study of the City-Lament Genre in the Hebrew Bible.* Rome: Editrice Pontifico Istituto Biblico, 1993.

Donoghue, Daniel. *Lady Godiva: A Literary History of the Legend.* Oxford: Blackwell, 2003.

Doob, Penelope B.R. *Nebuchadnezzar's Children: Conventions of Madness in Middle English Literature.* New Haven: Yale University Press, 1974.

Dougherty, James. *The Fivesquare City: The City in the Religious Imagination.* Notre Dame: University of Notre Dame Press, 1980.

Dubrow, Heather. *Echoes of Desire: English Petrarchism and its Counterdiscourses.* Ithaca: Cornell University Press, 1995.

Eckhardt, Jason C. "Behind the Mountains of Madness: Lovecraft and the Antarctic in 1930." *Lovecraft Studies* 14 (1987): 31–8.

Edmonds, Ennis B. *Rastafari: From Outcasts to Culture Bearers.* Oxford: Oxford University Press, 2003.

Emerson, Oliver F. "Legends of Cain, Especially in Old and Middle English." *PMLA* 21.4 (1906): 831–929.

Emmerson, Richard Kenneth. *Antichrist in the Middle Ages: A Study of Medieval Apocalypticism, Art, and Literature.* Seattle: University of Washington Press, 1981.

Emmerson, Richard K., and Ronald B. Herzman. *The Apocalyptic Imagination in Medieval Literature.* Philadelphia: University of Pennsylvania Press, 1992.

Empson, William. *The Structure of Complex Words,* 1951. Reprint, Cambridge, MA: Harvard University Press, 1989.

Erdman, David V. *Blake: Prophet Against Empire.* 2nd ed. Garden City, NY: Doubleday, 1969.

Evans, William McKee. "From the Land of Canaan to the Land of Guinea: The Strange Odyssey of the 'Sons of Ham.'" *AHR* 85.1 (1980): 14–43.

Eze, Emmanuel Chukwudi, ed. *Race and the Enlightenment: A Reader.* Oxford: Blackwell, 1997.

Fagan, Brian. *From Stonehenge to Samarkand: An Anthology of Archaeological Travel Writing.* Oxford: Oxford University Press, 2006.

Fainck, Guy. *Paul Orose et sa conception de l'histoire.* Doctoral thesis, Université d'Aix-en-Provence, 1951.

Favier, Jean. *Les papes d'Avignon.* Fayard, 2006.

Feerick, Jean E. *Strangers in Blood: Relocating Race in the Renaissance.* Toronto: University of Toronto Press, 2010.

Fell, Christine. "Perceptions of transience." *The Cambridge Companion to Old English Literature.* Edited by Malcolm Godden and Michael Lapidge. Cambridge: Cambridge University Press, 1991. 172–89.

Felski, Rita. "Context Stinks!" *NLH* 42 (2011): 573–91.

Felski, Rita. *Uses of Literature.* Oxford: Blackwell, 2008.

Finkel, I.L., and M.J. Seymour, eds. *Babylon: Myth and Reality.* London: The British Museum Press, 2008.

Firth, Katharine R. *The Apocalyptic Tradition in Reformation Britain, 1530–1645.* Oxford: Oxford University Press, 1979.

Fisch, Harold. *A Remembered Future: A Study in Literary Mythology.* Bloomington: Indiana University Press, 1984.

Fisch, Harold. *The Biblical Presence in Shakespeare, Milton, and Blake: A Comparative Study.* Oxford: Oxford University Press, 1999.

Fitzpatrick, Joan, ed. *The Idea of the City: Early-Modern, Modern and Post-Modern Locations and Communities.* Newcastle upon Tyne: Cambridge Scholars, 2009.

Flint, Valerie I.J. *The Imaginative Landscape of Christopher Columbus.* Princeton: Princeton University Press, 1992.

Flori, Jean. "La caricature de l'Islam dans l'occident médiéval: Origine et signification de quelques stéréotypes concernant l'Islam." *Aevum* 2 (1992): 245–56.

Foley, John Miles. *Immanent Art: From Structure to Meaning in Traditional Oral Epic.* Bloomington and Indianapolis: Indiana University Press, 1991.

Foley, John Miles. *The Singer of Tales in Performance.* Bloomington and Indianapolis: Indiana University Press, 1995.

Foley, John Miles. *How to Read an Oral Poem.* Urbana and Chicago: University of Illinois Press, 2002.

Forbes, Bruce David and Jeanne Halgren Kilde, eds. *Rapture, Revelation, and the End Times: Exploring the* Left Behind *Series.* New York: Palgrave Macmillan, 2004.

Foucault, Michel. "Nietzsche, Genealogy, History." In his *Language, Counter-Memory, Practice: Selected Essays and Interviews*, translated by Donald Bouchard and Sherry Simon. Ithaca: Cornell University Press, 1977. Reprinted in *The Foucault Reader*. Edited by Paul Rabinow. New York: Pantheon, 1984. 76–100.

Foucault, Michel. *The Order of Things: An Archaeology of the Human Sciences*. New York: Vintage, 1973.

Fraser, Robert. *Victorian Quest Romance: Stevenson, Haggard, Kipling, and Conan Doyle*. Plymouth: Northcote House, 1998.

Freedman, Paul. *Images of the Medieval Peasant*. Stanford: Stanford University Press, 1999.

Friedman, John Block. *The Monstrous Races in Medieval Art and Thought*. Cambridge, MA: Harvard University Press, 1981. Reprint, Syracuse: Syracuse University Press, 2000.

Frye, Northrop. *Anatomy of Criticism: Four Essays*. Princeton: Princeton University Press, 1957.

Frye, Northrop. *Fearful Symmetry: A Study of William Blake*. Princeton: Princeton University Press, 1947.

Frye, Northrop. *The Great Code: The Bible and Literature*. Toronto: Academic Press Canada, 1981.

Frye, Northrop. *The Secular Scripture: A Study of the Structure of Romance*. Cambridge, MA: Harvard University Press, 1976.

Frye, Northrop. *Words with Power: Being a Second Study of The Bible and Literature*. New York: Harcourt, Brace, Jovanovich, 1990.

Fuchs, Barbara. *Mimesis and Empire: The New World, Islam, and European Identities*. Cambridge: Cambridge University Press, 2001.

Fuchs, Barbara. *Romance*. New York: Routledge, 2004.

Gamer, Michael. *Romanticism and the Gothic: Genre, Reception, and Canon Formation*. Cambridge: Cambridge University Press, 2000.

Garner, Lori Ann. *Structuring Spaces: Oral Poetics and Architecture in Early Medieval England*. Notre Dame, IN: University of Notre Dame Press, 2011.

Gasper, Julia. *The Dragon and the Dove: The Plays of Thomas Dekker*. Oxford: Clarendon, 1990.

Gibbon, Edward. *The Decline and Fall of the Roman Empire*. Edited by J.B. Bury. Introduction by Hugh Trevor-Roper. 3 vols. London: Everyman, 1993.

Glasson, Travis. *Mastering Christianity: Missionary Anglicanism and Slavery in the Atlantic World*. Oxford: Oxford University Press, 2012.

Godden, Malcolm. "King and Counsellor in the Alfredian Boethius." In *Intertexts: Studies in Anglo-Saxon Culture Presented to Paul E. Szarmach*, edited by Virginia Blanton and Helene Scheck. Tempe: Arizona Center for Medieval and Renaissance Studies, 2008. 193–209.

Goetz, Rebecca Anne. *The Baptism of Early Virginia: How Christianity Created Race.* Baltimore: Johns Hopkins University Press, 2012.

Goetz, Werner. *Translatio imperii: Ein Beitrag zur Geschichte des Geschichtsdenkens und der politischen Theorien im Mittelalter und in der frühen Neuzeit.* Tübingen: Mohr, 1948.

Goldenberg, David M. *The Curse of Ham: Race and Slavery in Early Judaism, Christianity, and Islam.* Princeton: Princeton University Press, 2003.

Goldstein, Laurence. *Ruins and Empire: The Evolution of a Theme in Augustan and Romantic Literature.* Pittsburgh: University of Pittsburgh Press, 1977.

Goodman, Jennifer R. *Chivalry and Exploration, 1298–1630.* Woodbridge, Suffolk: Boydell and Brewer, 1998.

Grafton, Anthony, with April Shelford and Nancy Siraisi. *New Worlds, Ancient Texts: The Power of Tradition and the Shock of Discovery.* Cambridge, MA: Belknap Press of Harvard University Press, 1992.

Grafton, Anthony, Glenn W. Most, and Salvatore Settis, eds. *The Classical Tradition.* Cambridge, MA: Belknap Press of Harvard University Press, 2010.

Greene, Roland. *Five Words: Critical Semantics in the Age of Shakespeare and Cervantes.* Chicago: University of Chicago Press, 2013.

Grieve, Patricia E. *Floire and Blancheflor and the European Romance.* Cambridge: Cambridge University Press, 1997.

Hachicho, Mohammed Ali. "English Travel Books about the Arab near East in the Eighteenth Century." *Die Welt des Islams* 9 (1964): 1–206.

Hagendahl, Harald. "Orosius und Iustinus: Ein Beitrag zur Iustinischen Textgeschichte." *Göteborgs Högskolas Årsskrift* 47.12 (1941): 3–48.

Hahn, Thomas. "The Difference the Middle Ages Makes: Color and Race Before the Modern World." *JMEMS* 31.1 (2001): 1–37.

Hallo, William W., and William K. Simpson. *The Ancient Near East: A History.* 2nd ed. New York: Harcourt Brace, 1998.

Hallock, Ann. "The Pre-Eminent Role of *Babilonia* in Petrarch's Theme of the Two Cities." *Italica* 54 (1977): 290–7.

Hamlin, Hannibal. *Psalm Culture and Early Modern English Literature.* Cambridge: Cambridge University Press, 2004.

Hannaford, Ivan. *Race: The History of an Idea in the West.* Baltimore: Johns Hopkins University Press, 1996.

Harbus, Antonina. "Nebuchadnezzar's Dreams in the Old English *Daniel.*" *ES* 75.6 (1994): 489–508.

Harris, Jonathan Gil. "Four Exoskeletons and No Funeral." *NLH* 42 (2011): 615–39.

Haynes, Stephen R. *Noah's Curse: The Biblical Justification of American Slavery.* Oxford: Oxford University Press, 2002.

Heffernan, Carol F. *The Orient in Chaucer and Medieval Romance.* Cambridge: D.S. Brewer, 2003.

Helms, Mary W. *Ulysses' Sail: An Ethnographic Odyssey of Power, Knowledge and Geographical Distance.* Princeton: Princeton University Press, 1988.

Heng, Geraldine. "The Invention of Race in the European Middle Ages I: Race Studies, Modernity, and the Middle Ages." *Literature Compass* 8.5 (2011): 315–31.

Heng, Geraldine. "The Invention of Race in the European Middle Ages II: Locations of Medieval Race." *Literature Compass* 8.5 (2011): 332–50.

Heng, Geraldine. *Empire of Magic: Medieval Romance and the Politics of Cultural Fantasy.* New York: Columbia University Press, 2003.

Higgins, Iain. *Writing East; The "Travels" of Sir John Mandeville.* Philadelphia: University of Pennsylvania Press, 1997.

Hill, John. *Friend or Foe? The Figure of Babylon in the Book of Jeremiah MT.* Leiden: Brill, 1999.

Hillgarth, Jocelyn N. "L'Influence de la Cité de Dieu de saint Augustin au Haut Moyen Âge." *Sacris Erudiri* 28 (1985): 5–34.

Hillgarth, Jocelyn N. "The *Historiae* of Orosius in the Early Middle Ages." In *De Tertullian aux Mozarabes II: antiquité tardive et Christianisme ancient (VIe–IXe siècles). Mélanges offerts à Jacques Fontaine,* edited by Louis Holz and Jean-Claude Fredoville. Paris: Institut d'études augustinienne, 1992. 157–70.

Hollander, John. *The Figure of Echo: A Mode of Allusion in Milton and After.* Berkeley and Los Angeles: University of California Press, 1981.

Holsinger, Bruce. *Neomedievalism, Neoconservatism, and the War on Terror.* Chicago: Prickly Paradigm Press, 2007.

Hudson, Nicholas. "From 'Nation' to 'Race': The Origin of Racial Classification in Eighteenth-Century Thought." *Eighteenth-Century Studies* 29.3 (1996): 247–64.

Hume, Kathryn. "The 'ruin-motif' in Old English Poetry." *Anglia* 94 (1976): 339–60.

Hutcheon, Linda. *A Theory of Adaptation.* New York: Routledge, 2006.

Indick, Ben P. "Lovecraft's POElar Adventure." *Crypt of Cthulu* 32 (1985): 25–31.

Irvine, Alexander C. "Urban Fantasy." In *The Cambridge Companion to Fantasy Literature,* edited by Edward James and Farah Mendlesohn. Cambridge: Cambridge University Press, 2012. 200–13.

Irwin, Robert. *The Arabian Nights: A Companion.* New York: Penguin, 1994.

Isaacs, Benjamin. *The Invention of Racism in Classical Antiquity.* Princeton: Princeton University Press, 2004.

Ishiguro, Taro. "*Daniel*: the Old English Poem of Nebuchadnezzar against God." *Geibun Kenkyu* 73 (1997): 462–78.

Iyengar, Sujata. *Shades of Difference: Mythologies of Skin Color in Early Modern England.* Philadelphia: University of Pennsylvania Press, 2005.

Janowitz, Anne. *England's Ruins: Poetic Purpose and the National Landscape.* Oxford: Blackwell, 1990.

Jaye, Michael C. and Ann Chalmers Watts, eds. *Literature and the Urban Experience: Essays on the City and Literature.* New Brunswick, NJ: Rutgers University Press, 1981.

Johnson, Kenneth R. "Blake's Cities: Romantic Forms of Urban Renewal." In *Blake's Visionary Forms Dramatic,* edited by David V. Erdman and John E. Grant. Princeton: Princeton University Press, 1970. 413–42.

Jordan, Winthrop. *White Over Black: American Attitudes toward the Negro, 1550–1812.* 2nd ed. Chapel Hill: University of North Carolina Press, 2012.

Joshi, S.T. *A Dreamer and a Visionary: H.P. Lovecraft in His Time.* Liverpool: Liverpool University Press, 2001.

Joshi, S.T. "Lovecraft Criticism: A Study." In *H.P. Lovecraft: Four Decades of Criticism,* edited by S.T. Joshi. Athens: Ohio University Press, 1980. 20–6.

Joshi, S.T. *H.P. Lovecraft.* Mercer Island, WA: Starmont House, 1982.

Joshi, S.T. *H.P. Lovecraft: The Decline of the West.* Mercer Island, WA: Starmont House, 1990.

Joshi, S.T. *Lord Dunsany: Master of the Anglo-Irish Imagination.* Westport, CT: Greenwood Press, 1995.

Josipovici, Gabriel. *The Book of God: A Response to the Bible.* New Haven: Yale University Press, 1988.

Kaske, Robert E. "*Beowulf* and the Book of Enoch." *Speculum* 46 (1971): 421–31.

Keenan, Hugh T. "*The Ruin* as Babylon." *Tennessee Studies in Literature* 11 (1966): 109–17.

Kennedy, William J. *The Site of Petrarchism: Early Modern National Sentiment in Italy, France, and England.* Baltimore: Johns Hopkins University Press, 2003.

Kermode, Frank. *The Sense of an Ending: Studies in the Theory of Fiction.* New York: Oxford University Press, 1967. Reprinted with new epilogue, New York: Oxford University Press, 2000.

Kidd, Colin. *The Forging of Races: Race and Scripture in the Protestant Atlantic World, 1600–2000.* Cambridge: Cambridge University Press, 2006.

Kinsoshita, Sharon. *Medieval Boundaries: Rethinking Difference in Old French Literature.* Philadelphia: University of Pennsylvania Press, 2006.

Klaeber, Friedrich, ed. *Beowulf and The Fight at Finnsburg.* 3rd ed., with first and second supplements. Boston: D.C. Heath, 1950.

Krantz, Susan E. "Thomas Dekker's Political Commentary in *The Whore of Babylon.*" *SEL* 35 (1995): 271–91.

Kugel, James. *The Bible as It Was.* Cambridge, MA: Belknap Press of Harvard University Press, 1999.

Lacroix, Benoit. *Orose et ses idées*. Montreal: Institut d'études Médiévales; Paris: Librairie Philosophique J. Vrin, 1965.

Larsen, Mogens Trolle. *The Conquest of Assyria: Excavations in an Antique Land.* New York: Routledge, 1994.

Larson, Edward J. *Evolution: The Remarkable History of a Scientific Theory*. New York: Modern Library, 2004.

Leask, Nigel. *British Romantic Writers and the East: Anxieties of Empire*. Cambridge: Cambridge University Press, 1992.

Lee, Alexander. "Sin City? The Image of Babylon in Petrarch's *Canzoniere*." In *The Idea of the City*, edited by Joan Fitzpatrick, 39–51.

Lee, Anne Thompson. "*The Ruin*: Bath or Babylon? A Non-Archaeological Investigation." *NM* 74.3 (1973): 443–55.

Leiber, Fritz, Jr. "A Literary Copernicus." (1949) In *H.P. Lovecraft: Four Decades of Criticism*, edited by S.T. Joshi. Athens: Ohio University Press, 1980. 50–62.

Leick, Gwendolyn. *Mesopotamia: The Invention of the City*. New York: Penguin, 2002.

Levine, George. *Darwin and the Novelists: Patterns of Science in Victorian Fiction.* Cambridge, MA: Harvard University Press, 1988.

Lévy, Maurice. *Lovecraft: A Study in the Fantastic*. Translated by S.T. Joshi. Detroit: Wayne State University Press, 1988.

Lewis, Jack P. *A Study of the Interpretation of Noah and the Flood in Jewish and Christian Literature*. Leiden: E.J. Brill, 1968.

Lilley, Keith D. *City and Cosmos: The Medieval World in Urban Form*. London: Reaktion Books, 2009.

Linton, Joan Pong. *The Romance of the New World: Gender and the Literary Formation of English Colonialism*. Cambridge: Cambridge University Press, 1998.

Liuzza, R.M. "The Tower of Babel: *The Wanderer* and the Ruins of History." *Studies in the Literary Imagination* 36.1 (2003): 1–35.

Lloyd, Seton. *Foundations in the Dust: The Story of Mesopotamian Exploration* (1947). 2nd ed. London: Thames and Hudson, 1980.

Loomba, Ania. *Shakespeare, Race, and Colonialism*. Oxford: Oxford University Press, 2002.

Lundbom, Jack R. *The Hebrew Prophets: An Introduction*. Minneapolis: Fortress Press, 2010.

Macaulay, Rose. *Pleasure of Ruins* (1953). Reprint, New York: Walker and Co., 1966.

Machacek, Gregory. "Allusion." *PMLA* 122 (2007): 522–36.

Maguire, Laurie. *Helen of Troy: From Homer to Hollywood*. Oxford: Wiley-Blackwell, 2009.

Major, Tristan Gary. *Literary Developments of the Table of Nations and The Tower of Babel in Anglo-Saxon England*. PhD dissertation, University of Toronto, 2010.

Marcus, R.A. "The Latin Fathers." In *The Cambridge History of Medieval Political Thought, c. 350–c.1450,* edited by J.H. Burns. Cambridge: Cambridge University Press, 1988. 92–122.

Markus, R.A. *Saeculum: History and Society in the Theology of Saint Augustine.* Cambridge: Cambridge University Press, 1970.

Marrou, Henri. *St. Augustine and His Influence through the Ages.* New York: Harper, 1957.

Marshall, P.J., and Glyndwr Williams. *The Great Map of Mankind: Perceptions of New Worlds in the Age of Enlightenment.* Cambridge, MA: Harvard University Press, 1982.

Matthews, Gareth B. "Post-Medieval Augustinianism." In *The Cambridge Companion to Augustine,* edited by Eleonore Stump and Norman Kretzmann. Cambridge: Cambridge University Press, 2001. 267–79.

Matthews, Gareth B. ed. *The Augustinian Tradition.* Berkeley and Los Angeles: University of California Press, 1999.

McCoskey, Denise Eileen. *Race: Antiquity and Its Legacy.* Oxford: Oxford University Press, 2012.

McDermott, Hubert. *Novel and Romance: The Odyssey to Tom Jones.* London: Macmillan, 1989.

McFarland, Thomas. *Romanticism and the Forms of Ruin: Wordsworth, Coleridge, and Modalities of Fragmentation.* Princeton: Princeton University Press, 1981.

McGeough, Kevin M. *The Ancient Near East in the Nineteenth Century: Appreciations and Appropriations. III. Fantasy and Alternative Histories.* Hebrew Bible Monographs, 69. Sheffield: Sheffield Phoenix Press, 2015.

McGinn, Bernard. *Apocalyptic Spirituality.* New York: Paulist Press, 1979.

McGinn, Bernard. *Apocalyptic Traditions in the Middle Ages.* New York: Columbia University Press, 1979.

McLaughlin, Martin, and Letizia Panizza with Peter Hainsworth, eds. *Petrarch in Britain: Interpreters, Imitators, and Translators over 700 Years.* Oxford: Oxford University Press for The British Academy, 2007.

McNutt, Donald J. *Urban Revelations: Images of Ruin in the American City, 1790–1860.* New York: Routledge, 2006.

Mellinkoff, Ruth. "Cain's Monstrous Progeny in Beowulf: Part I, Noachic Tradition." *ASE* 8 (1979): 143–62.

Mellinkoff, Ruth. "Cain's Monstrous Progeny in Beowulf: Part II, Post-Diluvian Survival." *ASE* 9 (1981): 183–97.

Mellinkoff, Ruth. *The Mark of Cain.* Berkeley and Los Angeles: University of California Press, 1981.

Mendlesohn, Farah. *Rhetorics of Fantasy.* Middletown, CT: Wesleyan University Press, 2008.

Menegaldo, Gillies. "The City in H.P. Lovecraft's Work." *Lovecraft Studies* 4 (1981): 10–19.

Merrills, A.H. *History and Geography in Late Antiquity*. Cambridge: Cambridge University Press, 2005.

Metlitzki, Dorothee. *The Matter of Araby in Medieval England*. New Haven: Yale University Press, 1977.

Miéville, China. "Introduction." *At the Mountains of Madness: The Definitive Edition*. New York: Modern Library, 2005. xi–xxv.

Mighall, Robert. "Gothic Cities." In *The Routledge Companion to Gothic*, edited by Catherine Spooner and Emma McEvoy. New York: Routledge, 2007. 54–62.

Mighall, Robert. *A Geography of Victorian Gothic Fiction: Mapping History's Nightmares*. Oxford: Oxford University Press, 1999.

Mommsen, Theodor E. "Orosius and Augustine." In his *Medieval and Renaissance Studies*, edited by Eugene F. Rice. Ithaca: Cornell University Press, 1959. Reprint, Westport, CT: Greenwood Press, 1966. 325–48.

Morrison, K.F. *The Mimetic Tradition of Reform in the West*. Princeton: Princeton University Press, 1982.

Morrison, Karl F. *"I Am You": The Hermeneutics of Empathy in Western Literature, Theology, and Art*. Princeton: Princeton University Press, 1988.

Mortier, Roland. *La Poétique des ruines en France*. Geneva: Libraire Droz, 1974.

Murrell, Nathaniel Samuel, William David Spencer, and Adrian Anthony McFarlane, eds. *Chanting Down Babylon: The Rastafari Reader*. Philadelphia: Temple University Press, 1998.

Nead, Lynda. *Victorian Babylon: People, Streets and Images in Nineteenth-Century London*. New Haven: Yale University Press, 2000.

Nelson, Janet. "Kingship and Empire." In *The Cambridge History of Medieval Political Thought, c. 350–c.1450*, edited by J.H. Burns. Cambridge: Cambridge University Press, 1988. 211–51.

Nerlich, Michael. *Ideology of Adventure: Studies in Modern Consciousness, 1100–1750*. 2 vols. Minneapolis: University of Minnesota Press, 1987.

New Catholic Encyclopedia. 2nd ed. Washington, DC: Catholic University of America, 2003.

Norton, David. *A History of the Bible as Literature*. 2 vols. Cambridge: Cambridge University Press, 1993.

Norwich, John Julius. *Absolute Monarchs: A History of the Papacy*. New York: Random House, 2011.

O'Leary, Stephen D. *Arguing the Apocalypse: A Theory of Millennial Rhetoric*. New York: Oxford University Press, 1994.

O'Rourke Boyle, Marjorie. *Petrarch's Genius: Pentimento and Prophecy*. Berkeley and Los Angeles: University of California Press, 1991.

Oates, Joyce Carol. "Imaginary Cities: America." In *Literature and the Urban Experience: Essays on the City and Literature,* edited by Michael C. Jaye and Ann Chalmers Watts. New Brunswick, NJ: Rutgers University Press, 1981. 11–33.

Orchard, Andy. "Reconstructing *The Ruin.*" In *Intertexts: Studies in Anglo-Saxon Culture Presented to Paul E. Szarmach,* edited by Virginian Blanton and Helene Scheck. Tempe, AZ: Arizona Center for Medieval and Renaissance Studies, 2008. 45–68.

Orchard, Andy. *Pride and Prodigies: Studies in the Monsters of the Beowulf Manuscript.* 2nd ed. Toronto: University of Toronto Press, 2003.

Orr, Mary. *Intertextuality: Debates and Contexts.* Cambridge: Polity Press, 2003.

Overing, Gillian. "Nebuchadnezzar's Conversion in the Old English *Daniel*: a Psychological Portrait." *PLL* 20 (1984): 3–14.

Parker, Patricia. *Inescapable Romance: Studies in the Poetics of a Mode.* Princeton: Princeton University Press, 1979.

Paster, Gail Kern. *The Idea of the City in the Age of Shakespeare.* Athens: University of Georgia Press, 1985.

Patterson, Lee. "On the Margin: Postmodernism, Ironic History, and Medieval Studies." *Speculum* 65.1 (1990): 87–108.

Pearson, Roger. *The Fables of Reason: A Study of Voltaire's "Contes Philosophiques."* Oxford: Clarendon, 1993.

Peckham, Brian. *History and Prophecy: The Development of Late Judean Literary Traditions.* New York: Doubleday, 1994.

Peer, Larry H., ed. *Romanticism and the City.* New York: Palgrave Macmillan, 2011.

Peterson, Thomas Virgil. *Ham and Japheth: The Mythic World of Whites in the Antebellum South.* Metuchen, NJ and London: Scarecrow Press and The American Theological Library Association, 1978.

Phillips, Richard. *Mapping Men and Empire: A Geography of Adventure.* New York: Routledge, 1997.

Pick, Daniel. *Faces of Degeneration: A European Disorder, c. 1848–c. 1918.* Cambridge: Cambridge University Press, 1989.

Pike, Burton. *The Image of the City in Modern Literature.* Princeton: Princeton University Press, 1981.

Pucci, Joseph. *The Full-Knowing Reader: Allusion and the Power of the Reader in the Western Literary Tradition.* New Haven: Yale University Press, 1998.

Punter, David. *The Literature of Terror.* Vol. 1: *The Gothic Tradition.* 2nd ed. NY: Longman, 1996.

Quillen, Carol Everhart. *Rereading the Renaissance: Petrarch, Augustine, and the Language of Humanism.* Ann Arbor: University of Michigan Press, 1998.

Quinones, Ricardo J. *The Changes of Cain: Violence and the Lost Brother in Cain and Abel Literature.* Princeton: Princeton University Press, 1991.

Ramey, Lynn Tarte. *Christian, Saracen and Genre in Medieval French Literature.* New York: Routledge, 2001.

Raymond, André. *Cairo.* Translated by Willard Wood. Cambridge, MA: Harvard University Press, 2000.

Reimer, David J. *The Oracles Against Babylon in Jeremiah 50–51: A Horror Among the Nations.* San Francisco: Edwin Mellen, 1993.

Remley, Paul G. "*Daniel*, the Three Youths Fragment and the Transmission of Old English Verse." *ASE* 31 (2002): 81–140.

Remley, Paul. *Old English Biblical Verse: Studies in* Genesis, Exodus, and Daniel. Cambridge: Cambridge University Press, 1996.

Richey, Esther Gilman. *The Politics of Revelation in the English Renaissance.* Columbia: University of Missouri Press, 1998.

Ricks, Christopher. *Allusion to the Poets.* Oxford: Oxford University Press, 2002.

Robertson, D.W. *A Preface to Chaucer: Studies in Medieval Perspectives.* Princeton: Princeton University Press, 1962.

Robinson, Benedict. *Islam and Early Modern English Literature: The Politics of Romance from Spenser to Milton.* New York: Palgrave Macmillan, 2007.

Robinson, Fred C. "Medieval, the Middle Ages." *Speculum* 59.4 (1984): 745–56.

Romm, James S. *The Edges of the Earth in Ancient Thought: Geography, Exploration, and Fiction.* Princeton: Princeton University Press, 1992.

Roux, Georges. *Ancient Iraq.* 3rd ed. New York: Penguin, 1992.

Sack, Ronald H. *Images of Nebuchadnezzar: The Emergence of a Legend*, 2nd ed. Selinsgrove: Susquehanna University Press, 2004.

Said, Edward. *Orientalism.* New York: Vintage, 1978.

Sallis, Eva. *Sheherazade Through the Looking Glass: The Metamorphosis of the* Thousand and One Nights. Currey: Curzon Press, 1999.

Sals, Ulrike. *Die Biographie der "Hure Babylon": Studien zur Intertextualität der Babylon-Texte in der Bibel.* Tübingen: Mohr Sehr, 2004.

Samuel, Irene. "Semiramis in the Middle Ages: the History of a Legend." *MH* 2 (1943): 32–44.

Scheil, Andrew P. *The Footsteps of Israel: Understanding Jews in Anglo-Saxon England.* Ann Arbor: University of Michigan Press, 2004.

Scheil, Andrew. "Sacred History and Old English Religious Poetry." In *The Cambridge History of Early Medieval English Literature*, edited by Clare A. Lees. Cambridge: Cambridge University Press, 2013. 406–26.

Schein, Sylvia. "Babylon and Jerusalem: The Fall of Acre 1291–1996." [*sic*] In *From Clermont to Jerusalem: The Crusades and Crusader Societies, 1095–1500*, edited by Alan V. Murray. Turnhout: Brepols, 1998.

Schlauch, Margaret. "An Old English 'encomium urbis.'" *JEGP* 40 (1941): 14–28.

Schneidau, Herbert N. *Sacred Discontent: the Bible and Western Tradition.* Baton Rouge: Louisiana State University Press, 1976.

Schreckenberg, Heinz, and Kurt Schubert. *Jewish Historiography and Iconography in Early and Medieval Christianity.* Assen/Maastricht: Van Gorcum; Minneapolis: Fortress Press, 1992.

Schultz, David E., and S.T. Joshi, eds. *An Epicure in the Terrible: A Centennial Anthology of Essays in Honor of H.P. Lovecraft.* Rutherford, NJ: Fairleigh Dickinson University Press, 1991.

Schweitzer, Darrell. "Lovecraft and Lord Dunsany." In *Essays Lovecraftian,* edited by Darrell Schweitzer. Baltimore, MD: T-K Graphics, 1976. 91–107.

Seymour, Michael. *Babylon: Legend, History and the Ancient City.* London and New York: I.B. Tauris, 2014.

Sharma, Manish. "Nebuchadnezzar and the Defiance of Measure in the Old English *Daniel.*" *ES* 86.2 (2005): 103–26.

Shaw, Philip. *The Sublime.* New York: Routledge, 2005.

Shils, Edward. *Tradition.* Chicago: University of Chicago Press, 1981.

Slotkin, Richard. *Regeneration through Violence: The Mythology of the American Frontier, 1600–1860.* Middletown, CT: Wesleyan University Press, 1973.

Smedley, Audrey and Brian D. Smedley. *Race in North America: Origin and Evolution of a Worldview.* 4th ed. Boulder, CO: Westview Press, 2012.

Smith, Don G. *H.P. Lovecraft in Popular Culture: The Works and Their Adaptation in Film, Television, Comics, Music and Games.* Jefferson, NC: McFarland, 2006.

Southern, R.W. *Western Views of Islam in the Middle Ages.* Cambridge, MA: Harvard University Press, 1962.

Spitzer, Leo. *Classical and Christian Ideas of World Harmony: Prolegomena to an Interpretation of the Word "Stimmung."* Baltimore: Johns Hopkins University Press, 1963.

Steiner, George. *Grammars of Creation.* New Haven: Yale University Press, 2002.

Stepan, Nancy. *The Idea of Race in Science: Great Britain 1800–1960.* Hamden, CT: Archon Books, 1982.

Stephens, Walter. *Giants in Those Days: Folklore, Ancient History, and Nationalism.* Lincoln: University of Nebraska Press, 1989.

Stone, M.W.F. "Augustine and Medieval Philosophy." In *The Cambridge Companion to Augustine,* edited by Eleonore Stump and Norman Kretzmann. Cambridge: Cambridge University Press, 2001. 253–66.

Tinkler-Villani, Valeria, ed. *Babylon or New Jerusalem? Perceptions of the City in Literature.* Amsterdam: Rodopi, 2005.

Tolan, John. *Saracens: Islam in the Medieval European Imagination.* New York: Columbia University Press, 2002.

Trilling, Renée R. "Sovereignty and Social Order: Archbishop Wulfstan and the *Institutes of Polity*." In *The Bishop Reformed: Studies of Episcopal Power and Culture in the Central Middle Ages*, edited by John S. Ott and Anna Trumbore Jones. Aldershot, Hampshire: Ashgate, 2007. 58–85.

Trompf, G.W. *Early Christian Historiography: Narratives of Retributive Justice.* London: Continuum, 2000.

Trompf, G.W. *The Idea of Historical Recurrence in Western Thought: From Antiquity to the Reformation.* Berkeley and Los Angeles: University of California Press, 1979.

Ullmann, Walter. *Medieval Political Thought.* New York: Penguin, 1965. Reprint, 1975.

Ullmann, Walter. *Principles of Government and Politics in the Middle Ages.* London: Butler and Tanner, 1961.

Van De Mieroop, Marc. *A History of the Ancient Near East, ca. 3000–323 BC.* 2nd ed. Oxford: Blackwell, 2007.

van Oort, Johannes. *Jerusalem and Babylon: A Study into Augustine's City of God and the Sources of his Doctrine of the Two Cities.* Leiden: Brill, 1991.

Vanderhooft, David Stephen. *The Neo-Babylonian Empire and Babylon in the Latter Prophets.* Atlanta: Scholars Press, 1999.

Vendler, Helen. *Poets Thinking: Pope, Whitman, Dickinson, Yeats.* Cambridge, MA: Harvard University Press, 2004.

Voller, Jack G. *The Supernatural Sublime: The Metaphysics of Terror in Anglo-American Romanticism.* DeKalb, IL: Northern Illinois University Press, 1994.

Wacholder, Ben Zion. "Josephus, Flavius." In *The Oxford Companion to the Bible*, edited by Bruce M. Metzger and Michael D. Coogan. Oxford: Oxford University Press, 1993.

Wallace, David. *Premodern Places: Calais to Surinam, Chaucer to Aphra Behn.* Malden, MA and Oxford: Blackwell, 2004.

Walzer, Michael. *Exodus and Revolution.* New York: Basic Books, 1985.

Warner, Marina. *Stranger Magic: Charmed States and the Arabian Nights.* Cambridge, MA: Belknap Press of Harvard University Press, 2012.

Warwick, Alexandra. "Lost Cities: London's Apocalypse." *Spectral Readings: Towards a Gothic Geography.* London: Macmillan, 1999. 73–87.

Waswo, Richard. *The Founding Legend of Western Civilization: From Virgil to Vietnam.* Hanover and London: Wesleyan University Press / University Press of New England, 1997.

Weber, Eugen. *Apocalypses: Prophecies, Cults, and Millennial Beliefs through the Ages.* Cambridge, MA: Harvard University Press, 1999.

Weber, Max. *The City.* Translated and edited by Don Martindale and Gertrud Neuwirth. Glencoe: IL: Free Press, 1958.

Weimer, David R. *The City as Metaphor.* New York: Random House, 1966.

Weithman, Paul. "Augustine's Political Philosophy." In *The Cambridge Companion to Augustine*, edited by Eleonore Stump and Norman Kretzmann. Cambridge: Cambridge University Press, 2001. 234–52.

Westrem, Scott D. *Broader Horizons: A Study of Johannes Witte de Hese's* Itinerarius *and Medieval Travel Narratives.* Cambridge, MA: Medieval Academy of America, 2001.

Westrem, Scott D. *The Hereford Map: A Transcription and Translation of the Legends with Commentary.* Turnhout: Brepols, 2001.

Wheatley, Paul. *City as Symbol.* London: H.K. Lewis, 1969.

Wheeler, Roxanne. *The Complexion of Race: Categories of Difference in Eighteenth-Century British Culture.* Philadelphia: University of Pennsylvania Press, 2000.

White, Hayden. "The Forms of Wildness: Archaeology of an Idea." In *The Wild Man Within: An Image in Western Thought from the Renaissance to Romanticism*, edited by Edward Dudley and Maximillian Novak. Pittsburgh: University of Pittsburgh Press, 1972. 3–38.

Whitford, David M. *The Curse of Ham in the Early Modern Era: The Bible and the Justifications for Slavery.* Farnham, Surrey: Ashgate, 2009.

Williams, David. *Deformed Discourse: The Function of the Monster in Mediaeval Thought and Literature.* Montreal and Kingston: McGill-Queen's University Press, 1996.

Williams, Raymond. *Keywords: A Vocabulary of Culture and Society.* New York: Oxford University Press, 1976; revised ed. 1985.

Williams, Raymond. *The Country and the City.* Oxford: Oxford University Press, 1973.

Wiseman, D.J. *Nebuchadrezzar and Babylon.* Oxford: Oxford University Press for The British Academy, 1985.

Wolfe, Gar K. *The Known and the Unknown: The Iconography of Science Fiction.* Kent, Ohio: Kent State University Press, 1979.

Wolff, Anne. *How Many Miles to Babylon? Travels and Adventures to Egypt and Beyond, 1300–1640.* Liverpool: Liverpool University Press, 2003.

Wood, Forest. *The Arrogance of Faith: Christianity and Race in America from the Colonial Era to the Twentieth Century.* New York: Knopf, 1990.

Woodward, Christopher. *In Ruins.* New York: Pantheon, 2001.

Wormald, Patrick. "Kings and Kingship." In *The New Cambridge Medieval History.* Vol. I: c.500–700, edited by Paul Fouracre. Cambridge: Cambridge University Press, 2005. 571–604.

Yardley, J.C. *Justin and Pompeius Trogus: A Study in the Language of Justin's Epitome.* Toronto: University of Toronto Press, 2003.

Yeager, Suzanne M. *Jerusalem in Medieval Narrative.* Cambridge: Cambridge University Press, 2008.

Young, Robert M. *Darwin's Metaphor: Nature's Place in Victorian Culture.* Cambridge: Cambridge University Press, 1985.

Zanger, Jules. "Poe's Endless Voyage: *The Narrative of Arthur Gordon Pym.*" *PLL* 22.3 (1986): 276–83.

Ziolkowski, Theodore. *Gilgamesh Among Us: Modern Encounters with the Ancient Epic.* Ithaca: Cornell University Press, 2011.

Index

www.ingramcontent.com/pod-product-compliance
Lightning Source LLC
LaVergne TN
LVHW090148080826
844660LV00013B/720/J

* 9 7 8 1 4 4 2 6 3 7 3 3 7 *